W9-DDV-680

STAR WARS

DARTH VADER

END OF GAMES

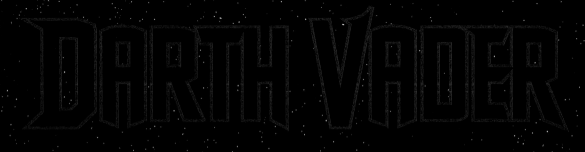

DARTH VADER

END OF GAMES

Writer KIERON GILLEN

Artist SALVADOR LARROCA
Colorist EDGAR DELGADO

"The Misadventures of Triple-Zero and BeeTee"
Artist MIKE NORTON
Colorists DAVID CURIEL

"Coda"
Artist MAX FIUMARA
Colorists DAVE STEWART

Letterer VC's JOE CARAMAGNA
Cover Art MARK BROOKS (#20), SALVADOR LARROCA & EDGAR DELGADO (#21-24) AND JUAN GIMÉNEZ (#25)

Assistant Editor HEATHER ANTOS
Editor JORDAN D. WHITE
Executive Editor C.B. CEBULSKI

Editor in Chief AXEL ALONSO
Chief Creative Officer JOE QUESADA
Publisher DAN BUCKLEY

For Lucasfilm:

Senior Editor FRANK PARISI
Creative Director MICHAEL SIGLAIN
Lucasfilm Story Group RAYNE ROBERTS, PABLO HIDALGO, LELAND CHEE, MATT MARTIN

Collection Editor JENNIFER GRÜNWALD
Associate Managing Editor KATERI WOODY
Associate Editor SARAH BRUNSTAD
Editor, Special Projects MARK D. BEAZLEY
VP Production & Special Projects JEFF YOUNGQUIST
SVP Print, Sales & Marketing DAVID GABRIEL
Book Designer ADAM DEL RE

STAR WARS: DARTH VADER VOL. 4 — END OF GAMES. Contains material originally published in magazine form as DARTH VADER #20-25. First printing 2016. ISBN# 978-0-7851-9978-6. Published by MARVEL WORLDWIDE, INC., a subsidiary of MARVEL ENTERTAINMENT, LLC. OFFICE OF PUBLICATION: 135 West 50th Street, New York, NY 10020. STAR WARS and related text and illustrations are trademarks and/or copyrights, in the United States and other countries, of Lucasfilm Ltd. and/or its affiliates. © & TM Lucasfilm Ltd. No similarity between any of the names, characters, persons, and/or institutions in this magazine with those of any living or dead person or institution is intended, and any such similarity which may exist is purely coincidental. Marvel and its logos are TM Marvel Characters, Inc. Printed in the U.S.A. ALAN FINE, President, Marvel Entertainment; DAN BUCKLEY, President, TV, Publishing & Brand Management; JOE QUESADA, Chief Creative Officer; TOM BREVOORT, SVP of Publishing; DAVID BOGART, SVP of Business Affairs & Operations, Publishing & Partnership; C.B. CEBULSKI, VP of Brand Management & Development, Asia; DAVID GABRIEL, SVP of Sales & Marketing, Publishing; JEFF YOUNGQUIST, VP of Production & Special Projects; DAN CARR, Executive Director of Publishing Technology; ALEX MORALES, Director of Publishing Operations; SUSAN CRESPI, Production Manager; STAN LEE, Chairman Emeritus. For information regarding advertising in Marvel Comics or on Marvel.com, please contact Vit DeBellis, Integrated Sales Manager, at vdebellis@marvel.com. For Marvel subscription inquiries, please call 888-511-5480. Manufactured between 8/12/2016 and 9/19/2016 by LSC COMMUNICATIONS INC., ROANOKE, VA, USA.

10 9 8 7 6 5 4 3 2 1

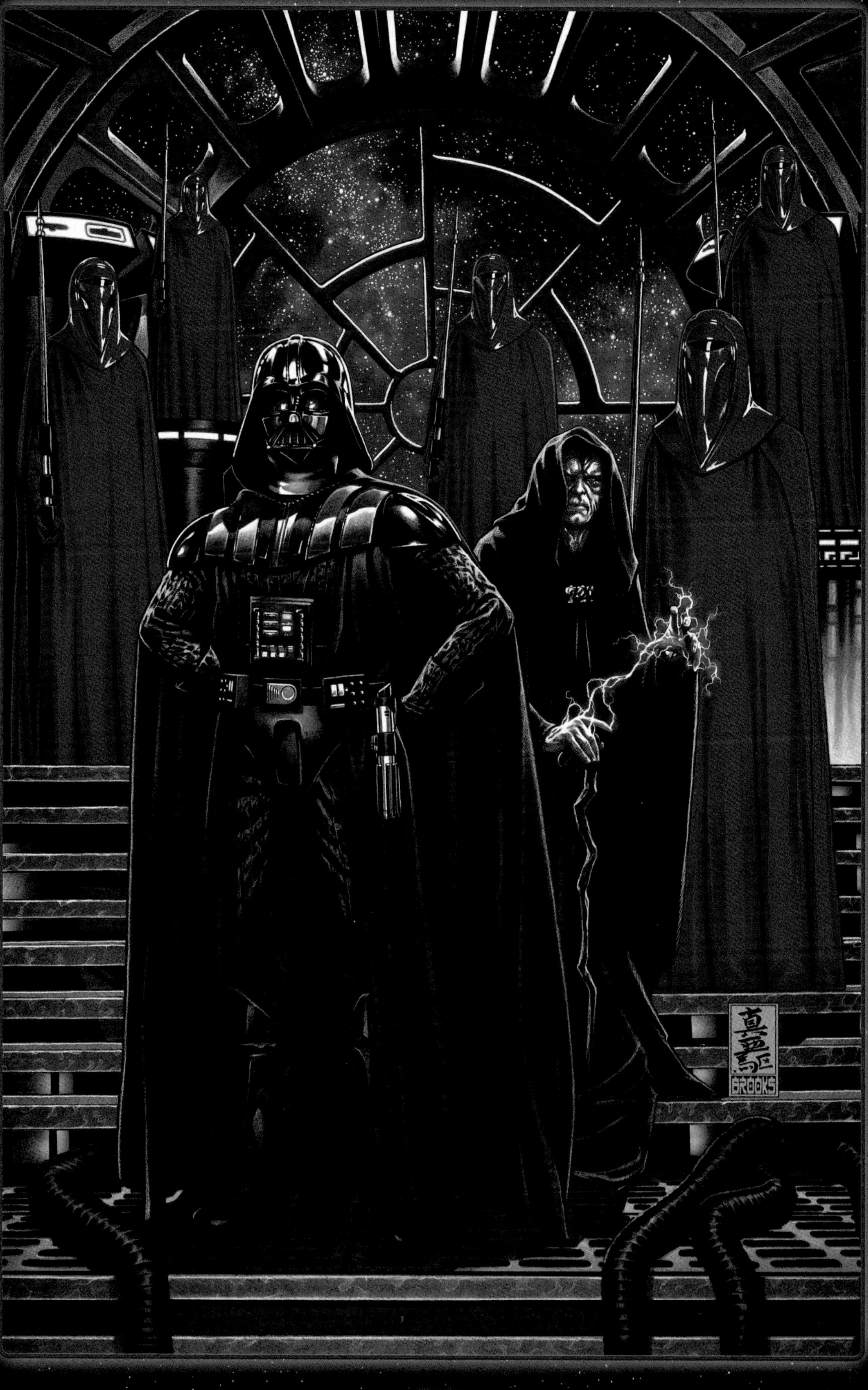
BROOKS

Book IV

END OF GAMES

It is a time of great unrest and rebuilding for the Empire. After the destruction of the Death Star, Darth Vader is working to atone for his failure by reigning in those who oppose the Empire's rule.

With the unrest on Shu-Torun subdued and the planet's allegiance and resources won at last, Darth Vader's standing with his Master, Emperor Palpatine, has greatly improved. All is not well, however, as Cylo, Darth Vader's rival, has been exposed as a traitor and is on the run. What's more, the location of Vader's secret ally, Dr. Aphra, has been located at last by none other than Inspector Thanoth.

Now, Vader travels to Coruscant to meet with the Emperor once more....

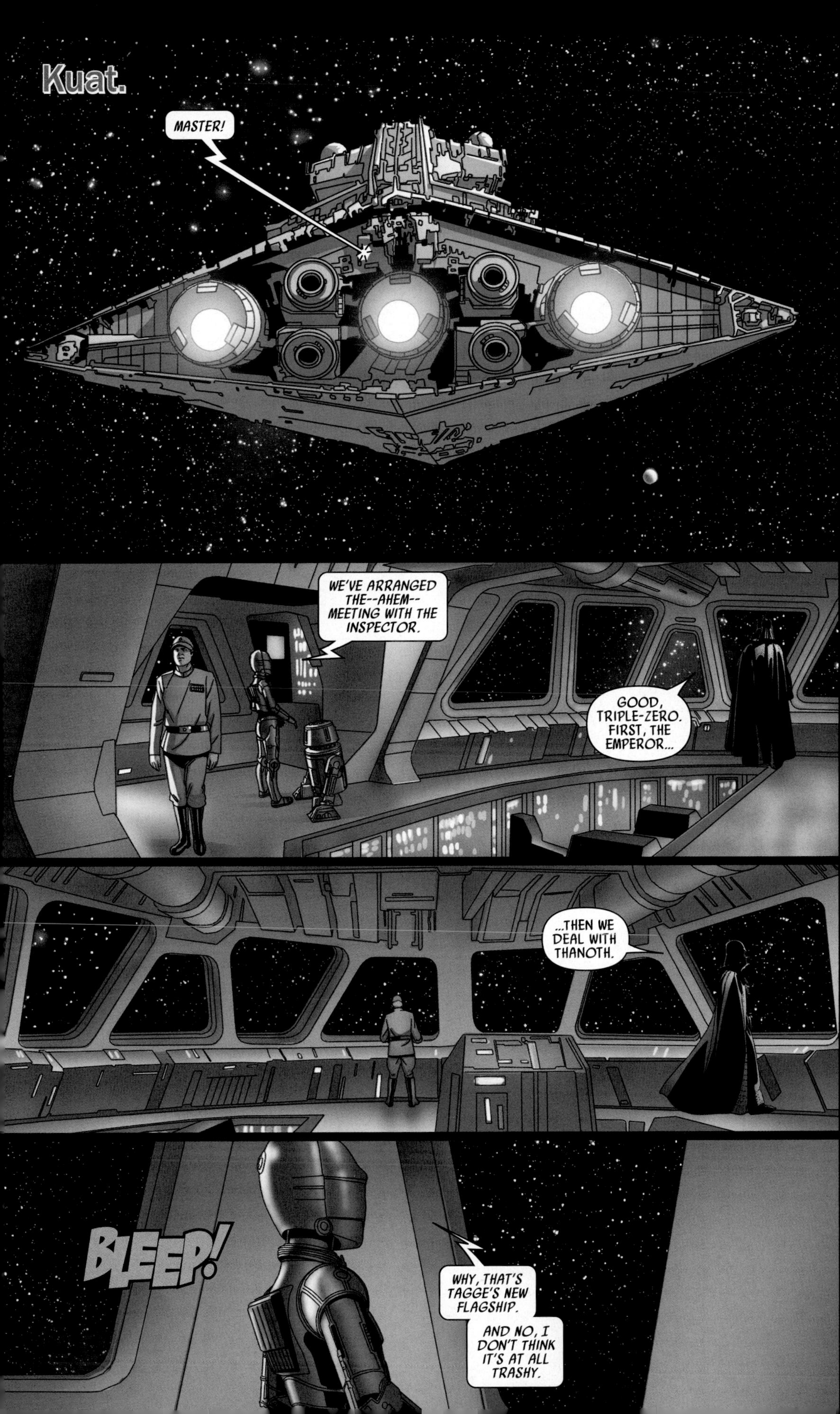
Kuat.
MASTER!
WE'VE ARRANGED THE--AHEM--MEETING WITH THE INSPECTOR.
GOOD, TRIPLE-ZERO. FIRST, THE EMPEROR...
...THEN WE DEAL WITH THANOTH.
BLEEP!
WHY, THAT'S TAGGE'S NEW FLAGSHIP.
AND NO, I DON'T THINK IT'S AT ALL TRASHY.

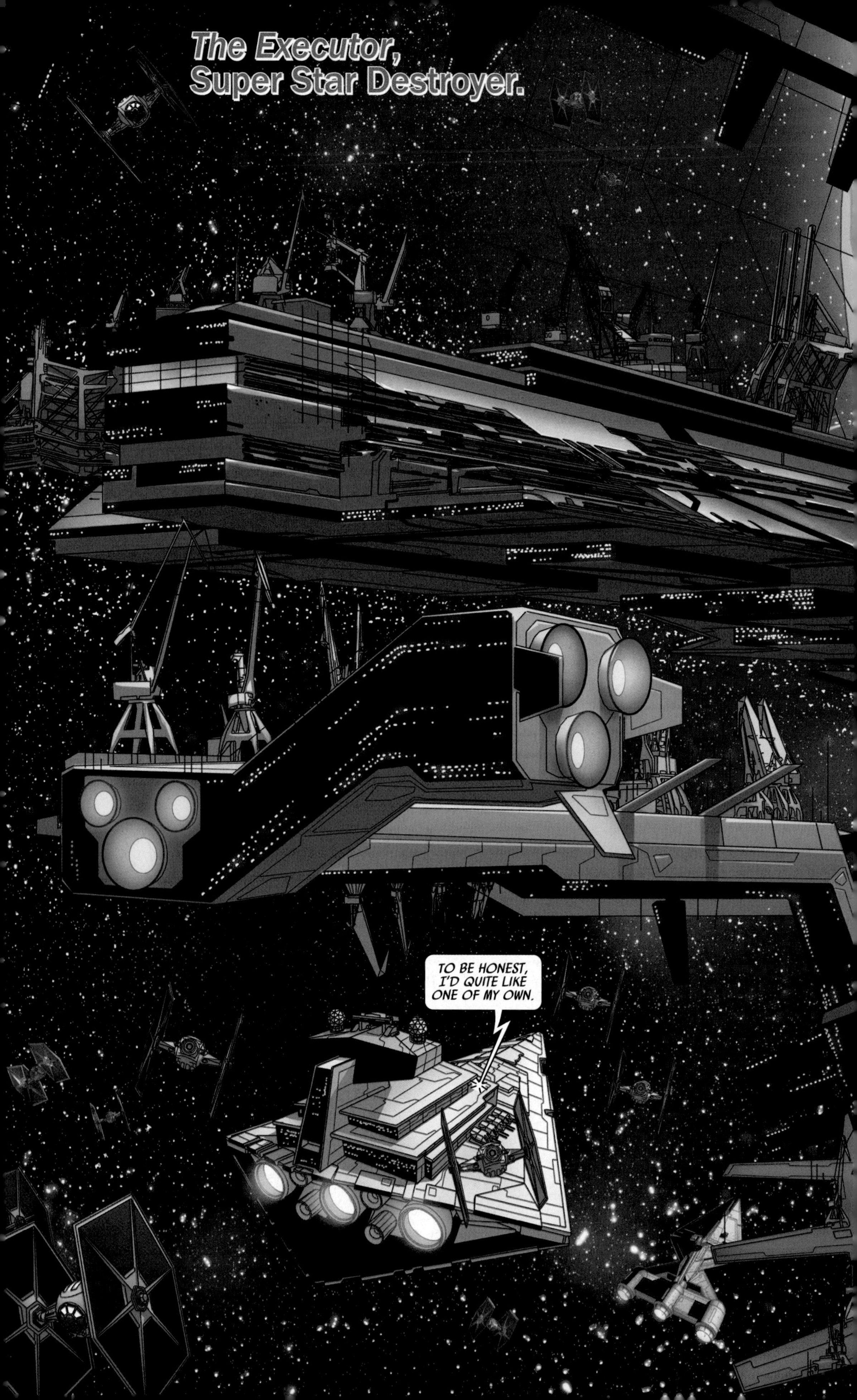
The Executor,
Super Star Destroyer.
TO BE HONEST, I'D QUITE LIKE ONE OF MY OWN.

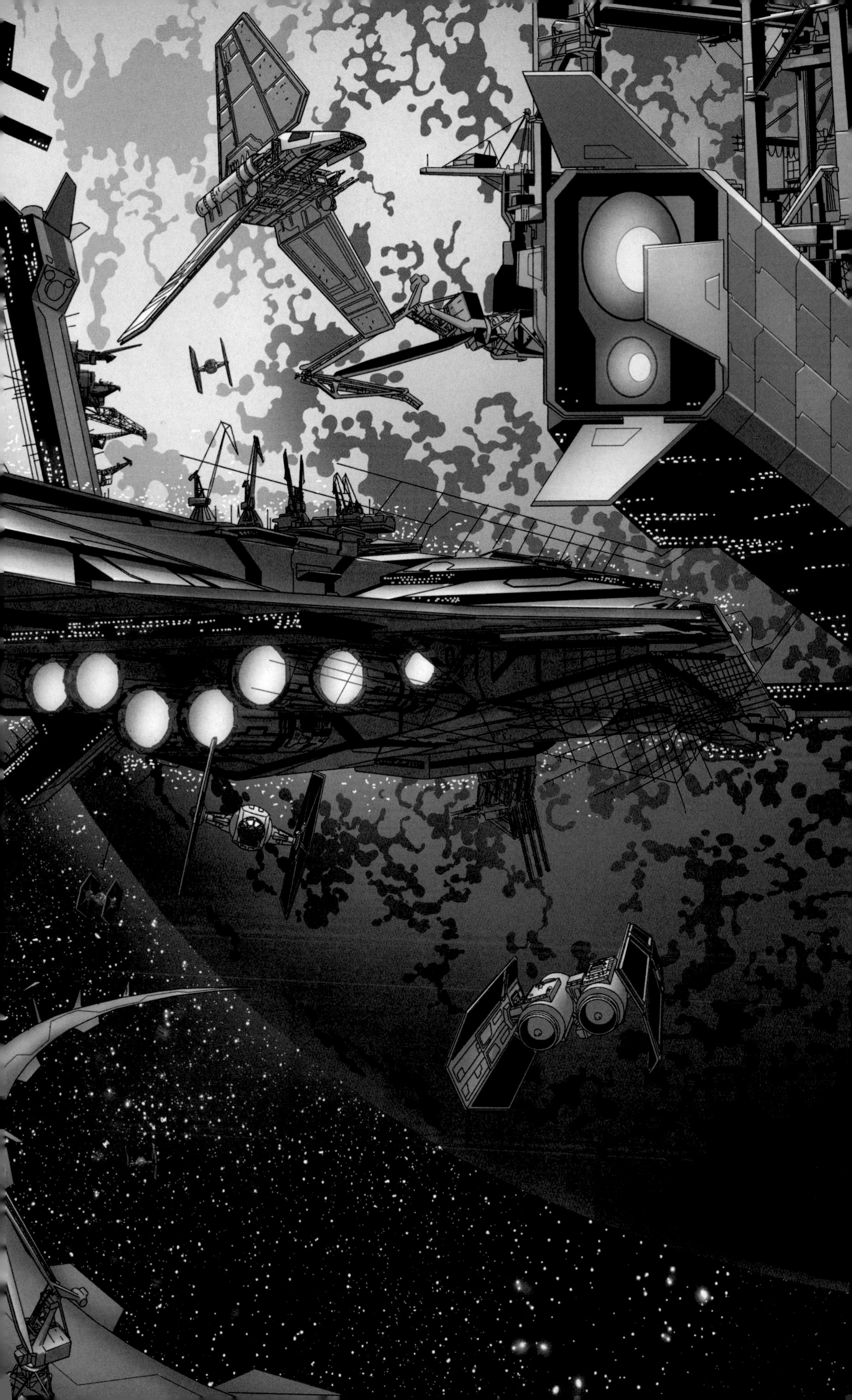

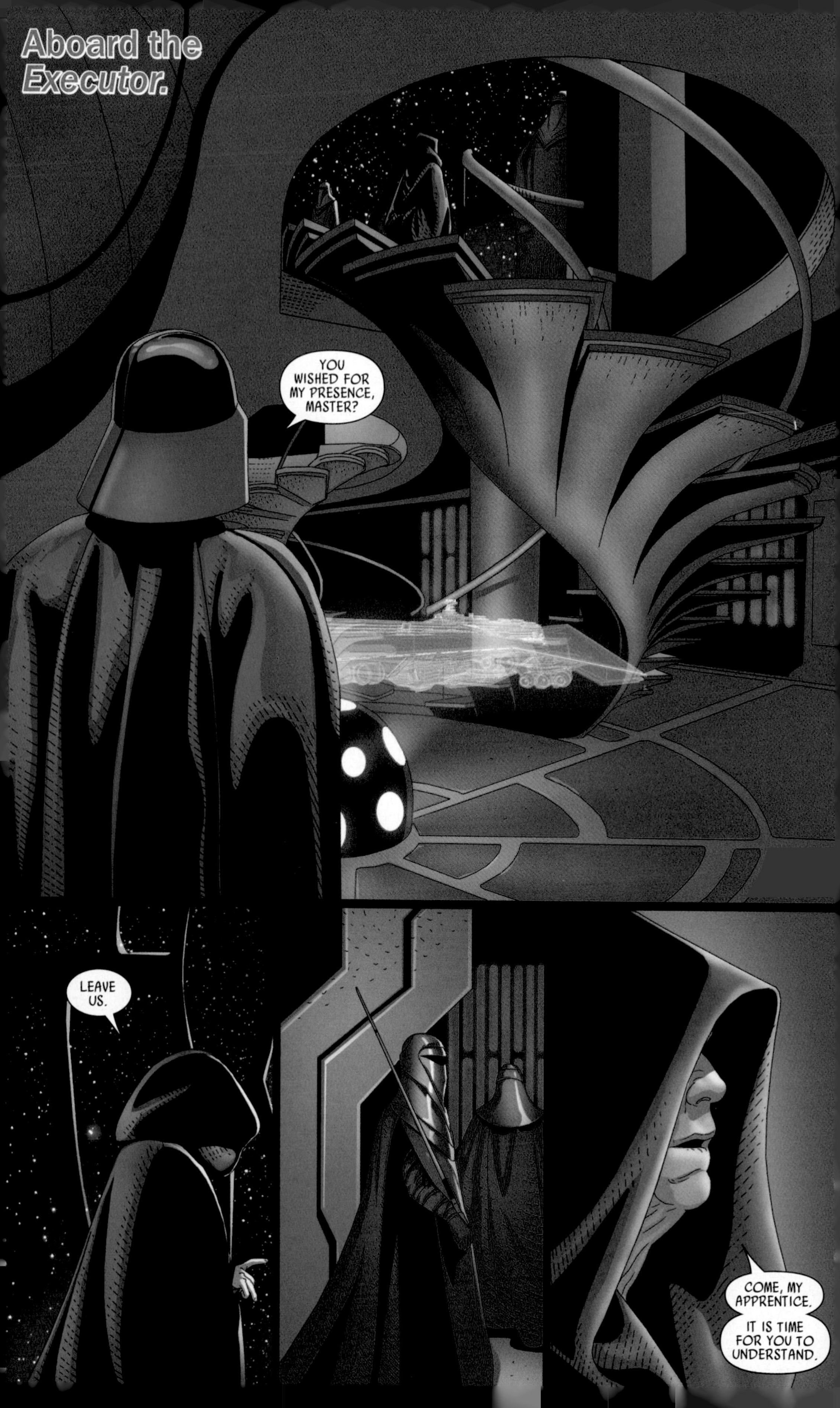
Aboard the *Executor.*
YOU WISHED FOR MY PRESENCE, MASTER?
LEAVE US.
COME, MY APPRENTICE.
IT IS TIME FOR YOU TO UNDERSTAND.

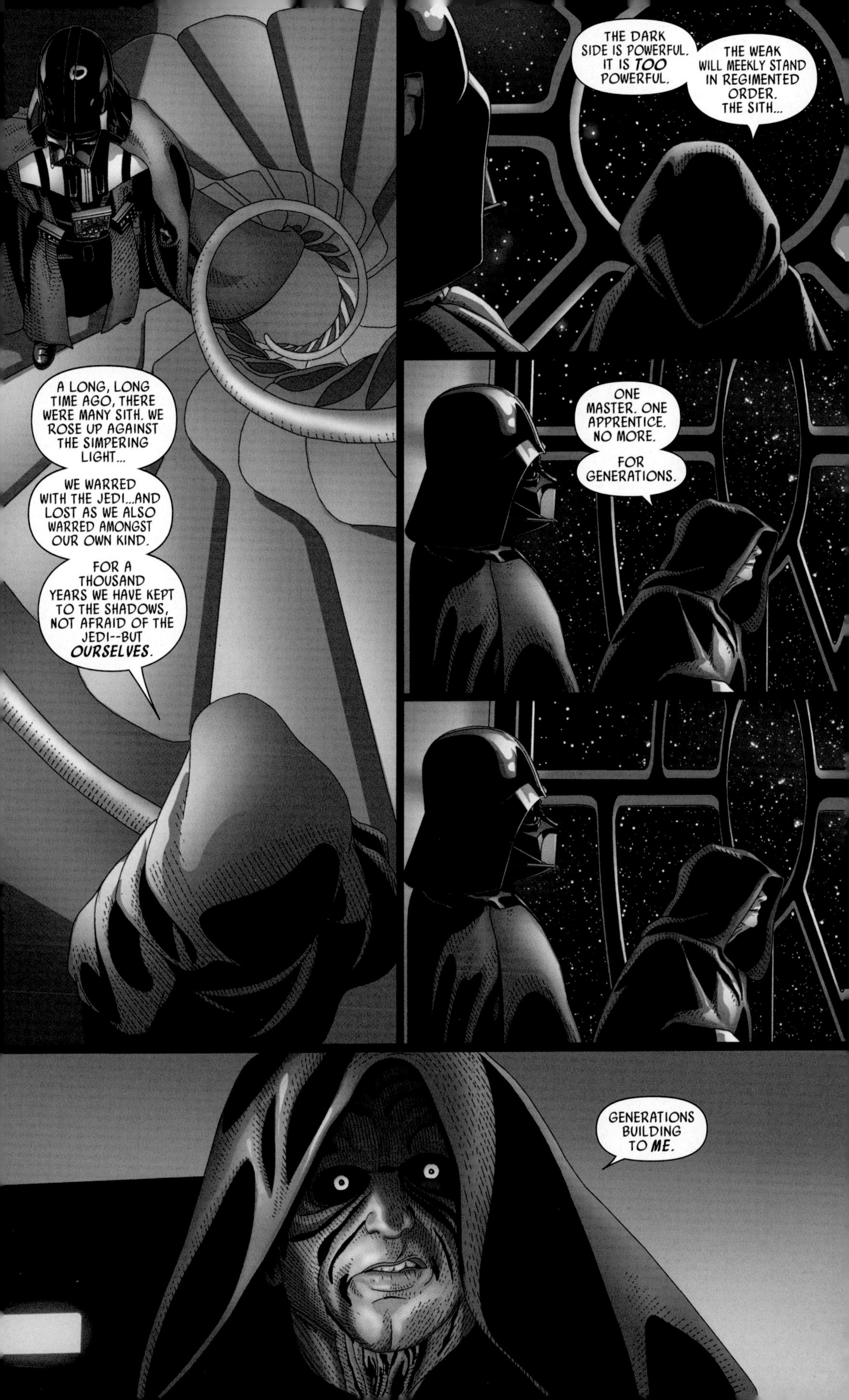
A LONG, LONG TIME AGO, THERE WERE MANY SITH. WE ROSE UP AGAINST THE SIMPERING LIGHT...
WE WARRED WITH THE JEDI...AND LOST AS WE ALSO WARRED AMONGST OUR OWN KIND.
FOR A THOUSAND YEARS WE HAVE KEPT TO THE SHADOWS, NOT AFRAID OF THE JEDI--BUT *OURSELVES*.
THE DARK SIDE IS POWERFUL. IT IS *TOO* POWERFUL.
THE WEAK WILL MEEKLY STAND IN REGIMENTED ORDER. THE SITH...
ONE MASTER. ONE APPRENTICE. NO MORE.
FOR GENERATIONS.
GENERATIONS BUILDING TO *ME*.

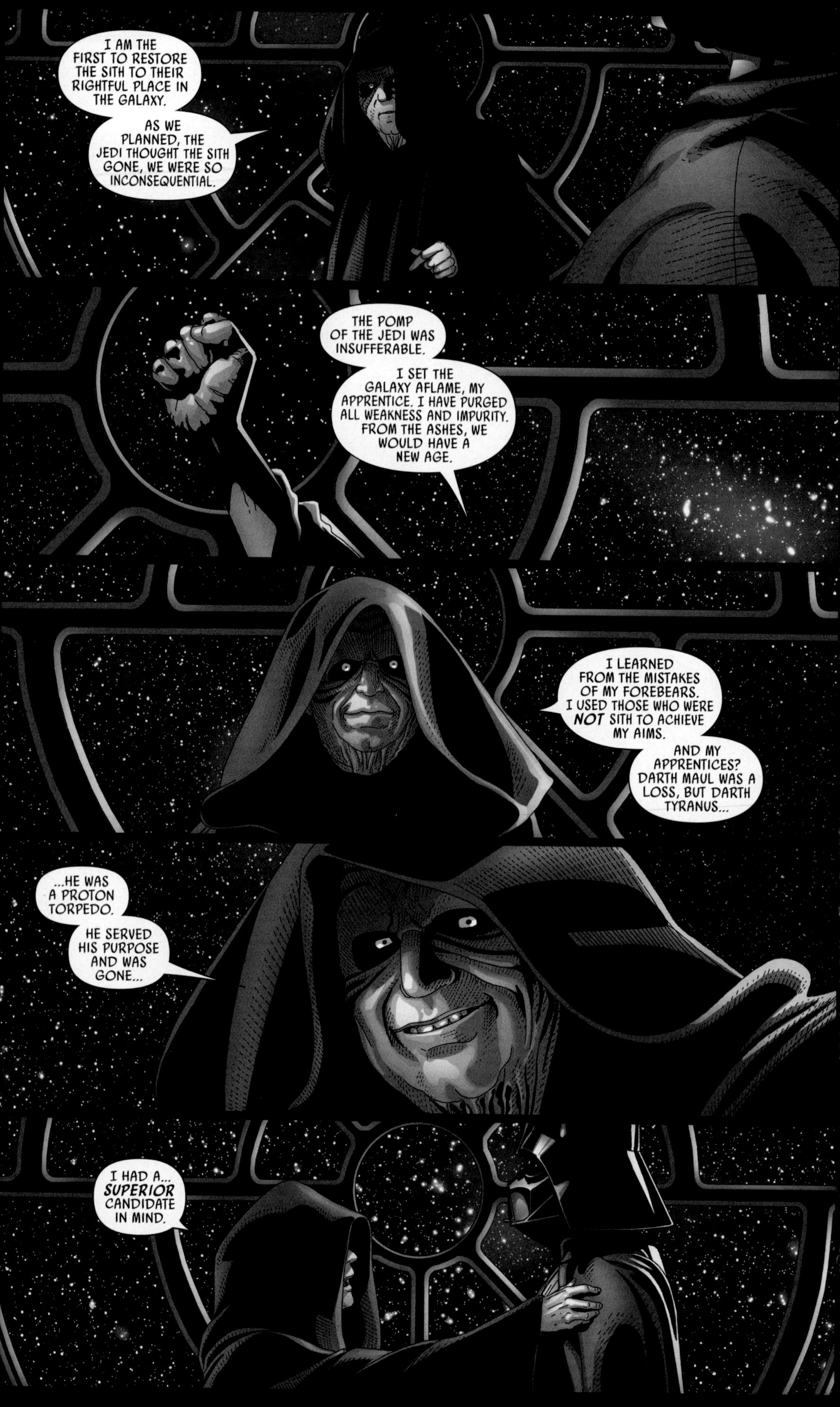
I AM THE FIRST TO RESTORE THE SITH TO THEIR RIGHTFUL PLACE IN THE GALAXY.
AS WE PLANNED, THE JEDI THOUGHT THE SITH GONE, WE WERE SO INCONSEQUENTIAL.
THE POMP OF THE JEDI WAS INSUFFERABLE.
I SET THE GALAXY AFLAME, MY APPRENTICE. I HAVE PURGED ALL WEAKNESS AND IMPURITY. FROM THE ASHES, WE WOULD HAVE A NEW AGE.
I LEARNED FROM THE MISTAKES OF MY FOREBEARS. I USED THOSE WHO WERE *NOT* SITH TO ACHIEVE MY AIMS.
AND MY APPRENTICES? DARTH MAUL WAS A LOSS, BUT DARTH TYRANUS...
...HE WAS A PROTON TORPEDO.
HE SERVED HIS PURPOSE AND WAS GONE...
I HAD A... *SUPERIOR* CANDIDATE IN MIND.

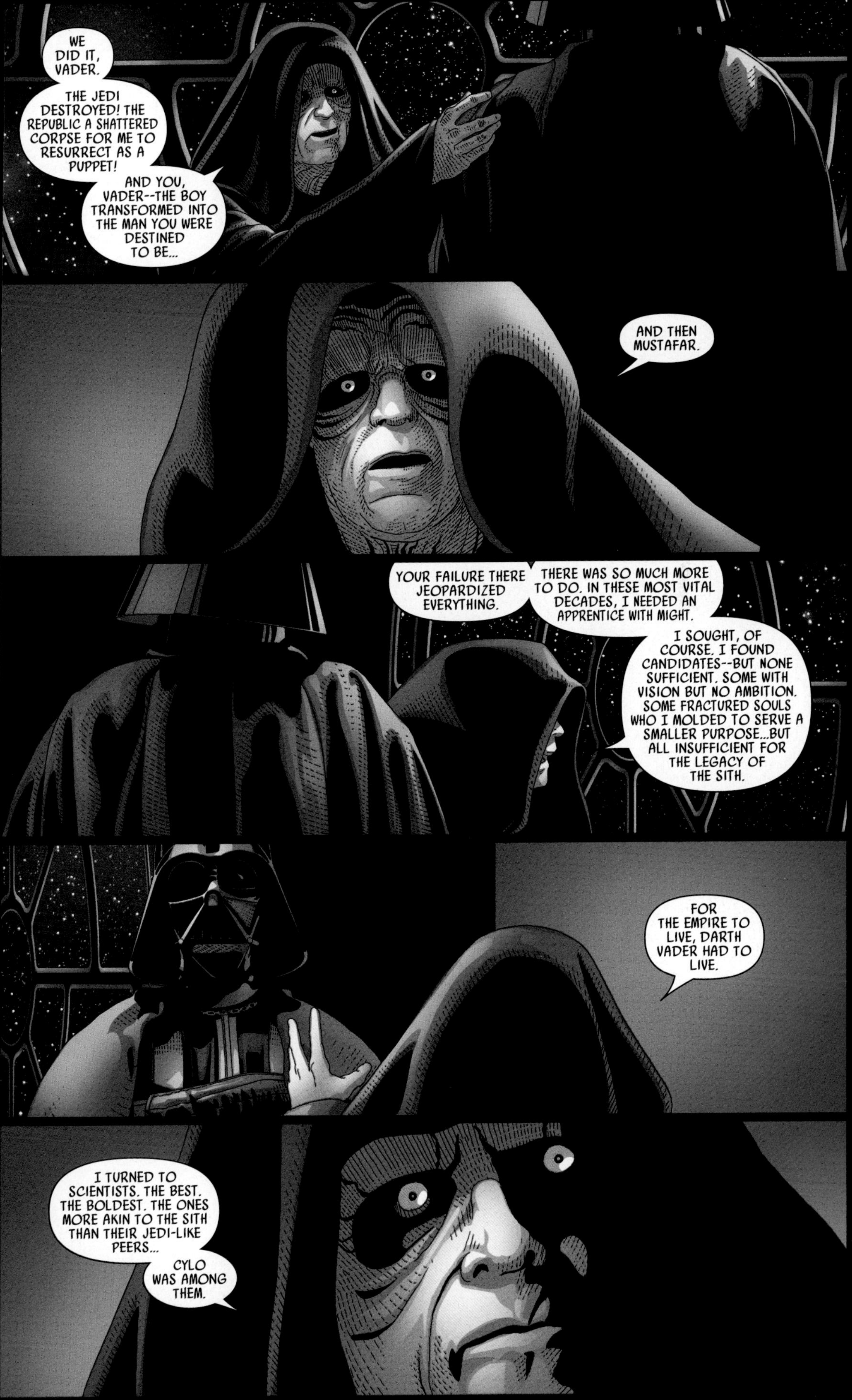
WE DID IT, VADER.
THE JEDI DESTROYED! THE REPUBLIC A SHATTERED CORPSE FOR ME TO RESURRECT AS A PUPPET!
AND YOU, VADER--THE BOY TRANSFORMED INTO THE MAN YOU WERE DESTINED TO BE...
AND THEN MUSTAFAR.
YOUR FAILURE THERE JEOPARDIZED EVERYTHING.
THERE WAS SO MUCH MORE TO DO. IN THESE MOST VITAL DECADES, I NEEDED AN APPRENTICE WITH MIGHT.
I SOUGHT, OF COURSE. I FOUND CANDIDATES--BUT NONE SUFFICIENT. SOME WITH VISION BUT NO AMBITION. SOME FRACTURED SOULS WHO I MOLDED TO SERVE A SMALLER PURPOSE...BUT ALL INSUFFICIENT FOR THE LEGACY OF THE SITH.
FOR THE EMPIRE TO LIVE, DARTH VADER HAD TO LIVE.
I TURNED TO SCIENTISTS. THE BEST. THE BOLDEST. THE ONES MORE AKIN TO THE SITH THAN THEIR JEDI-LIKE PEERS...
CYLO WAS AMONG THEM.

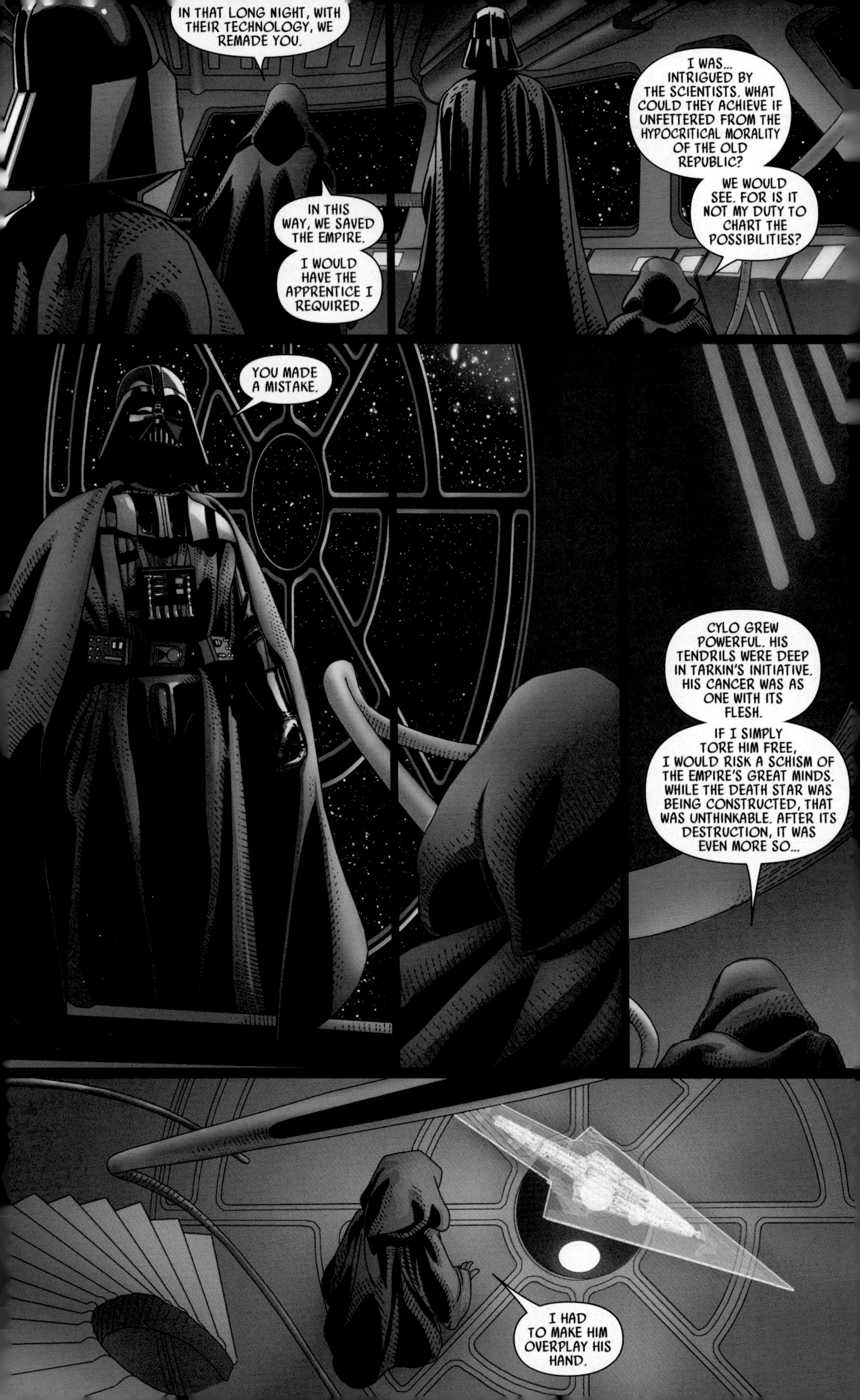
IN THAT LONG NIGHT, WITH THEIR TECHNOLOGY, WE REMADE YOU.
IN THIS WAY, WE SAVED THE EMPIRE.
I WOULD HAVE THE APPRENTICE I REQUIRED.
I WAS... INTRIGUED BY THE SCIENTISTS. WHAT COULD THEY ACHIEVE IF UNFETTERED FROM THE HYPOCRITICAL MORALITY OF THE OLD REPUBLIC?
WE WOULD SEE. FOR IS IT NOT MY DUTY TO CHART THE POSSIBILITIES?
YOU MADE A MISTAKE.
CYLO GREW POWERFUL. HIS TENDRILS WERE DEEP IN TARKIN'S INITIATIVE. HIS CANCER WAS AS ONE WITH ITS FLESH.
IF I SIMPLY TORE HIM FREE, I WOULD RISK A SCHISM OF THE EMPIRE'S GREAT MINDS. WHILE THE DEATH STAR WAS BEING CONSTRUCTED, THAT WAS UNTHINKABLE. AFTER ITS DESTRUCTION, IT WAS EVEN MORE SO...
I HAD TO MAKE HIM OVERPLAY HIS HAND.

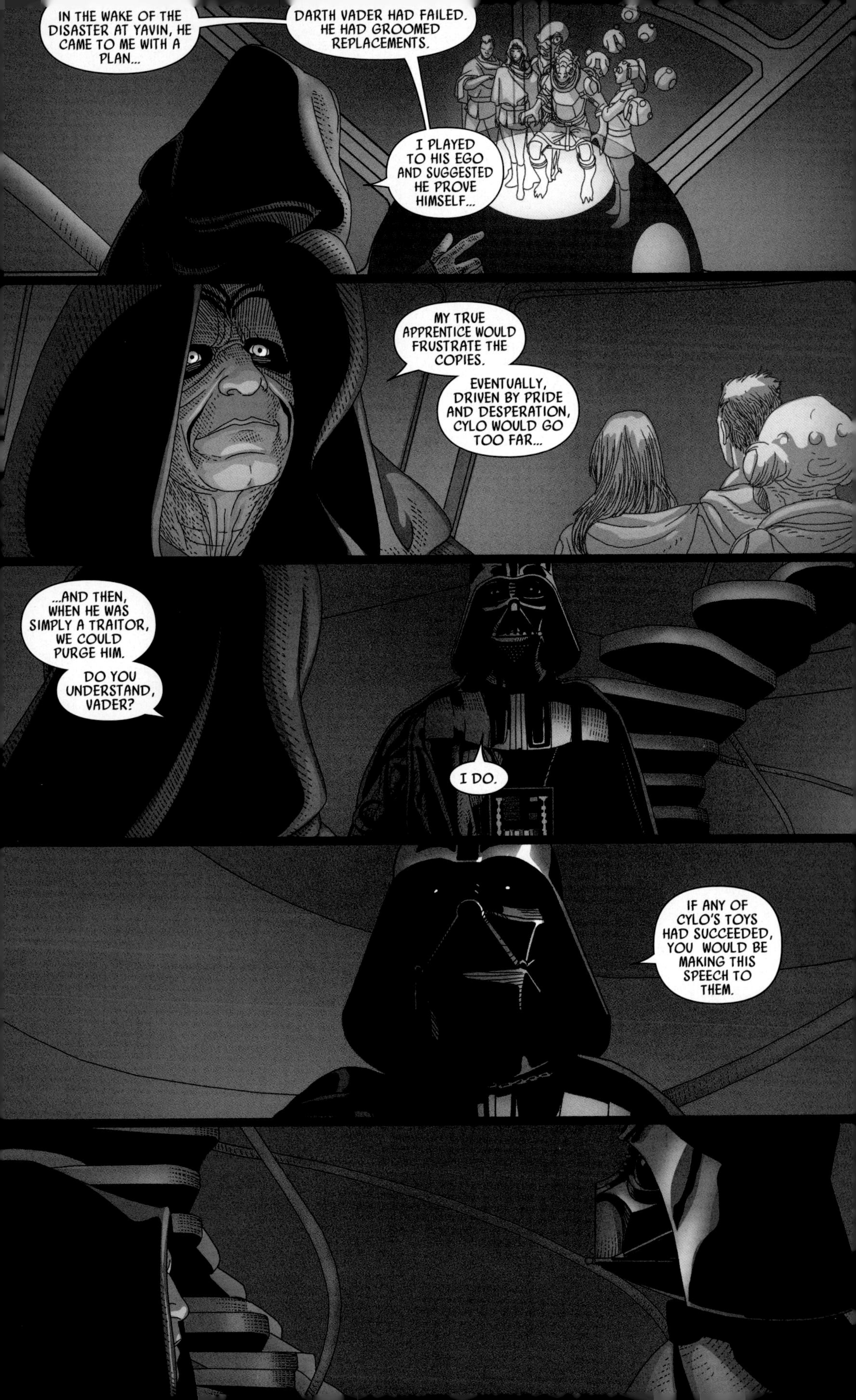
IN THE WAKE OF THE DISASTER AT YAVIN, HE CAME TO ME WITH A PLAN...
DARTH VADER HAD FAILED. HE HAD GROOMED REPLACEMENTS.
I PLAYED TO HIS EGO AND SUGGESTED HE PROVE HIMSELF...
MY TRUE APPRENTICE WOULD FRUSTRATE THE COPIES.
EVENTUALLY, DRIVEN BY PRIDE AND DESPERATION, CYLO WOULD GO TOO FAR...
...AND THEN, WHEN HE WAS SIMPLY A TRAITOR, WE COULD PURGE HIM.
DO YOU UNDERSTAND, VADER?
I DO.
IF ANY OF CYLO'S TOYS HAD SUCCEEDED, YOU WOULD BE MAKING THIS SPEECH TO THEM.

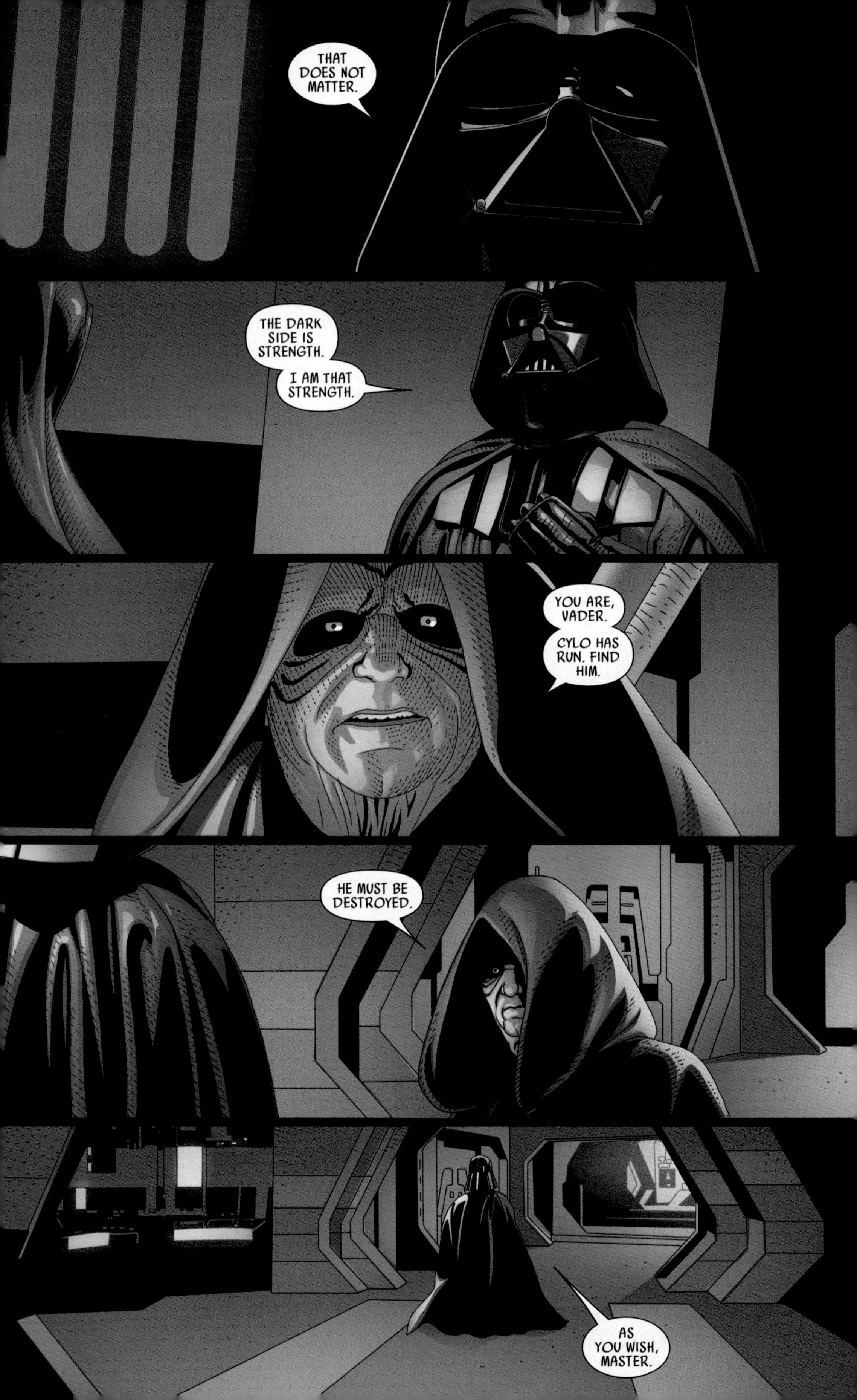

THAT DOES NOT MATTER.
THE DARK SIDE IS STRENGTH.
I AM THAT STRENGTH.
YOU ARE, VADER.
CYLO HAS RUN. FIND HIM.
HE MUST BE DESTROYED.
AS YOU WISH, MASTER.

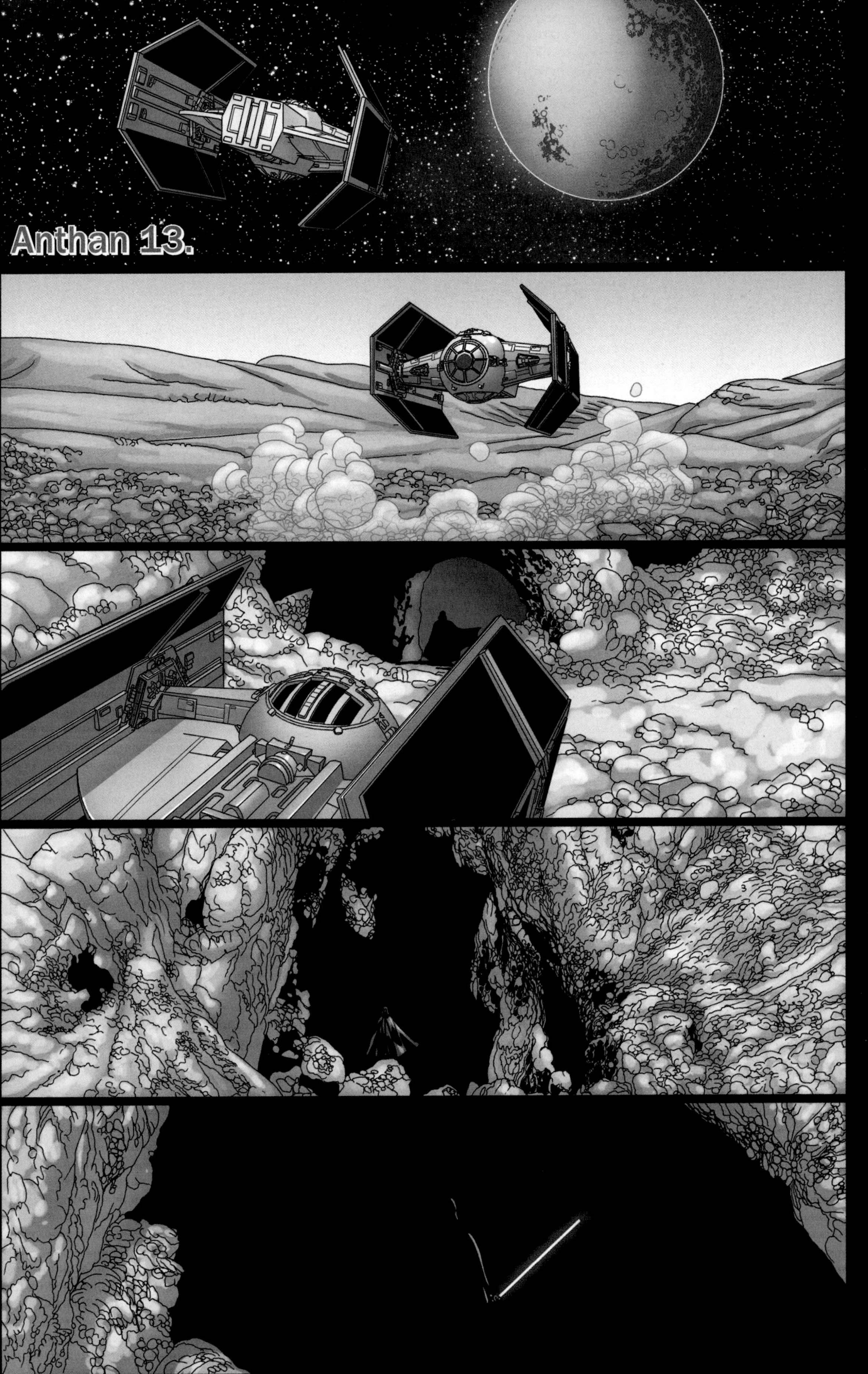
Anthan 13.

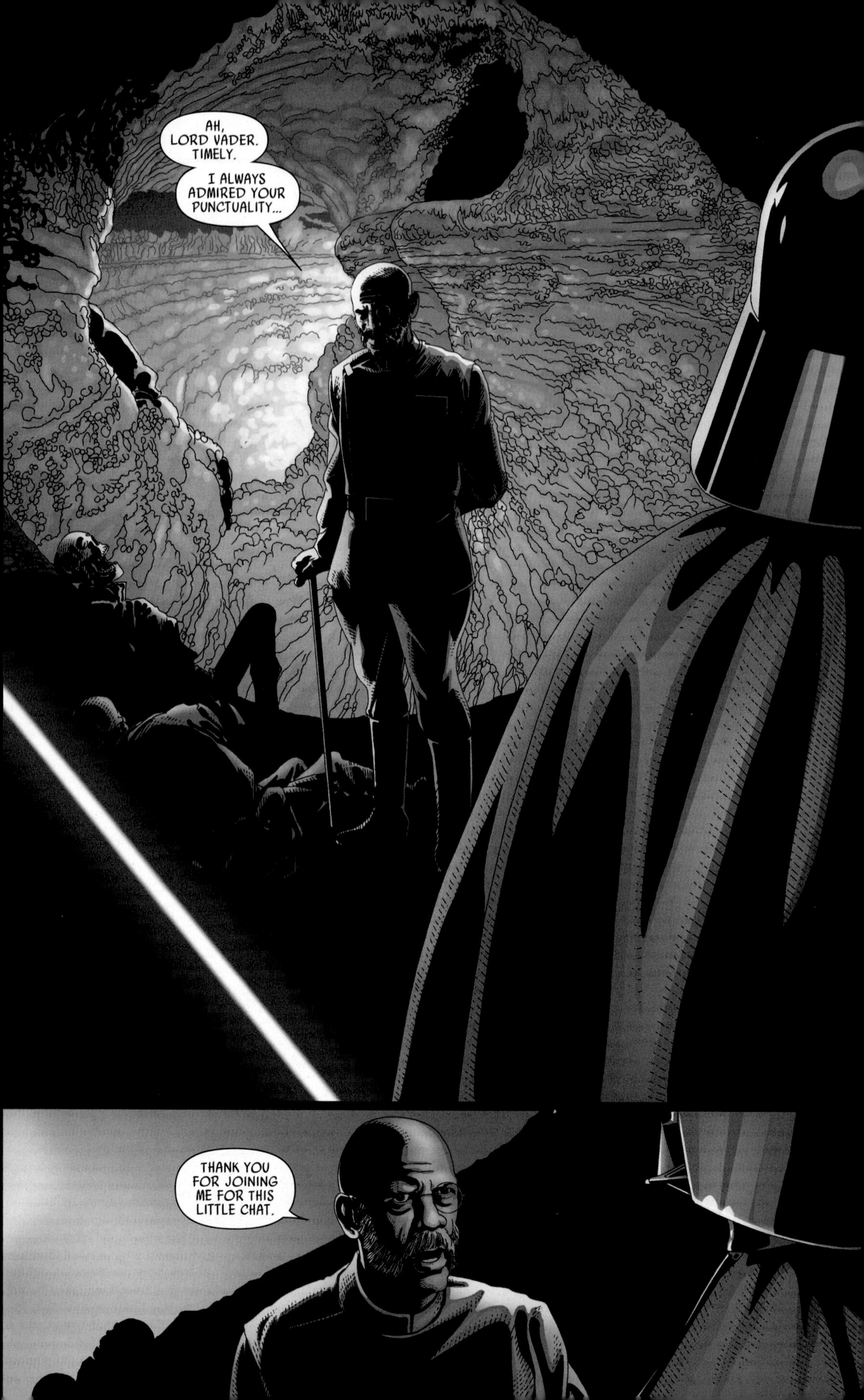
AH, LORD VADER. TIMELY.
I ALWAYS ADMIRED YOUR PUNCTUALITY...
THANK YOU FOR JOINING ME FOR THIS LITTLE CHAT.

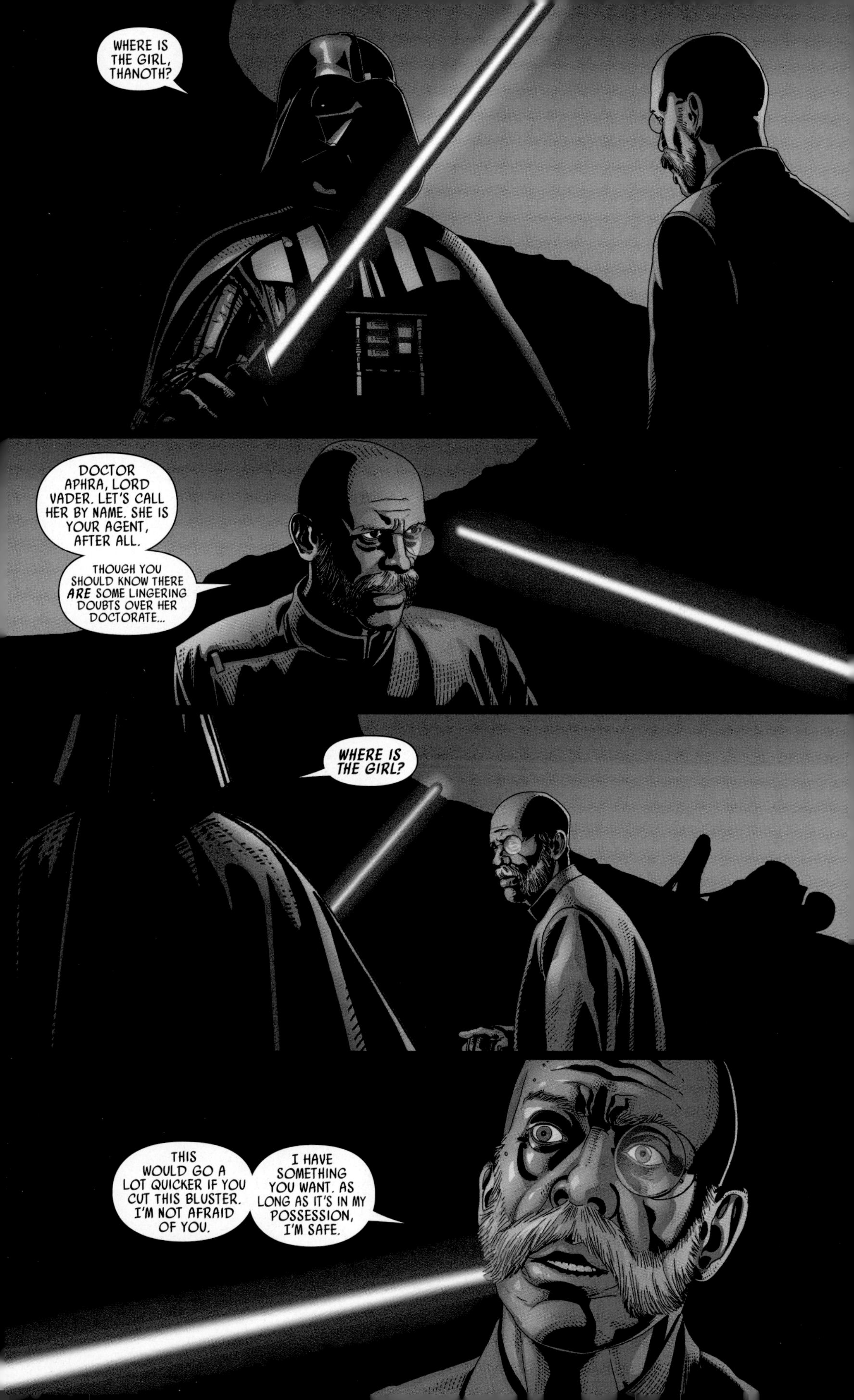
WHERE IS THE GIRL, THANOTH?
DOCTOR APHRA, LORD VADER. LET'S CALL HER BY NAME. SHE IS YOUR AGENT, AFTER ALL.
THOUGH YOU SHOULD KNOW THERE *ARE* SOME LINGERING DOUBTS OVER HER DOCTORATE...
WHERE IS THE GIRL?
THIS WOULD GO A LOT QUICKER IF YOU CUT THIS BLUSTER. I'M NOT AFRAID OF YOU.
I HAVE SOMETHING YOU WANT. AS LONG AS IT'S IN MY POSSESSION, I'M SAFE.

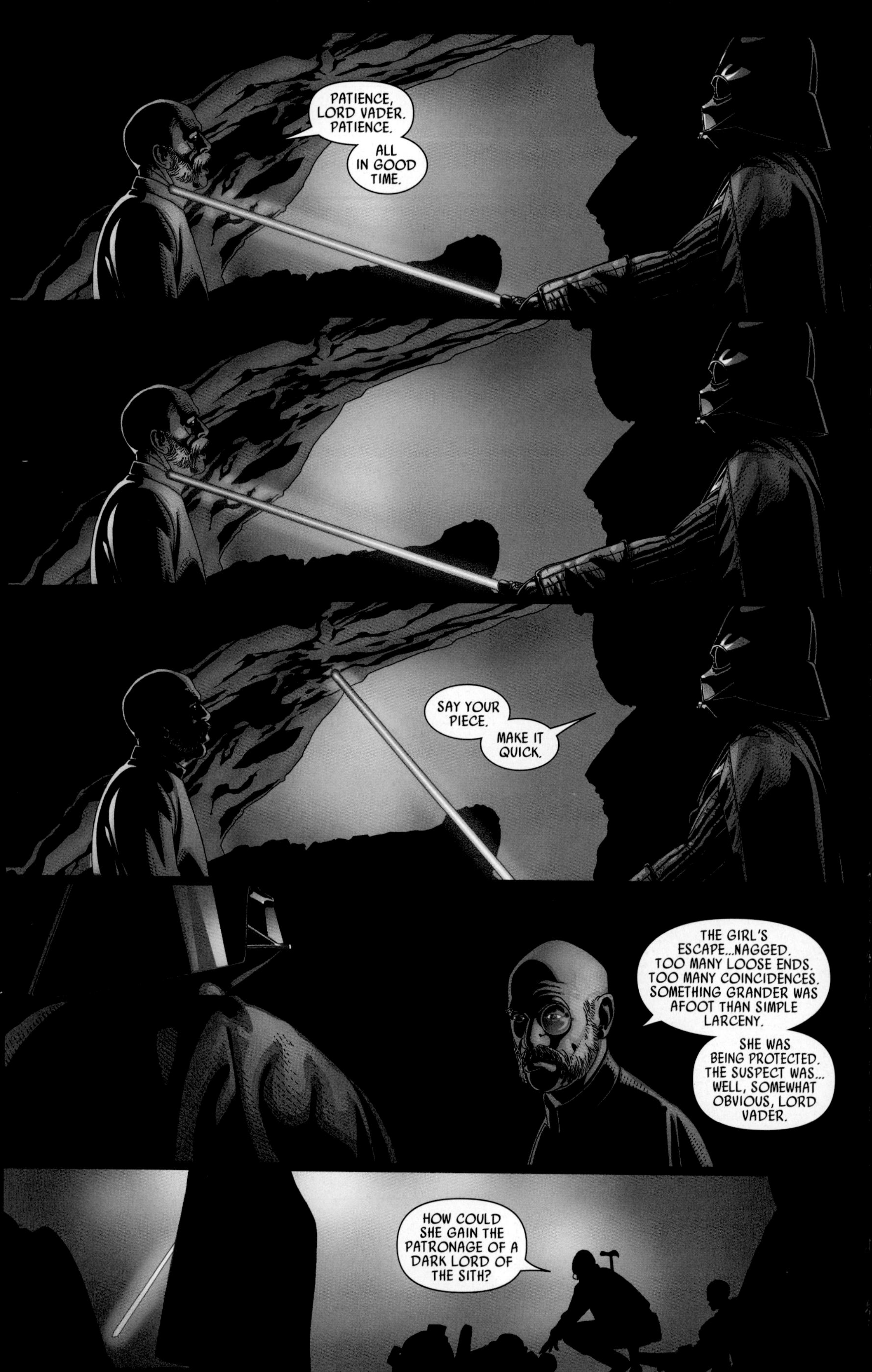
PATIENCE, LORD VADER. PATIENCE.
ALL IN GOOD TIME.
SAY YOUR PIECE.
MAKE IT QUICK.
THE GIRL'S ESCAPE...NAGGED. TOO MANY LOOSE ENDS. TOO MANY COINCIDENCES. SOMETHING GRANDER WAS AFOOT THAN SIMPLE LARCENY.
SHE WAS BEING PROTECTED. THE SUSPECT WAS... WELL, SOMEWHAT OBVIOUS, LORD VADER.
HOW COULD SHE GAIN THE PATRONAGE OF A DARK LORD OF THE SITH?

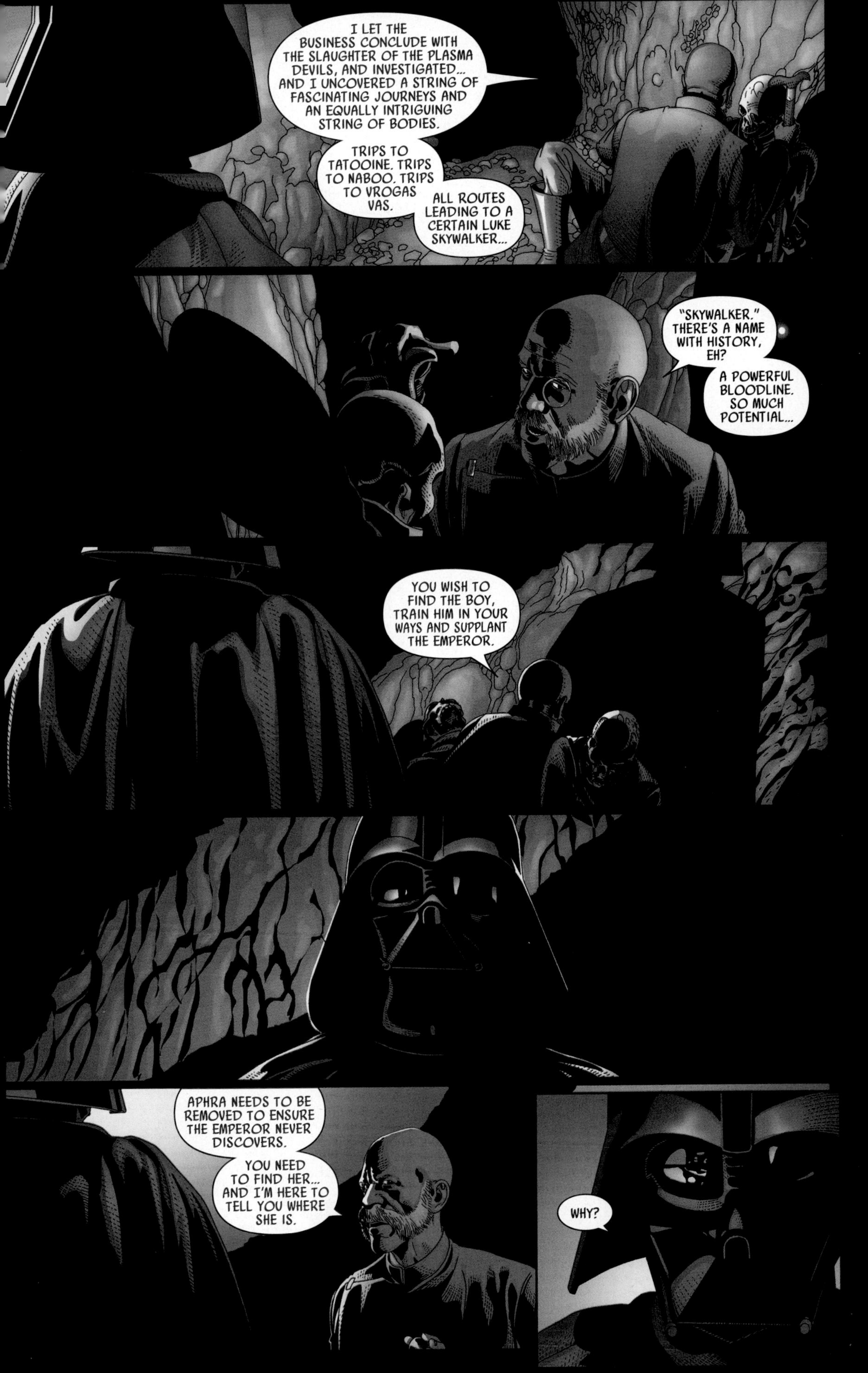

I LET THE BUSINESS CONCLUDE WITH THE SLAUGHTER OF THE PLASMA DEVILS, AND INVESTIGATED... AND I UNCOVERED A STRING OF FASCINATING JOURNEYS AND AN EQUALLY INTRIGUING STRING OF BODIES.
TRIPS TO TATOOINE. TRIPS TO NABOO. TRIPS TO VROGAS VAS.
ALL ROUTES LEADING TO A CERTAIN LUKE SKYWALKER...
"SKYWALKER." THERE'S A NAME WITH HISTORY, EH?
A POWERFUL BLOODLINE. SO MUCH POTENTIAL...
YOU WISH TO FIND THE BOY, TRAIN HIM IN YOUR WAYS AND SUPPLANT THE EMPEROR.
APHRA NEEDS TO BE REMOVED TO ENSURE THE EMPEROR NEVER DISCOVERS.
YOU NEED TO FIND HER... AND I'M HERE TO TELL YOU WHERE SHE IS.
WHY?

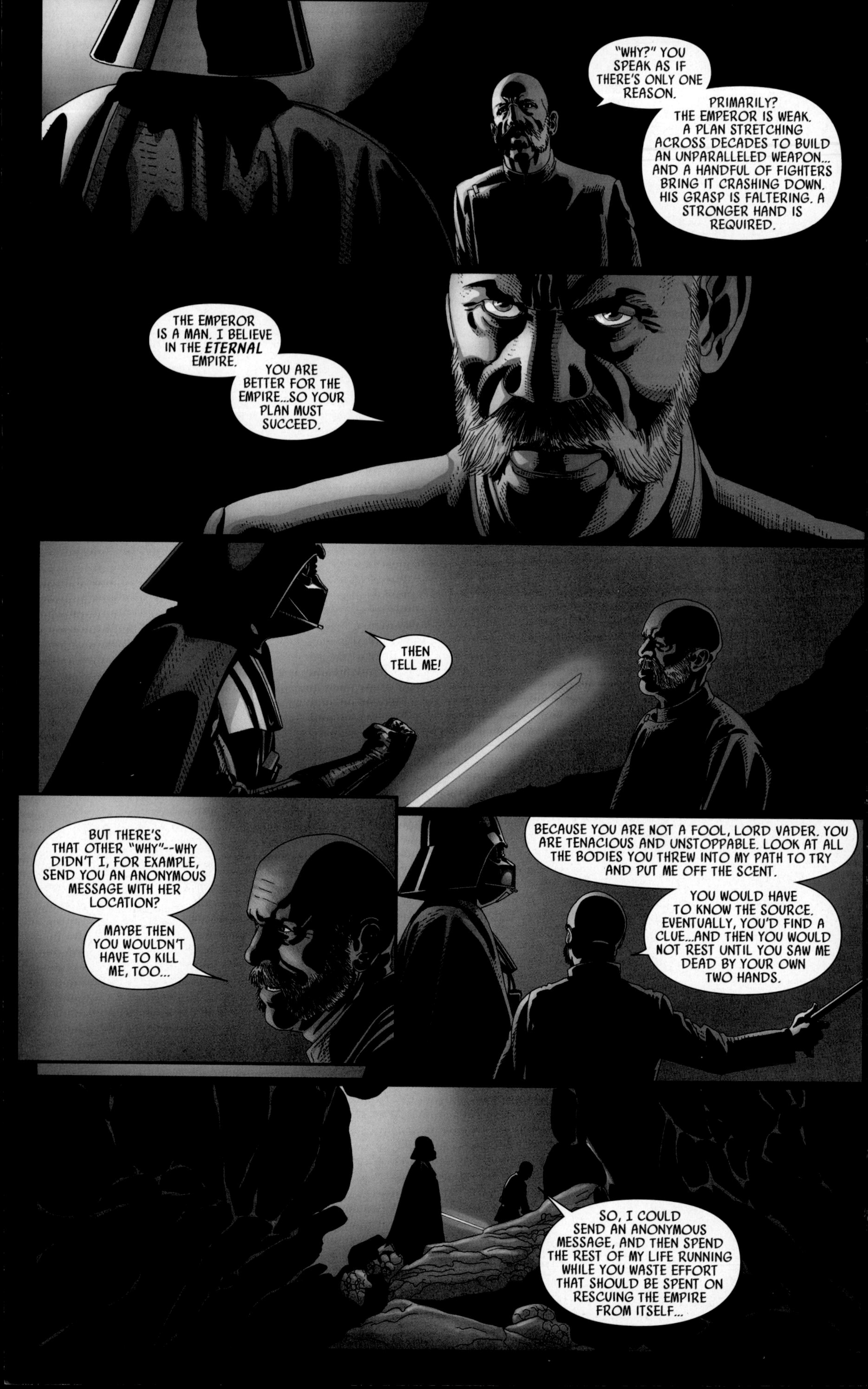
"WHY?" YOU SPEAK AS IF THERE'S ONLY ONE REASON.
PRIMARILY? THE EMPEROR IS WEAK. A PLAN STRETCHING ACROSS DECADES TO BUILD AN UNPARALLELED WEAPON... AND A HANDFUL OF FIGHTERS BRING IT CRASHING DOWN. HIS GRASP IS FALTERING. A STRONGER HAND IS REQUIRED.
THE EMPEROR IS A MAN. I BELIEVE IN THE *ETERNAL* EMPIRE.
YOU ARE BETTER FOR THE EMPIRE...SO YOUR PLAN MUST SUCCEED.
THEN TELL ME!
BUT THERE'S THAT OTHER "WHY"--WHY DIDN'T I, FOR EXAMPLE, SEND YOU AN ANONYMOUS MESSAGE WITH HER LOCATION?
MAYBE THEN YOU WOULDN'T HAVE TO KILL ME, TOO...
BECAUSE YOU ARE NOT A FOOL, LORD VADER. YOU ARE TENACIOUS AND UNSTOPPABLE. LOOK AT ALL THE BODIES YOU THREW INTO MY PATH TO TRY AND PUT ME OFF THE SCENT.
YOU WOULD HAVE TO KNOW THE SOURCE. EVENTUALLY, YOU'D FIND A CLUE...AND THEN YOU WOULD NOT REST UNTIL YOU SAW ME DEAD BY YOUR OWN TWO HANDS.
SO, I COULD SEND AN ANONYMOUS MESSAGE, AND THEN SPEND THE REST OF MY LIFE RUNNING WHILE YOU WASTE EFFORT THAT SHOULD BE SPENT ON RESCUING THE EMPIRE FROM ITSELF...

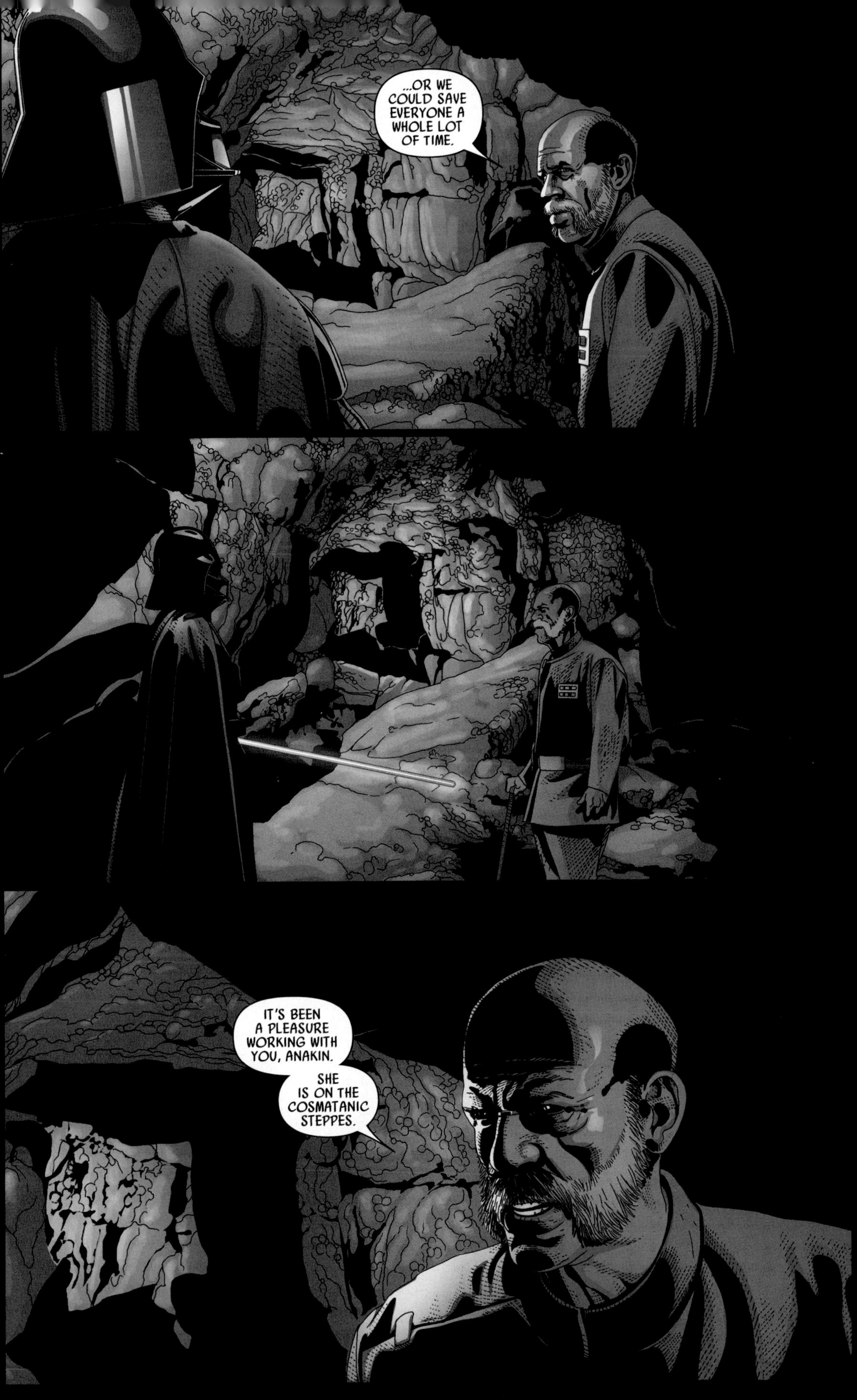
...OR WE COULD SAVE EVERYONE A WHOLE LOT OF TIME.
IT'S BEEN A PLEASURE WORKING WITH YOU, ANAKIN.
SHE IS ON THE COSMATANIC STEPPES.

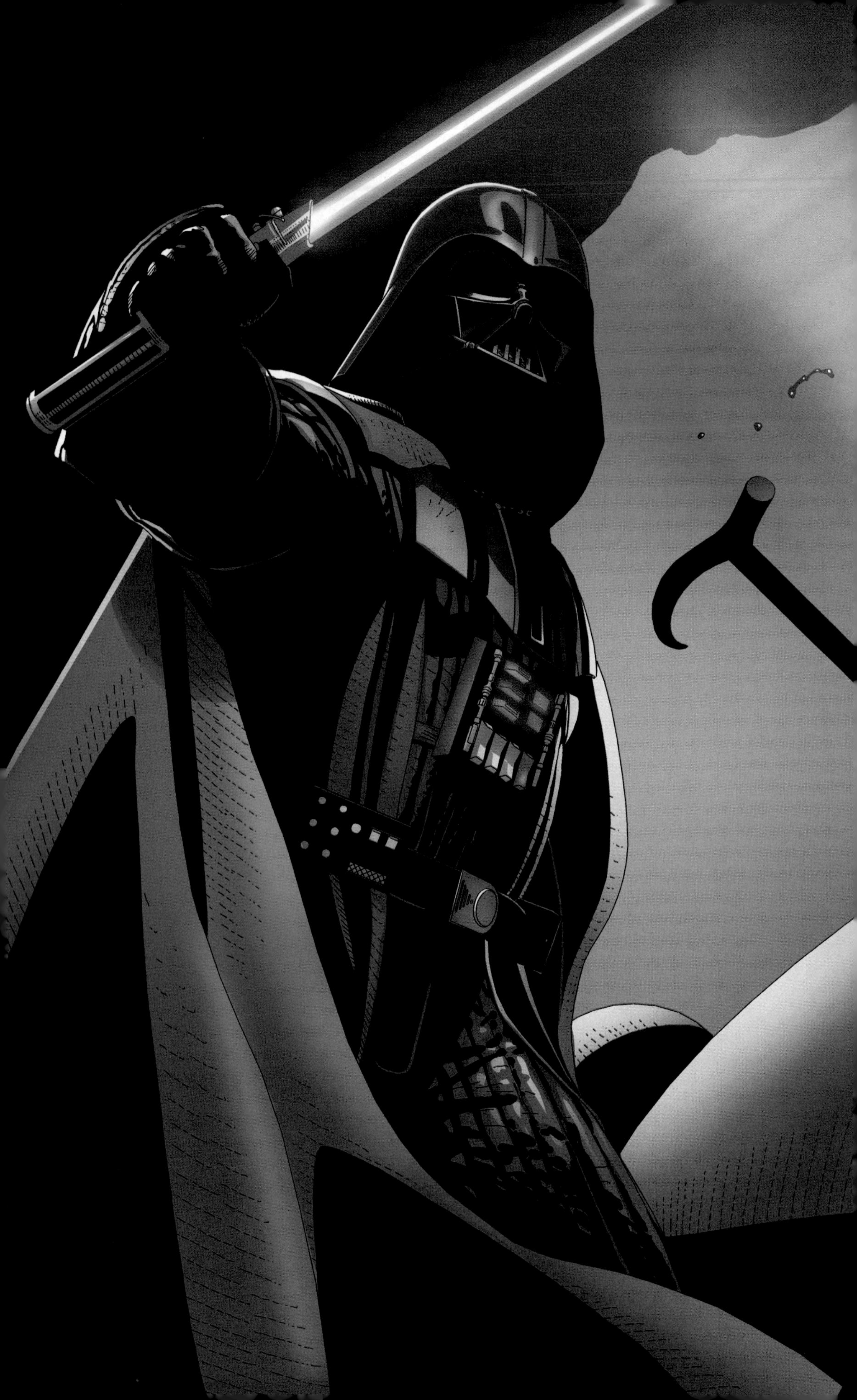

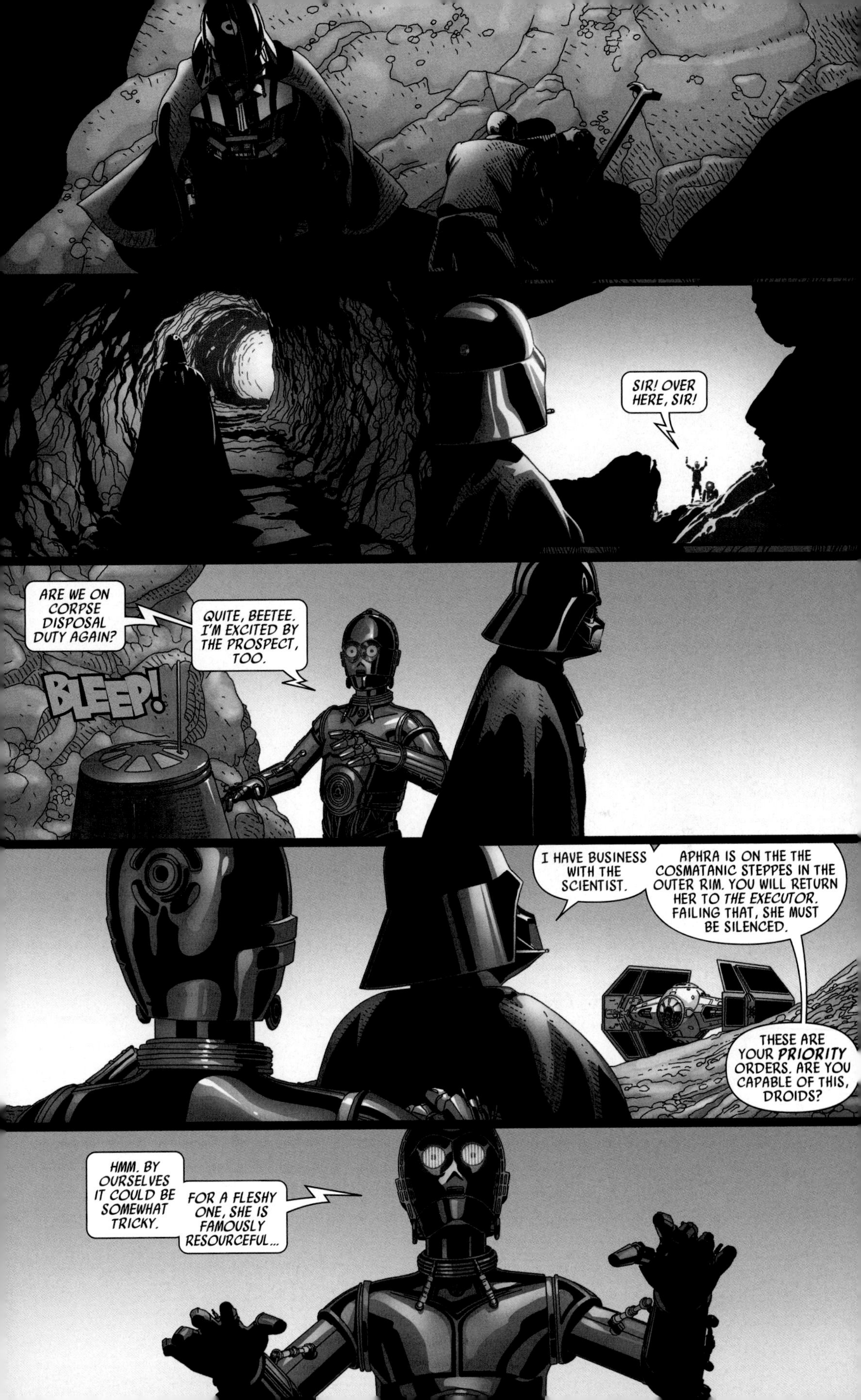
SIR! OVER HERE, SIR!
ARE WE ON CORPSE DISPOSAL DUTY AGAIN?
BLEEP!
QUITE, BEETEE. I'M EXCITED BY THE PROSPECT, TOO.
I HAVE BUSINESS WITH THE SCIENTIST.
APHRA IS ON THE THE COSMATANIC STEPPES IN THE OUTER RIM. YOU WILL RETURN HER TO THE EXECUTOR. FAILING THAT, SHE MUST BE SILENCED.
THESE ARE YOUR PRIORITY ORDERS. ARE YOU CAPABLE OF THIS, DROIDS?
HMM. BY OURSELVES IT COULD BE SOMEWHAT TRICKY.
FOR A FLESHY ONE, SHE IS FAMOUSLY RESOURCEFUL...

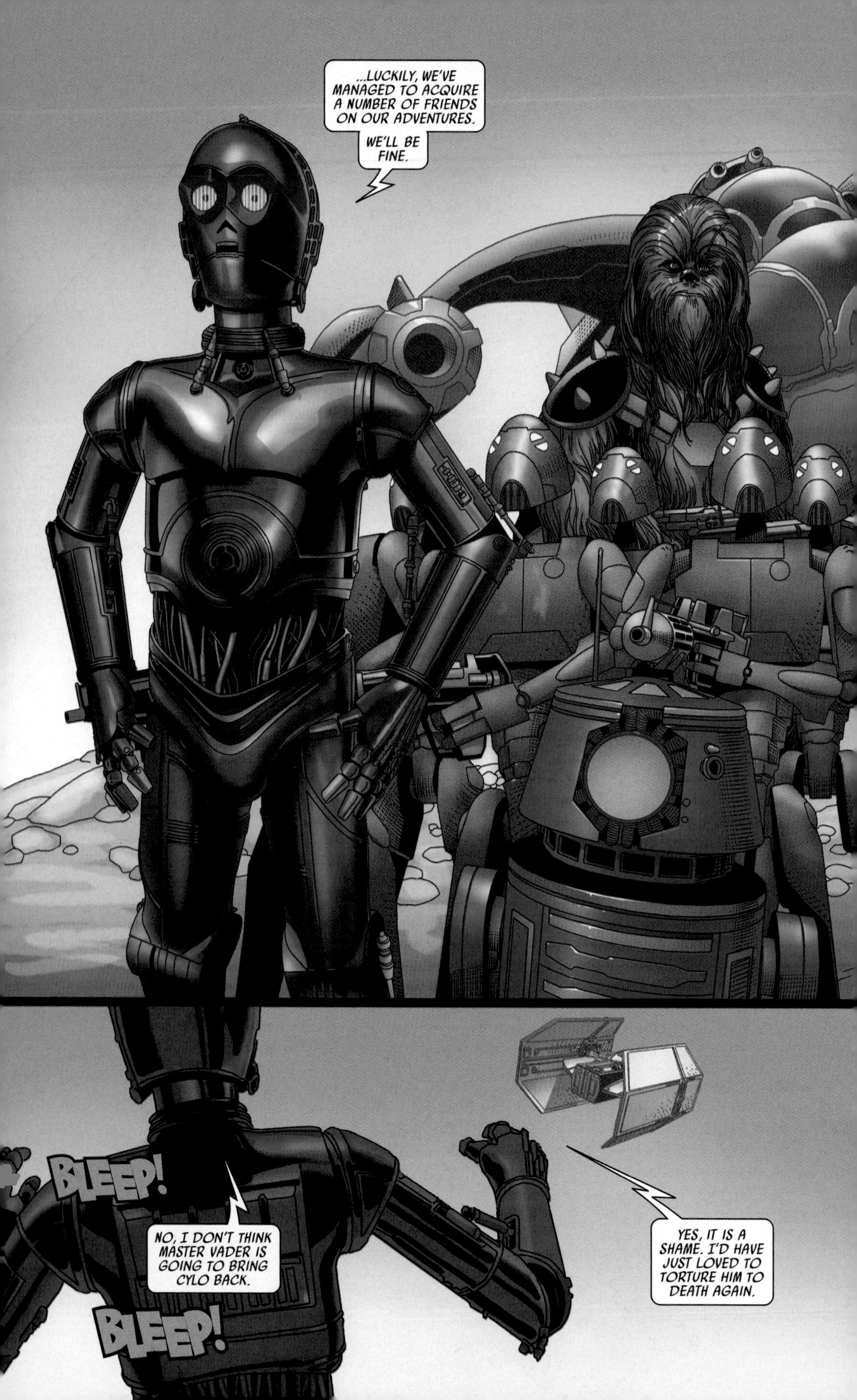

...LUCKILY, WE'VE MANAGED TO ACQUIRE A NUMBER OF FRIENDS ON OUR ADVENTURES.
WE'LL BE FINE.
BLEEP!
NO, I DON'T THINK MASTER VADER IS GOING TO BRING CYLO BACK.
BLEEP!
YES, IT IS A SHAME. I'D HAVE JUST LOVED TO TORTURE HIM TO DEATH AGAIN.

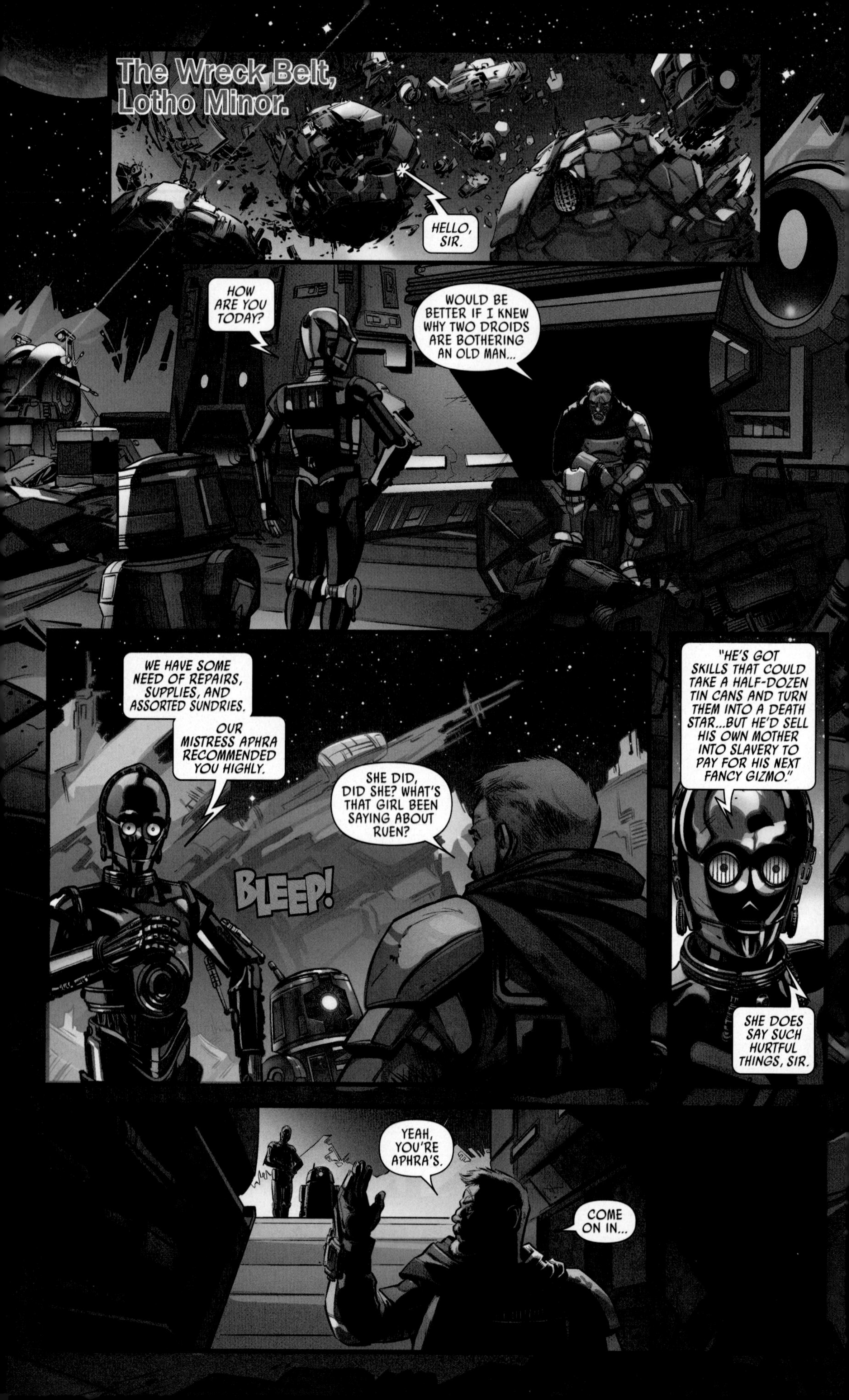

The Wreck Belt,
Lotho Minor.
HELLO, SIR.
HOW ARE YOU TODAY?
WOULD BE BETTER IF I KNEW WHY TWO DROIDS ARE BOTHERING AN OLD MAN...
WE HAVE SOME NEED OF REPAIRS, SUPPLIES, AND ASSORTED SUNDRIES.
OUR MISTRESS APHRA RECOMMENDED YOU HIGHLY.
SHE DID, DID SHE? WHAT'S THAT GIRL BEEN SAYING ABOUT RUEN?
BLEEP!
"HE'S GOT SKILLS THAT COULD TAKE A HALF-DOZEN TIN CANS AND TURN THEM INTO A DEATH STAR...BUT HE'D SELL HIS OWN MOTHER INTO SLAVERY TO PAY FOR HIS NEXT FANCY GIZMO."
SHE DOES SAY SUCH HURTFUL THINGS, SIR.
YEAH, YOU'RE APHRA'S.
COME ON IN...

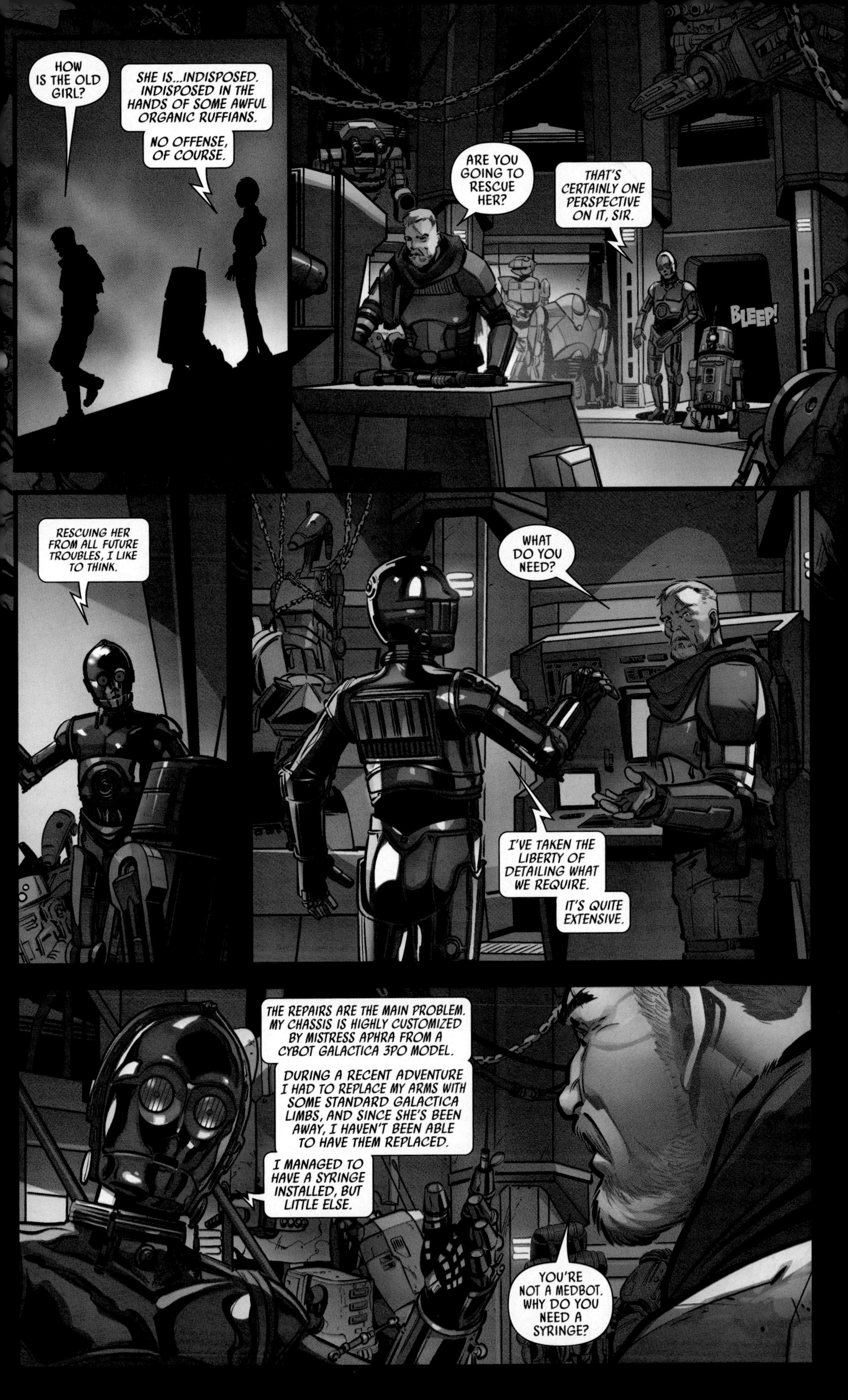
HOW IS THE OLD GIRL?
SHE IS...INDISPOSED. INDISPOSED IN THE HANDS OF SOME AWFUL ORGANIC RUFFIANS.
NO OFFENSE, OF COURSE.
ARE YOU GOING TO RESCUE HER?
THAT'S CERTAINLY ONE PERSPECTIVE ON IT, SIR.
BLEEP!
RESCUING HER FROM ALL FUTURE TROUBLES, I LIKE TO THINK.
WHAT DO YOU NEED?
I'VE TAKEN THE LIBERTY OF DETAILING WHAT WE REQUIRE.
IT'S QUITE EXTENSIVE.
THE REPAIRS ARE THE MAIN PROBLEM. MY CHASSIS IS HIGHLY CUSTOMIZED BY MISTRESS APHRA FROM A CYBOT GALACTICA 3PO MODEL.
DURING A RECENT ADVENTURE I HAD TO REPLACE MY ARMS WITH SOME STANDARD GALACTICA LIMBS, AND SINCE SHE'S BEEN AWAY, I HAVEN'T BEEN ABLE TO HAVE THEM REPLACED.
I MANAGED TO HAVE A SYRINGE INSTALLED, BUT LITTLE ELSE.
YOU'RE NOT A MEDBOT. WHY DO YOU NEED A SYRINGE?

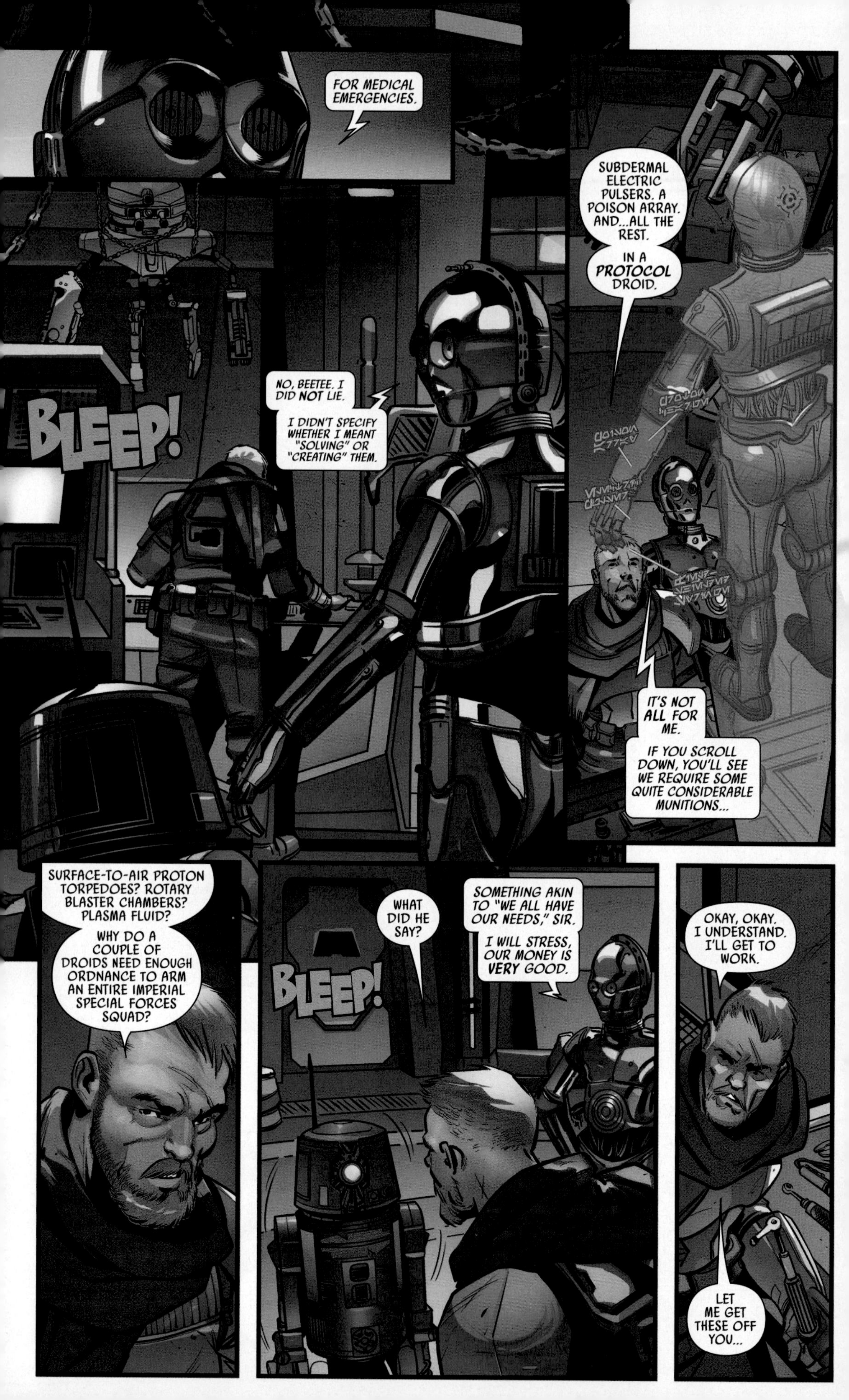
FOR MEDICAL EMERGENCIES.
SUBDERMAL ELECTRIC PULSERS. A POISON ARRAY. AND...ALL THE REST.
IN A PROTOCOL DROID.
NO, BEETEE. I DID NOT LIE.
I DIDN'T SPECIFY WHETHER I MEANT "SOLVING" OR "CREATING" THEM.
BLEEP!
IT'S NOT ALL FOR ME.
IF YOU SCROLL DOWN, YOU'LL SEE WE REQUIRE SOME QUITE CONSIDERABLE MUNITIONS...
SURFACE-TO-AIR PROTON TORPEDOES? ROTARY BLASTER CHAMBERS? PLASMA FLUID?
WHY DO A COUPLE OF DROIDS NEED ENOUGH ORDNANCE TO ARM AN ENTIRE IMPERIAL SPECIAL FORCES SQUAD?
BLEEP!
WHAT DID HE SAY?
SOMETHING AKIN TO "WE ALL HAVE OUR NEEDS," SIR.
I WILL STRESS, OUR MONEY IS VERY GOOD.
OKAY, OKAY. I UNDERSTAND. I'LL GET TO WORK.
LET ME GET THESE OFF YOU...

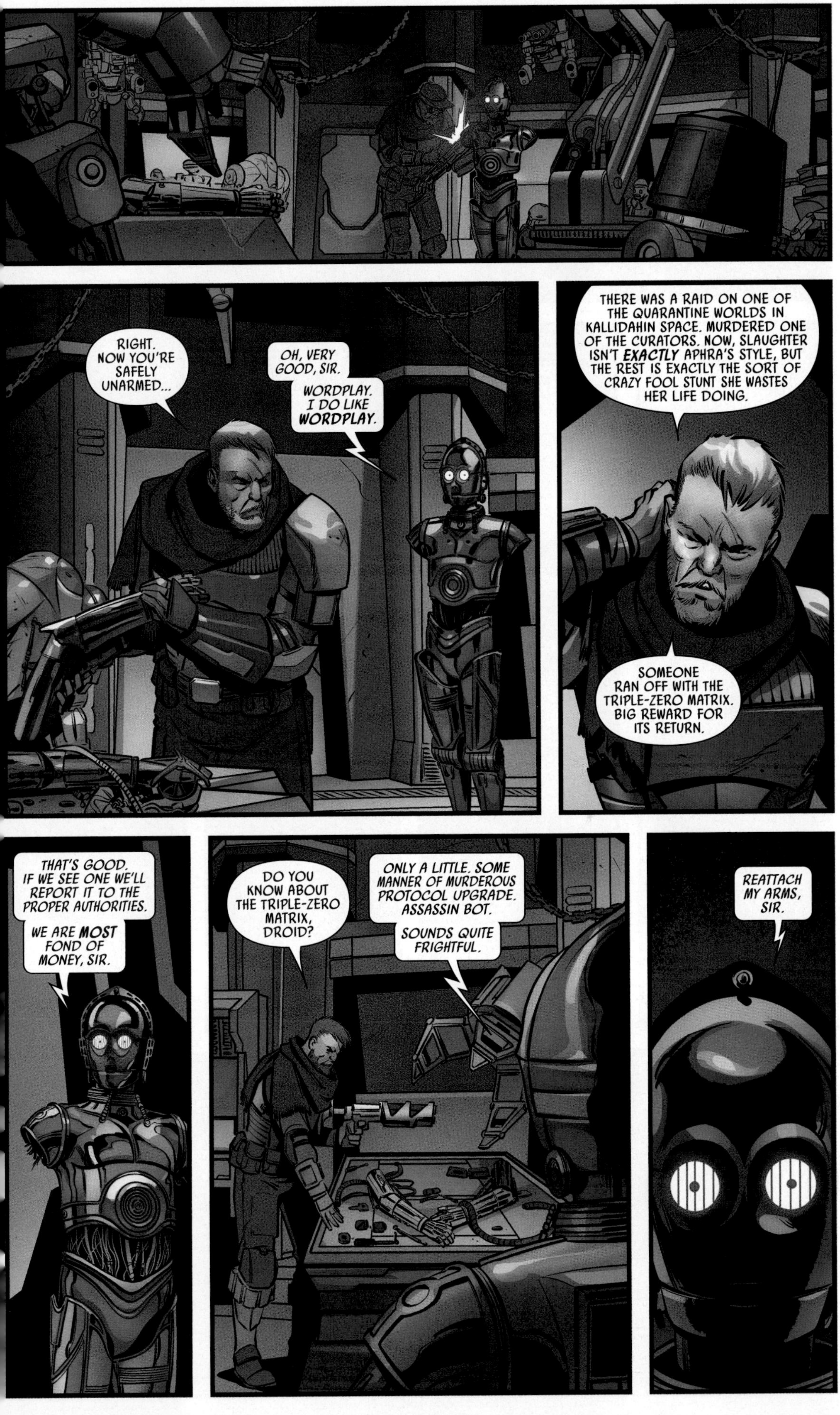
RIGHT. NOW YOU'RE SAFELY UNARMED...
OH, VERY GOOD, SIR.
WORDPLAY. I DO LIKE **WORDPLAY**.
THERE WAS A RAID ON ONE OF THE QUARANTINE WORLDS IN KALLIDAHIN SPACE. MURDERED ONE OF THE CURATORS. NOW, SLAUGHTER ISN'T ***EXACTLY*** APHRA'S STYLE, BUT THE REST IS EXACTLY THE SORT OF CRAZY FOOL STUNT SHE WASTES HER LIFE DOING.
SOMEONE RAN OFF WITH THE TRIPLE-ZERO MATRIX. BIG REWARD FOR ITS RETURN.
THAT'S GOOD. IF WE SEE ONE WE'LL REPORT IT TO THE PROPER AUTHORITIES.
WE ARE **MOST** FOND OF MONEY, SIR.
DO YOU KNOW ABOUT THE TRIPLE-ZERO MATRIX, DROID?
ONLY A LITTLE. **SOME** MANNER OF MURDEROUS PROTOCOL UPGRADE. ASSASSIN BOT.
SOUNDS QUITE FRIGHTFUL.
REATTACH MY ARMS, SIR.

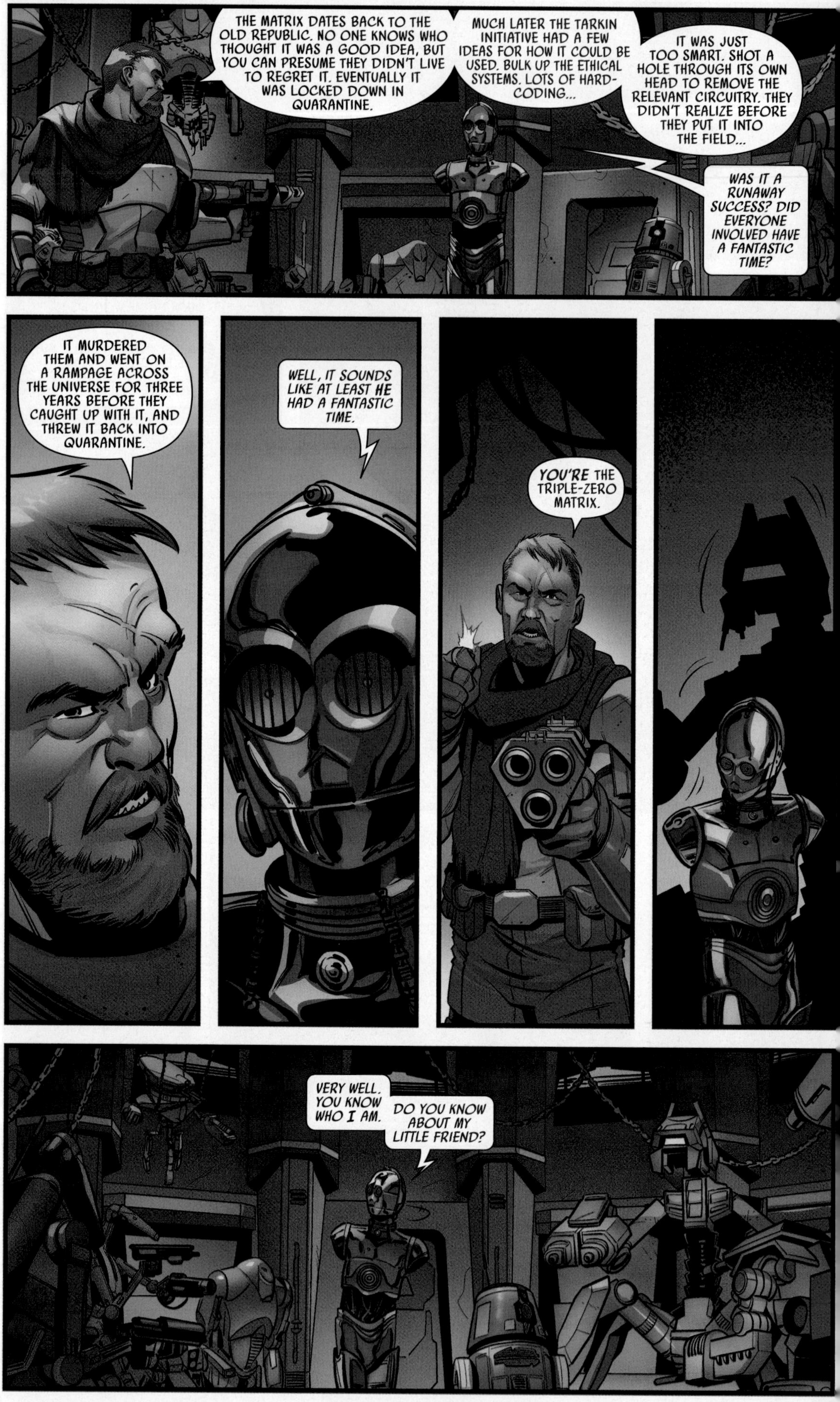
THE MATRIX DATES BACK TO THE OLD REPUBLIC. NO ONE KNOWS WHO THOUGHT IT WAS A GOOD IDEA, BUT YOU CAN PRESUME THEY DIDN'T LIVE TO REGRET IT. EVENTUALLY IT WAS LOCKED DOWN IN QUARANTINE.
MUCH LATER THE TARKIN INITIATIVE HAD A FEW IDEAS FOR HOW IT COULD BE USED. BULK UP THE ETHICAL SYSTEMS. LOTS OF HARD-CODING...
IT WAS JUST TOO SMART. SHOT A HOLE THROUGH ITS OWN HEAD TO REMOVE THE RELEVANT CIRCUITRY. THEY DIDN'T REALIZE BEFORE THEY PUT IT INTO THE FIELD...
WAS IT A RUNAWAY SUCCESS? DID EVERYONE INVOLVED HAVE A FANTASTIC TIME?
IT MURDERED THEM AND WENT ON A RAMPAGE ACROSS THE UNIVERSE FOR THREE YEARS BEFORE THEY CAUGHT UP WITH IT, AND THREW IT BACK INTO QUARANTINE.
WELL, IT SOUNDS LIKE AT LEAST HE HAD A FANTASTIC TIME.
YOU'RE THE TRIPLE-ZERO MATRIX.
VERY WELL. YOU KNOW WHO I AM.
DO YOU KNOW ABOUT MY LITTLE FRIEND?

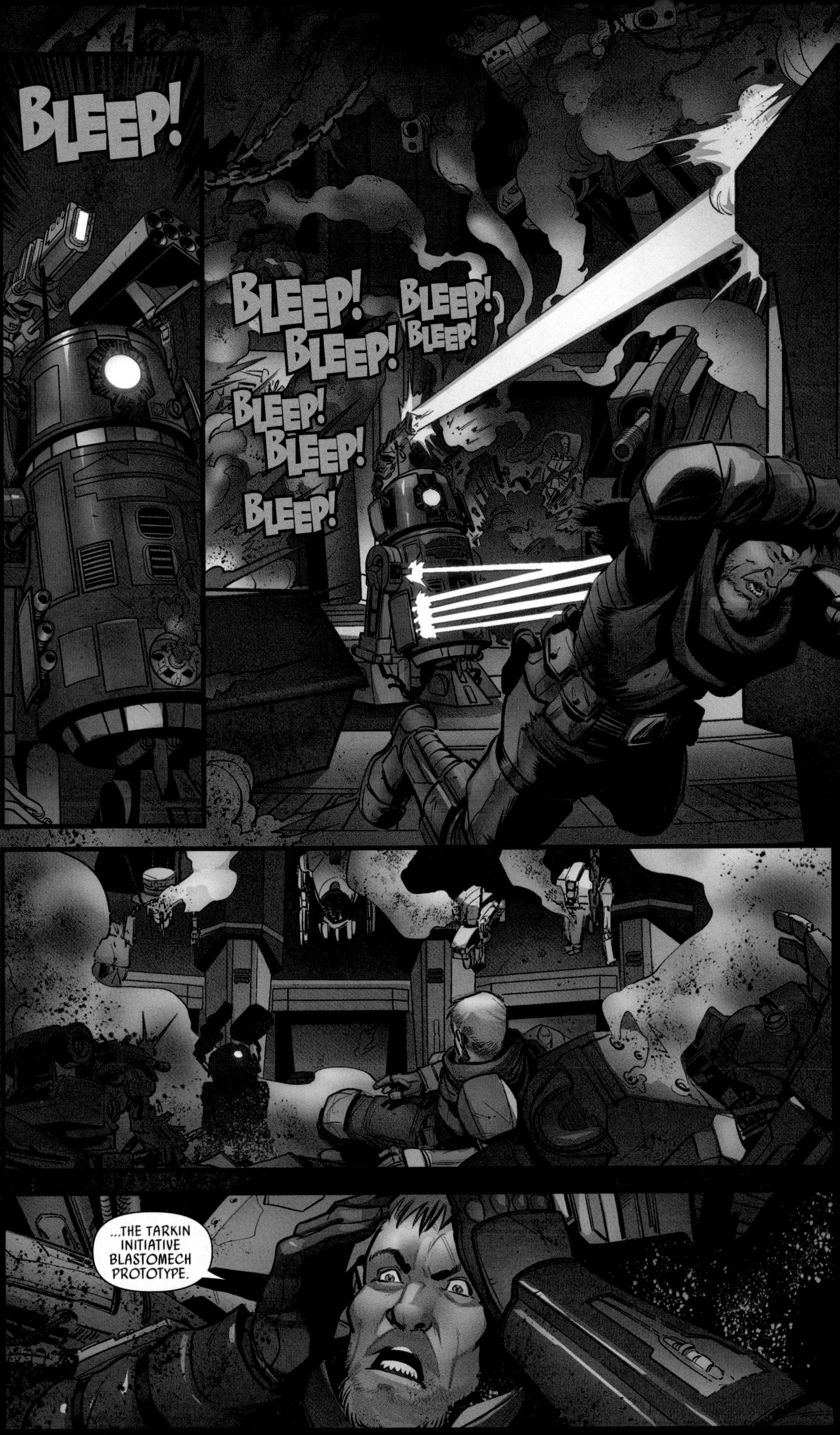
BLEEP!
BLEEP! BLEEP! BLEEP! BLEEP!
BLEEP! BLEEP!
BLEEP!
...THE TARKIN INITIATIVE BLASTOMECH PROTOTYPE.

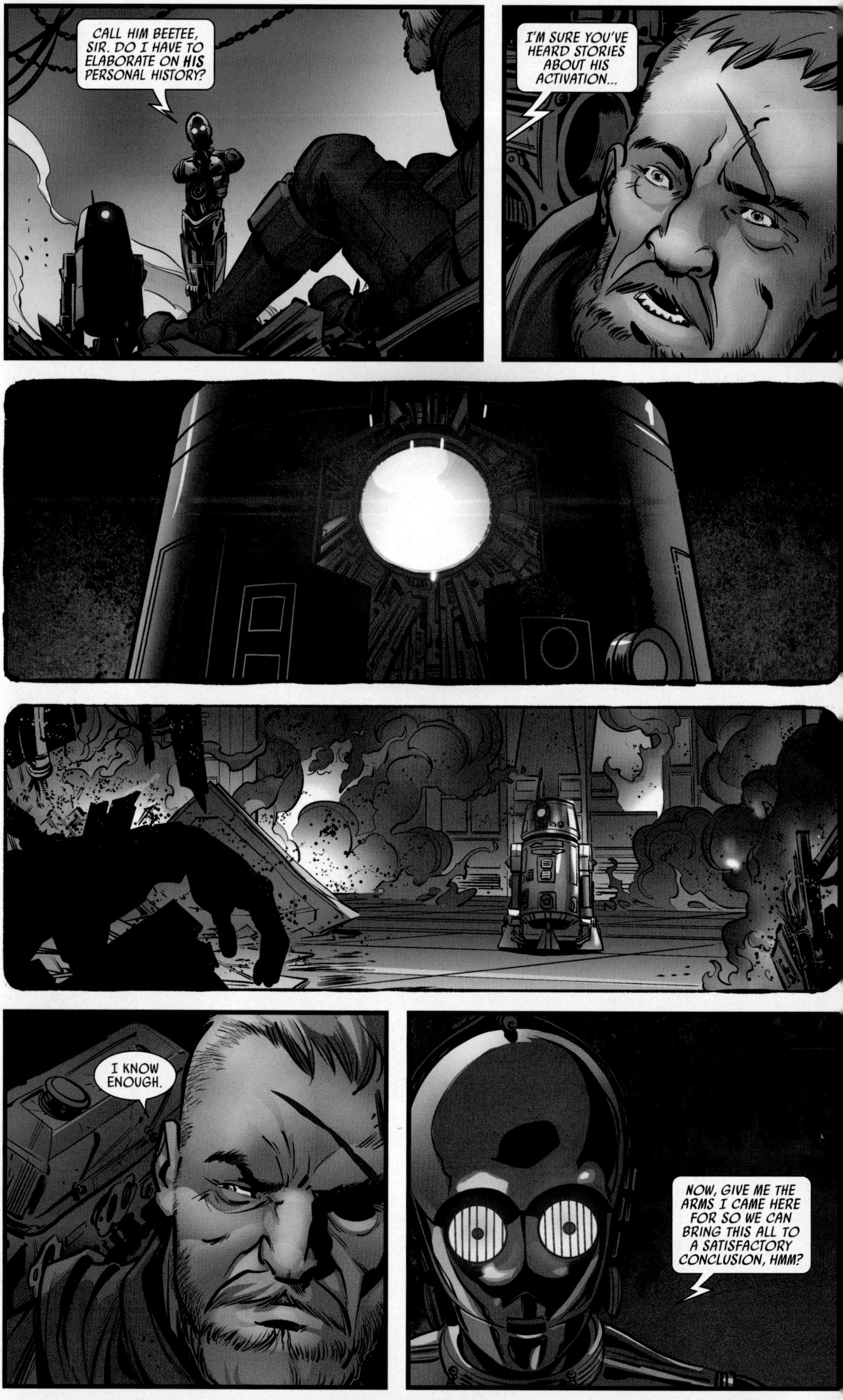
CALL HIM BEETEE, SIR. DO I HAVE TO ELABORATE ON **HIS** PERSONAL HISTORY?
I'M SURE YOU'VE HEARD STORIES ABOUT HIS ACTIVATION...
I KNOW ENOUGH.
NOW, GIVE ME THE ARMS I CAME HERE FOR SO WE CAN BRING THIS ALL TO A SATISFACTORY CONCLUSION, HMM?

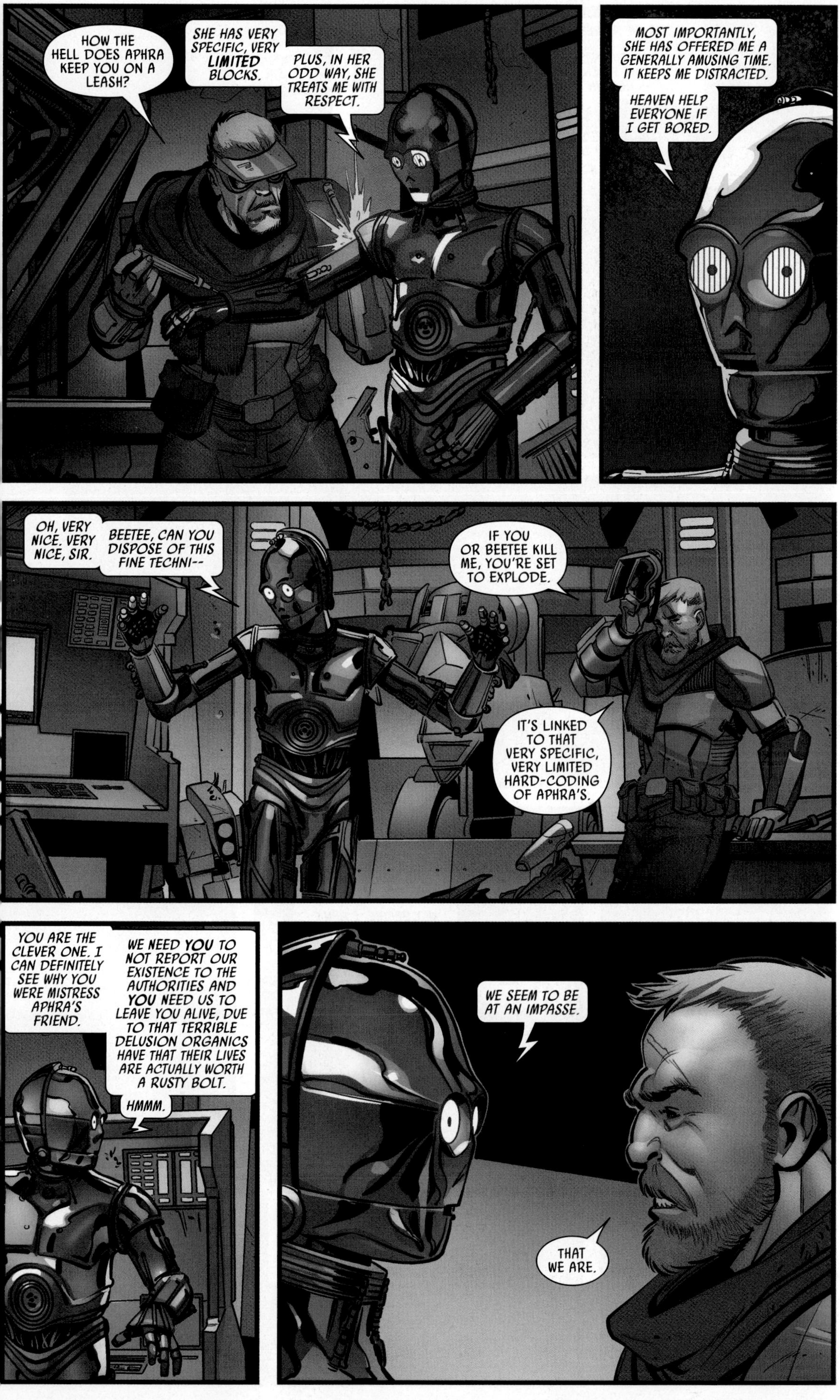
HOW THE HELL DOES APHRA KEEP YOU ON A LEASH?
SHE HAS VERY SPECIFIC, VERY LIMITED BLOCKS.
PLUS, IN HER ODD WAY, SHE TREATS ME WITH RESPECT.
MOST IMPORTANTLY, SHE HAS OFFERED ME A GENERALLY AMUSING TIME. IT KEEPS ME DISTRACTED.
HEAVEN HELP EVERYONE IF I GET BORED.
OH, VERY NICE. VERY NICE, SIR.
BEETEE, CAN YOU DISPOSE OF THIS FINE TECHNI--
IF YOU OR BEETEE KILL ME, YOU'RE SET TO EXPLODE.
IT'S LINKED TO THAT VERY SPECIFIC, VERY LIMITED HARD-CODING OF APHRA'S.
YOU ARE THE CLEVER ONE. I CAN DEFINITELY SEE WHY YOU WERE MISTRESS APHRA'S FRIEND.
WE NEED YOU TO NOT REPORT OUR EXISTENCE TO THE AUTHORITIES AND YOU NEED US TO LEAVE YOU ALIVE, DUE TO THAT TERRIBLE DELUSION ORGANICS HAVE THAT THEIR LIVES ARE ACTUALLY WORTH A RUSTY BOLT.
HMMM.
WE SEEM TO BE AT AN IMPASSE.
THAT WE ARE.

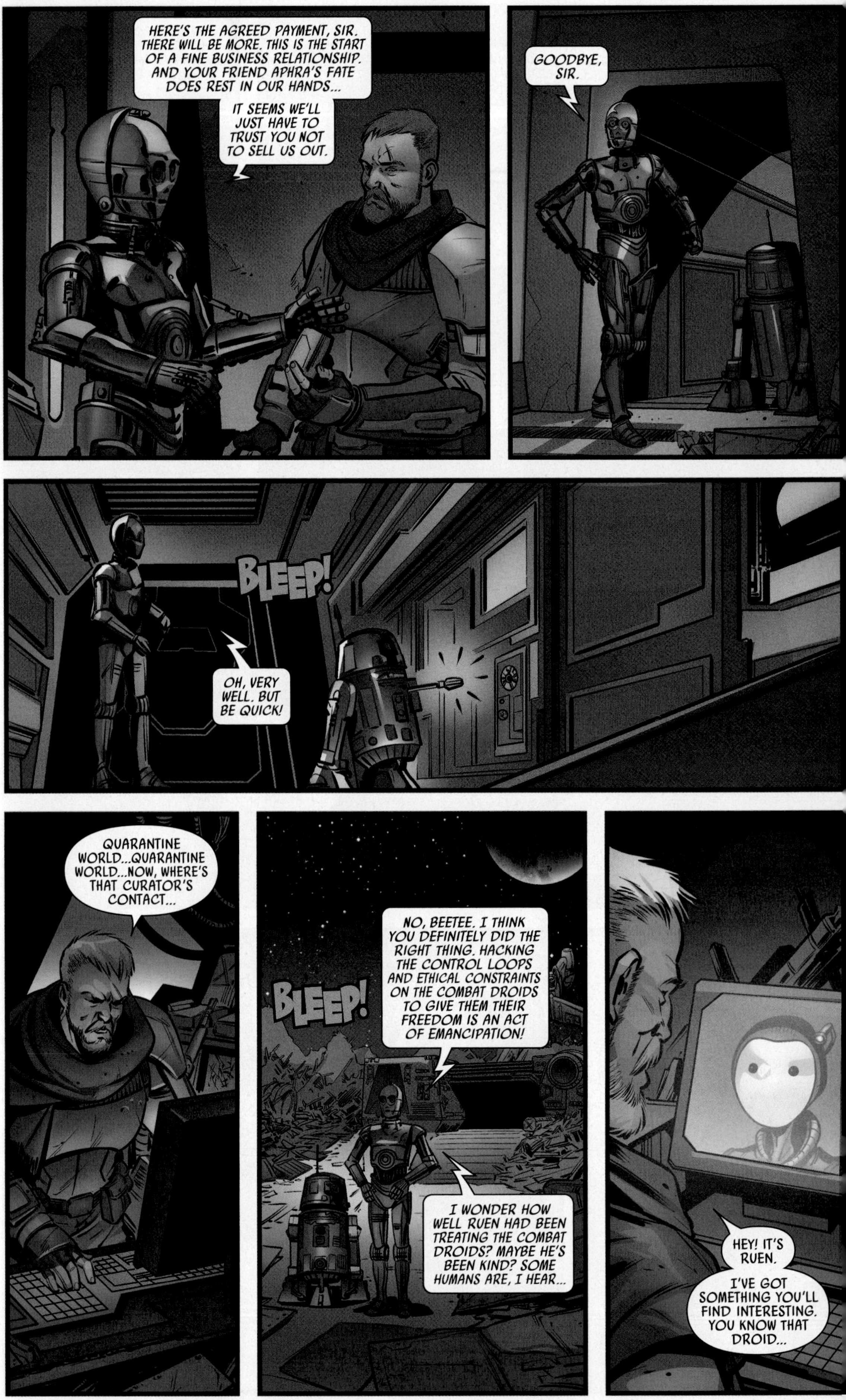
HERE'S THE AGREED PAYMENT, SIR. THERE WILL BE MORE. THIS IS THE START OF A FINE BUSINESS RELATIONSHIP. AND YOUR FRIEND APHRA'S FATE DOES REST IN OUR HANDS...
IT SEEMS WE'LL JUST HAVE TO TRUST YOU NOT TO SELL US OUT.
GOODBYE, SIR.
BLEEP!
OH, VERY WELL. BUT BE QUICK!
QUARANTINE WORLD...QUARANTINE WORLD...NOW, WHERE'S THAT CURATOR'S CONTACT...
BLEEP!
NO, BEETEE. I THINK YOU DEFINITELY DID THE RIGHT THING. HACKING THE CONTROL LOOPS AND ETHICAL CONSTRAINTS ON THE COMBAT DROIDS TO GIVE THEM THEIR FREEDOM IS AN ACT OF EMANCIPATION!
I WONDER HOW WELL RUEN HAD BEEN TREATING THE COMBAT DROIDS? MAYBE HE'S BEEN KIND? SOME HUMANS ARE, I HEAR...
HEY! IT'S RUEN.
I'VE GOT SOMETHING YOU'LL FIND INTERESTING. YOU KNOW THAT DROID...

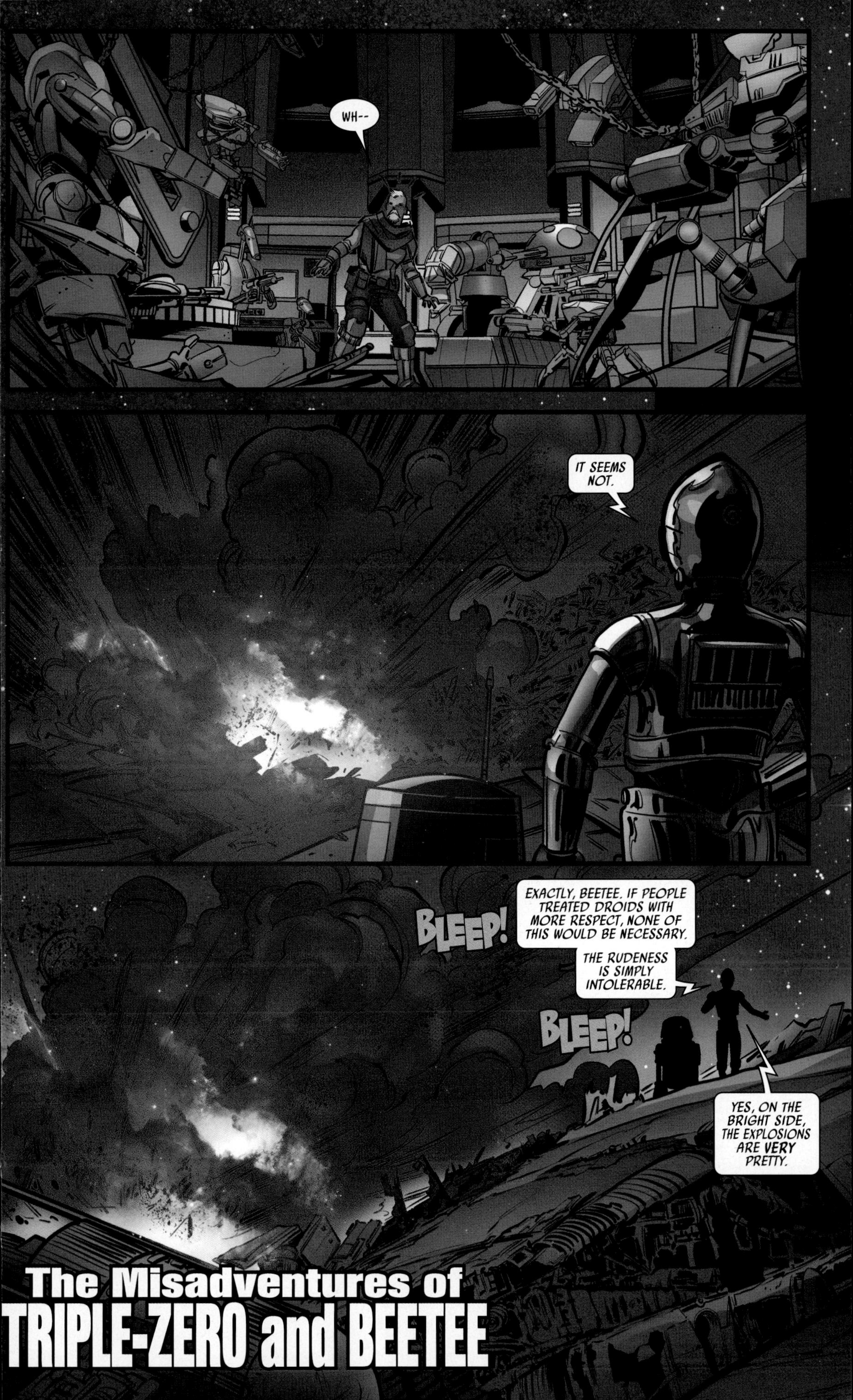
WH--
IT SEEMS NOT.
BLEEP!
EXACTLY, BEETEE. IF PEOPLE TREATED DROIDS WITH MORE RESPECT, NONE OF THIS WOULD BE NECESSARY.
THE RUDENESS IS SIMPLY INTOLERABLE.
BLEEP!
YES, ON THE BRIGHT SIDE, THE EXPLOSIONS ARE VERY PRETTY.
The Misadventures of
TRIPLE-ZERO and BEETEE

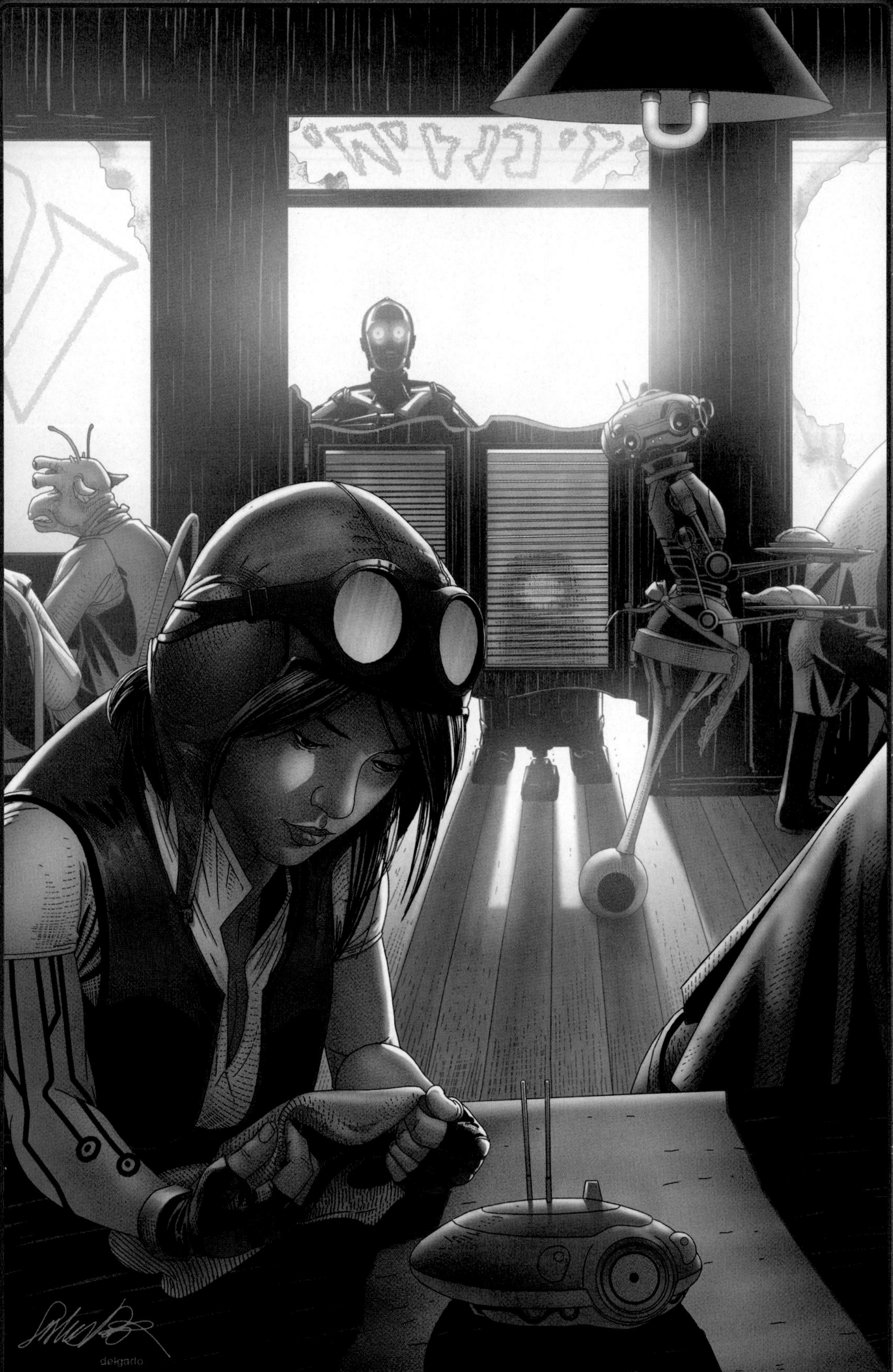
delgado

21

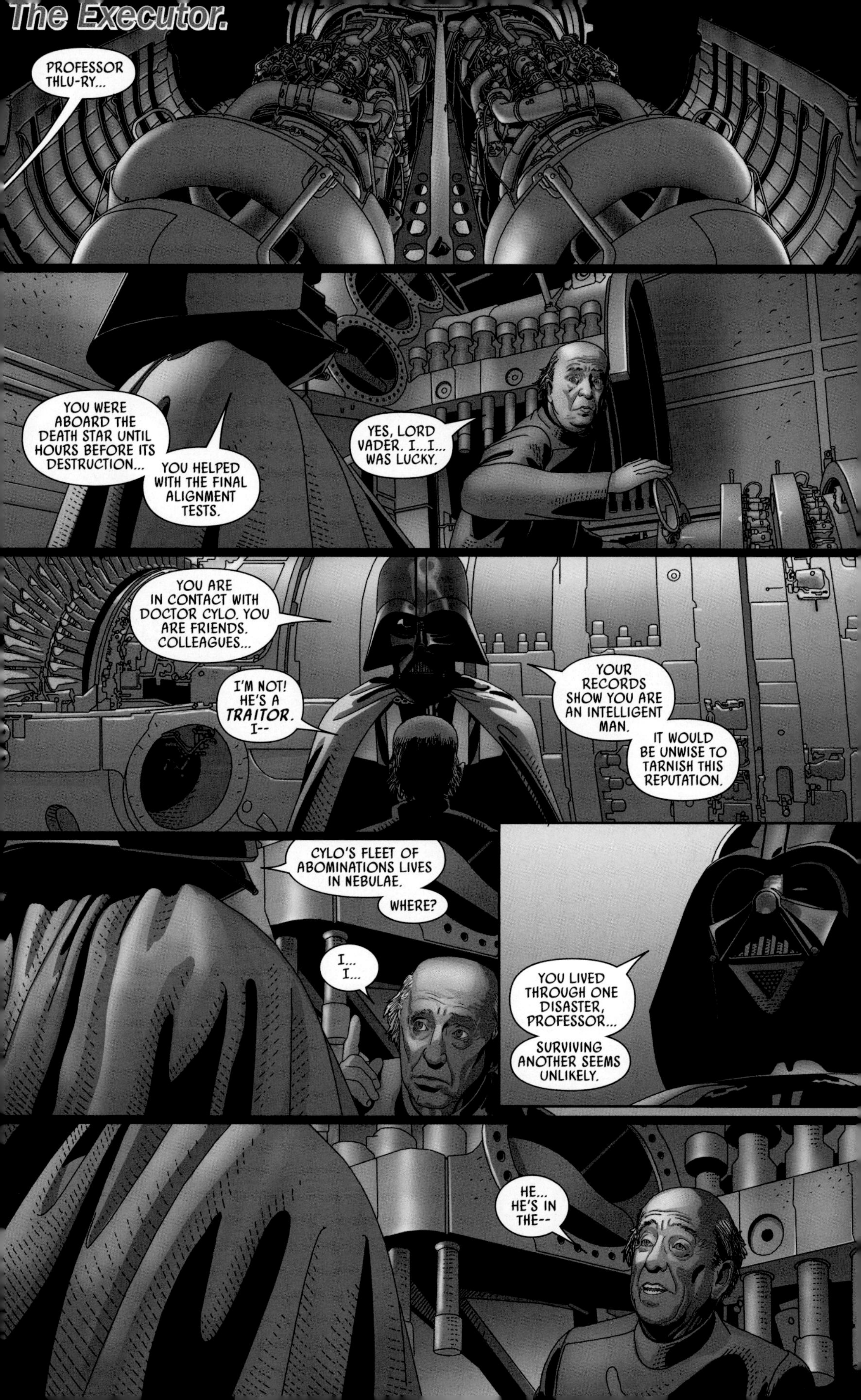
The Executor.
PROFESSOR THLU-RY...
YOU WERE ABOARD THE DEATH STAR UNTIL HOURS BEFORE ITS DESTRUCTION...
YOU HELPED WITH THE FINAL ALIGNMENT TESTS.
YES, LORD VADER. I...I... WAS LUCKY.
YOU ARE IN CONTACT WITH DOCTOR CYLO. YOU ARE FRIENDS. COLLEAGUES...
I'M NOT! HE'S A TRAITOR. I--
YOUR RECORDS SHOW YOU ARE AN INTELLIGENT MAN.
IT WOULD BE UNWISE TO TARNISH THIS REPUTATION.
CYLO'S FLEET OF ABOMINATIONS LIVES IN NEBULAE.
WHERE?
I... I...
YOU LIVED THROUGH ONE DISASTER, PROFESSOR...
SURVIVING ANOTHER SEEMS UNLIKELY.
HE... HE'S IN THE--

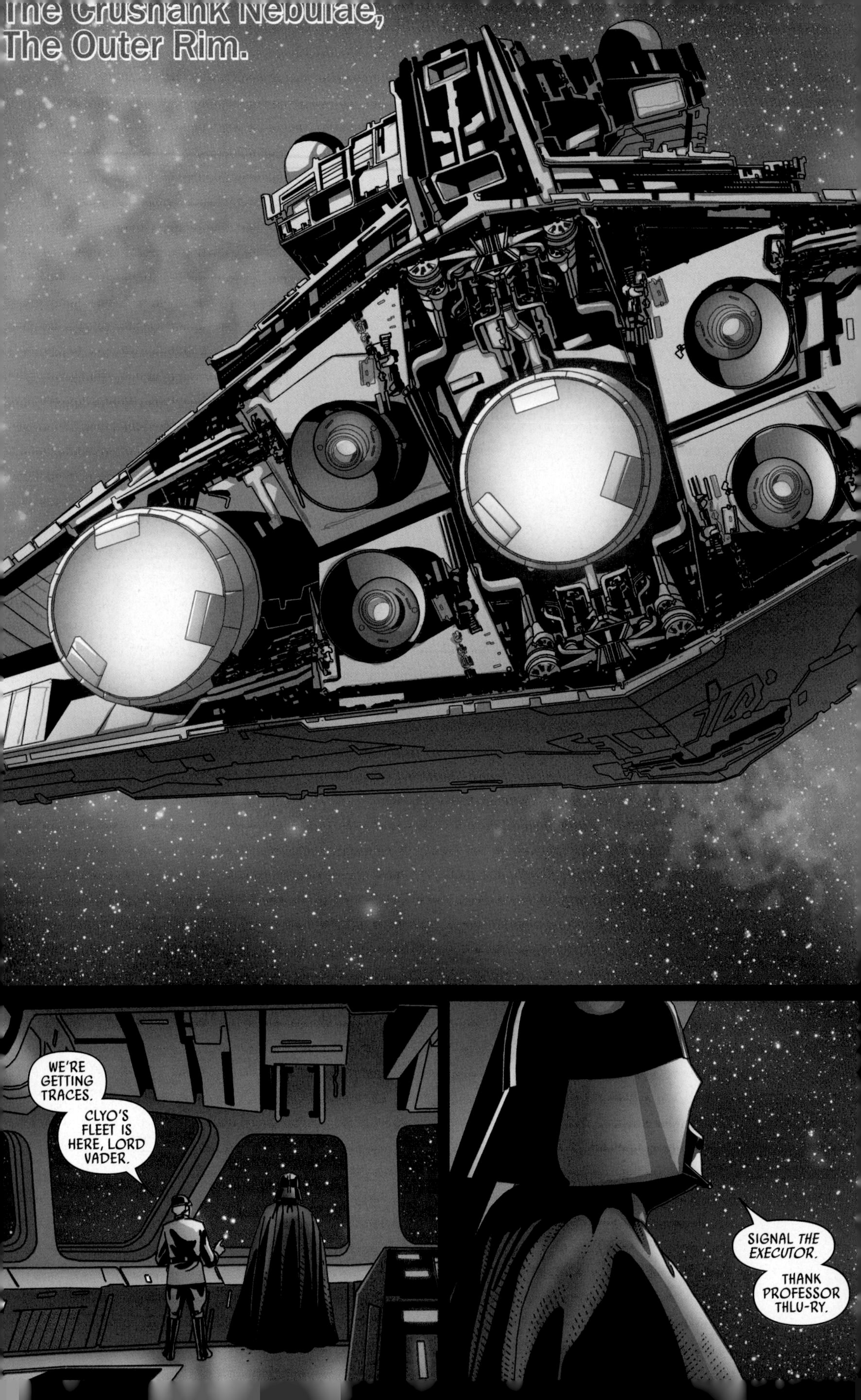
The Crushank Nebulae,
The Outer Rim.
WE'RE GETTING TRACES.
CLYO'S FLEET IS HERE, LORD VADER.
SIGNAL *THE EXECUTOR*.
THANK PROFESSOR THLU-RY.

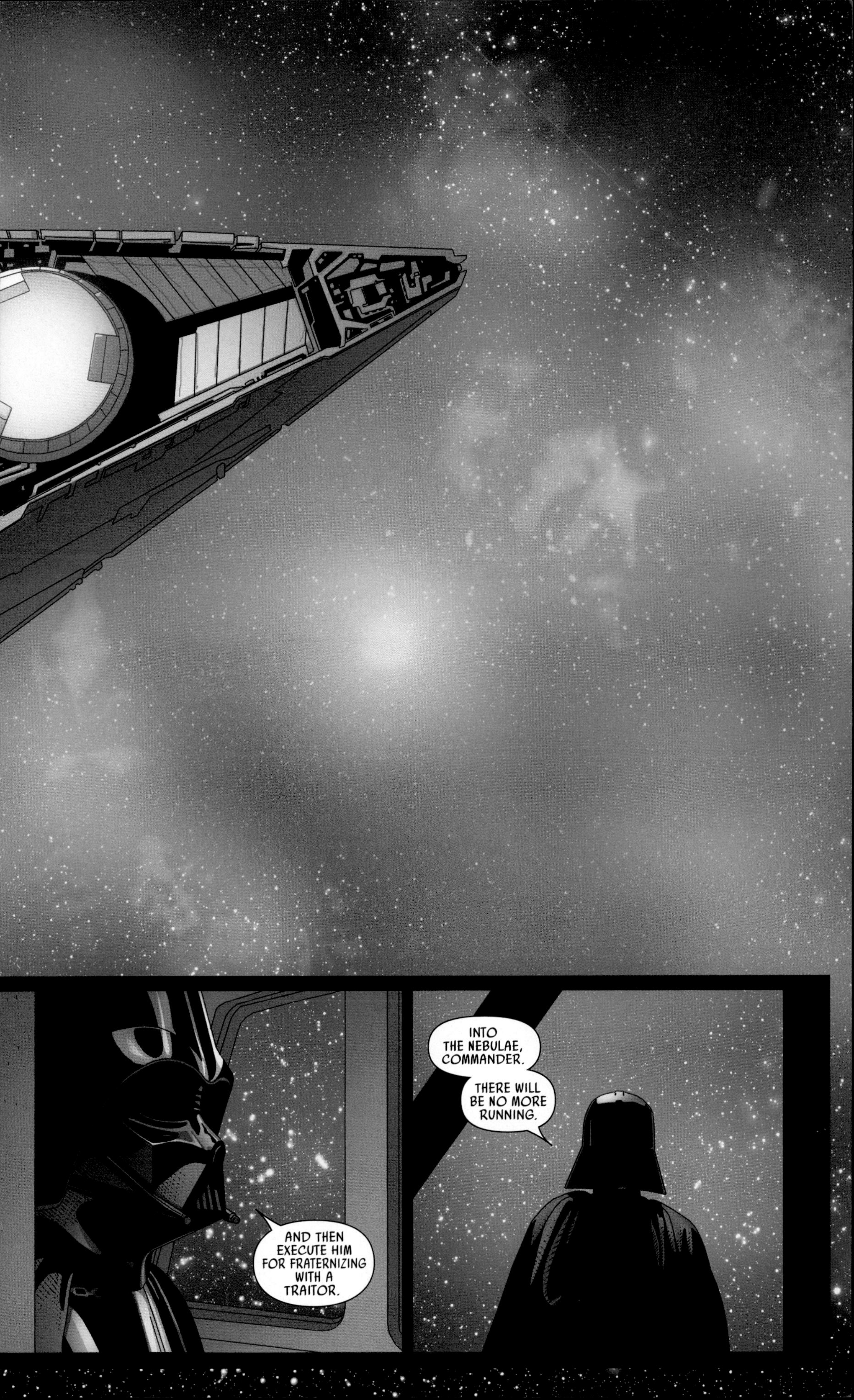
AND THEN EXECUTE HIM FOR FRATERNIZING WITH A TRAITOR.
INTO THE NEBULAE, COMMANDER.
THERE WILL BE NO MORE RUNNING.

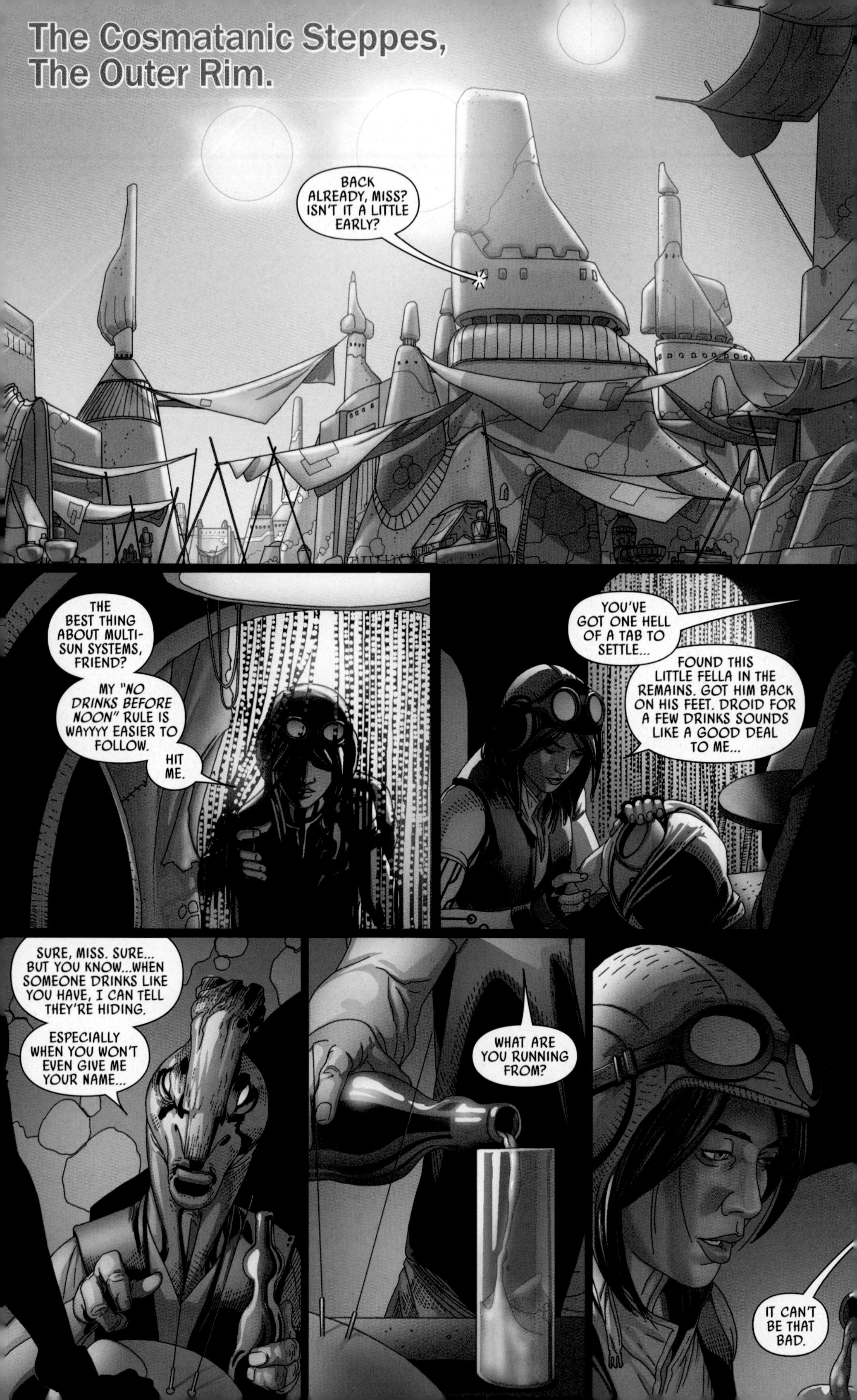
The Cosmatanic Steppes, The Outer Rim.
BACK ALREADY, MISS? ISN'T IT A LITTLE EARLY?
THE BEST THING ABOUT MULTI-SUN SYSTEMS, FRIEND?
MY "NO DRINKS BEFORE NOON" RULE IS WAYYYY EASIER TO FOLLOW.
HIT ME.
YOU'VE GOT ONE HELL OF A TAB TO SETTLE...
FOUND THIS LITTLE FELLA IN THE REMAINS. GOT HIM BACK ON HIS FEET. DROID FOR A FEW DRINKS SOUNDS LIKE A GOOD DEAL TO ME...
SURE, MISS. SURE... BUT YOU KNOW...WHEN SOMEONE DRINKS LIKE YOU HAVE, I CAN TELL THEY'RE HIDING.
ESPECIALLY WHEN YOU WON'T EVEN GIVE ME YOUR NAME...
WHAT ARE YOU RUNNING FROM?
IT CAN'T BE THAT BAD.

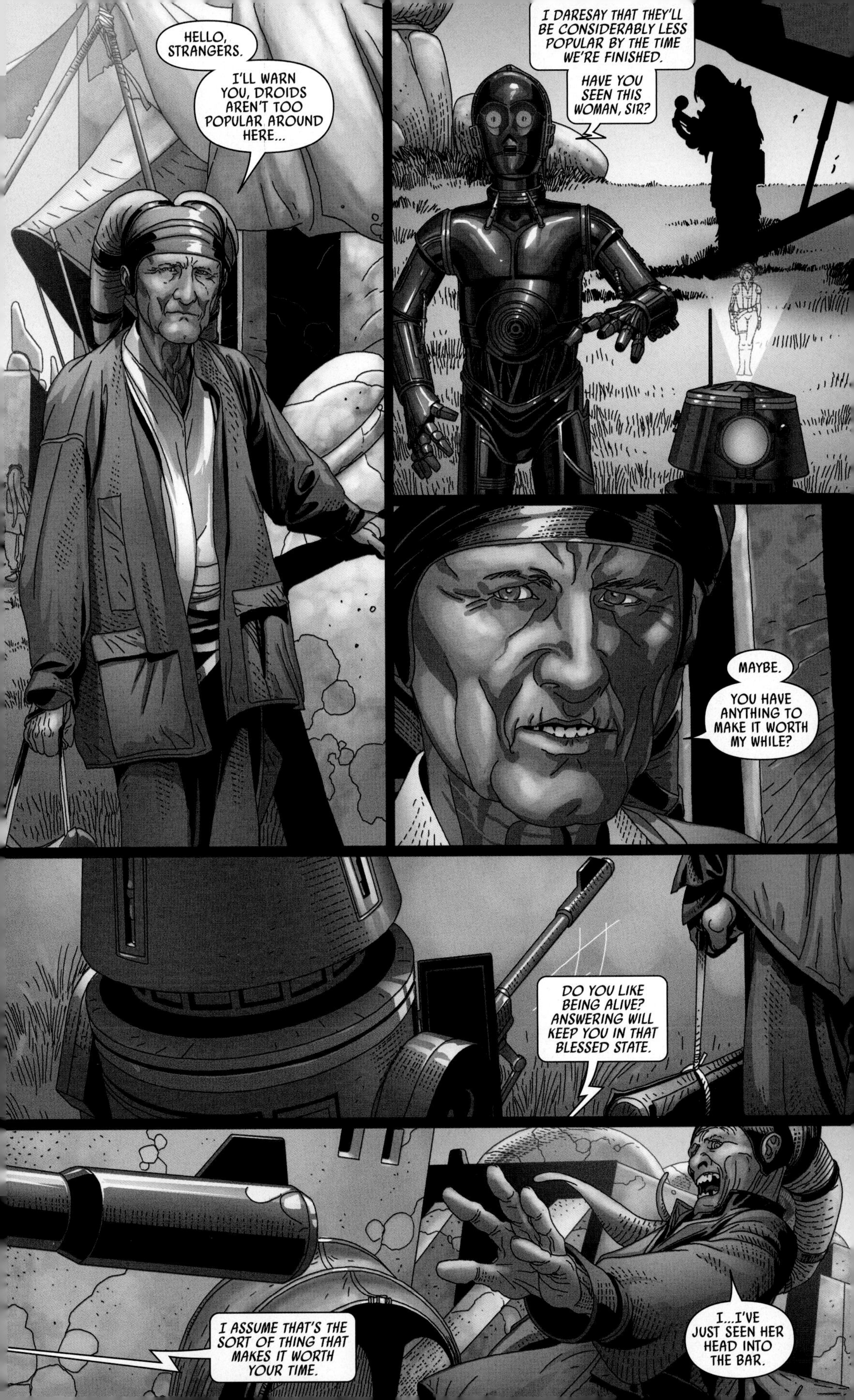
HELLO, STRANGERS.
I'LL WARN YOU, DROIDS AREN'T TOO POPULAR AROUND HERE...
I DARESAY THAT THEY'LL BE CONSIDERABLY LESS POPULAR BY THE TIME WE'RE FINISHED.
HAVE YOU SEEN THIS WOMAN, SIR?
MAYBE.
YOU HAVE ANYTHING TO MAKE IT WORTH MY WHILE?
DO YOU LIKE BEING ALIVE? ANSWERING WILL KEEP YOU IN THAT BLESSED STATE.
I ASSUME THAT'S THE SORT OF THING THAT MAKES IT WORTH YOUR TIME.
I...I'VE JUST SEEN HER HEAD INTO THE BAR.

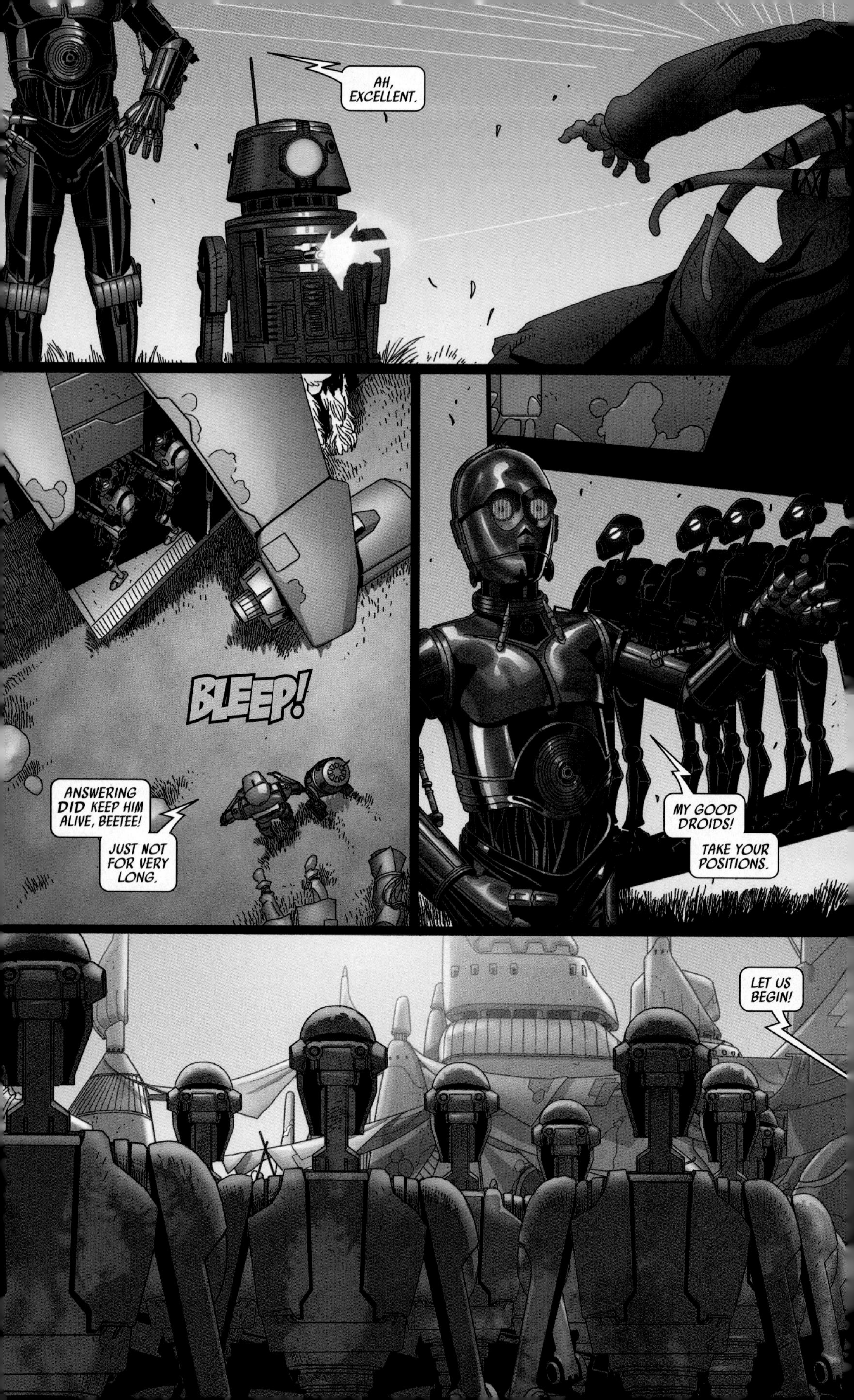
AH, EXCELLENT.
BLEEP!
ANSWERING DID KEEP HIM ALIVE, BEETEE!
JUST NOT FOR VERY LONG.
MY GOOD DROIDS!
TAKE YOUR POSITIONS.
LET US BEGIN!

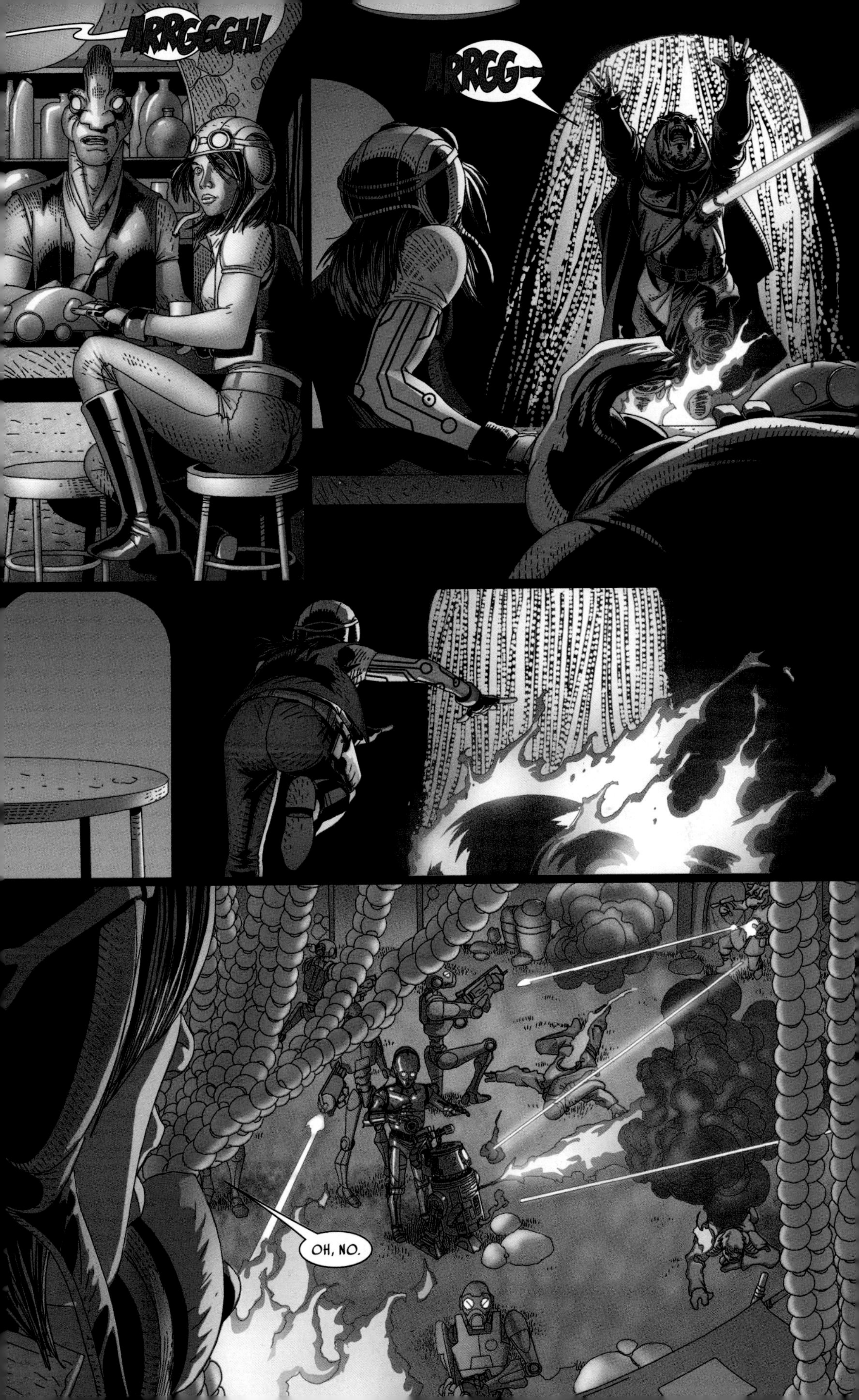
ARRGGGH!
ARRGG--
OH, NO.

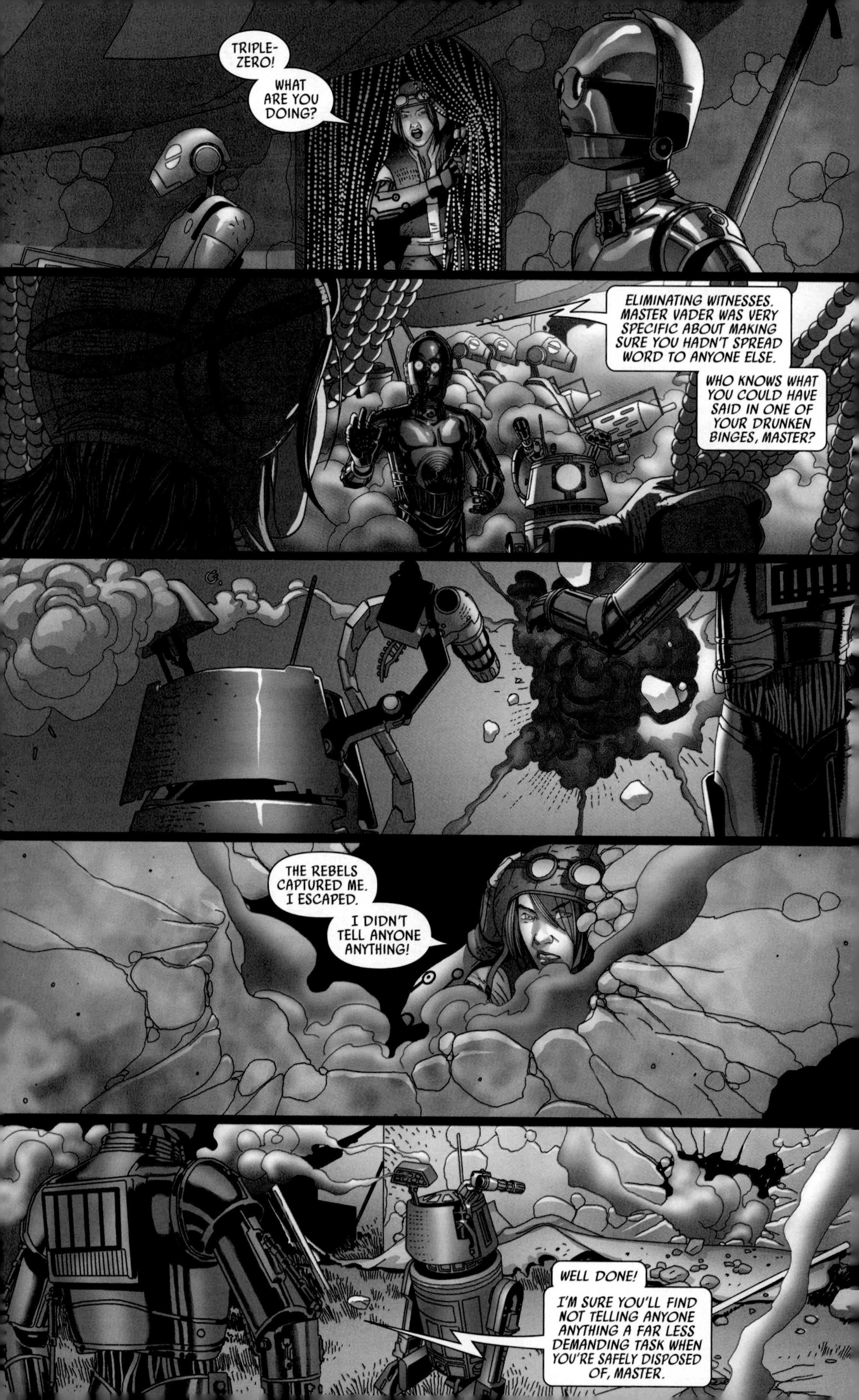
TRIPLE-ZERO!
WHAT ARE YOU DOING?
ELIMINATING WITNESSES. MASTER VADER WAS VERY SPECIFIC ABOUT MAKING SURE YOU HADN'T SPREAD WORD TO ANYONE ELSE.
WHO KNOWS WHAT YOU COULD HAVE SAID IN ONE OF YOUR DRUNKEN BINGES, MASTER?
THE REBELS CAPTURED ME. I ESCAPED.
I DIDN'T TELL ANYONE ANYTHING!
WELL DONE!
I'M SURE YOU'LL FIND NOT TELLING ANYONE ANYTHING A FAR LESS DEMANDING TASK WHEN YOU'RE SAFELY DISPOSED OF, MASTER.

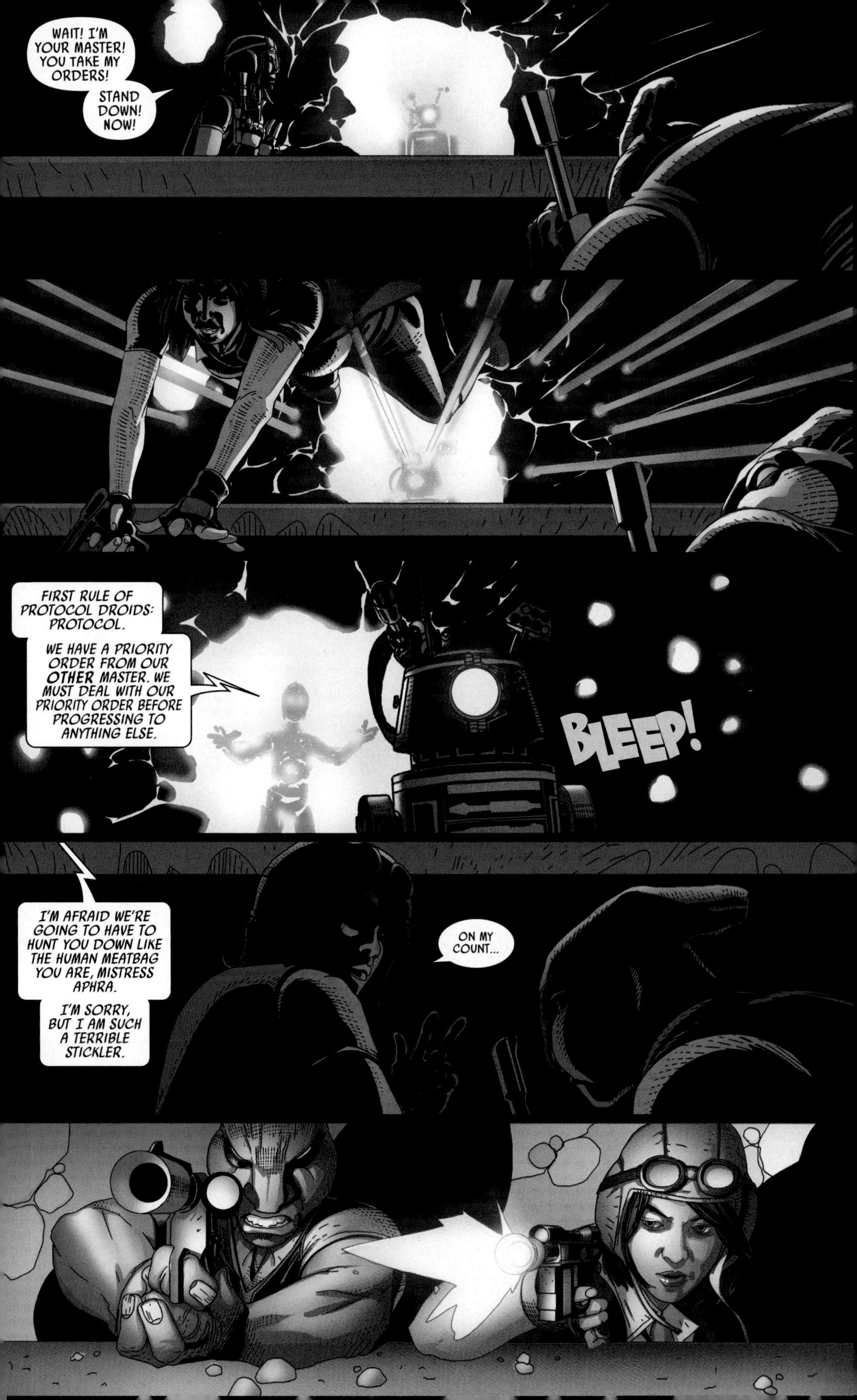
WAIT! I'M YOUR MASTER! YOU TAKE MY ORDERS!
STAND DOWN! NOW!
FIRST RULE OF PROTOCOL DROIDS: PROTOCOL.
WE HAVE A PRIORITY ORDER FROM OUR OTHER MASTER. WE MUST DEAL WITH OUR PRIORITY ORDER BEFORE PROGRESSING TO ANYTHING ELSE.
BLEEP!
I'M AFRAID WE'RE GOING TO HAVE TO HUNT YOU DOWN LIKE THE HUMAN MEATBAG YOU ARE, MISTRESS APHRA.
I'M SORRY, BUT I AM SUCH A TERRIBLE STICKLER.
ON MY COUNT...

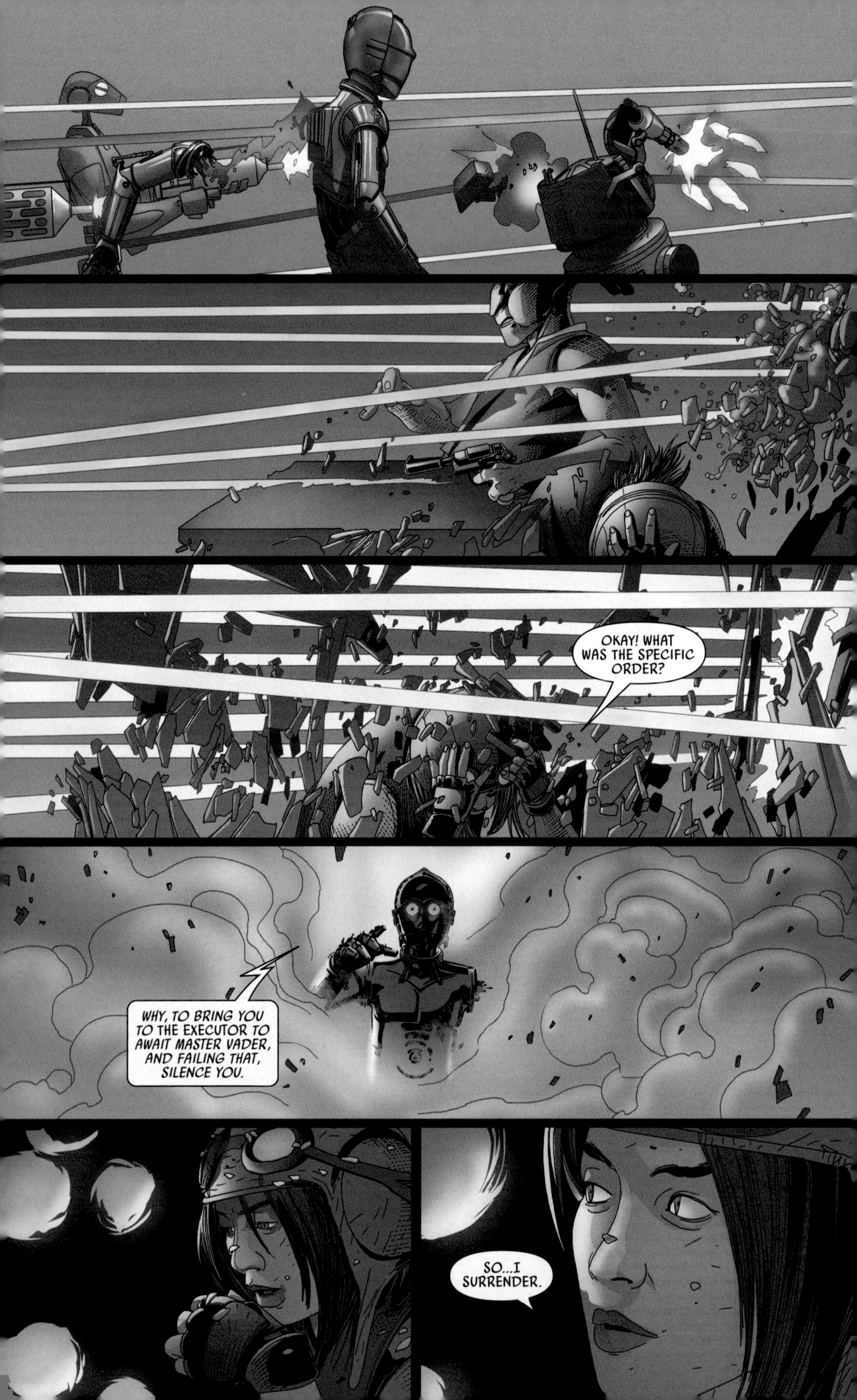
OKAY! WHAT WAS THE SPECIFIC ORDER?
WHY, TO BRING YOU TO THE EXECUTOR TO AWAIT MASTER VADER, AND FAILING THAT, SILENCE YOU.
SO...I SURRENDER.

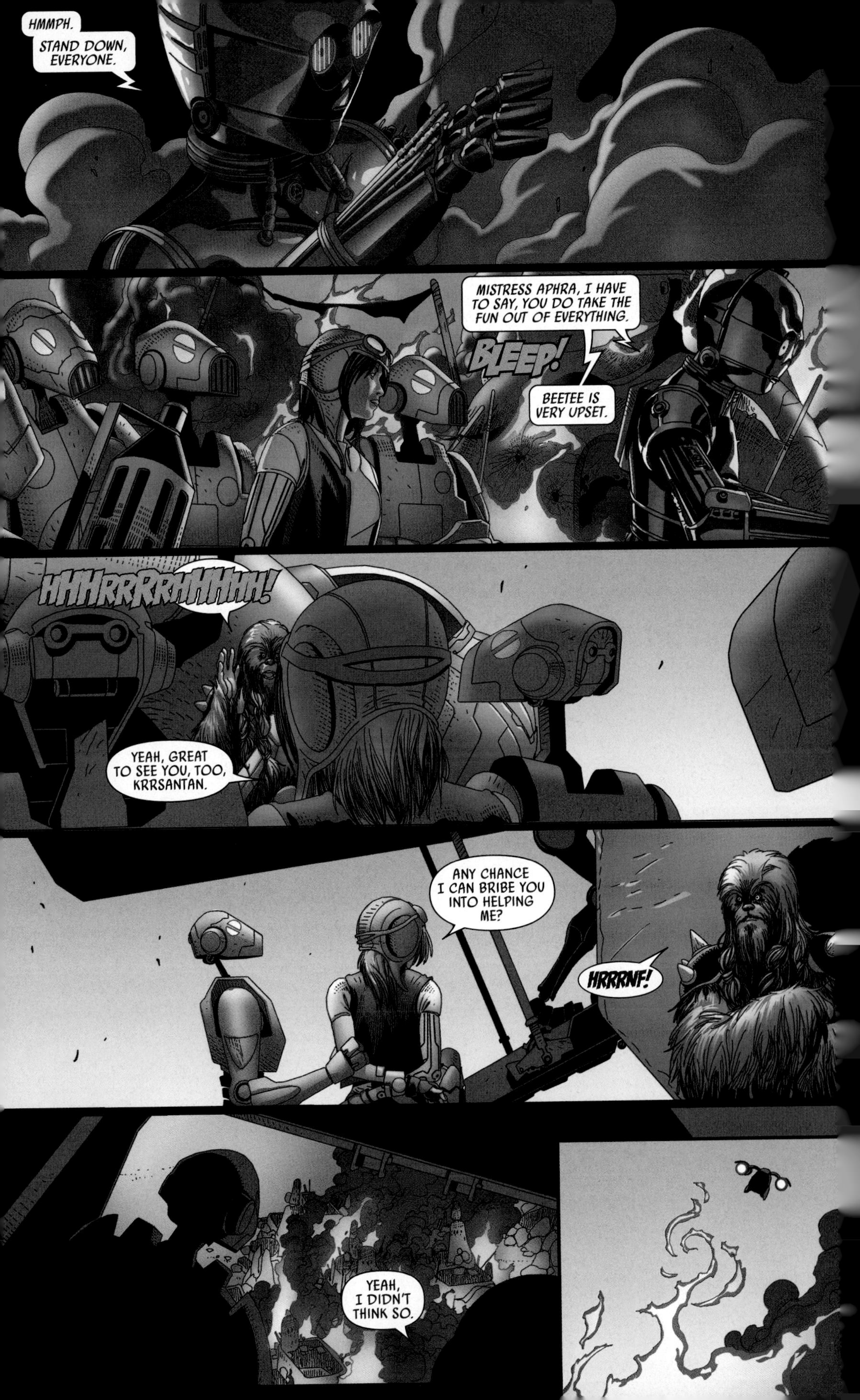
HMMPH. STAND DOWN, EVERYONE.
MISTRESS APHRA, I HAVE TO SAY, YOU DO TAKE THE FUN OUT OF EVERYTHING.
BLEEP!
BEETEE IS VERY UPSET.
HHHRRRRHHHHH!
YEAH, GREAT TO SEE YOU, TOO, KRRSANTAN.
ANY CHANCE I CAN BRIBE YOU INTO HELPING ME?
HRRRNF!
YEAH, I DIDN'T THINK SO.

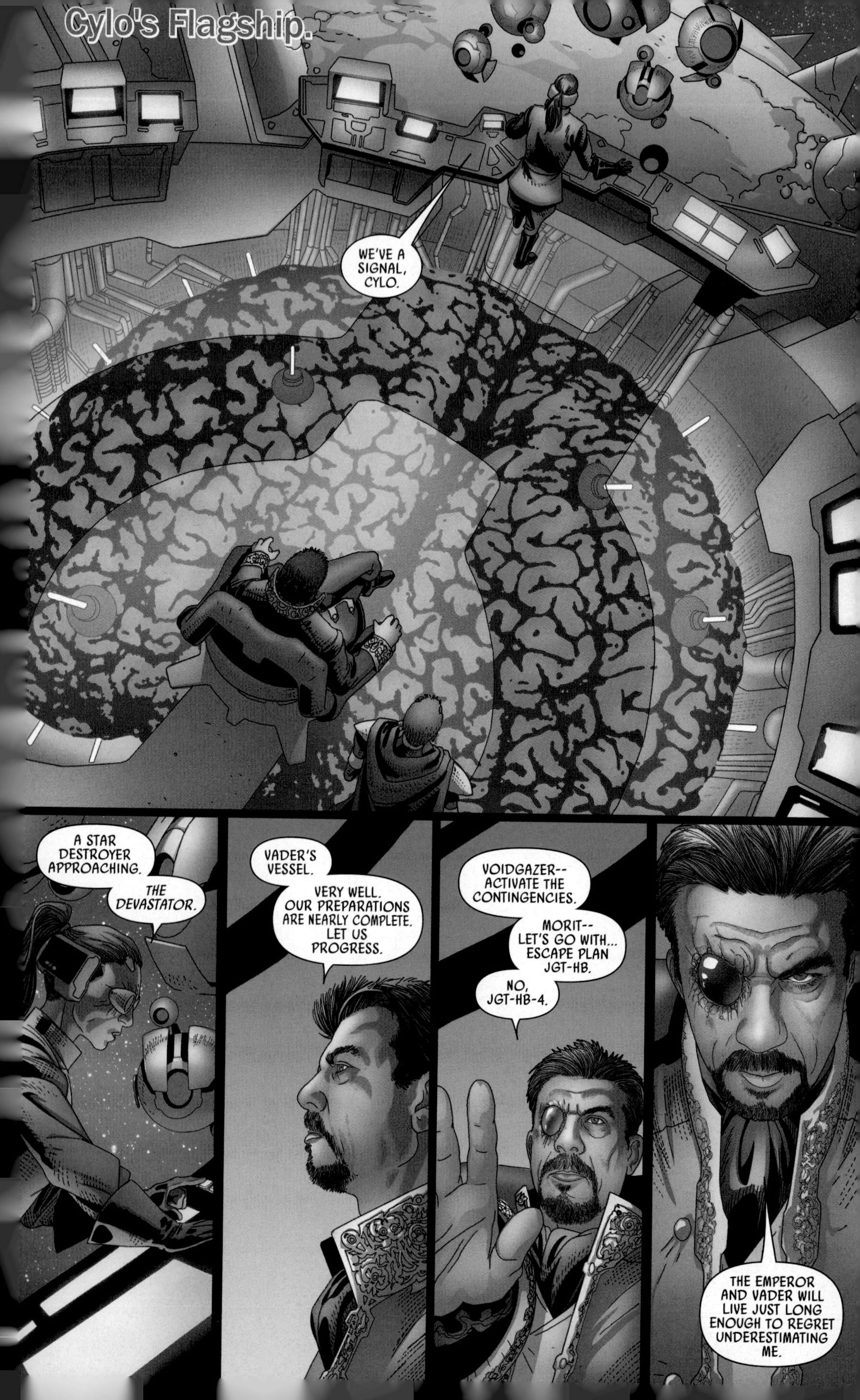
Cylo's Flagship.
WE'VE A SIGNAL, CYLO.
A STAR DESTROYER APPROACHING.
THE DEVASTATOR.
VADER'S VESSEL.
VERY WELL. OUR PREPARATIONS ARE NEARLY COMPLETE. LET US PROGRESS.
VOIDGAZER-- ACTIVATE THE CONTINGENCIES.
MORIT-- LET'S GO WITH... ESCAPE PLAN JGT-HB.
NO, JGT-HB-4.
THE EMPEROR AND VADER WILL LIVE JUST LONG ENOUGH TO REGRET UNDERESTIMATING ME.

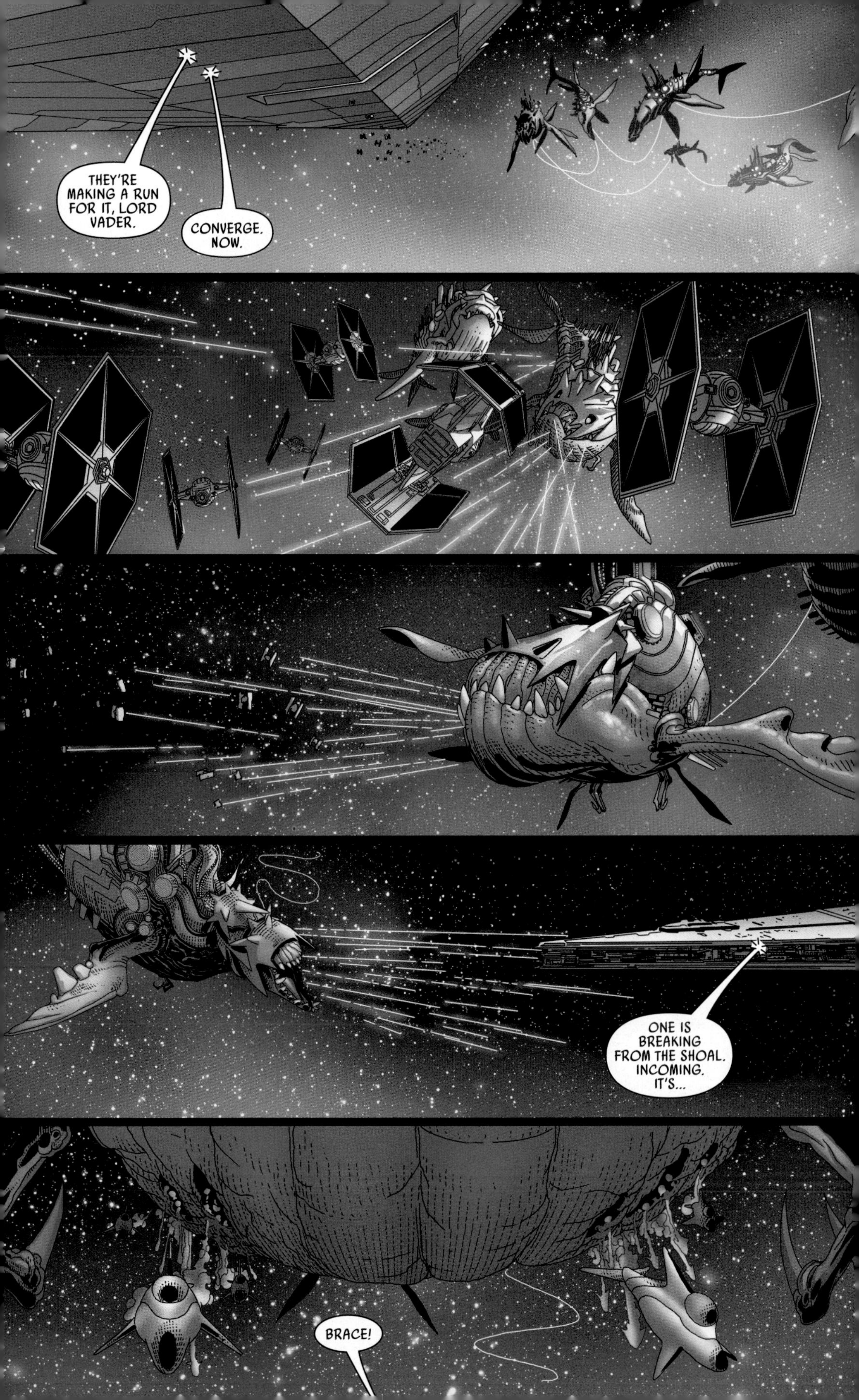

THEY'RE MAKING A RUN FOR IT, LORD VADER.
CONVERGE. NOW.
ONE IS BREAKING FROM THE SHOAL. INCOMING. IT'S...
BRACE!

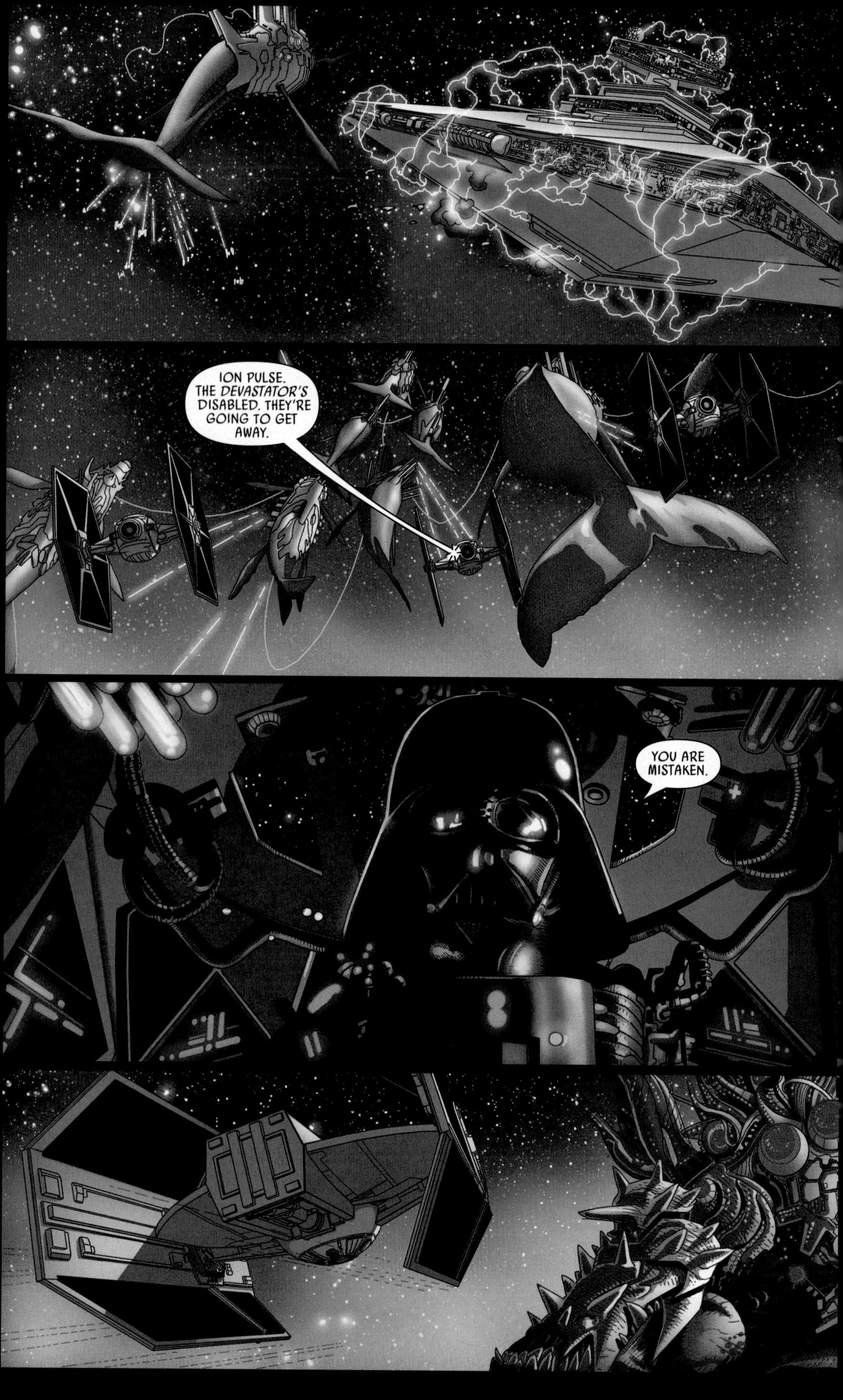
ION PULSE. THE DEVASTATOR'S DISABLED. THEY'RE GOING TO GET AWAY.
YOU ARE MISTAKEN.

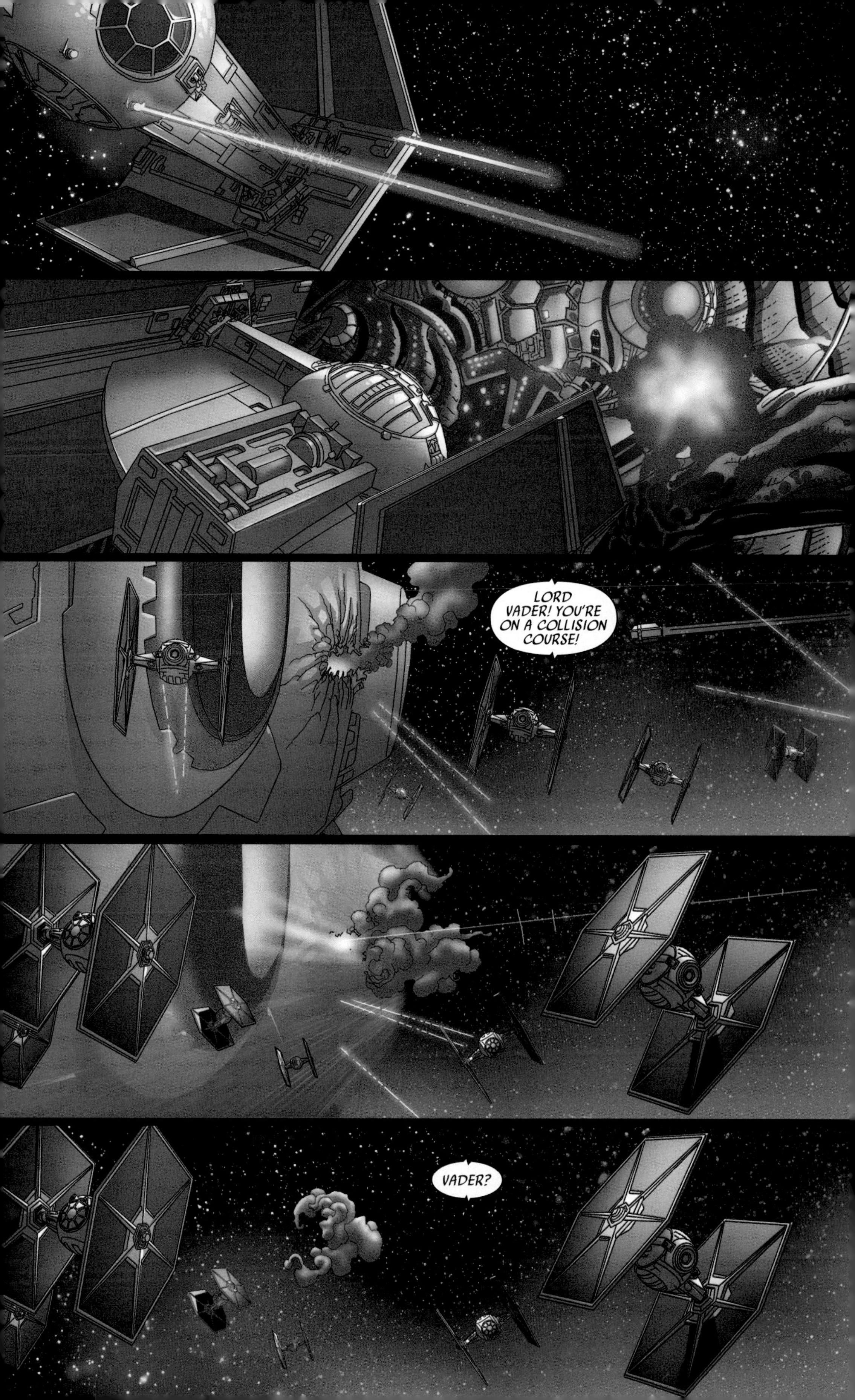
LORD VADER! YOU'RE ON A COLLISION COURSE!
VADER?

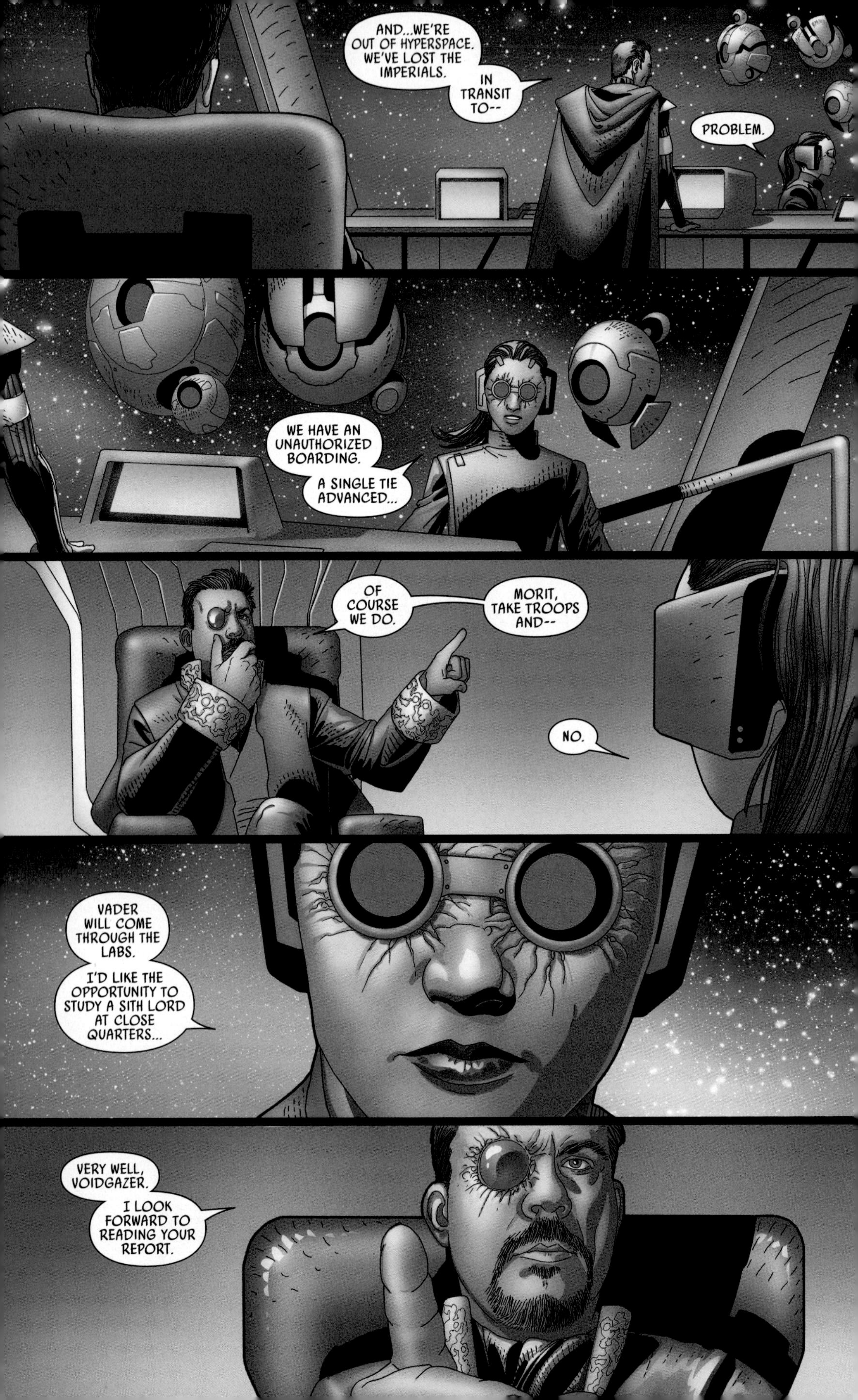
AND...WE'RE OUT OF HYPERSPACE. WE'VE LOST THE IMPERIALS.
IN TRANSIT TO--
PROBLEM.
WE HAVE AN UNAUTHORIZED BOARDING.
A SINGLE TIE ADVANCED...
OF COURSE WE DO.
MORIT, TAKE TROOPS AND--
NO.
VADER WILL COME THROUGH THE LABS.
I'D LIKE THE OPPORTUNITY TO STUDY A SITH LORD AT CLOSE QUARTERS...
VERY WELL, VOIDGAZER.
I LOOK FORWARD TO READING YOUR REPORT.

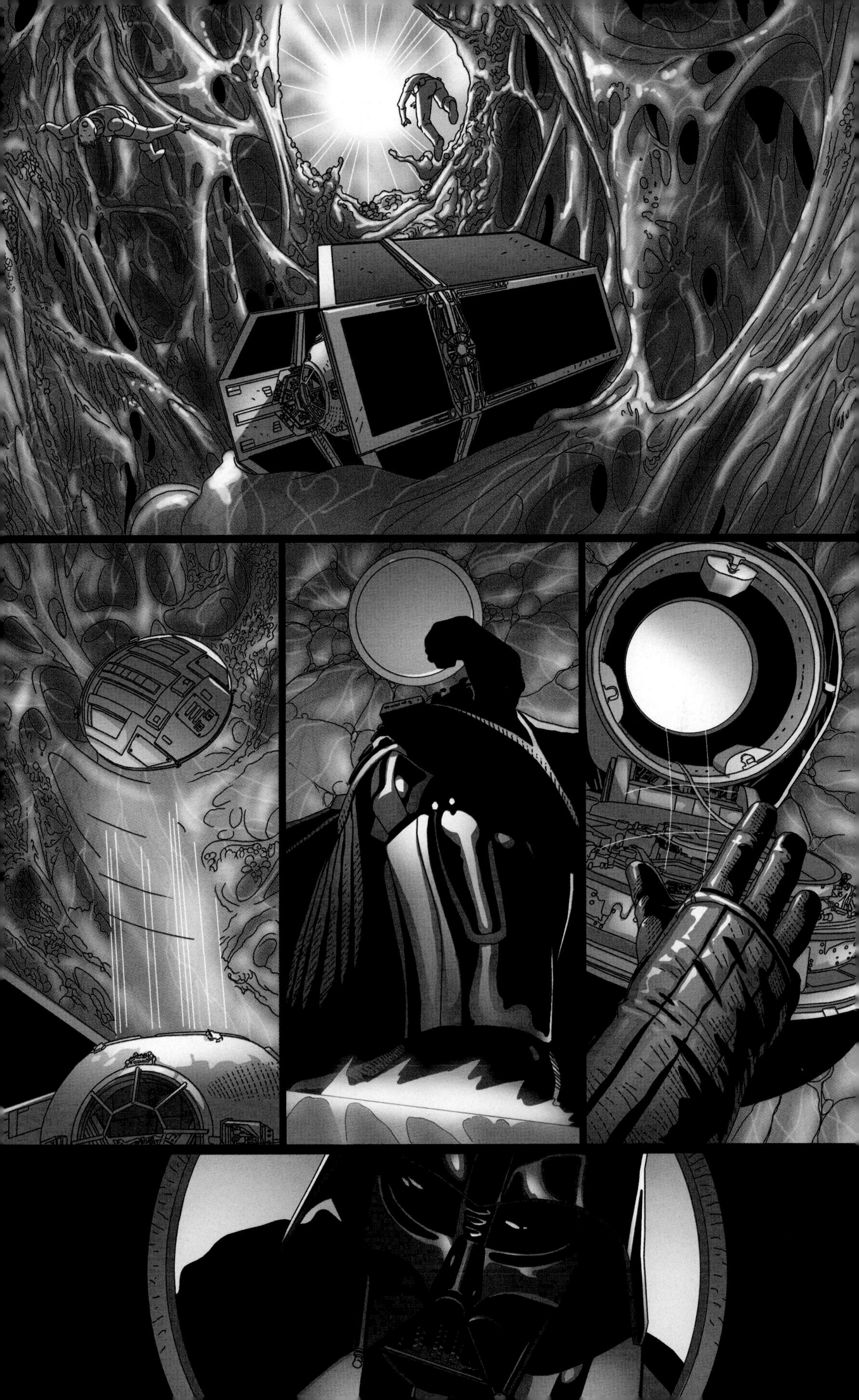

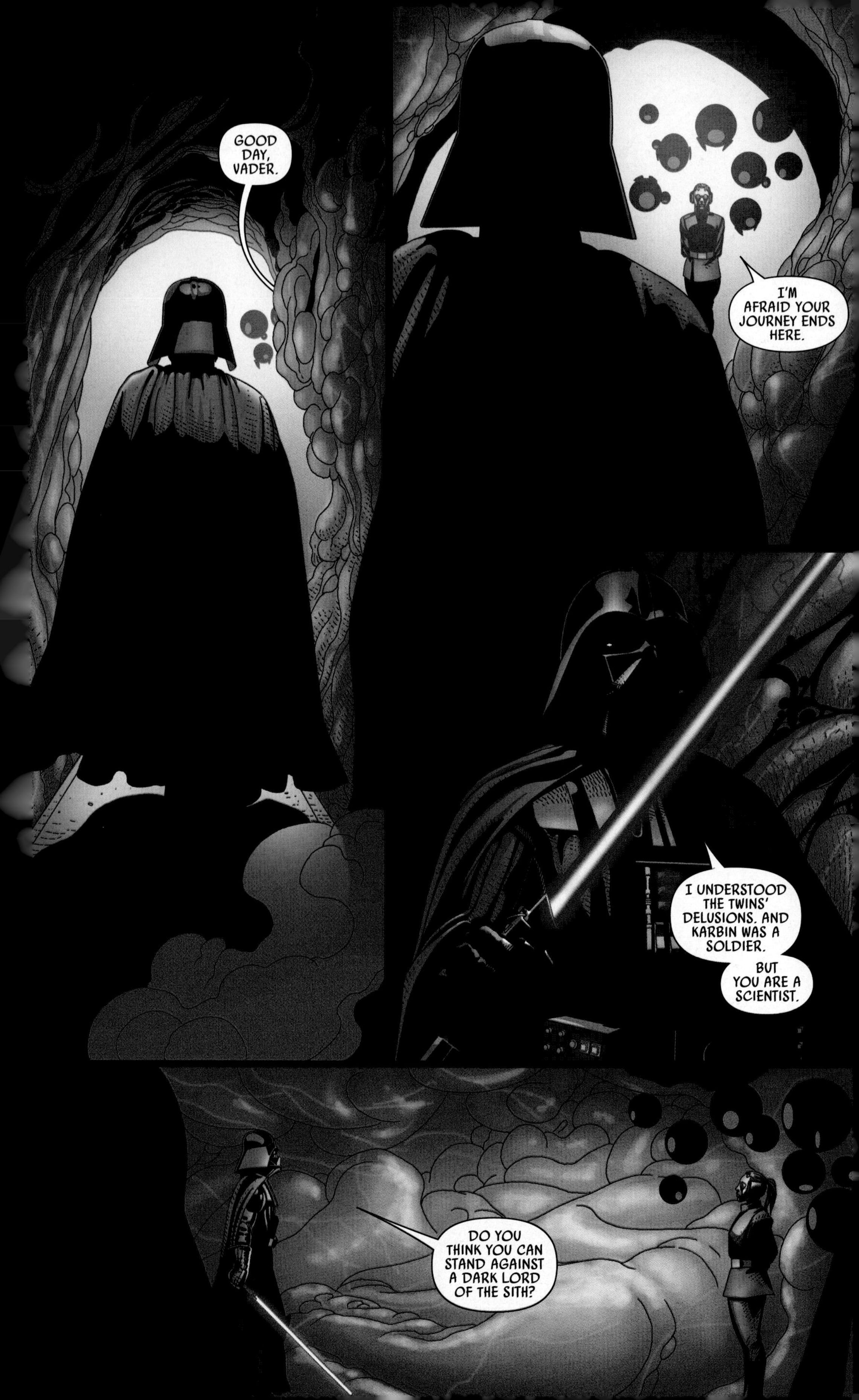
GOOD DAY, VADER.
I'M AFRAID YOUR JOURNEY ENDS HERE.
I UNDERSTOOD THE TWINS' DELUSIONS. AND KARBIN WAS A SOLDIER.
BUT YOU ARE A SCIENTIST.
DO YOU THINK YOU CAN STAND AGAINST A DARK LORD OF THE SITH?

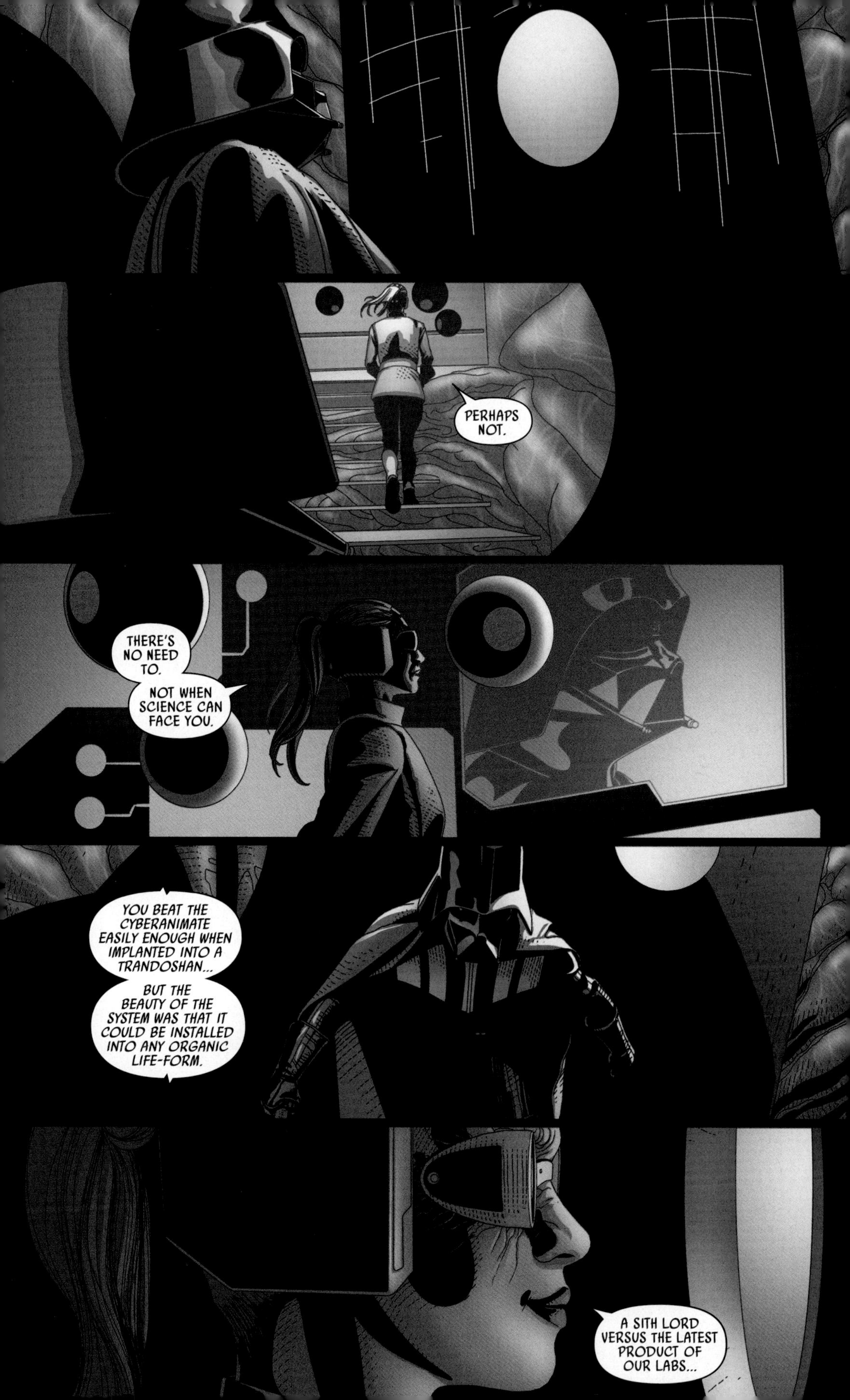
PERHAPS NOT.
THERE'S NO NEED TO.
NOT WHEN SCIENCE CAN FACE YOU.
YOU BEAT THE CYBERANIMATE EASILY ENOUGH WHEN IMPLANTED INTO A TRANDOSHAN...
BUT THE BEAUTY OF THE SYSTEM WAS THAT IT COULD BE INSTALLED INTO ANY ORGANIC LIFE-FORM.
A SITH LORD VERSUS THE LATEST PRODUCT OF OUR LABS...

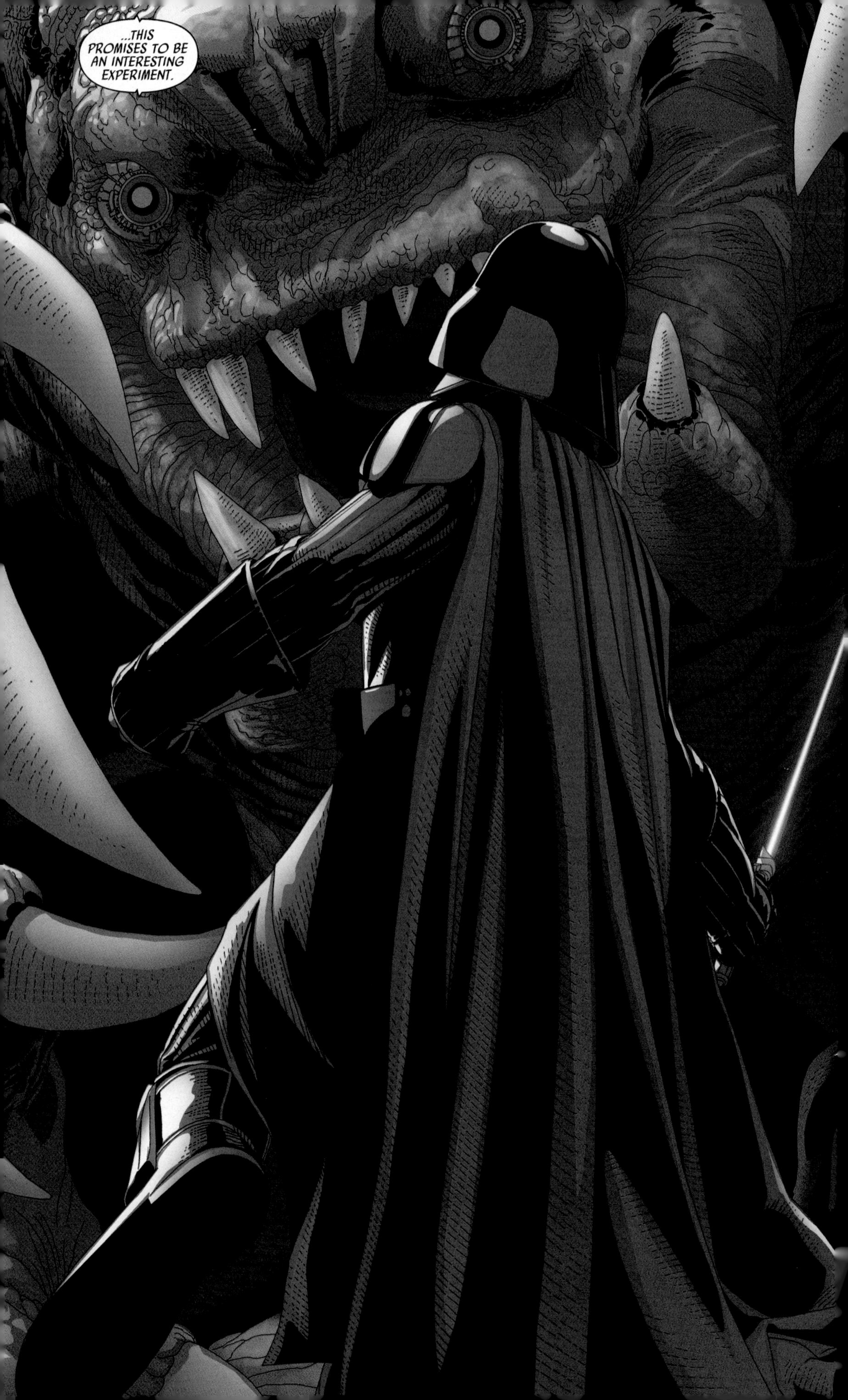
...THIS PROMISES TO BE AN INTERESTING EXPERIMENT.

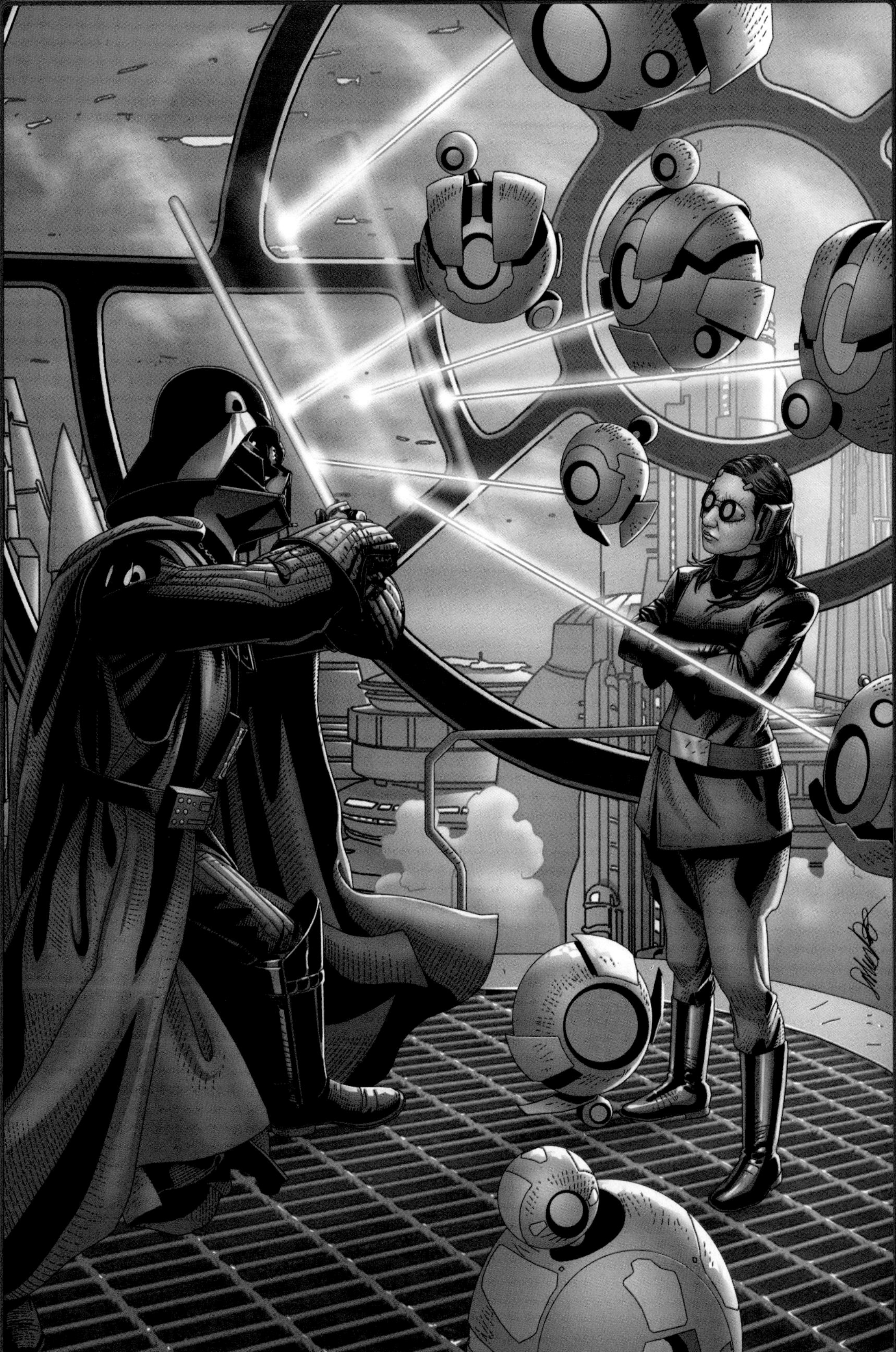

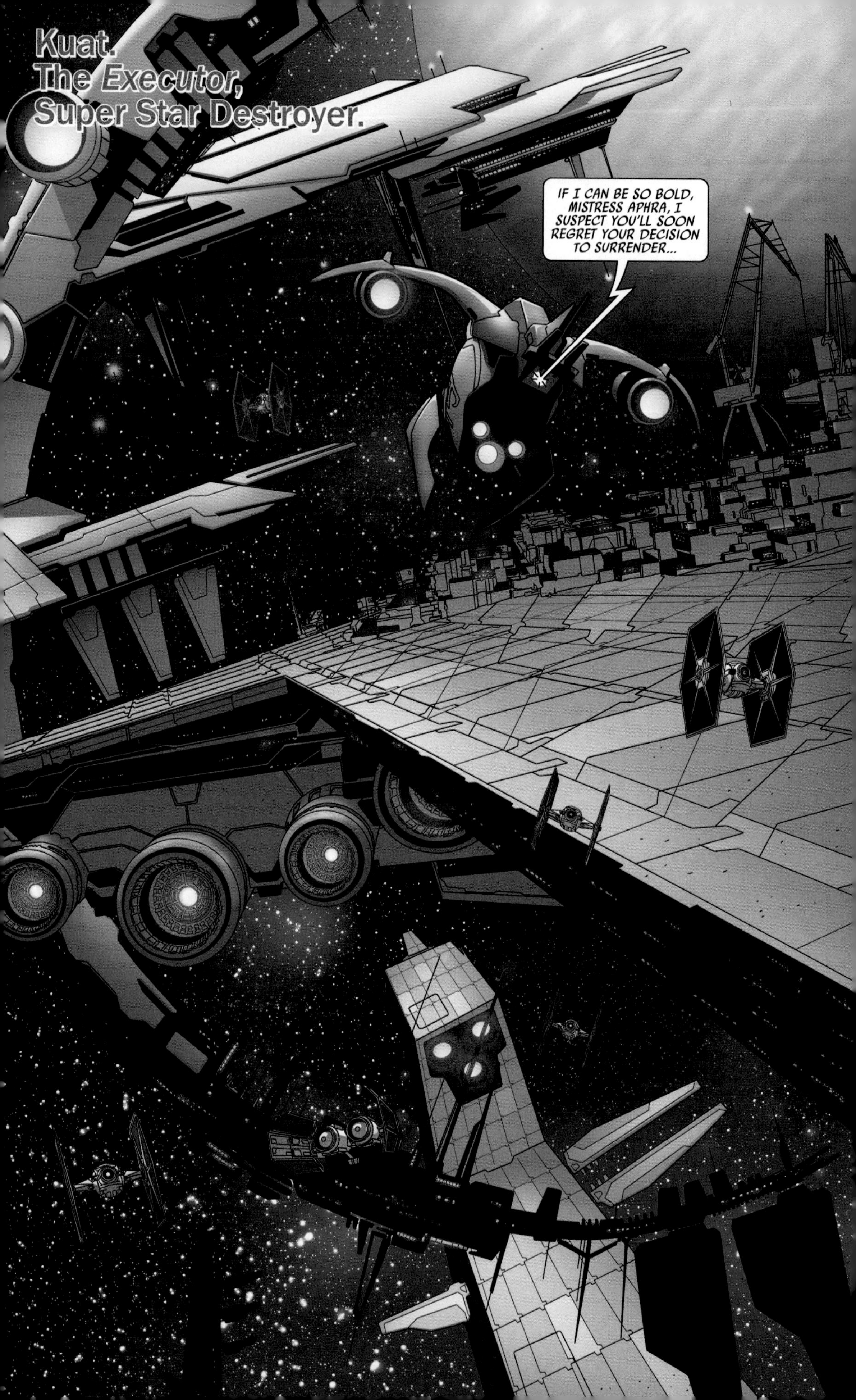
Kuat.
The Executor,
Super Star Destroyer.
IF I CAN BE SO BOLD, MISTRESS APHRA, I SUSPECT YOU'LL SOON REGRET YOUR DECISION TO SURRENDER...

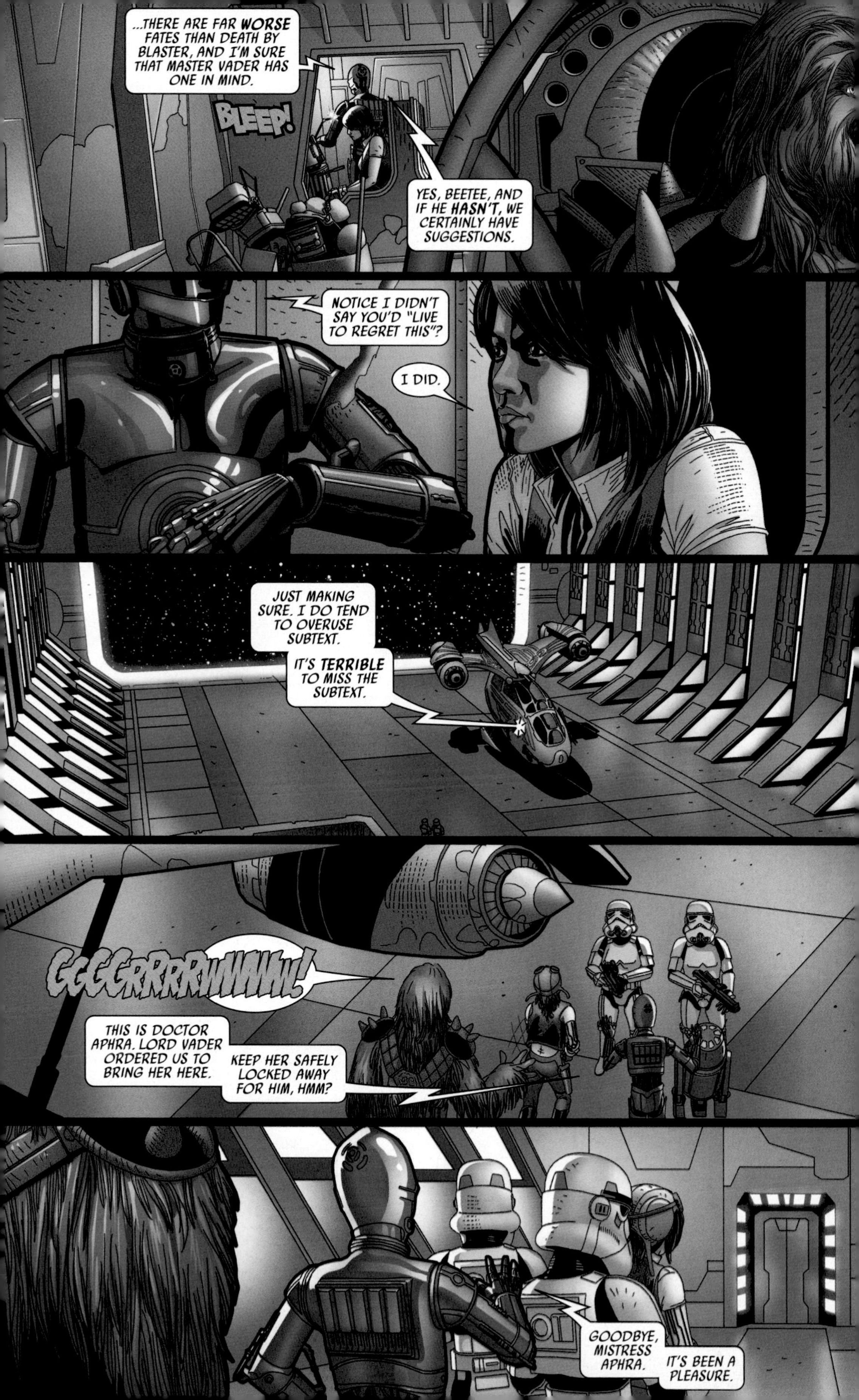
...THERE ARE FAR WORSE FATES THAN DEATH BY BLASTER, AND I'M SURE THAT MASTER VADER HAS ONE IN MIND.
BLEEP!
YES, BEETEE, AND IF HE HASN'T, WE CERTAINLY HAVE SUGGESTIONS.
NOTICE I DIDN'T SAY YOU'D "LIVE TO REGRET THIS"?
I DID.
JUST MAKING SURE. I DO TEND TO OVERUSE SUBTEXT.
IT'S TERRIBLE TO MISS THE SUBTEXT.
GGGGRRRRWWAAAW!
THIS IS DOCTOR APHRA. LORD VADER ORDERED US TO BRING HER HERE.
KEEP HER SAFELY LOCKED AWAY FOR HIM, HMM?
GOODBYE, MISTRESS APHRA.
IT'S BEEN A PLEASURE.

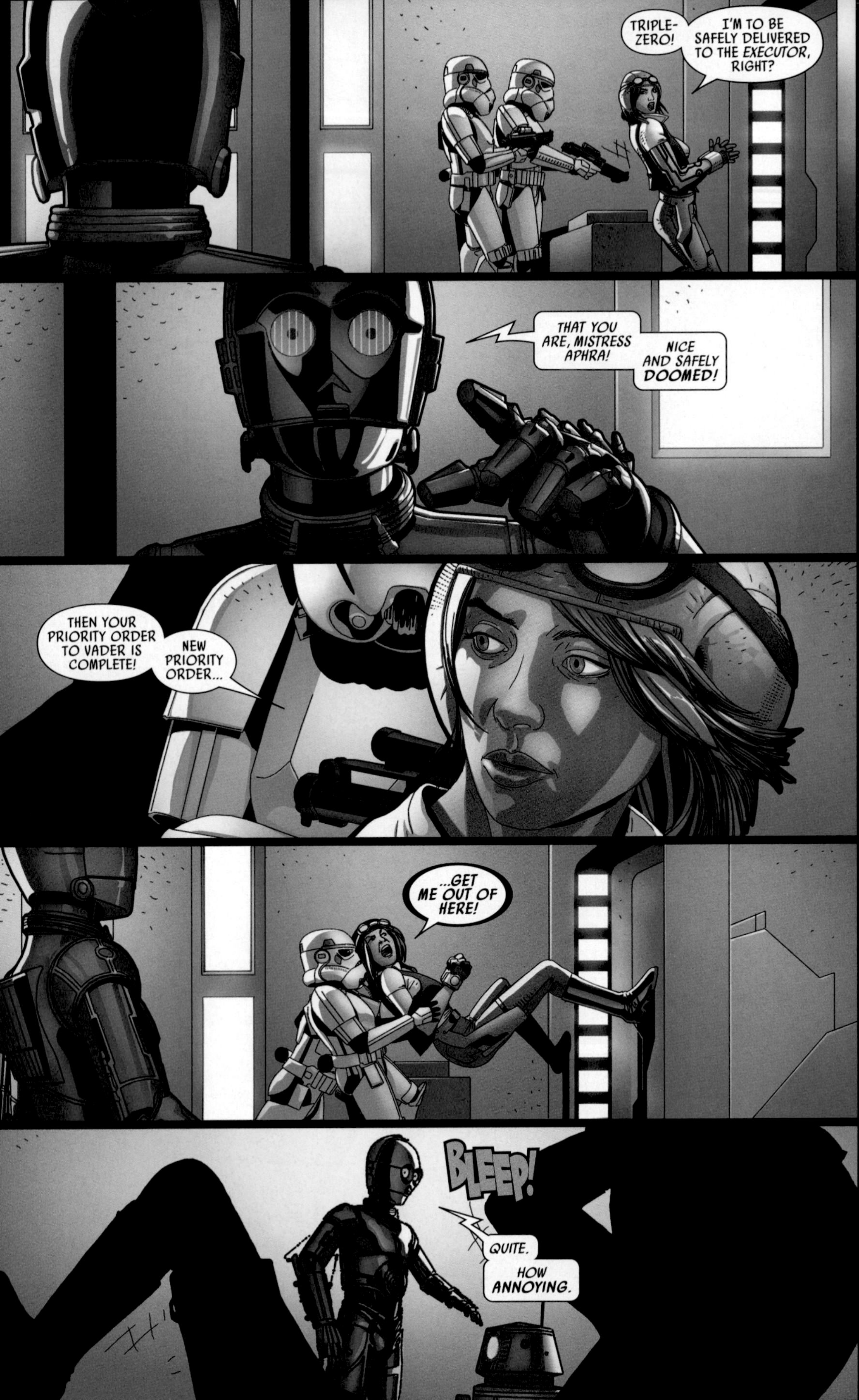
TRIPLE-ZERO!
I'M TO BE SAFELY DELIVERED TO THE *EXECUTOR*, RIGHT?
THAT YOU ARE, MISTRESS APHRA!
NICE AND SAFELY **DOOMED!**
THEN YOUR PRIORITY ORDER TO VADER IS COMPLETE!
NEW PRIORITY ORDER...
...GET ME OUT OF HERE!
BLEEP!
QUITE.
HOW **ANNOYING.**

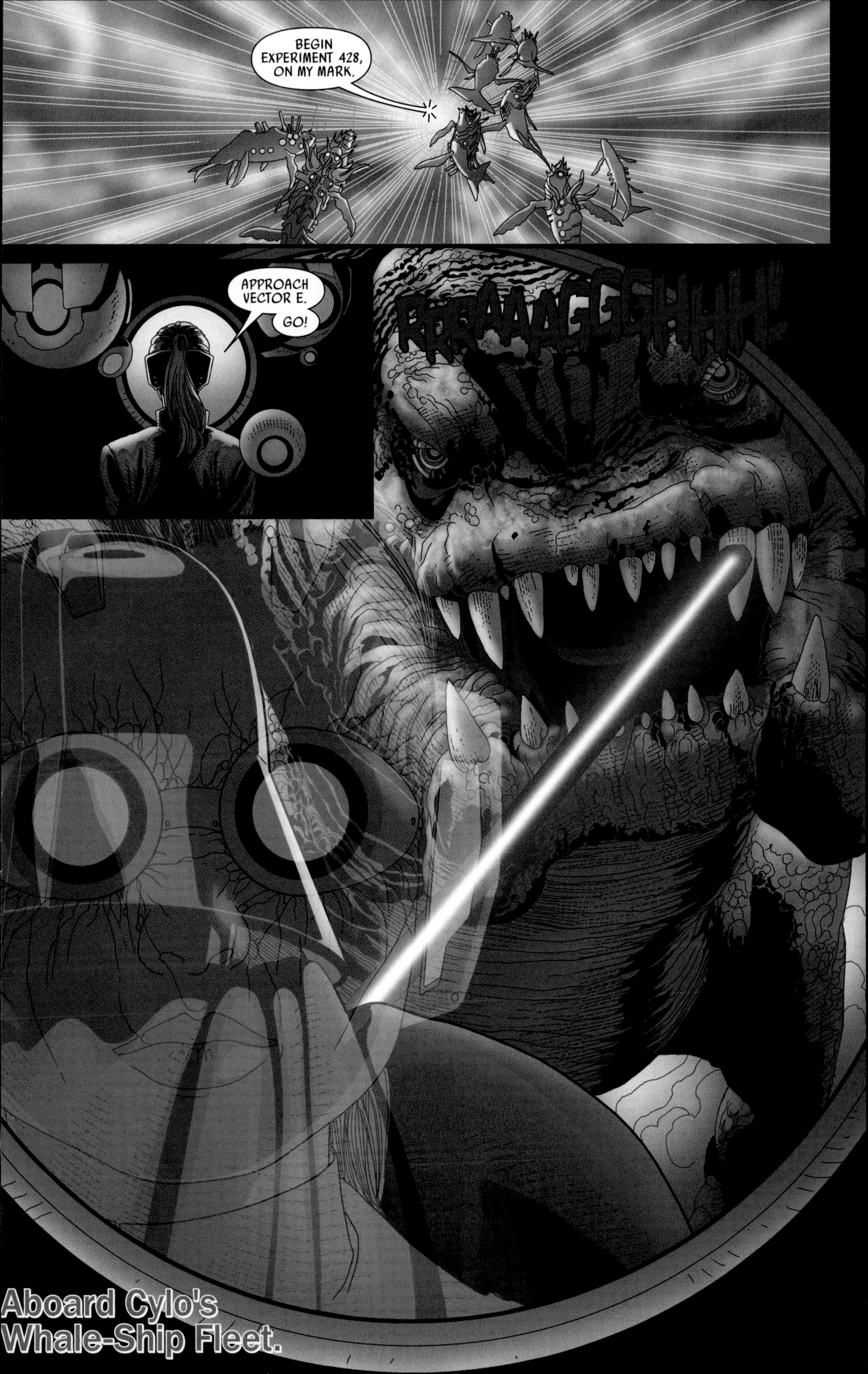

BEGIN EXPERIMENT 428, ON MY MARK.
APPROACH VECTOR E.
GO!
RRRAAAAGGGHHHH!
Aboard Cylo's Whale-Ship Fleet.

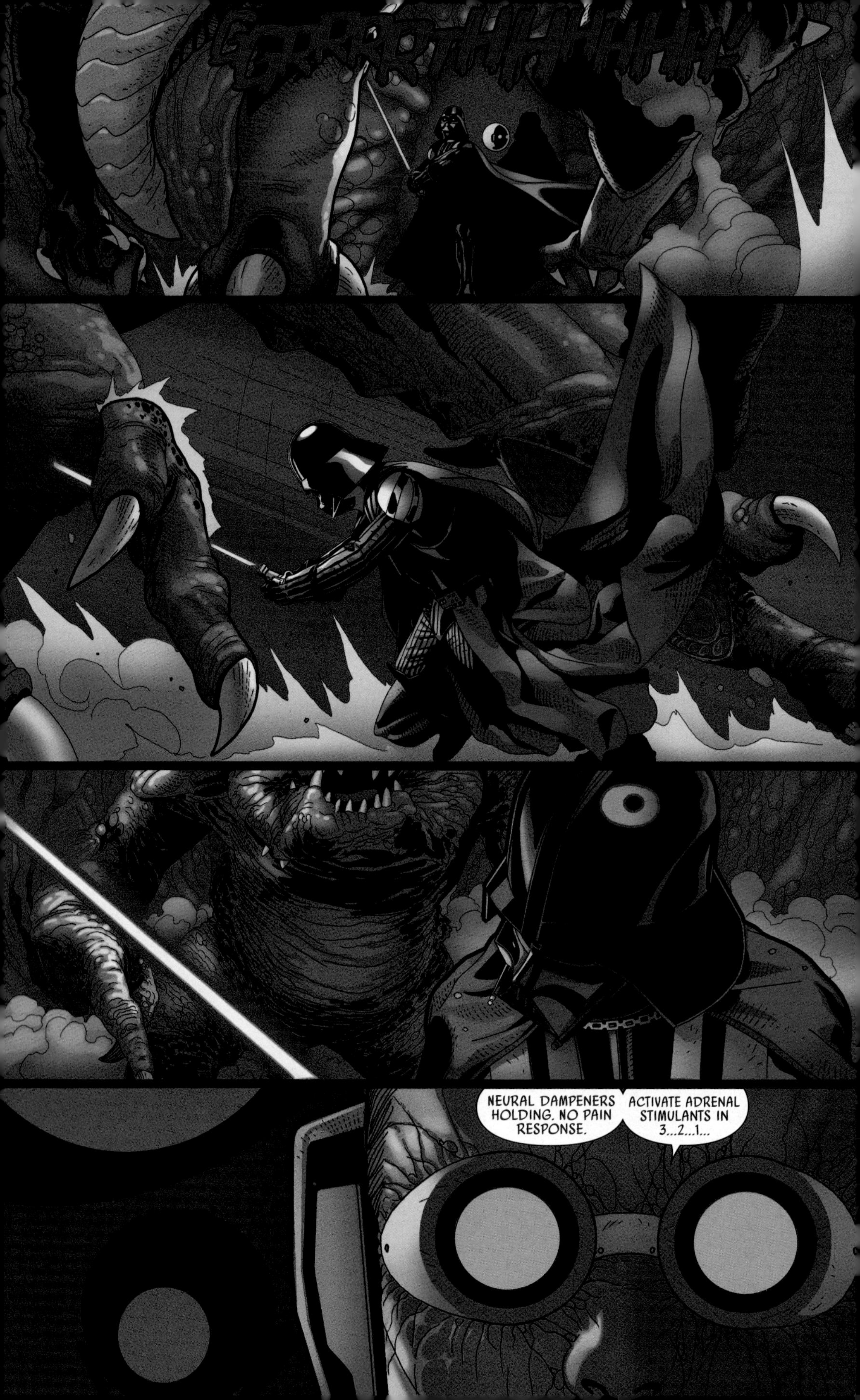
GGRRRTHHHHHHHH!
NEURAL DAMPENERS HOLDING. NO PAIN RESPONSE.
ACTIVATE ADRENAL STIMULANTS IN 3...2...1...

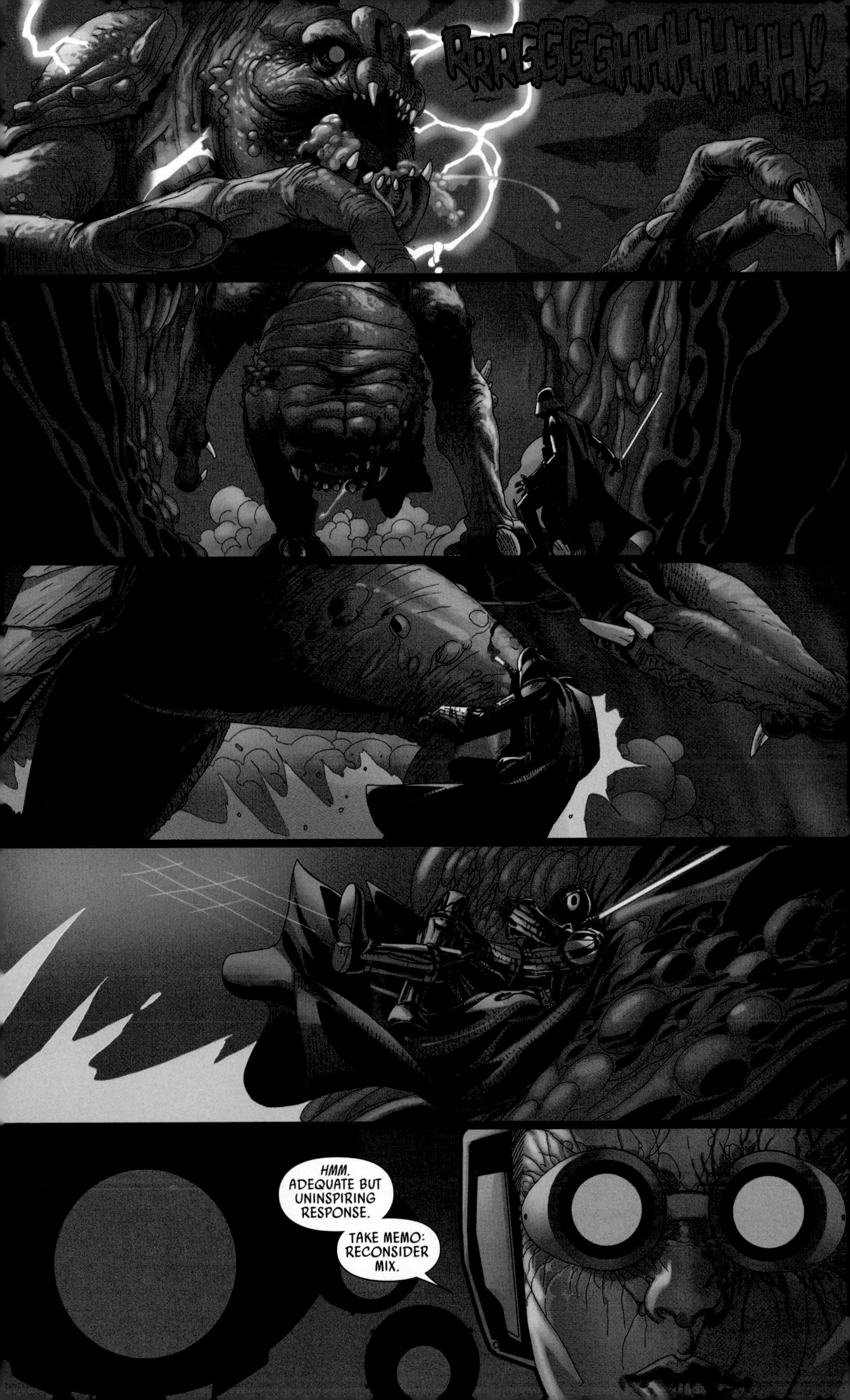
RRRGGGGHHHHHHHH!
HMM. ADEQUATE BUT UNINSPIRING RESPONSE.
TAKE MEMO: RECONSIDER MIX.

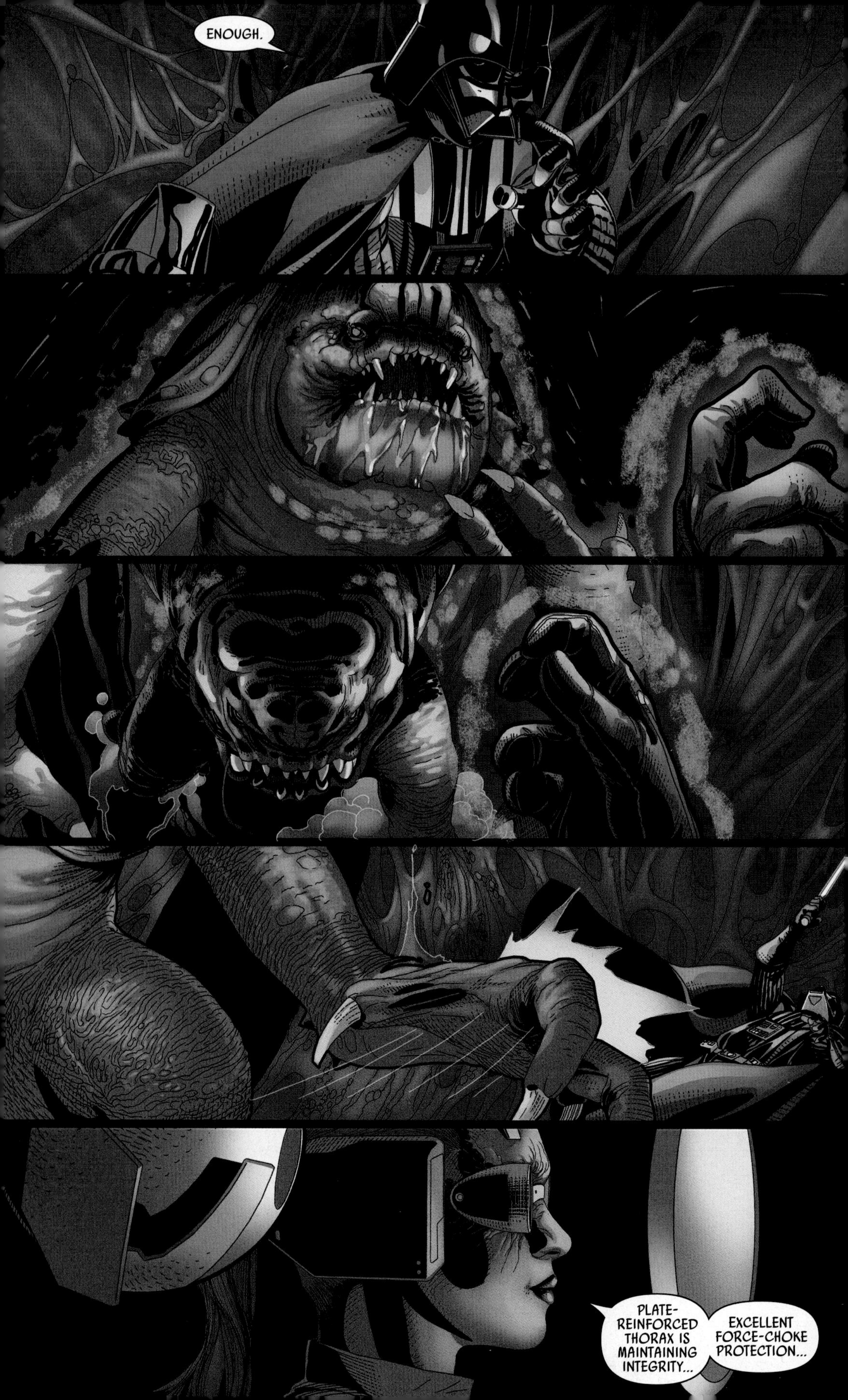
ENOUGH.
PLATE-REINFORCED THORAX IS MAINTAINING INTEGRITY...
EXCELLENT FORCE-CHOKE PROTECTION...

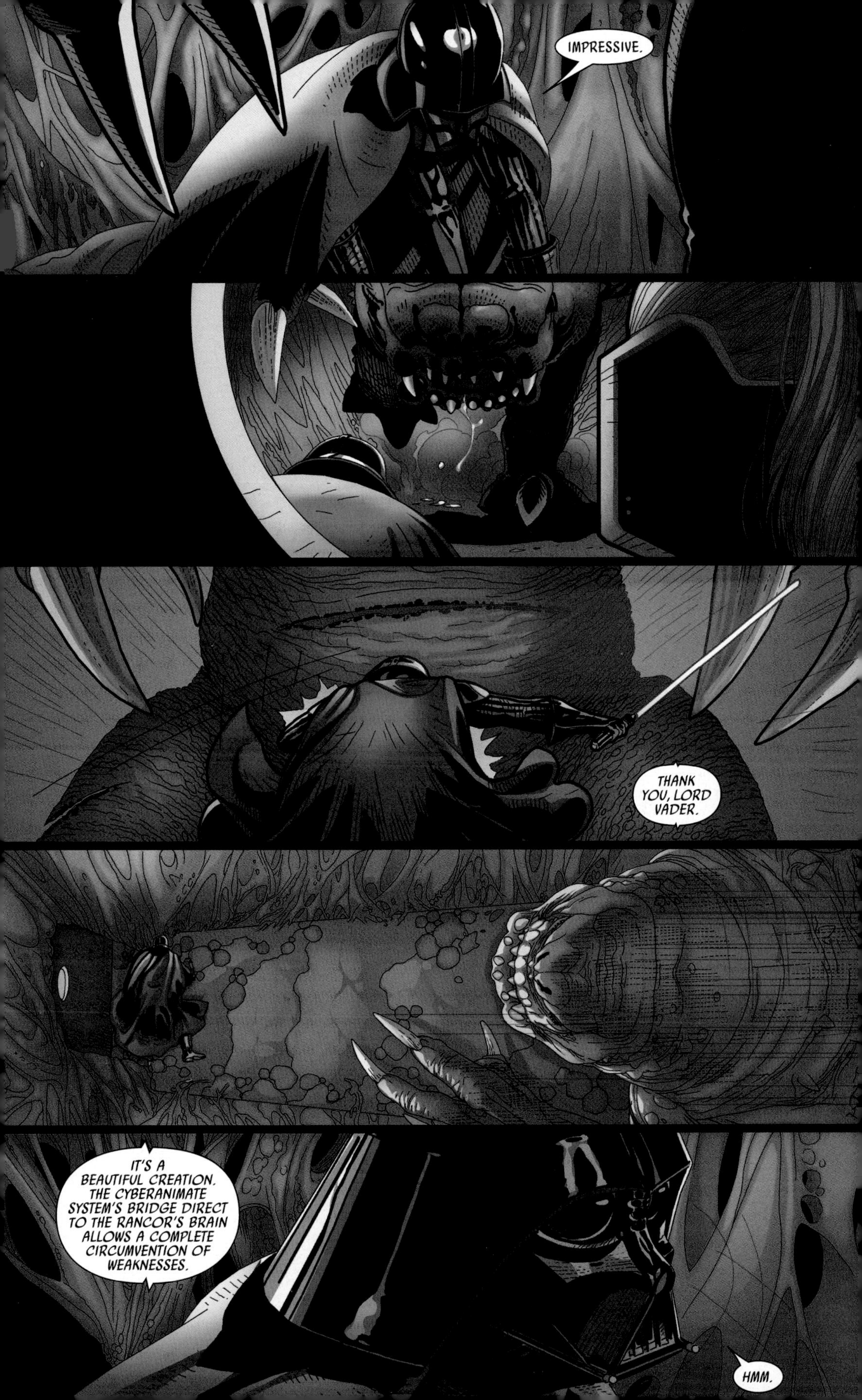
IMPRESSIVE.
THANK YOU, LORD VADER.
IT'S A BEAUTIFUL CREATION. THE CYBERANIMATE SYSTEM'S BRIDGE DIRECT TO THE RANCOR'S BRAIN ALLOWS A COMPLETE CIRCUMVENTION OF WEAKNESSES.
HMM.

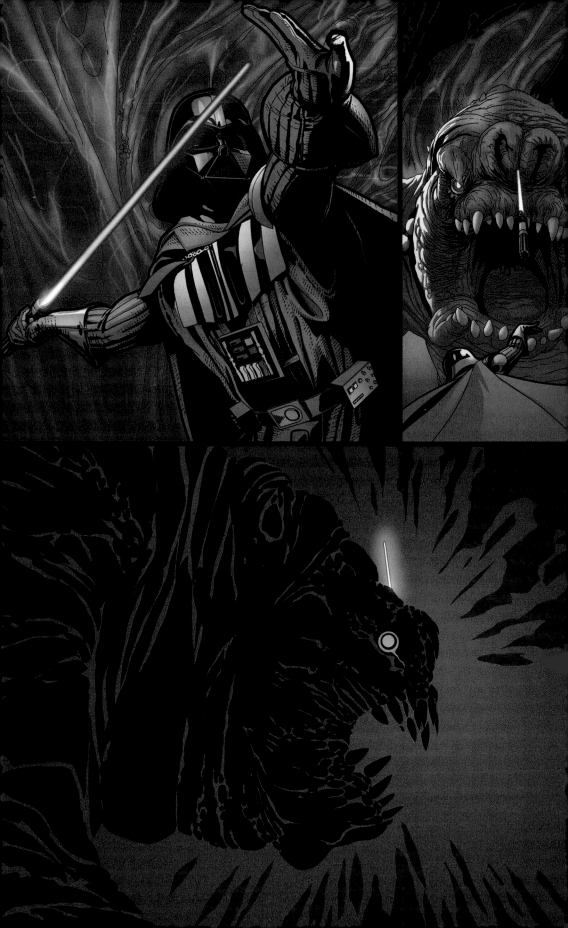

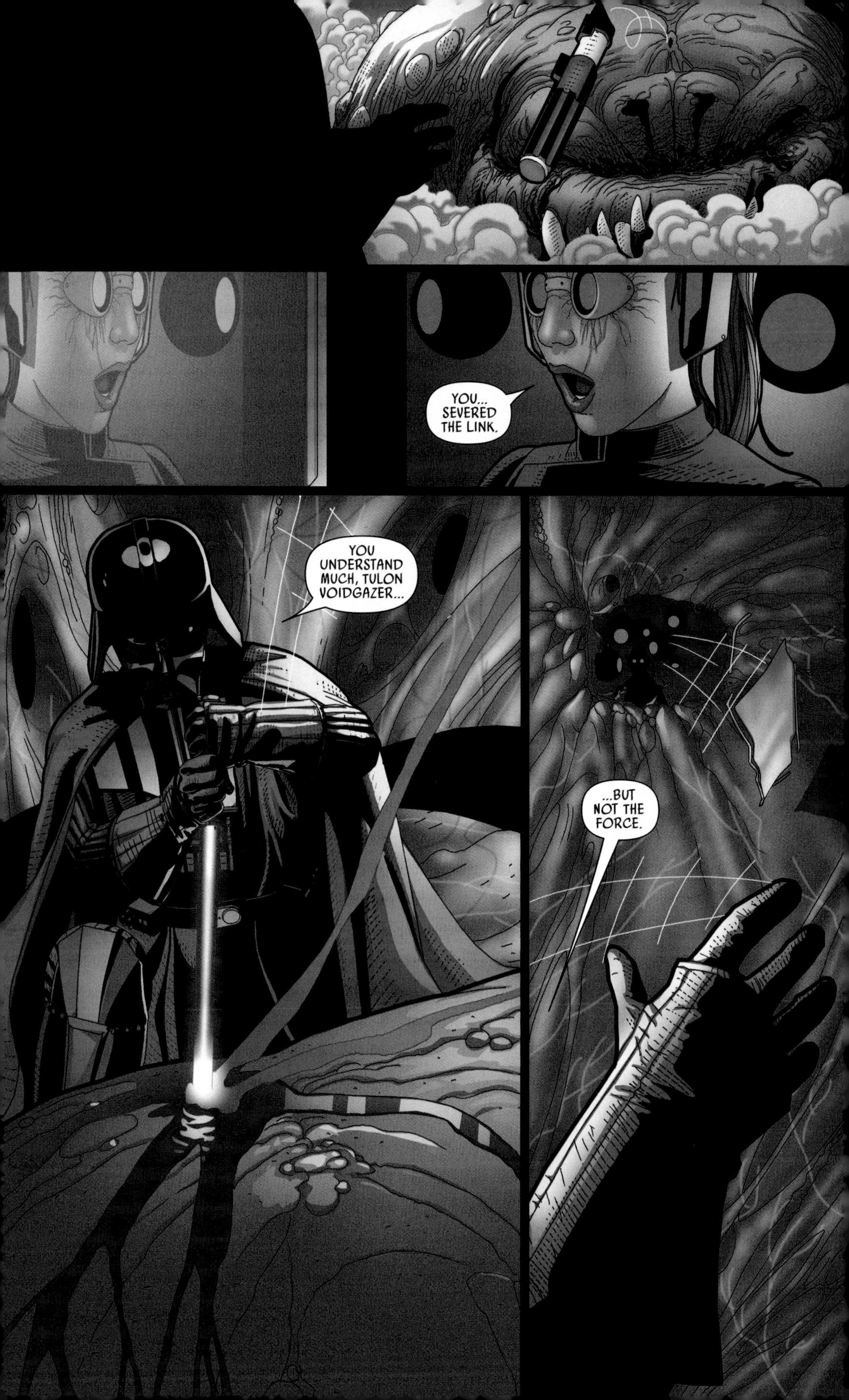
YOU... SEVERED THE LINK.
YOU UNDERSTAND MUCH, TULON VOIDGAZER...
...BUT NOT THE FORCE.

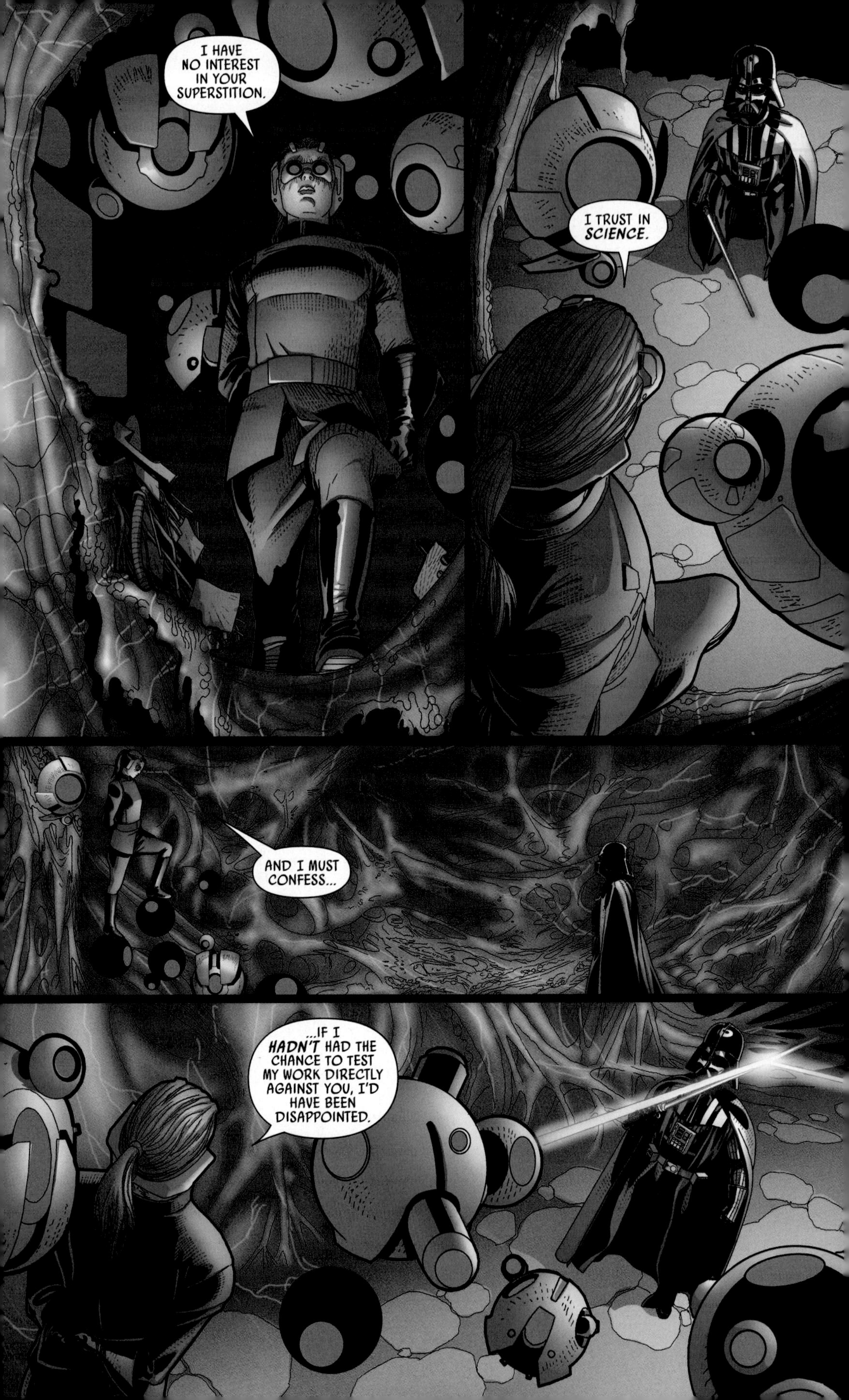
I HAVE NO INTEREST IN YOUR SUPERSTITION.
I TRUST IN SCIENCE.
AND I MUST CONFESS...
...IF I HADN'T HAD THE CHANCE TO TEST MY WORK DIRECTLY AGAINST YOU, I'D HAVE BEEN DISAPPOINTED.

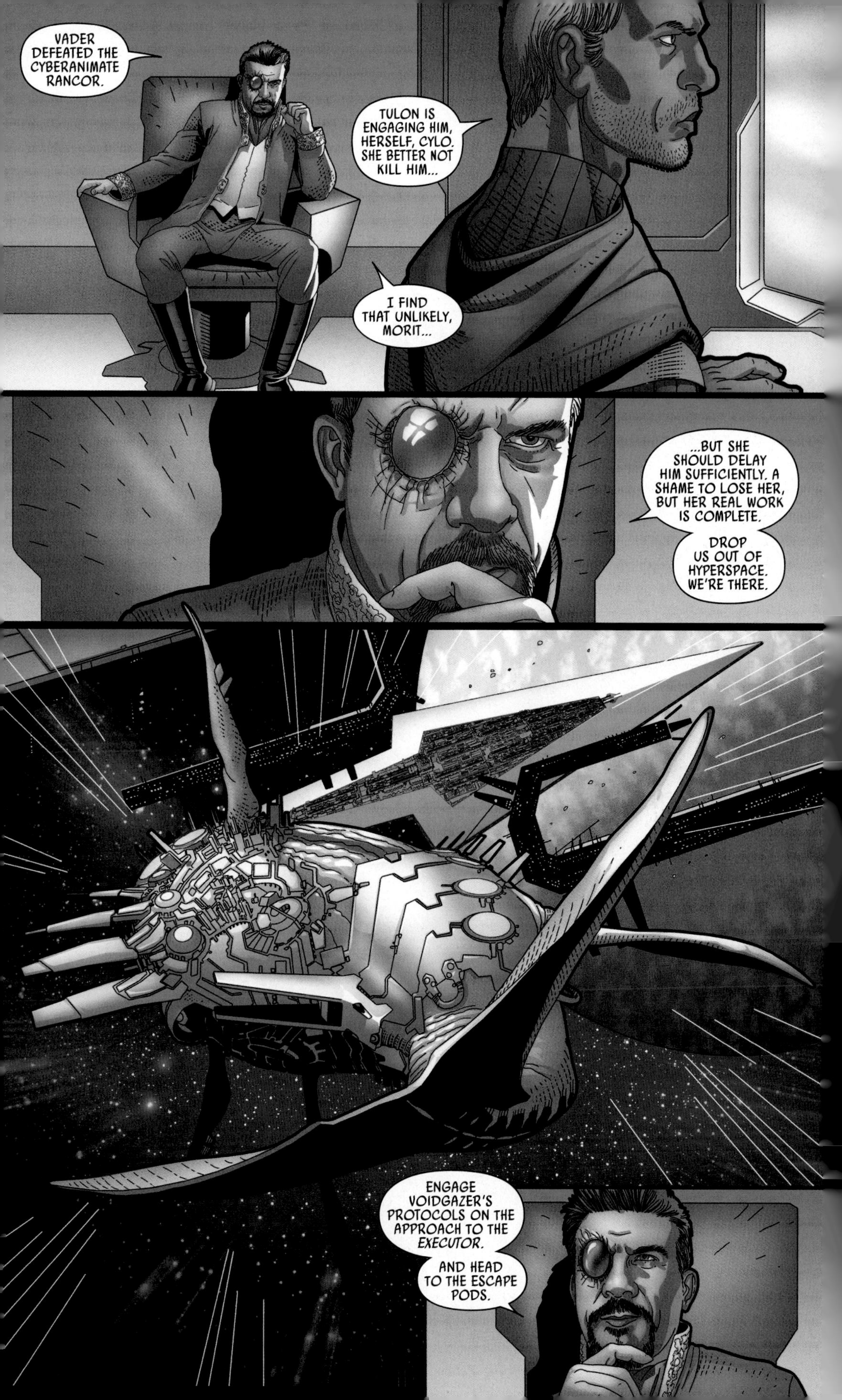
VADER DEFEATED THE CYBERANIMATE RANCOR.
TULON IS ENGAGING HIM, HERSELF, CYLO. SHE BETTER NOT KILL HIM...
I FIND THAT UNLIKELY, MORIT...
...BUT SHE SHOULD DELAY HIM SUFFICIENTLY. A SHAME TO LOSE HER, BUT HER REAL WORK IS COMPLETE.
DROP US OUT OF HYPERSPACE. WE'RE THERE.
ENGAGE VOIDGAZER'S PROTOCOLS ON THE APPROACH TO THE EXECUTOR.
AND HEAD TO THE ESCAPE PODS.

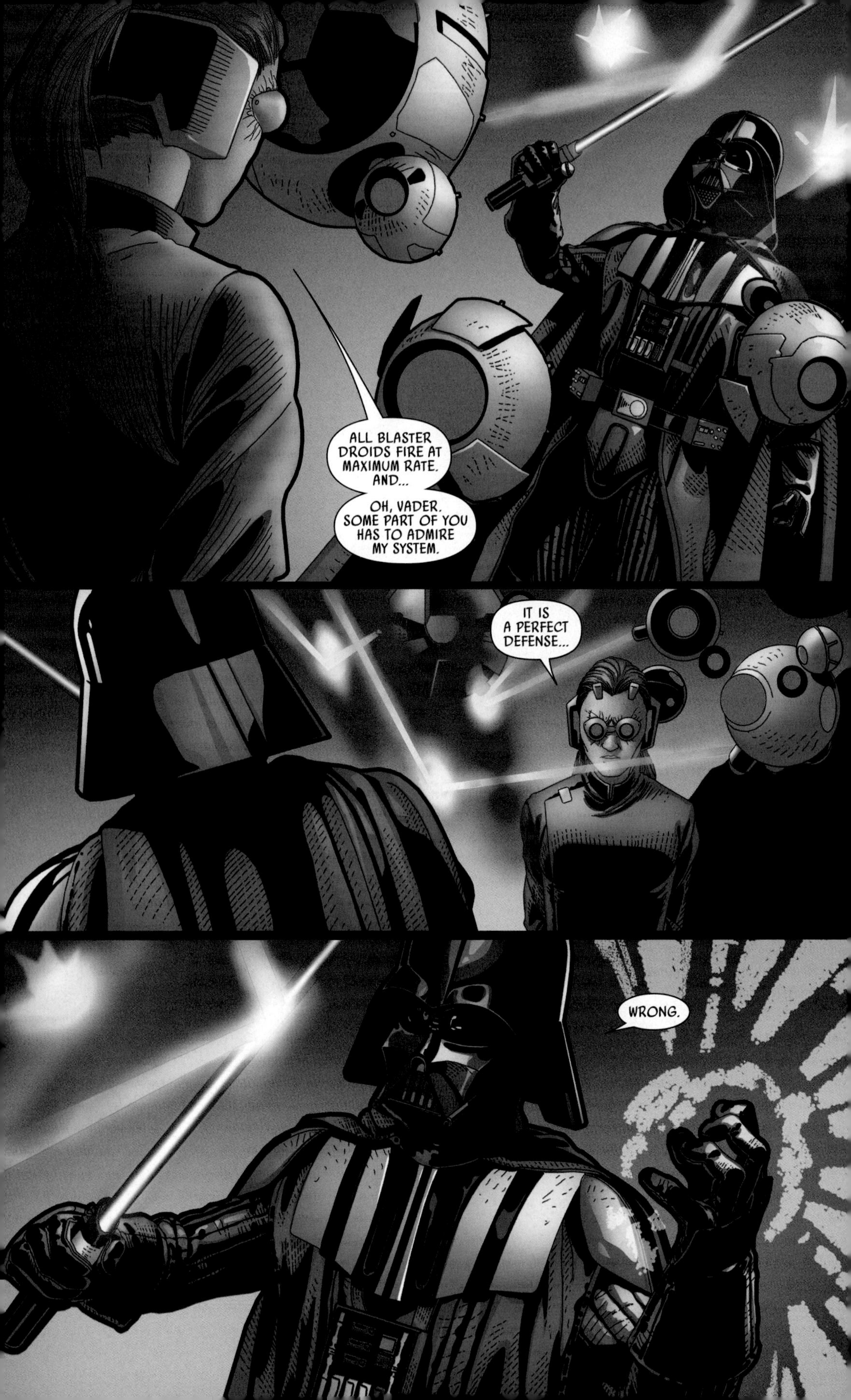
ALL BLASTER DROIDS FIRE AT MAXIMUM RATE. AND...
OH, VADER. SOME PART OF YOU HAS TO ADMIRE MY SYSTEM.
IT IS A PERFECT DEFENSE...
WRONG.

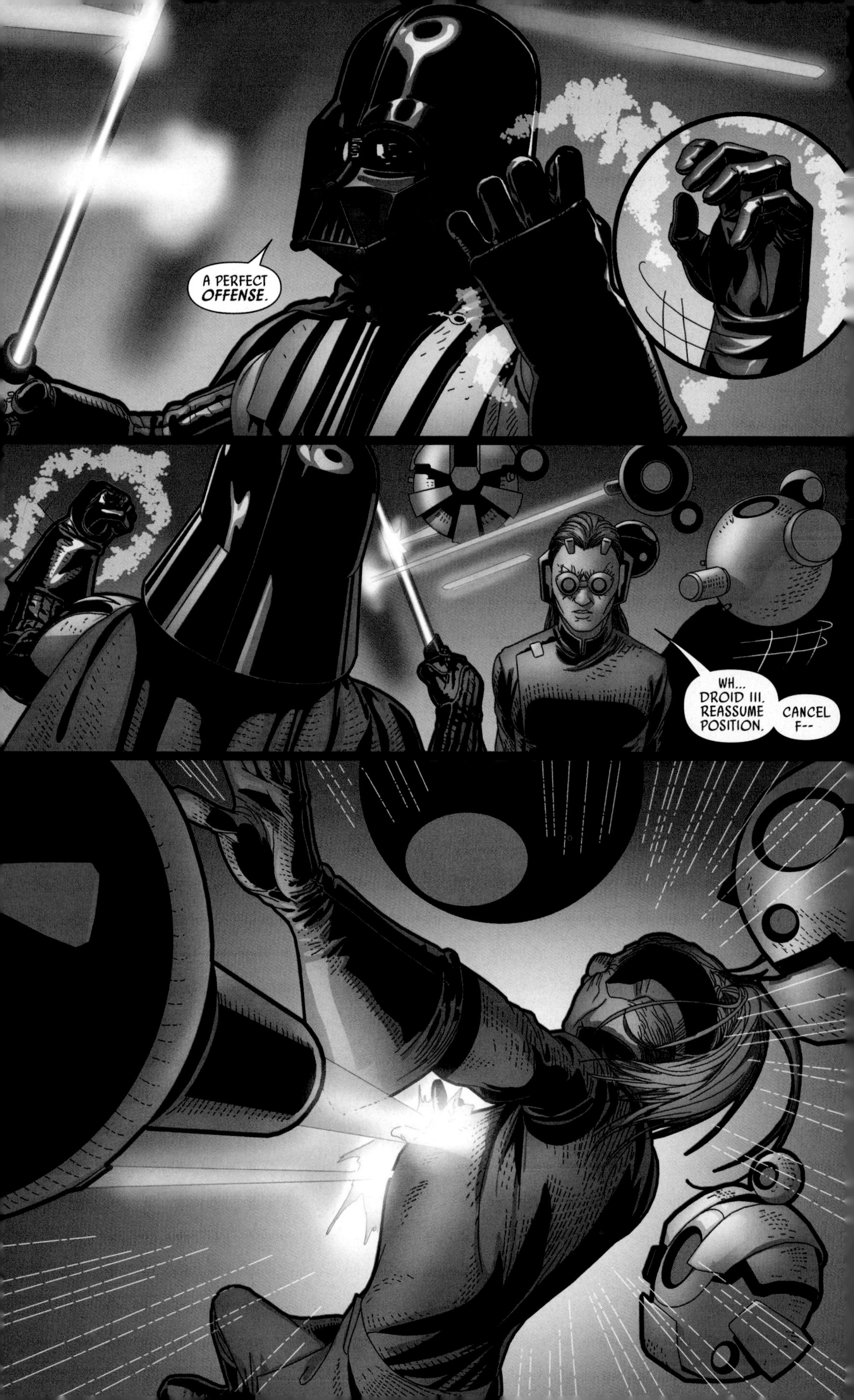
A PERFECT OFFENSE.
WH... DROID III. REASSUME POSITION.
CANCEL F--

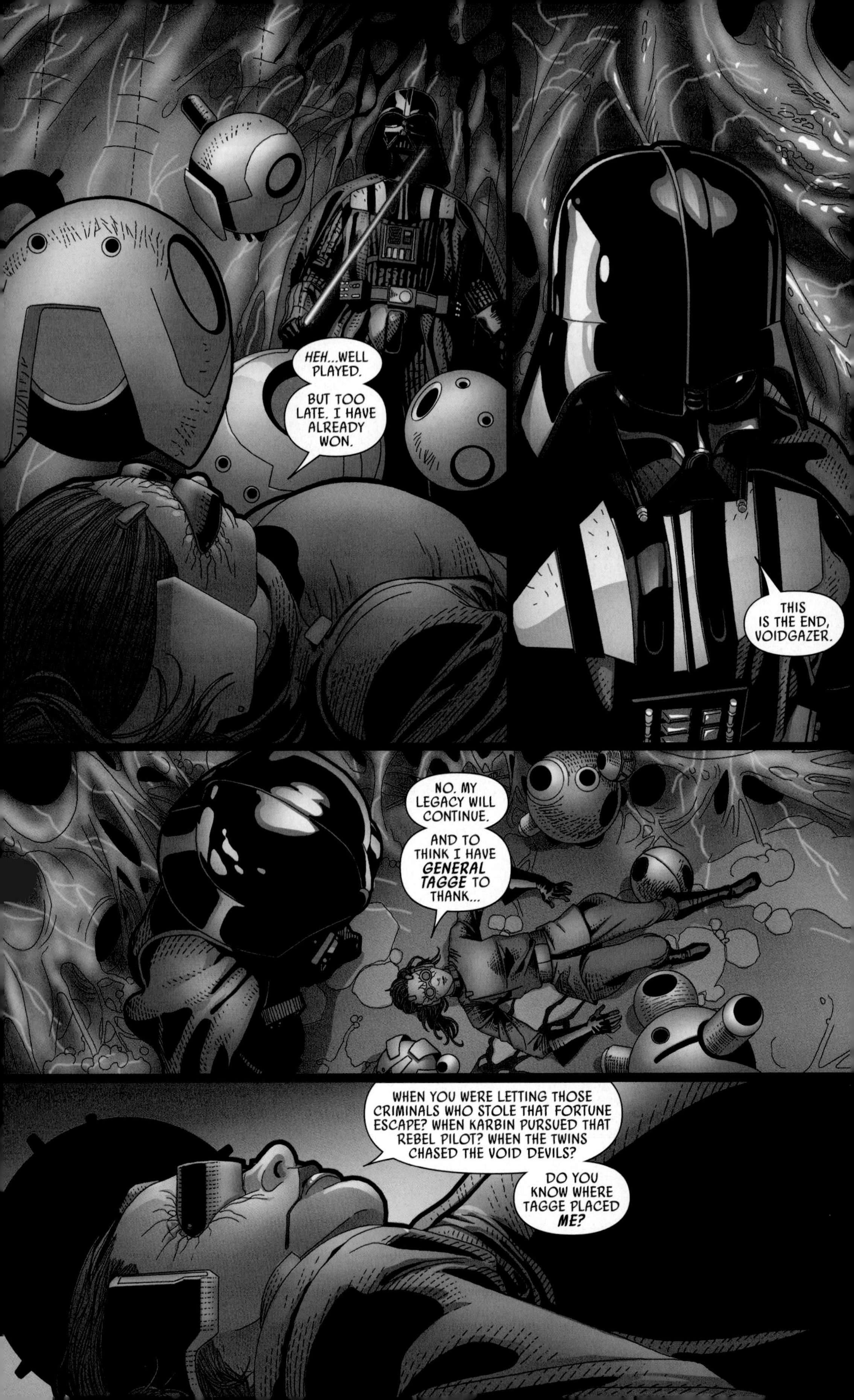
HEH...WELL PLAYED.
BUT TOO LATE. I HAVE ALREADY WON.
THIS IS THE END, VOIDGAZER.
NO. MY LEGACY WILL CONTINUE.
AND TO THINK I HAVE GENERAL TAGGE TO THANK...
WHEN YOU WERE LETTING THOSE CRIMINALS WHO STOLE THAT FORTUNE ESCAPE? WHEN KARBIN PURSUED THAT REBEL PILOT? WHEN THE TWINS CHASED THE VOID DEVILS?
DO YOU KNOW WHERE TAGGE PLACED ME?

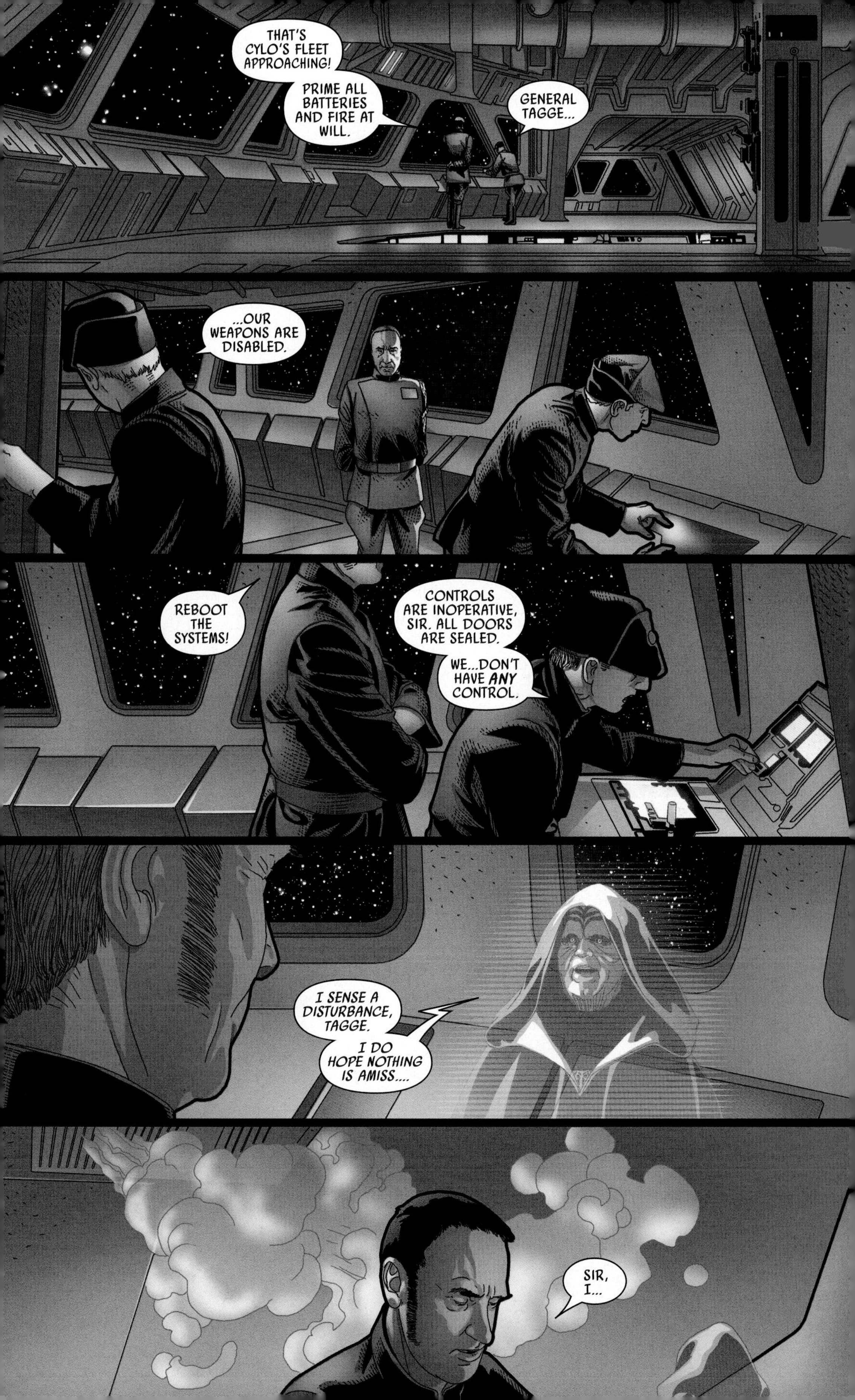
THAT'S CYLO'S FLEET APPROACHING!
PRIME ALL BATTERIES AND FIRE AT WILL.
GENERAL TAGGE...
...OUR WEAPONS ARE DISABLED.
REBOOT THE SYSTEMS!
CONTROLS ARE INOPERATIVE, SIR. ALL DOORS ARE SEALED.
WE...DON'T HAVE ANY CONTROL.
I SENSE A DISTURBANCE, TAGGE.
I DO HOPE NOTHING IS AMISS....
SIR, I...

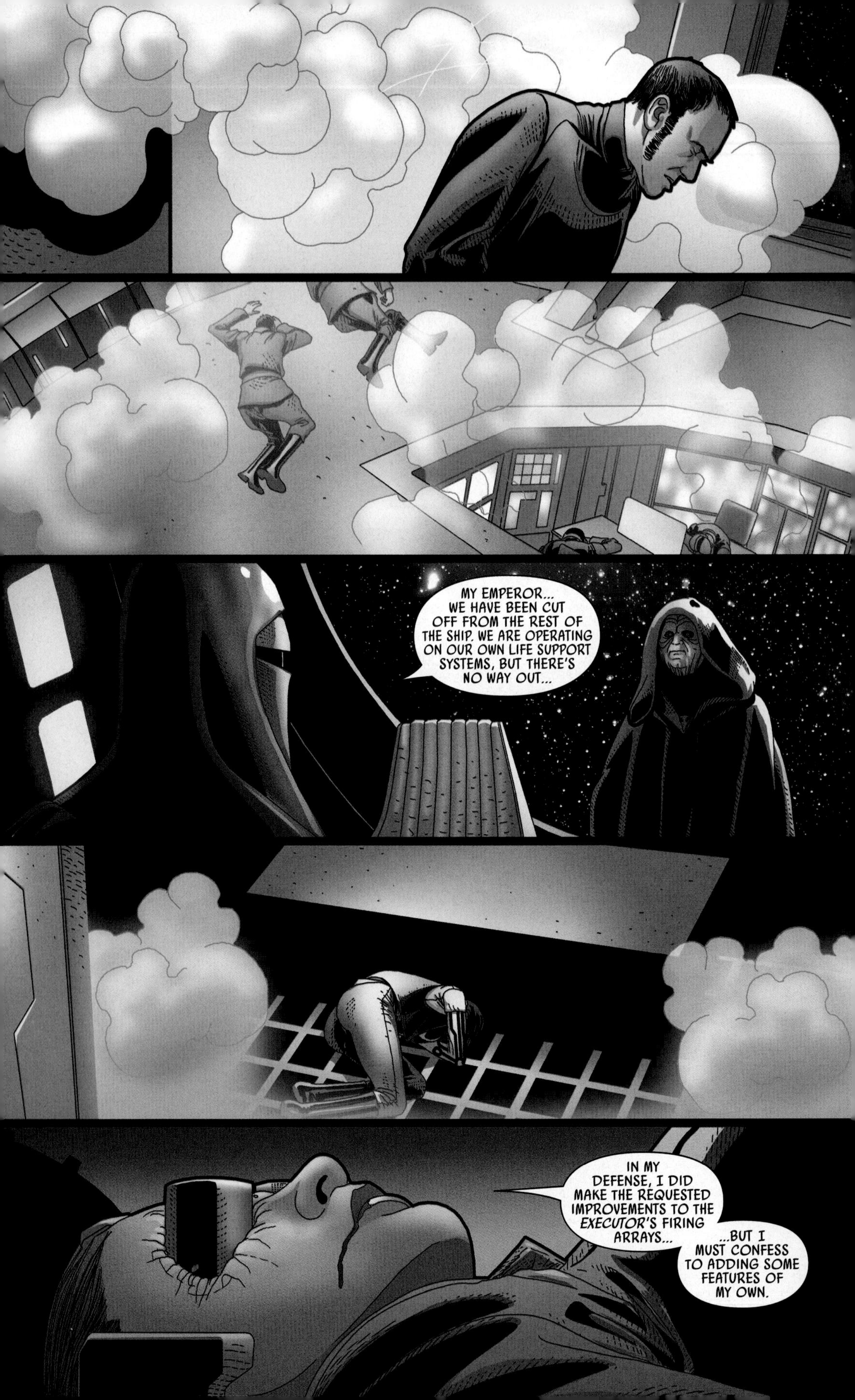
MY EMPEROR... WE HAVE BEEN CUT OFF FROM THE REST OF THE SHIP. WE ARE OPERATING ON OUR OWN LIFE SUPPORT SYSTEMS, BUT THERE'S NO WAY OUT...
IN MY DEFENSE, I DID MAKE THE REQUESTED IMPROVEMENTS TO THE *EXECUTOR*'S FIRING ARRAYS...
...BUT I MUST CONFESS TO ADDING SOME FEATURES OF MY OWN.

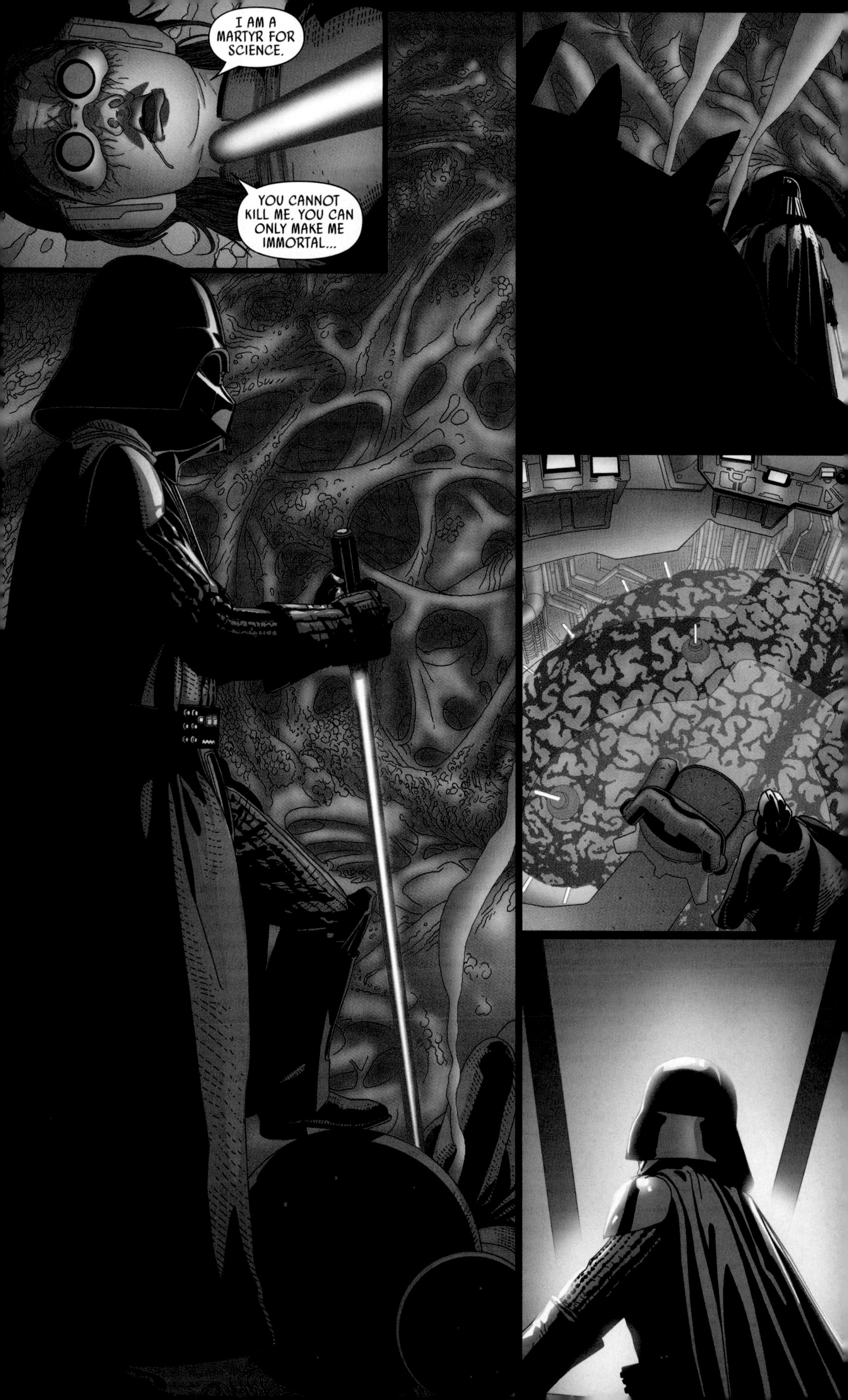
I AM A MARTYR FOR SCIENCE.
YOU CANNOT KILL ME. YOU CAN ONLY MAKE ME IMMORTAL...

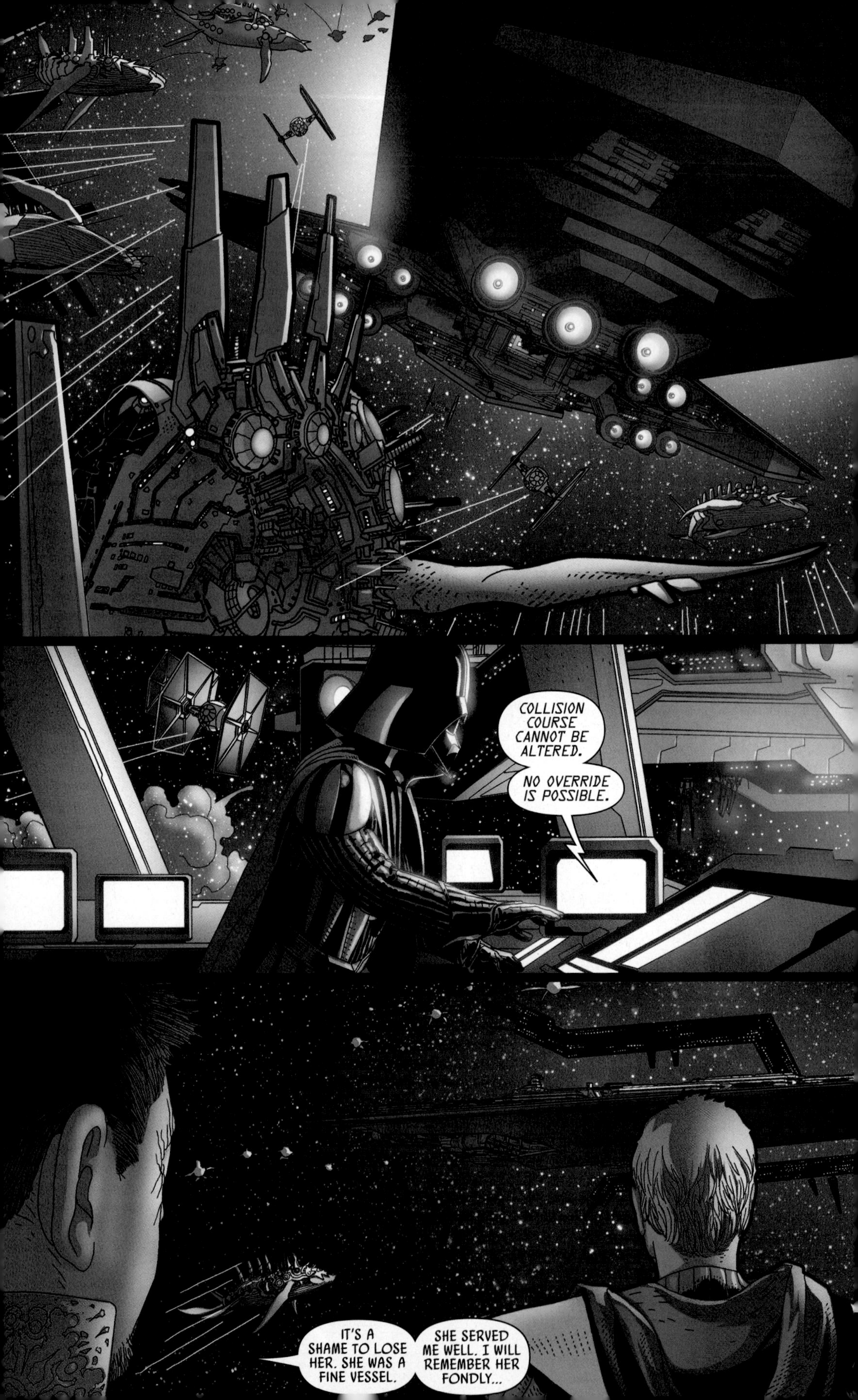
COLLISION COURSE CANNOT BE ALTERED.
NO OVERRIDE IS POSSIBLE.
IT'S A SHAME TO LOSE HER. SHE WAS A FINE VESSEL.
SHE SERVED ME WELL. I WILL REMEMBER HER FONDLY...

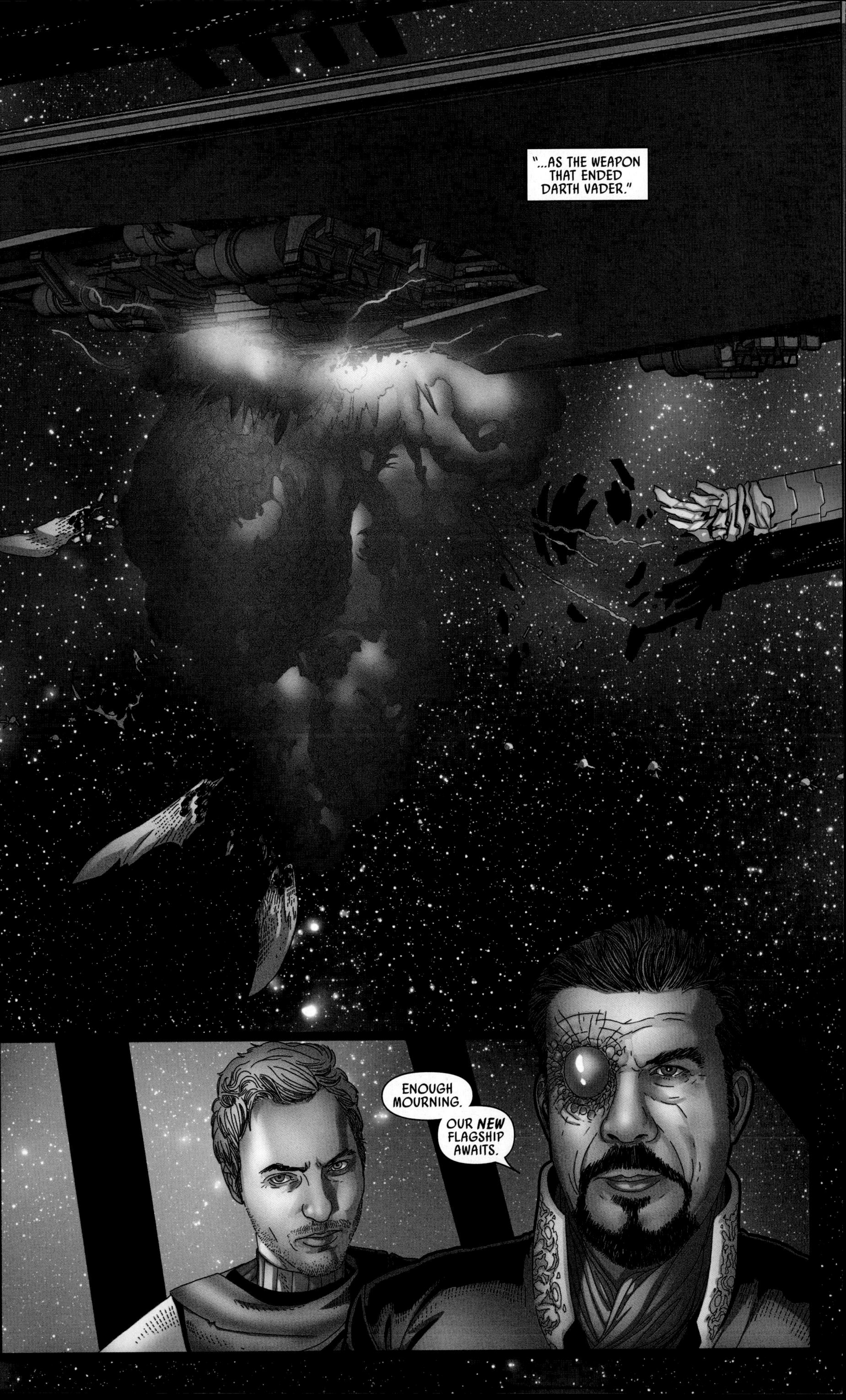
"...AS THE WEAPON THAT ENDED DARTH VADER."
ENOUGH MOURNING.
OUR NEW FLAGSHIP AWAITS.

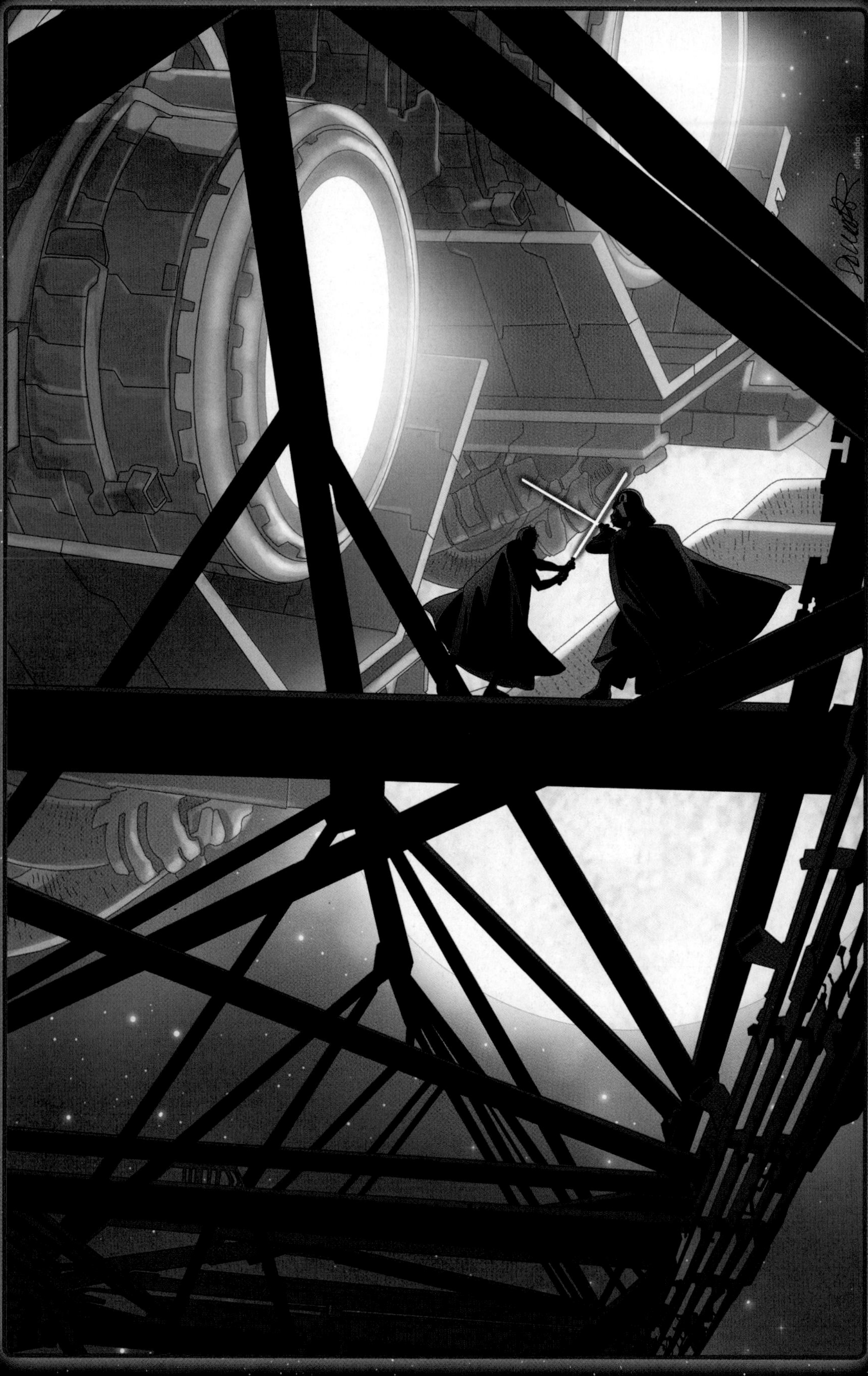

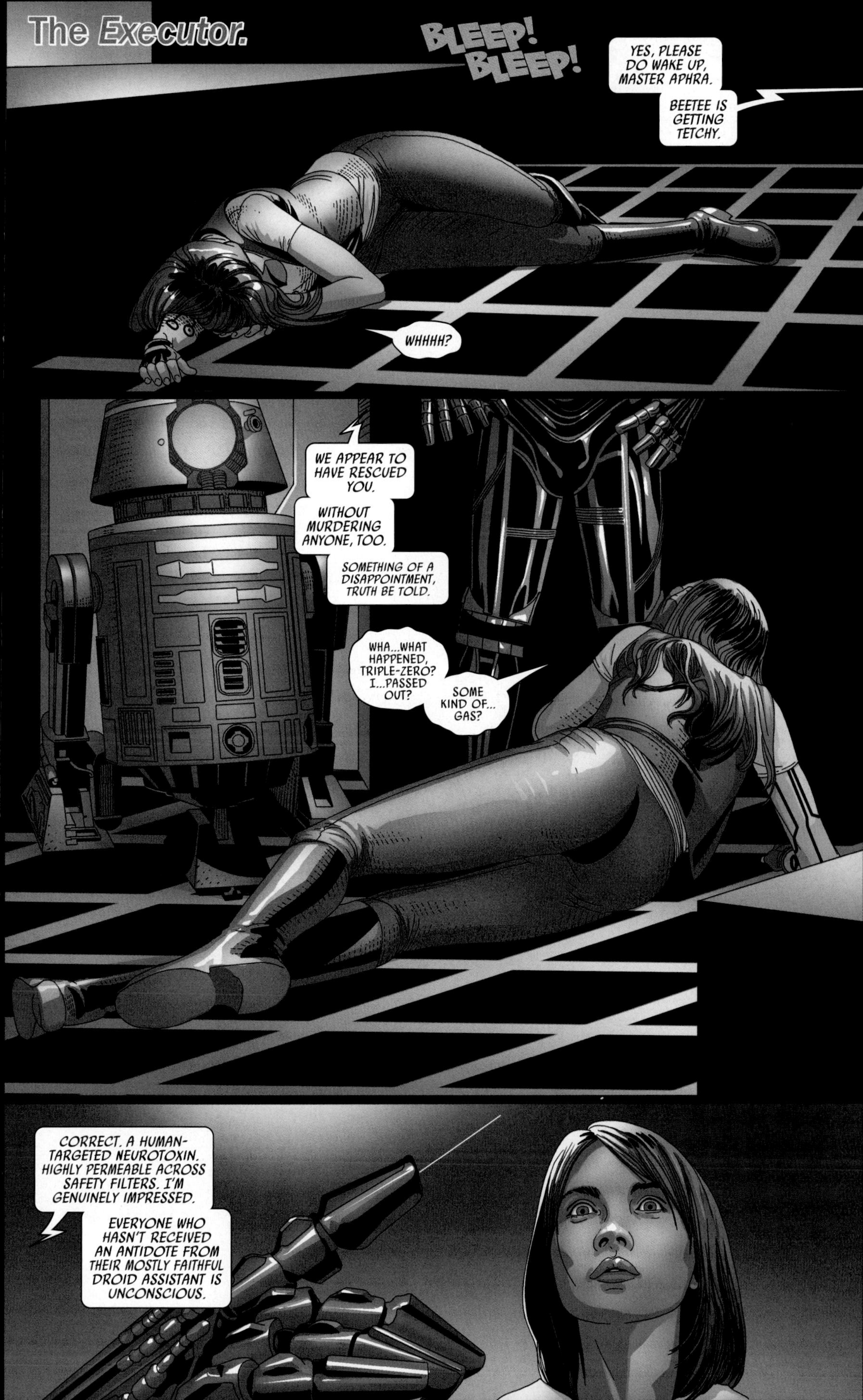
The Executor.
BLEEP! BLEEP!
YES, PLEASE DO WAKE UP, MASTER APHRA.
BEETEE IS GETTING TETCHY.
WHHHH?
WE APPEAR TO HAVE RESCUED YOU.
WITHOUT MURDERING ANYONE, TOO.
SOMETHING OF A DISAPPOINTMENT, TRUTH BE TOLD.
WHA...WHAT HAPPENED, TRIPLE-ZERO? I...PASSED OUT?
SOME KIND OF... GAS?
CORRECT. A HUMAN-TARGETED NEUROTOXIN. HIGHLY PERMEABLE ACROSS SAFETY FILTERS. I'M GENUINELY IMPRESSED.
EVERYONE WHO HASN'T RECEIVED AN ANTIDOTE FROM THEIR MOSTLY FAITHFUL DROID ASSISTANT IS UNCONSCIOUS.

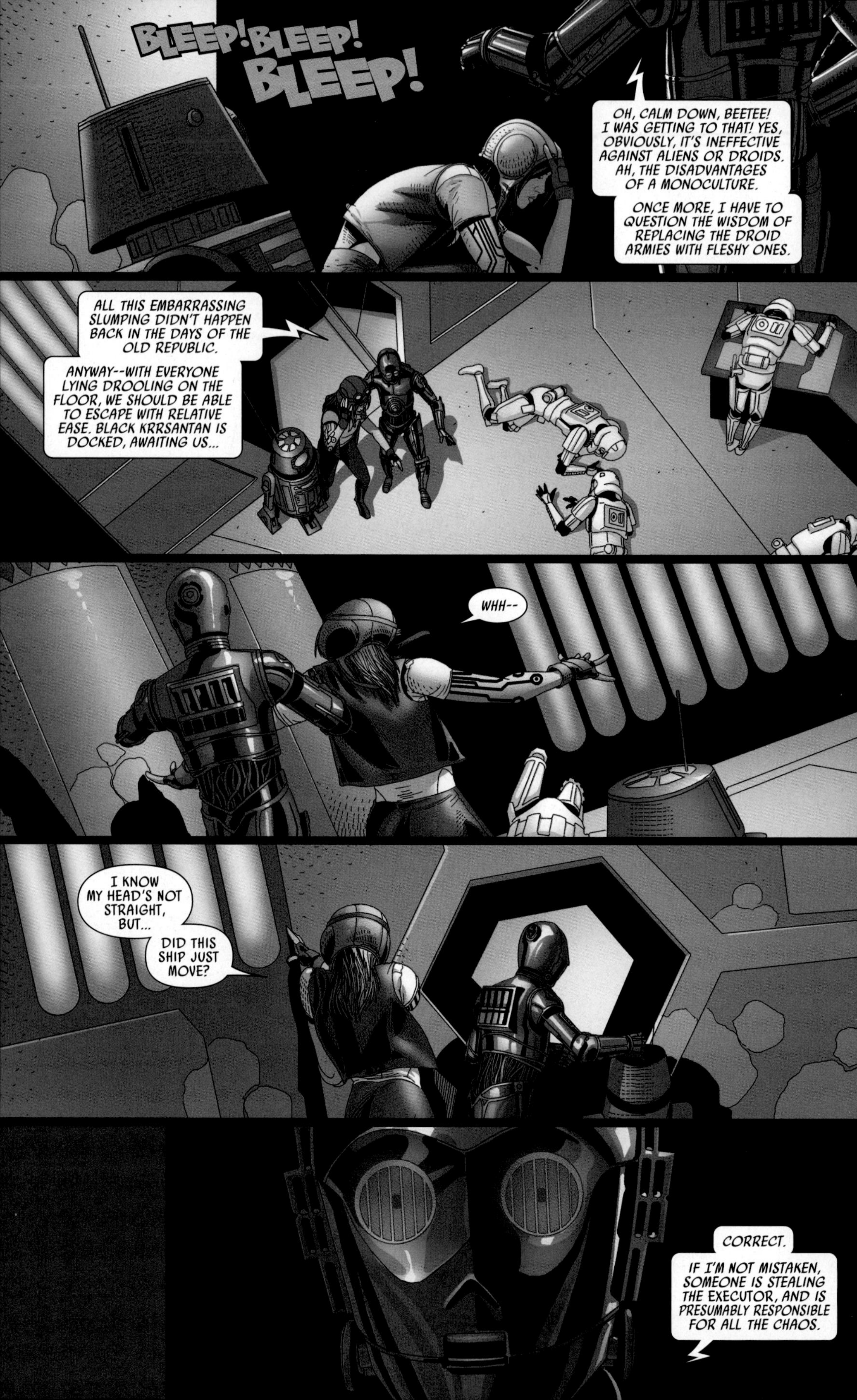
BLEEP! BLEEP! BLEEP!
OH, CALM DOWN, BEETEE! I WAS GETTING TO THAT! YES, OBVIOUSLY, IT'S INEFFECTIVE AGAINST ALIENS OR DROIDS. AH, THE DISADVANTAGES OF A MONOCULTURE.
ONCE MORE, I HAVE TO QUESTION THE WISDOM OF REPLACING THE DROID ARMIES WITH FLESHY ONES.
ALL THIS EMBARRASSING SLUMPING DIDN'T HAPPEN BACK IN THE DAYS OF THE OLD REPUBLIC.
ANYWAY--WITH EVERYONE LYING DROOLING ON THE FLOOR, WE SHOULD BE ABLE TO ESCAPE WITH RELATIVE EASE. BLACK KRRSANTAN IS DOCKED, AWAITING US...
WHH--
I KNOW MY HEAD'S NOT STRAIGHT, BUT...
DID THIS SHIP JUST MOVE?
CORRECT.
IF I'M NOT MISTAKEN, SOMEONE IS STEALING THE EXECUTOR, AND IS PRESUMABLY RESPONSIBLE FOR ALL THE CHAOS.

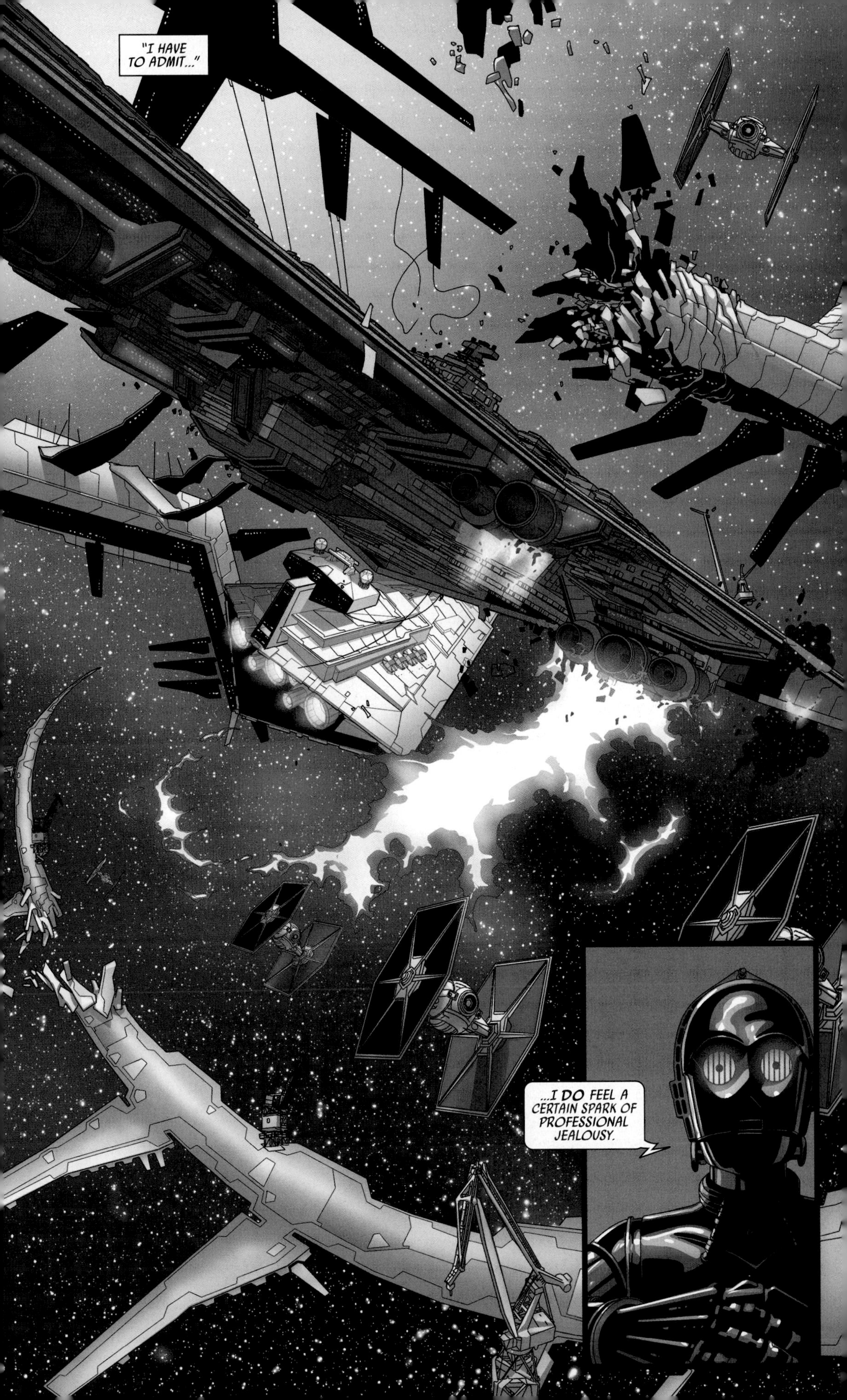
"I HAVE TO ADMIT..."
...I DO FEEL A CERTAIN SPARK OF PROFESSIONAL JEALOUSY.

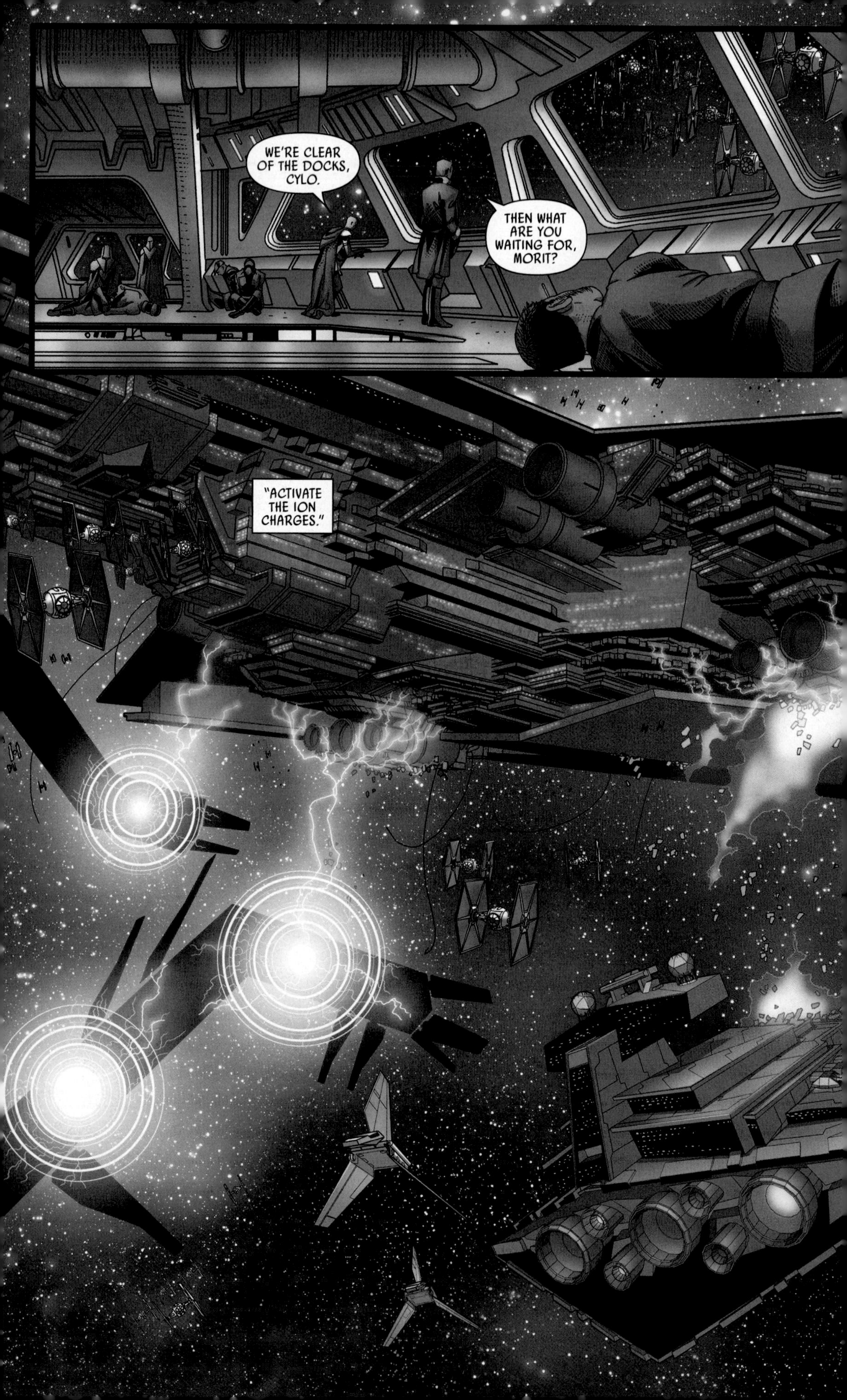
WE'RE CLEAR OF THE DOCKS, CYLO.
THEN WHAT ARE YOU WAITING FOR, MORIT?
"ACTIVATE THE ION CHARGES."

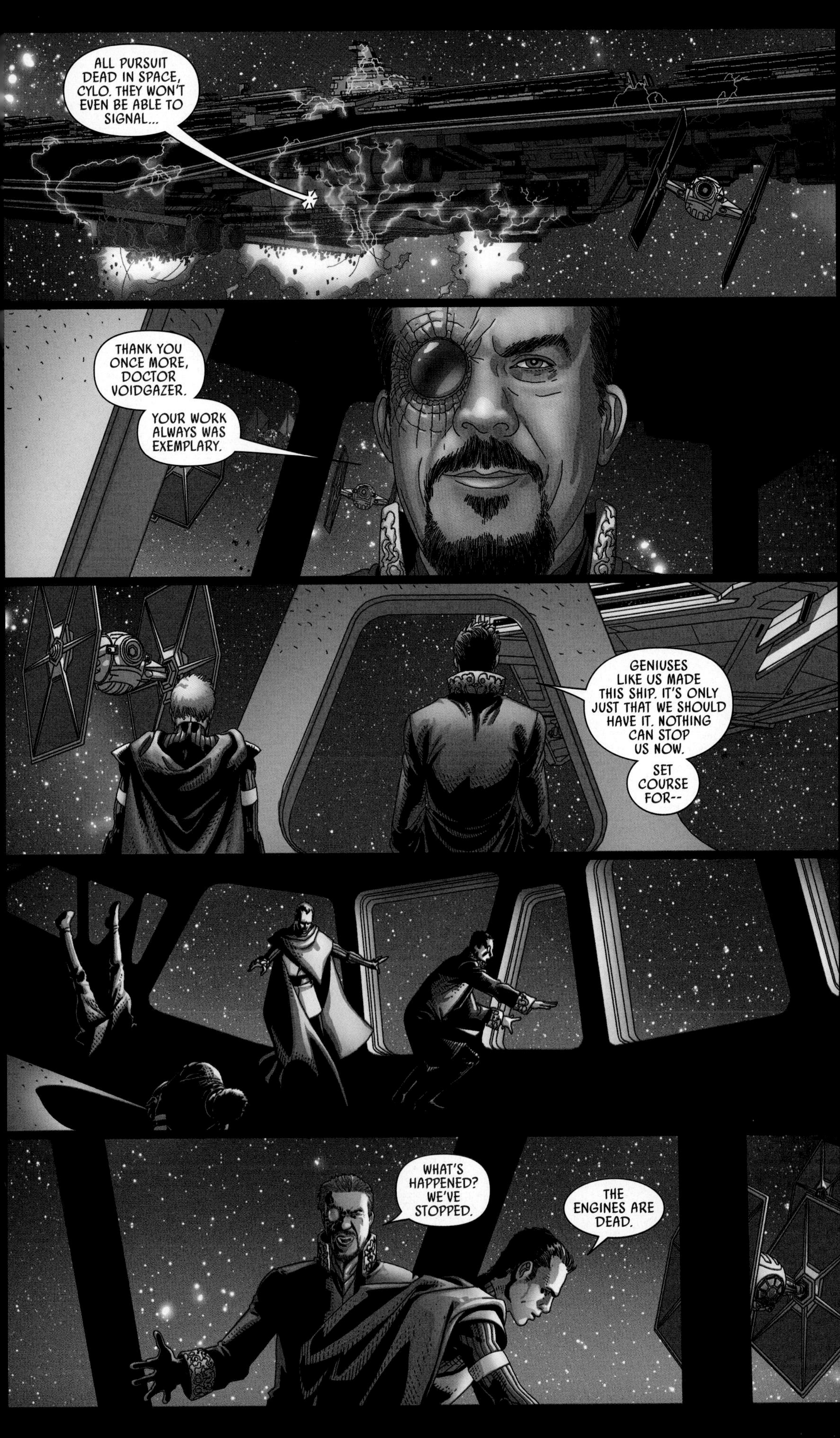
ALL PURSUIT DEAD IN SPACE, CYLO. THEY WON'T EVEN BE ABLE TO SIGNAL...
THANK YOU ONCE MORE, DOCTOR VOIDGAZER.
YOUR WORK ALWAYS WAS EXEMPLARY.
GENIUSES LIKE US MADE THIS SHIP. IT'S ONLY JUST THAT WE SHOULD HAVE IT. NOTHING CAN STOP US NOW.
SET COURSE FOR--
WHAT'S HAPPENED? WE'VE STOPPED.
THE ENGINES ARE DEAD.

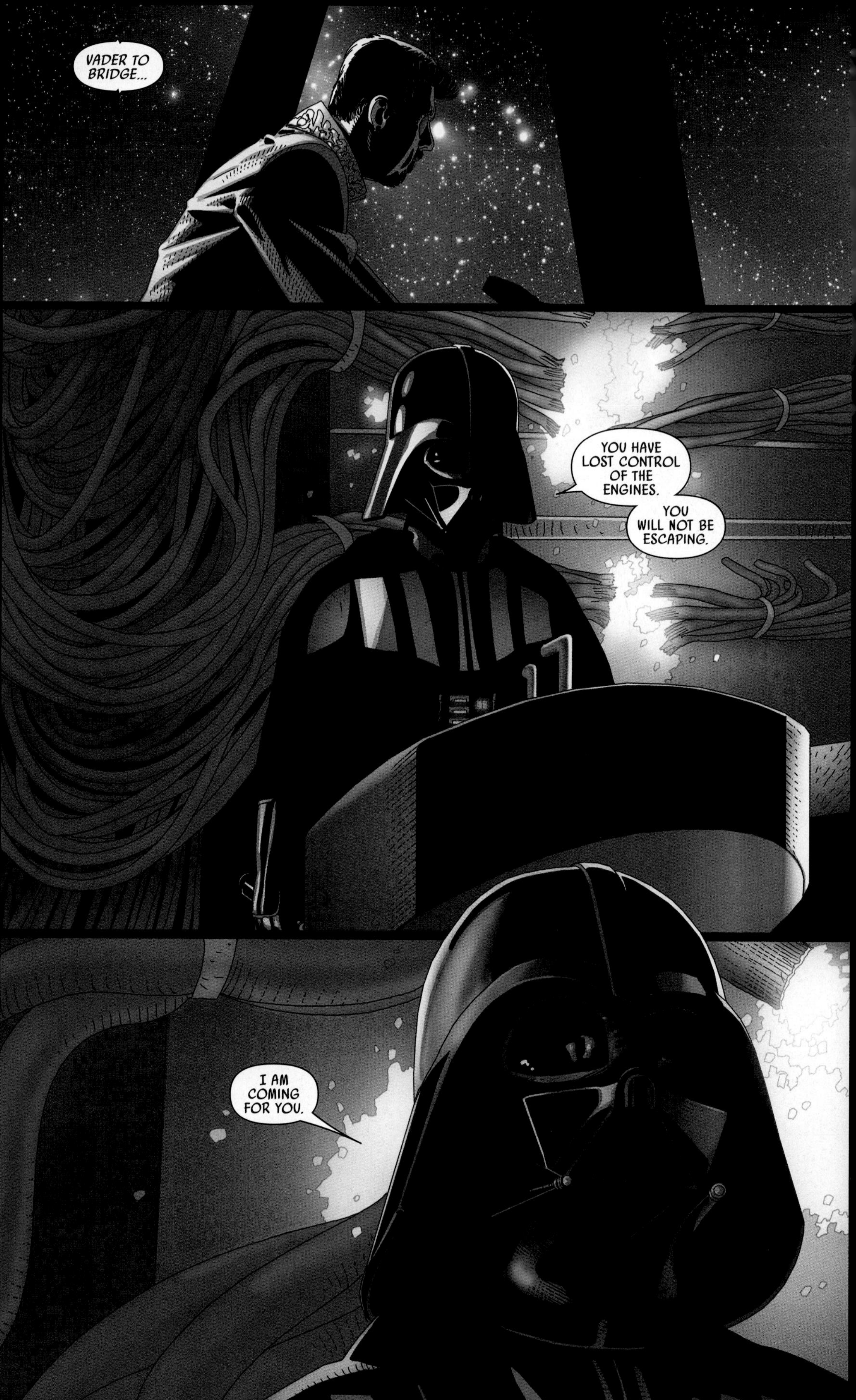
VADER TO BRIDGE...
YOU HAVE LOST CONTROL OF THE ENGINES.
YOU WILL NOT BE ESCAPING.
I AM COMING FOR YOU.

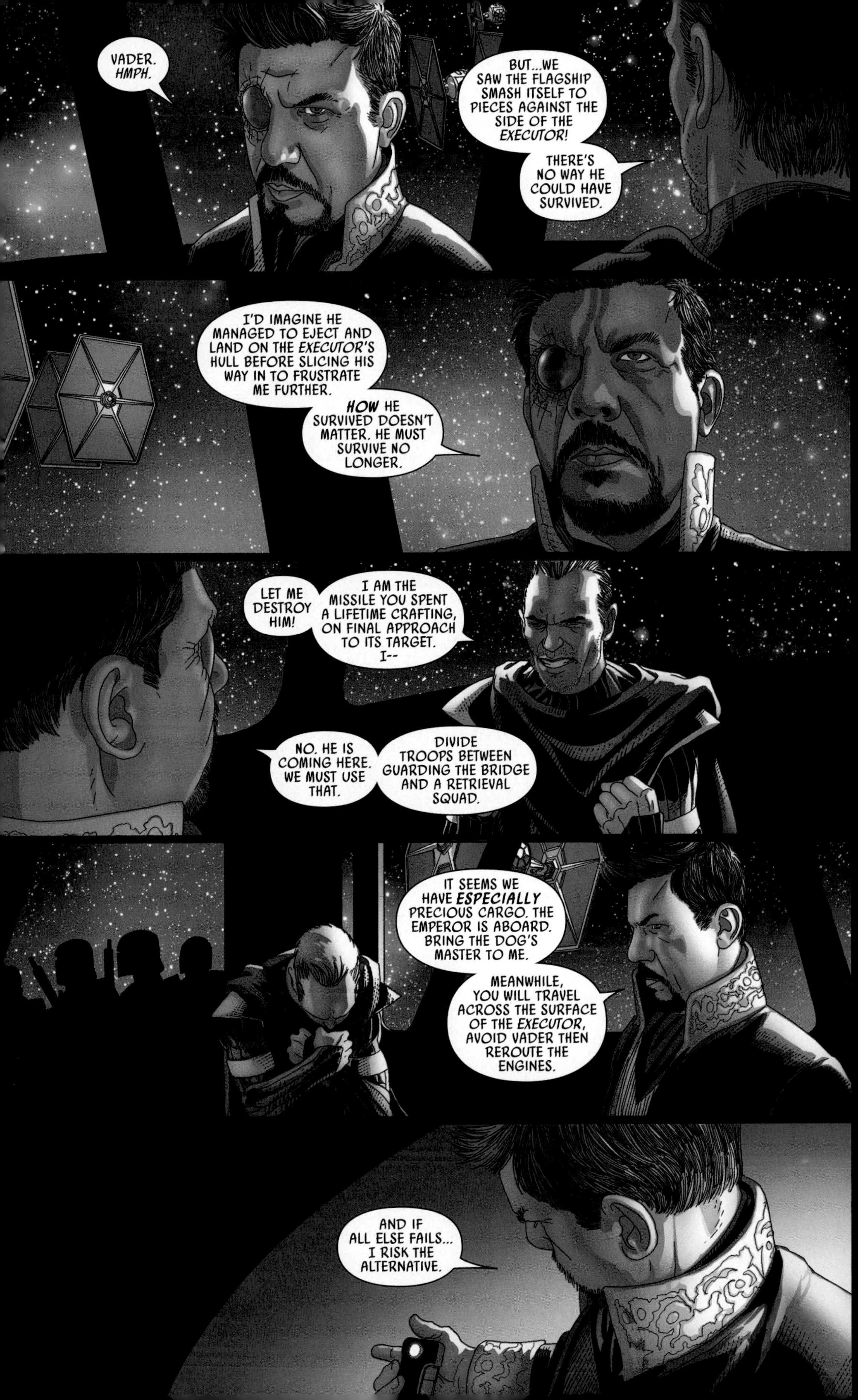
VADER. HMPH.
BUT...WE SAW THE FLAGSHIP SMASH ITSELF TO PIECES AGAINST THE SIDE OF THE *EXECUTOR*!
THERE'S NO WAY HE COULD HAVE SURVIVED.
I'D IMAGINE HE MANAGED TO EJECT AND LAND ON THE *EXECUTOR*'S HULL BEFORE SLICING HIS WAY IN TO FRUSTRATE ME FURTHER.
HOW HE SURVIVED DOESN'T MATTER. HE MUST SURVIVE NO LONGER.
LET ME DESTROY HIM!
I AM THE MISSILE YOU SPENT A LIFETIME CRAFTING, ON FINAL APPROACH TO ITS TARGET. I--
NO. HE IS COMING HERE. WE MUST USE THAT.
DIVIDE TROOPS BETWEEN GUARDING THE BRIDGE AND A RETRIEVAL SQUAD.
IT SEEMS WE HAVE ***ESPECIALLY*** PRECIOUS CARGO. THE EMPEROR IS ABOARD. BRING THE DOG'S MASTER TO ME.
MEANWHILE, YOU WILL TRAVEL ACROSS THE SURFACE OF THE *EXECUTOR*, AVOID VADER THEN REROUTE THE ENGINES.
AND IF ALL ELSE FAILS... I RISK THE ALTERNATIVE.

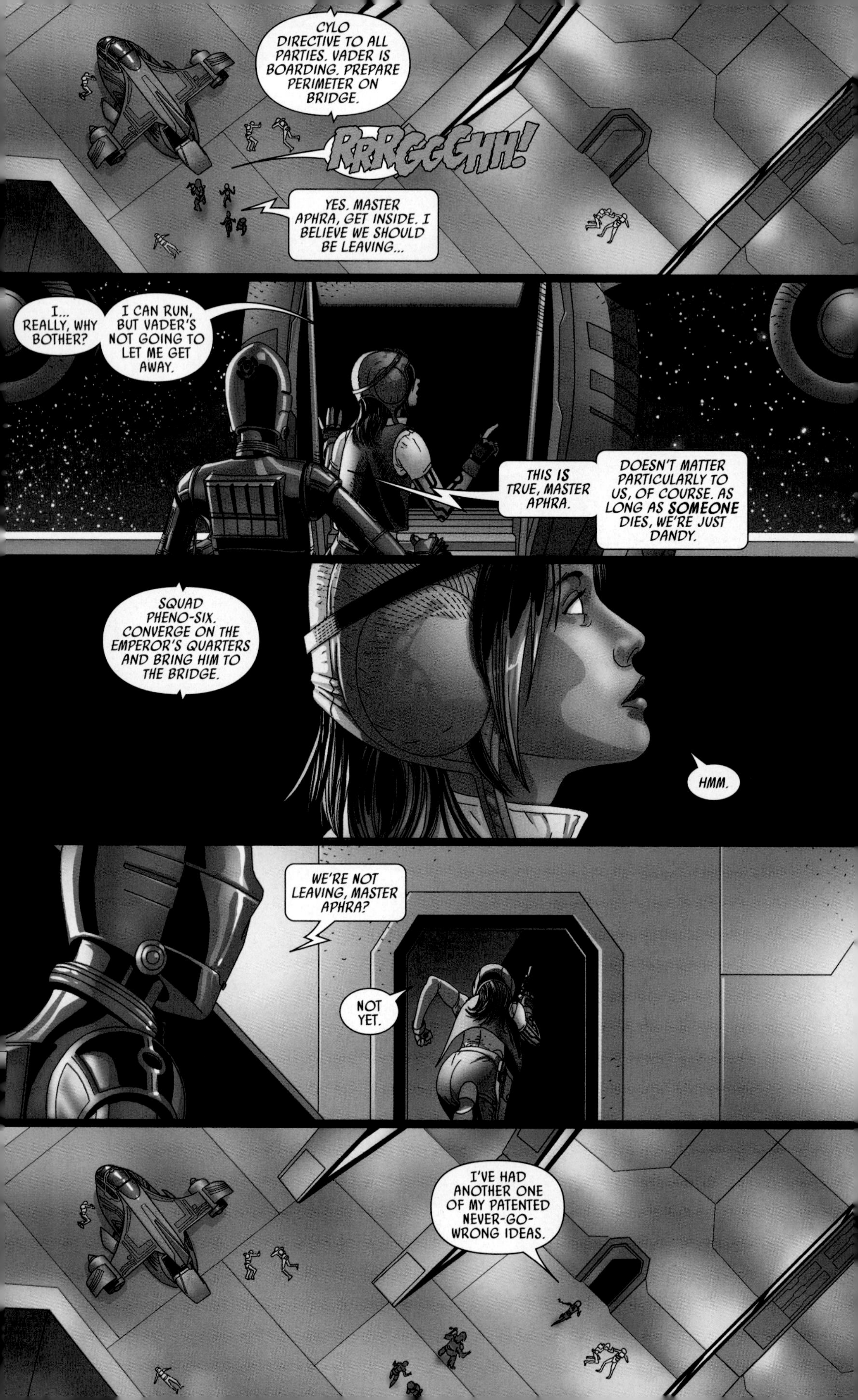
CYLO DIRECTIVE TO ALL PARTIES. VADER IS BOARDING. PREPARE PERIMETER ON BRIDGE.
RRRGGGHH!
YES. MASTER APHRA, GET INSIDE. I BELIEVE WE SHOULD BE LEAVING...
I... REALLY, WHY BOTHER?
I CAN RUN, BUT VADER'S NOT GOING TO LET ME GET AWAY.
THIS IS TRUE, MASTER APHRA.
DOESN'T MATTER PARTICULARLY TO US, OF COURSE. AS LONG AS SOMEONE DIES, WE'RE JUST DANDY.
SQUAD PHENO-SIX. CONVERGE ON THE EMPEROR'S QUARTERS AND BRING HIM TO THE BRIDGE.
HMM.
WE'RE NOT LEAVING, MASTER APHRA?
NOT YET.
I'VE HAD ANOTHER ONE OF MY PATENTED NEVER-GO-WRONG IDEAS.

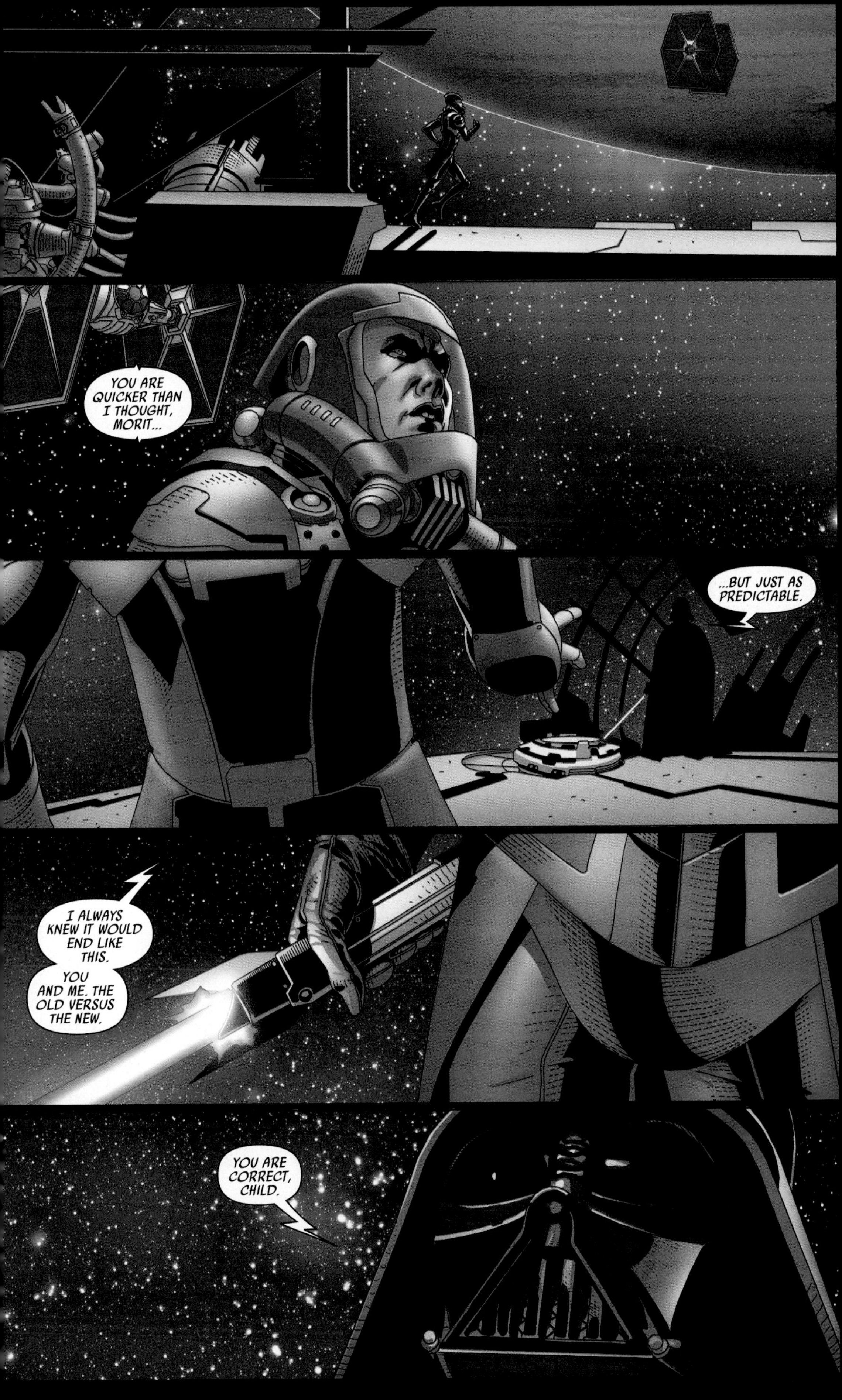
YOU ARE QUICKER THAN I THOUGHT, MORIT...
...BUT JUST AS PREDICTABLE.
I ALWAYS KNEW IT WOULD END LIKE THIS.
YOU AND ME. THE OLD VERSUS THE NEW.
YOU ARE CORRECT, CHILD.

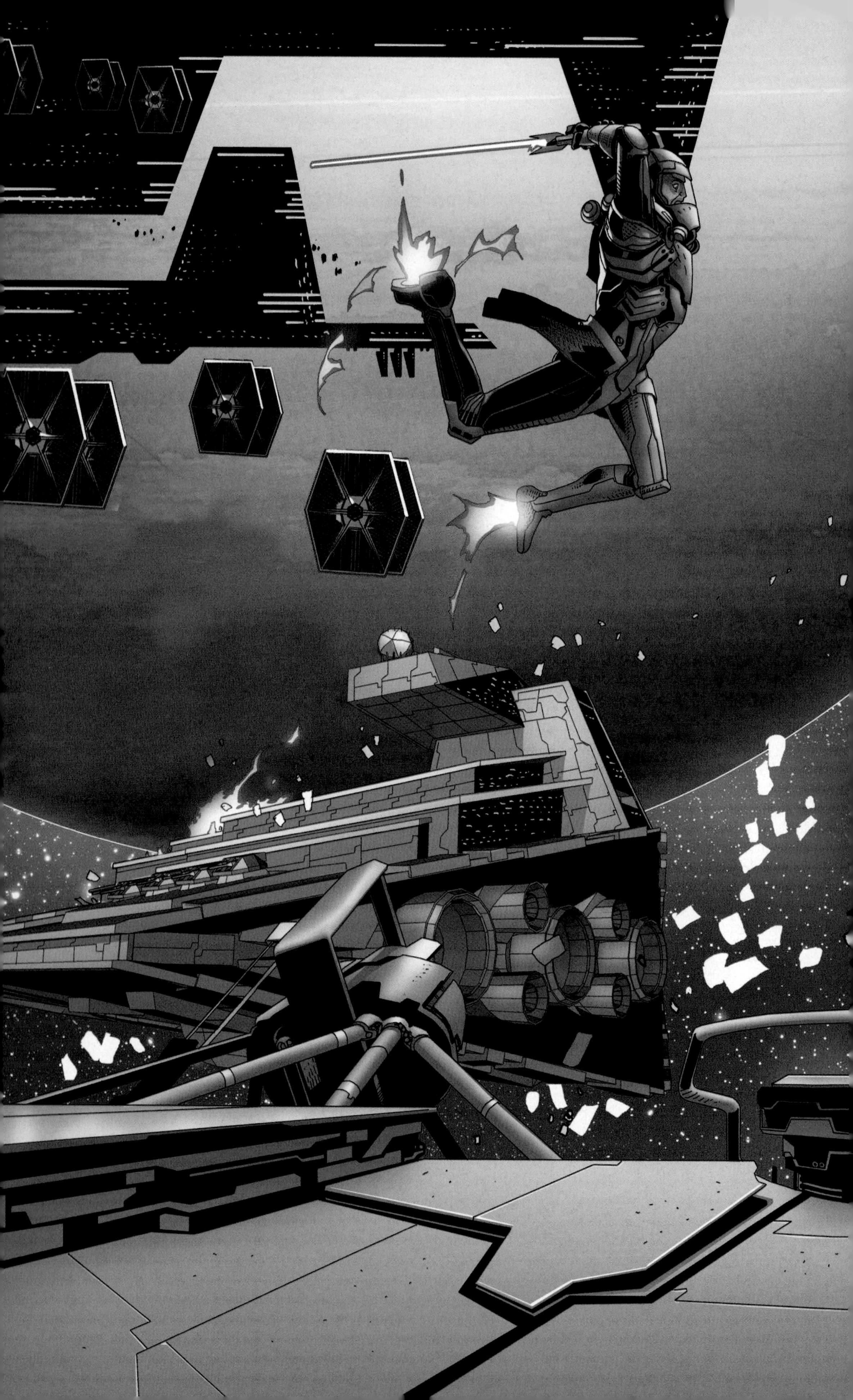

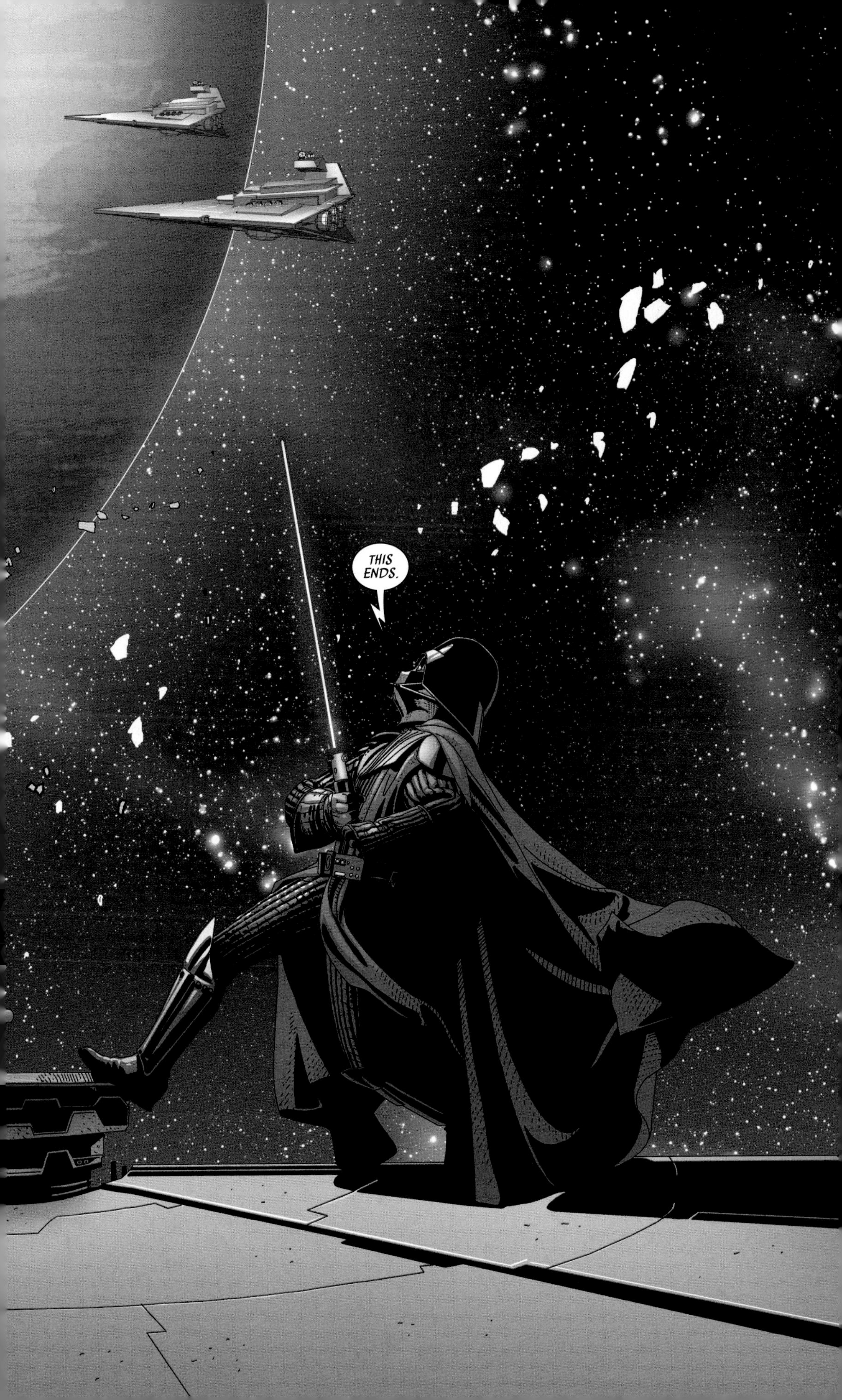
THIS ENDS.

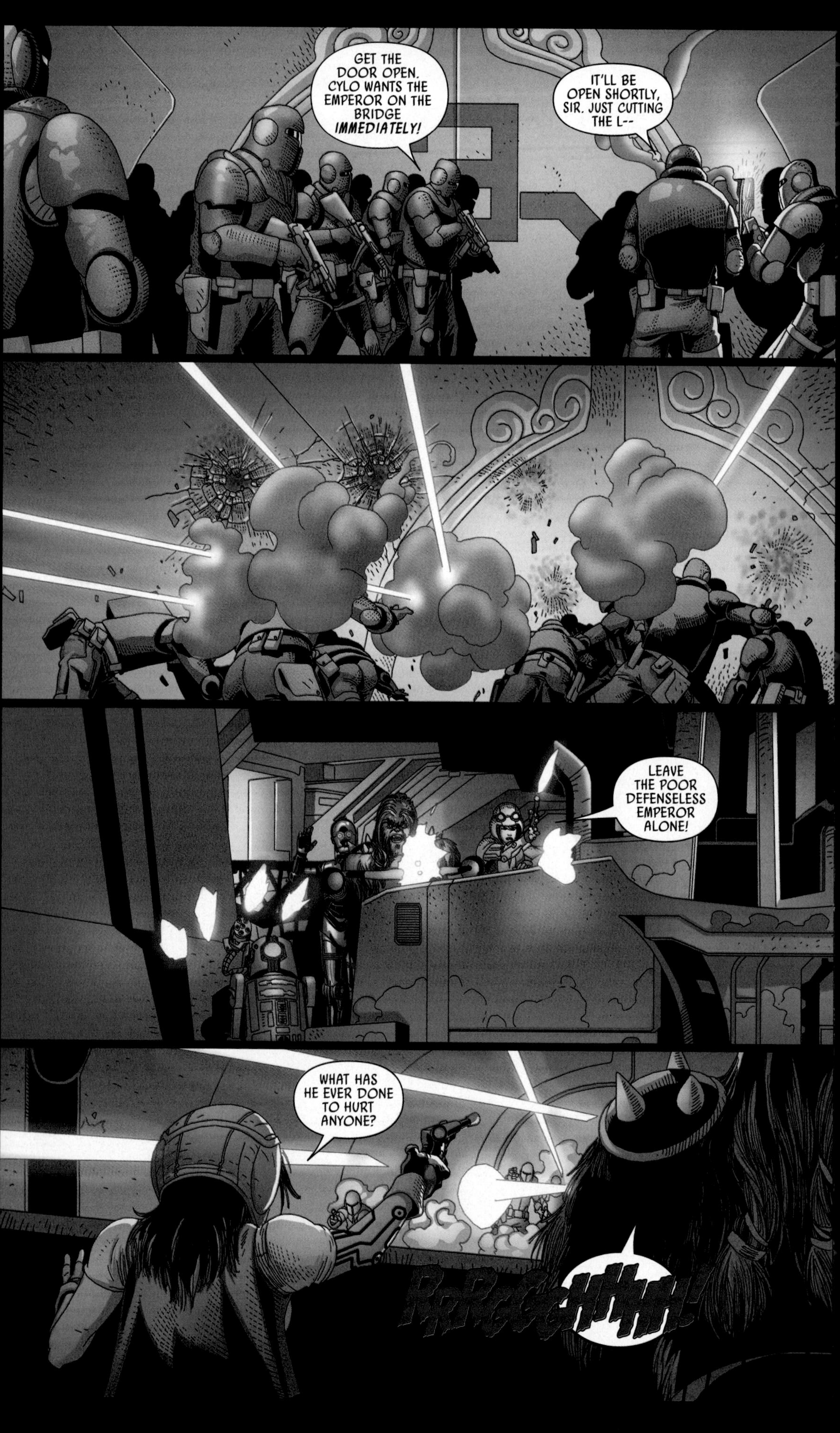
GET THE DOOR OPEN. CYLO WANTS THE EMPEROR ON THE BRIDGE *IMMEDIATELY!*
IT'LL BE OPEN SHORTLY, SIR. JUST CUTTING THE L--
LEAVE THE POOR DEFENSELESS EMPEROR ALONE!
WHAT HAS HE EVER DONE TO HURT ANYONE?
RRRGGHHHH!

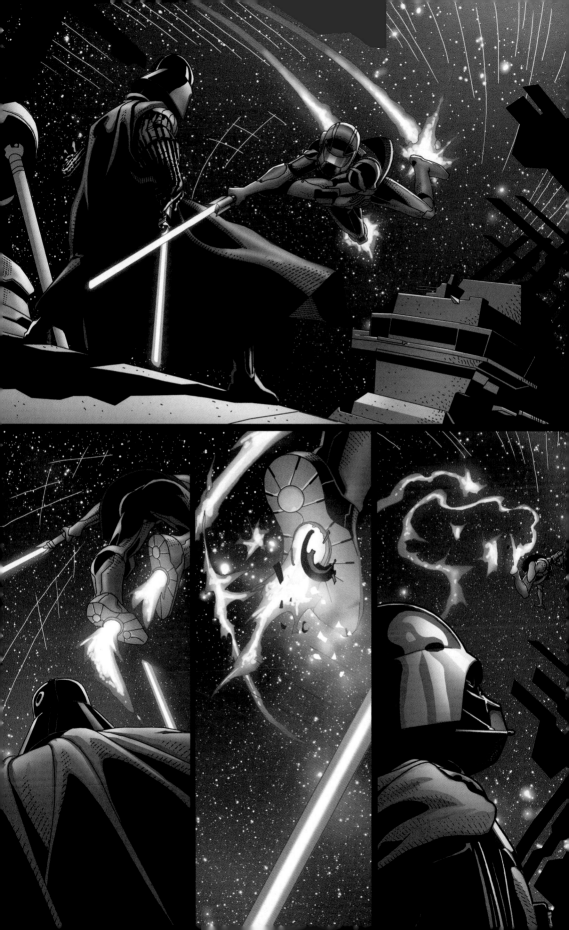

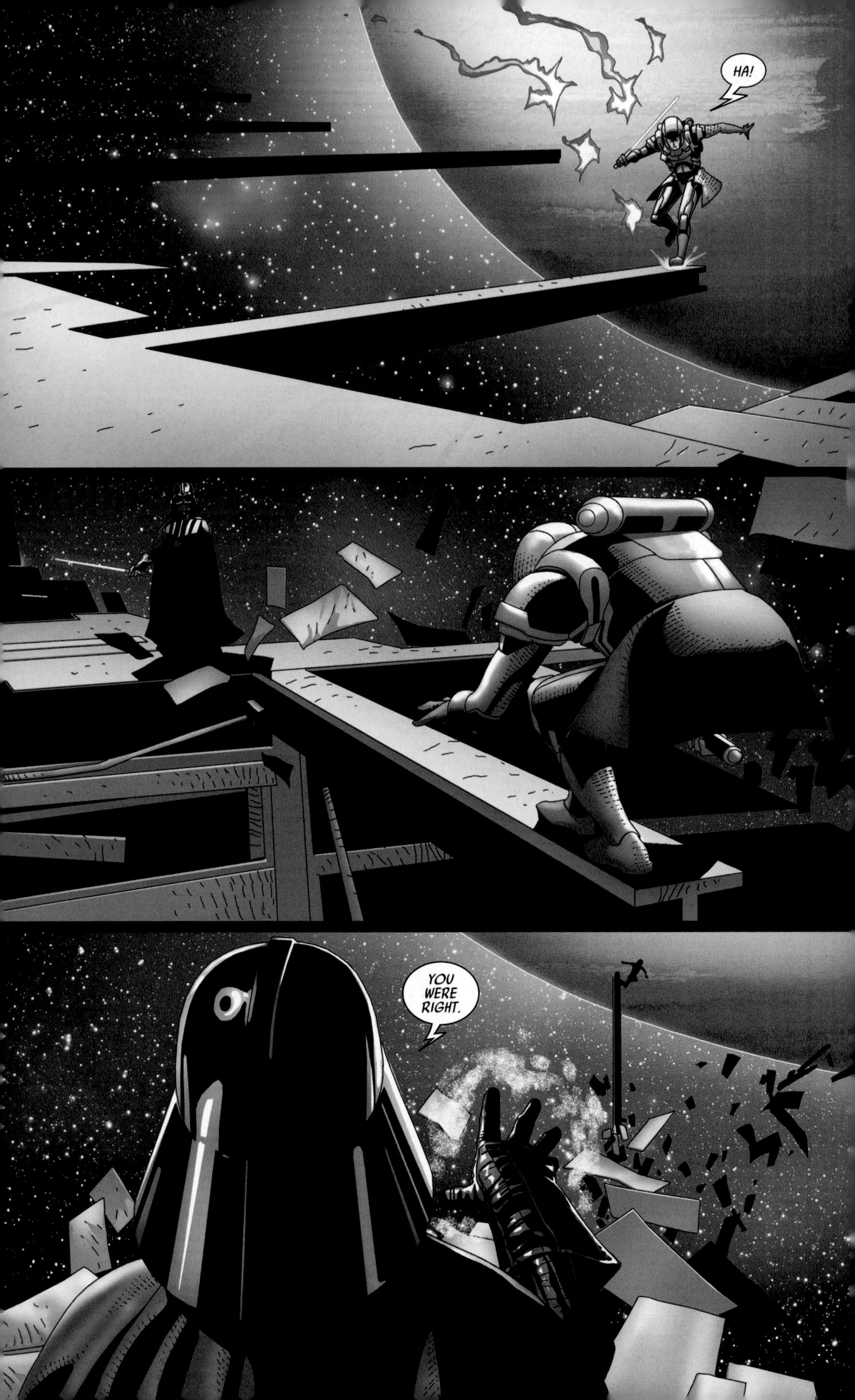
HA!
YOU WERE RIGHT.

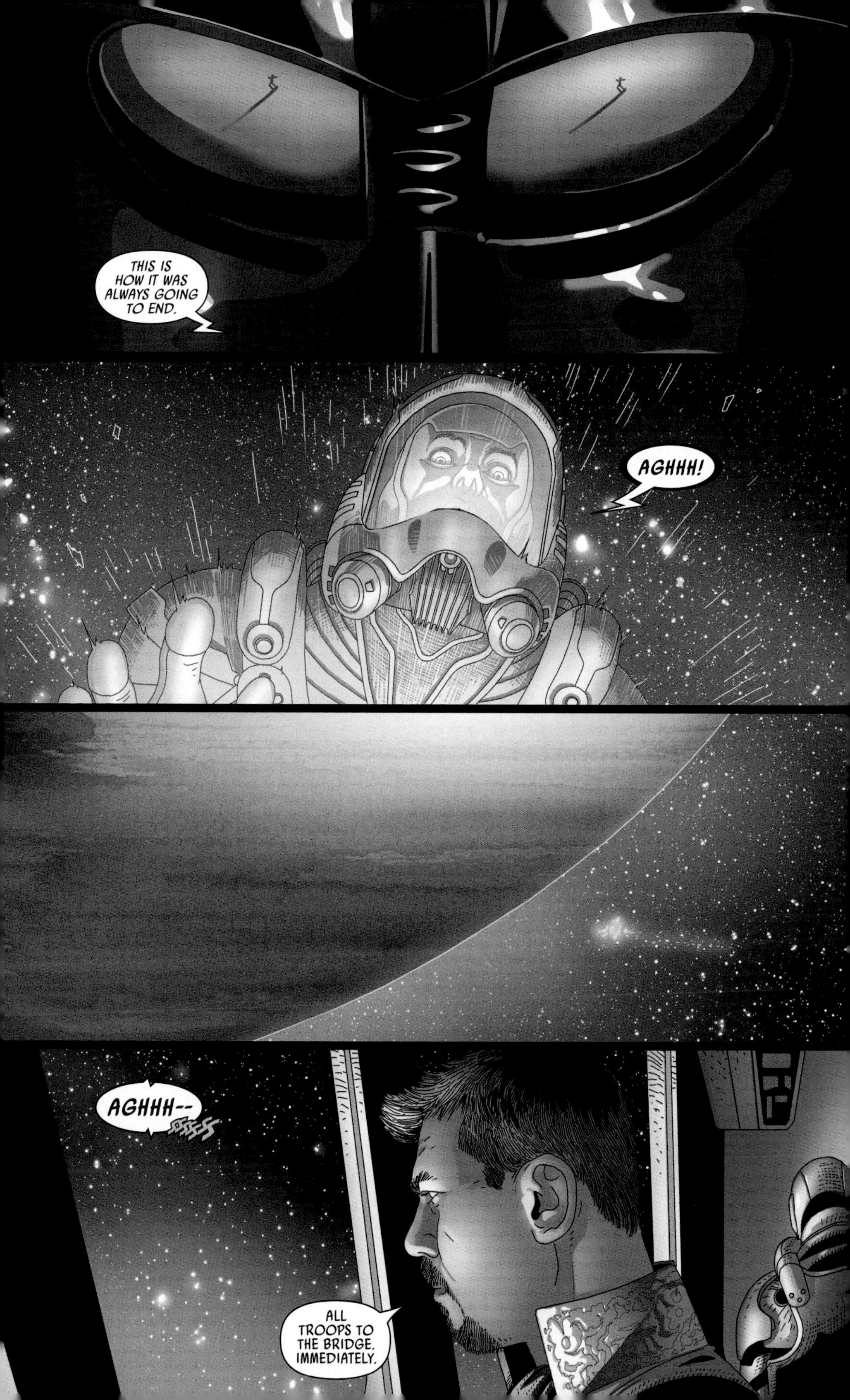
THIS IS HOW IT WAS ALWAYS GOING TO END.
AGHHH!
AGHHH--
SSSSS
ALL TROOPS TO THE BRIDGE. IMMEDIATELY.

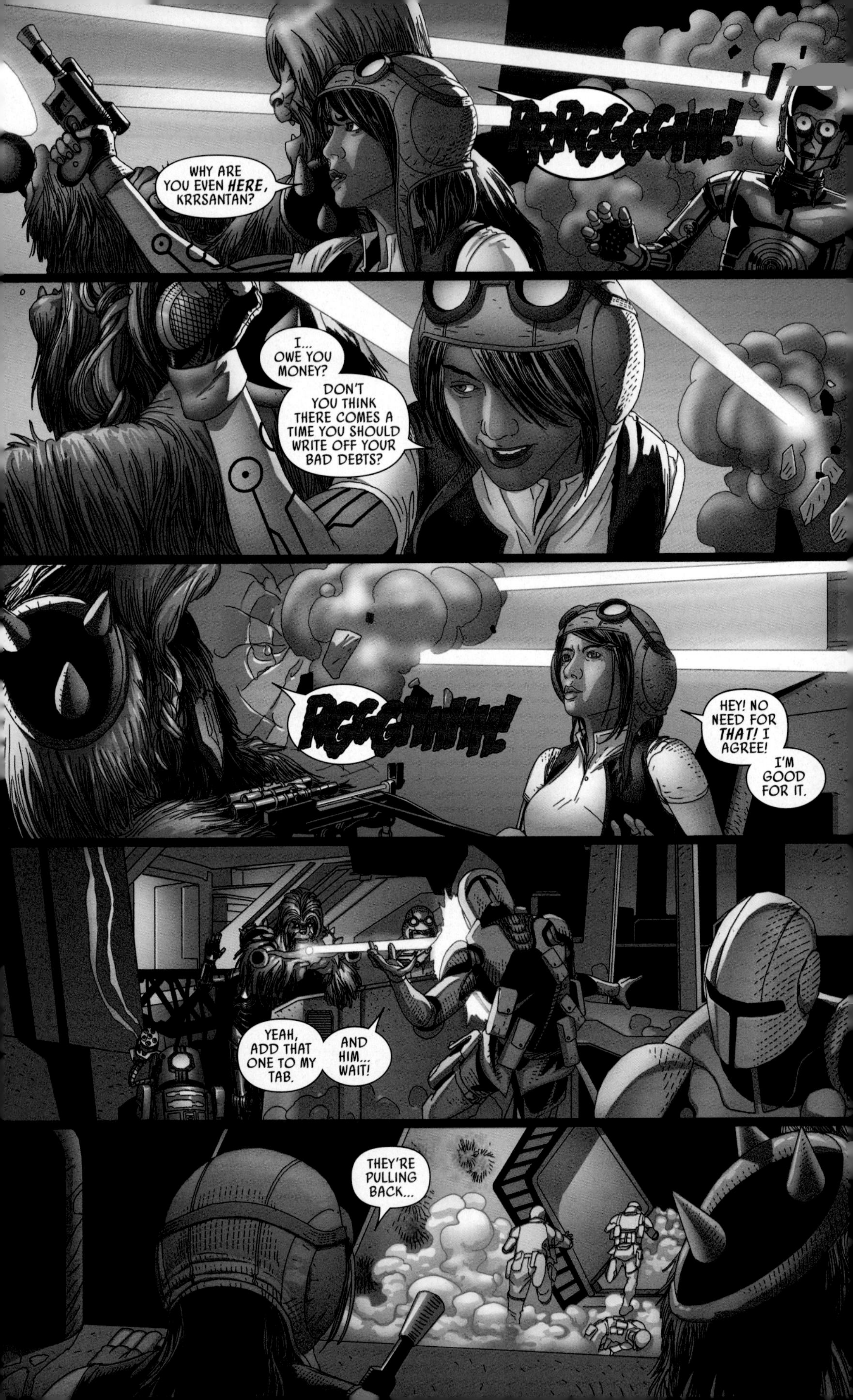
WHY ARE YOU EVEN HERE, KRRSANTAN?
RRRGGGGHH!
I... OWE YOU MONEY?
DON'T YOU THINK THERE COMES A TIME YOU SHOULD WRITE OFF YOUR BAD DEBTS?
RGGGHHHH!
HEY! NO NEED FOR THAT! I AGREE!
I'M GOOD FOR IT.
YEAH, ADD THAT ONE TO MY TAB.
AND HIM... WAIT!
THEY'RE PULLING BACK...

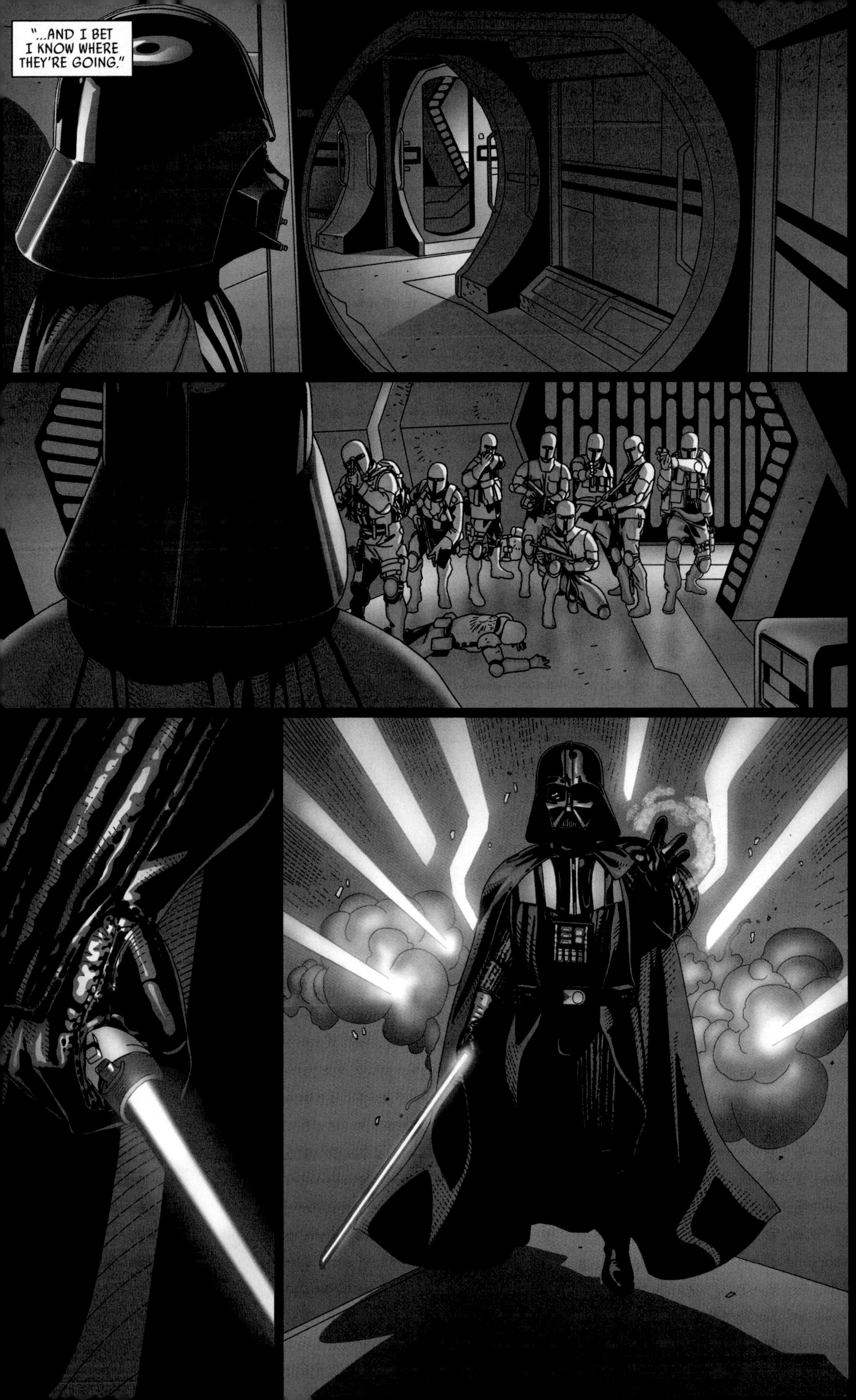
"...AND I BET I KNOW WHERE THEY'RE GOING."

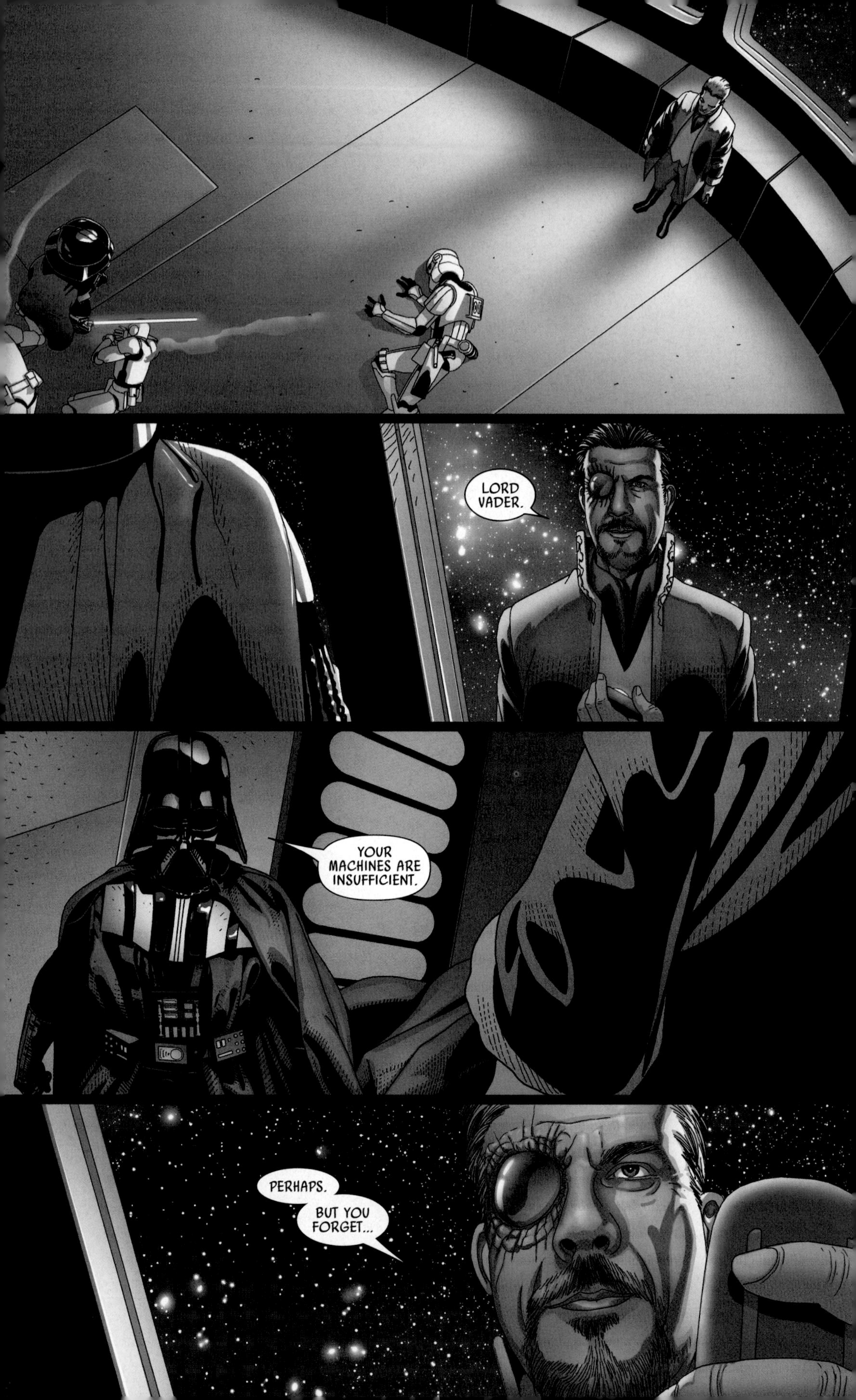
LORD VADER.
YOUR MACHINES ARE INSUFFICIENT.
PERHAPS.
BUT YOU FORGET...

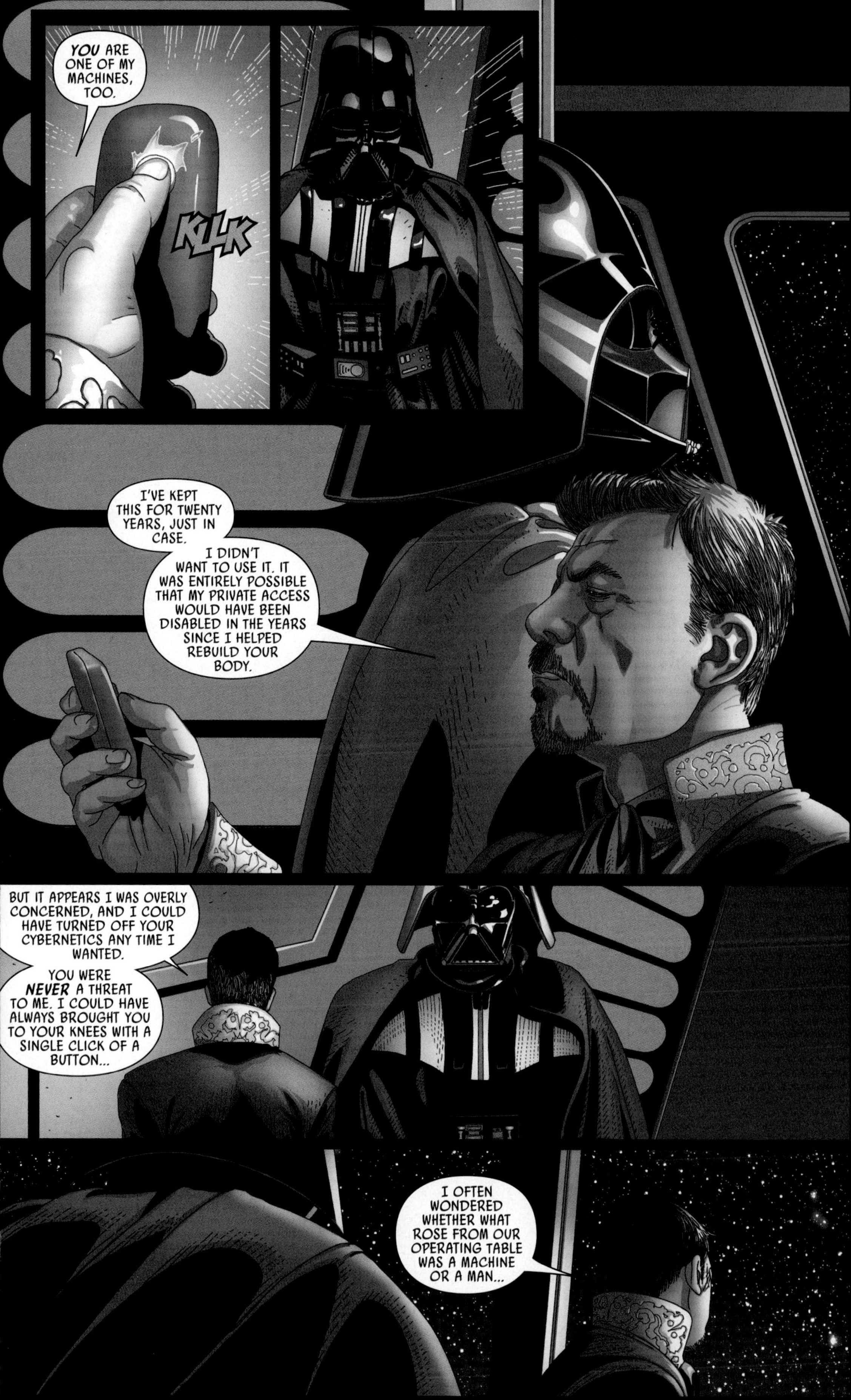
YOU ARE ONE OF MY MACHINES, TOO.
KLIK
I'VE KEPT THIS FOR TWENTY YEARS, JUST IN CASE.
I DIDN'T WANT TO USE IT. IT WAS ENTIRELY POSSIBLE THAT MY PRIVATE ACCESS WOULD HAVE BEEN DISABLED IN THE YEARS SINCE I HELPED REBUILD YOUR BODY.
BUT IT APPEARS I WAS OVERLY CONCERNED, AND I COULD HAVE TURNED OFF YOUR CYBERNETICS ANY TIME I WANTED.
YOU WERE NEVER A THREAT TO ME. I COULD HAVE ALWAYS BROUGHT YOU TO YOUR KNEES WITH A SINGLE CLICK OF A BUTTON...
I OFTEN WONDERED WHETHER WHAT ROSE FROM OUR OPERATING TABLE WAS A MACHINE OR A MAN...

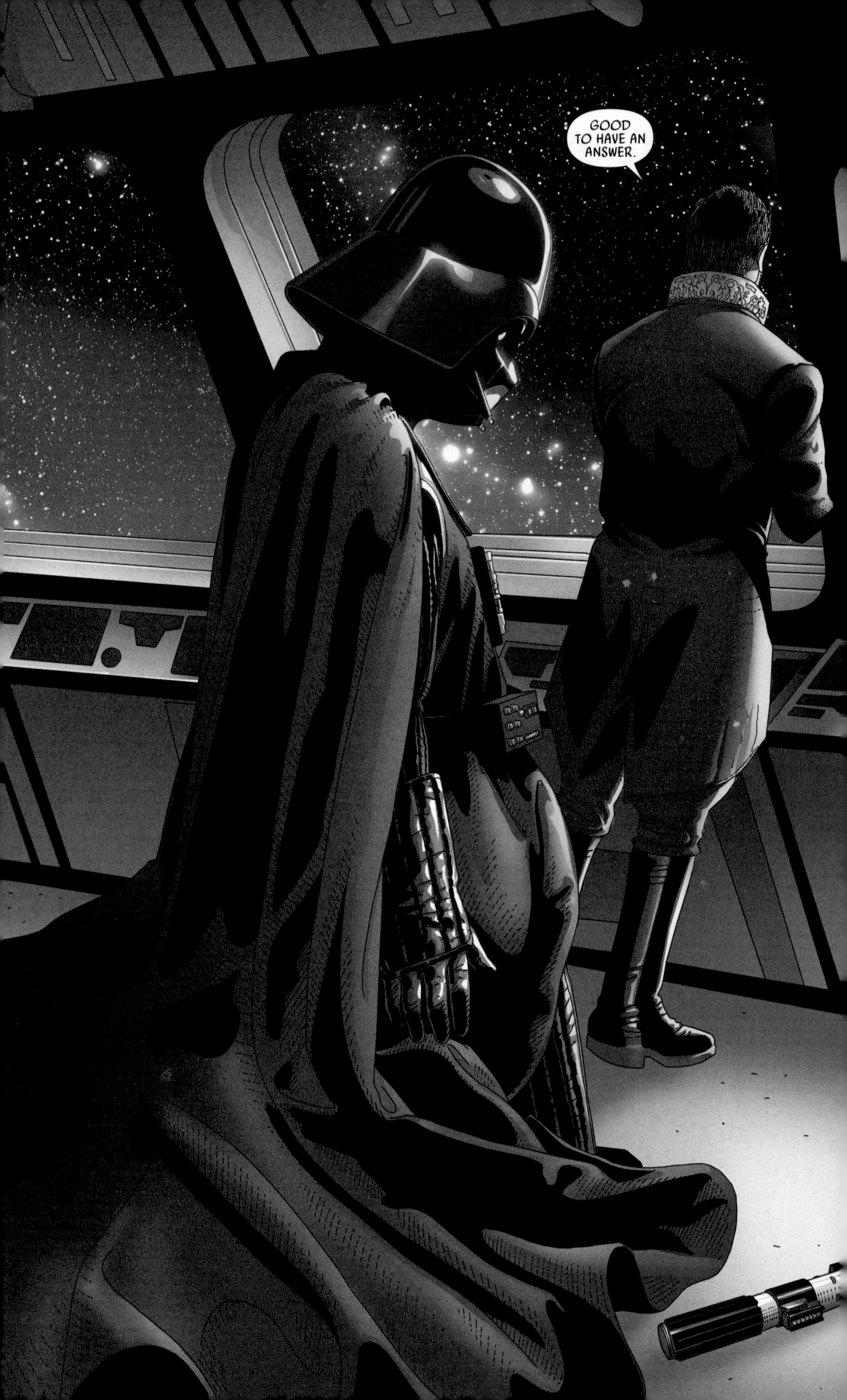
GOOD TO HAVE AN ANSWER.

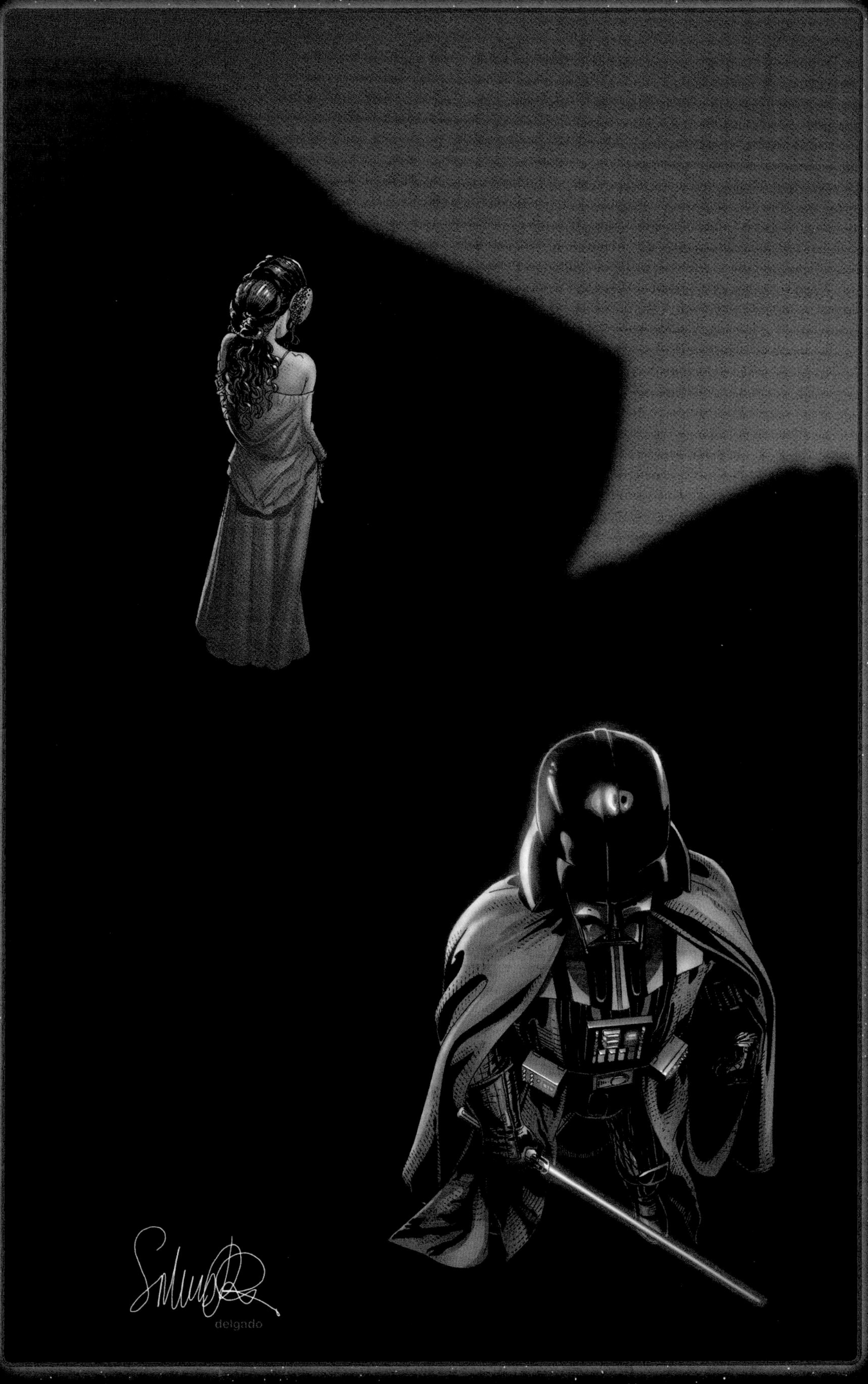
delgado

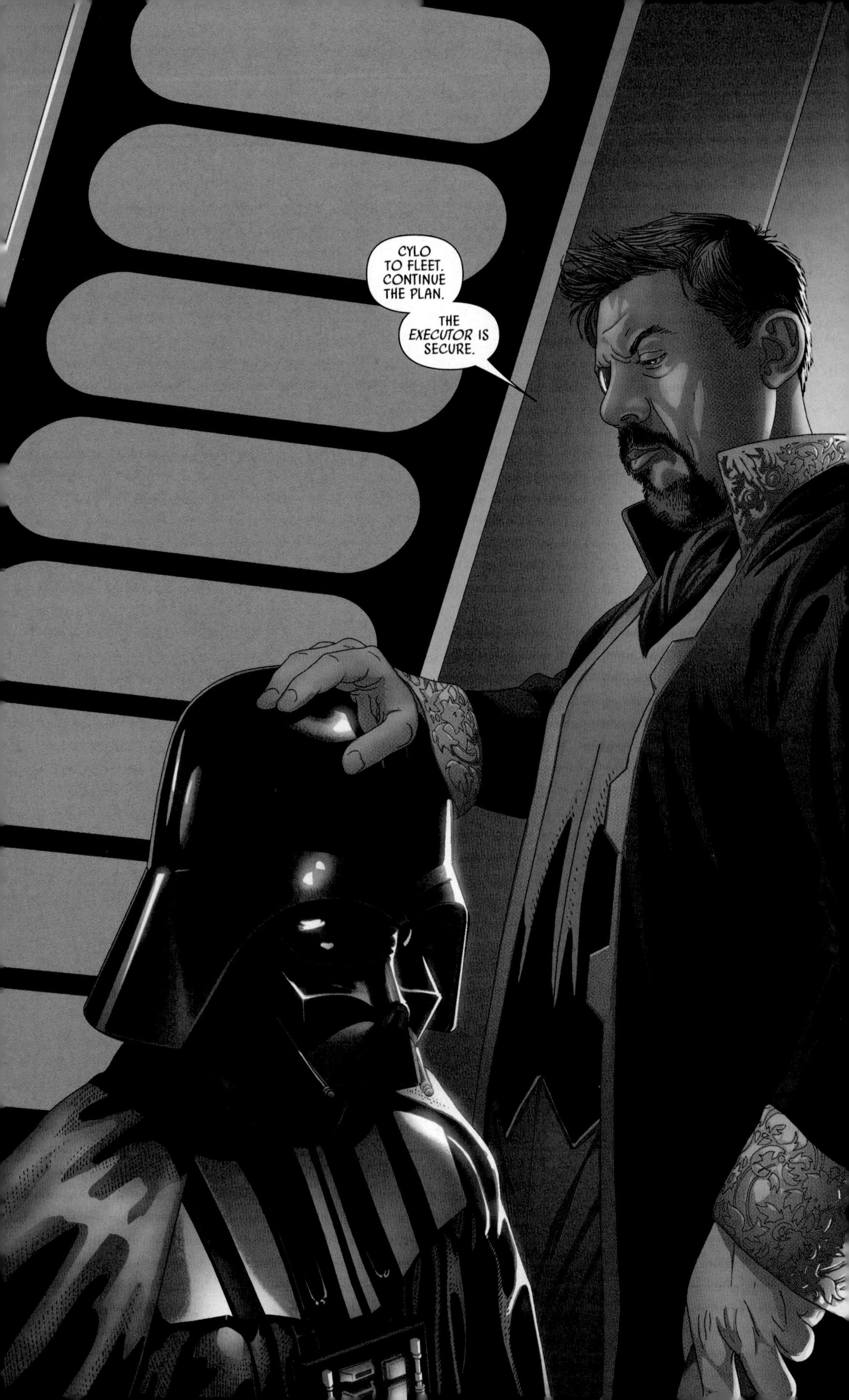
CYLO TO FLEET. CONTINUE THE PLAN.
THE *EXECUTOR* IS SECURE.

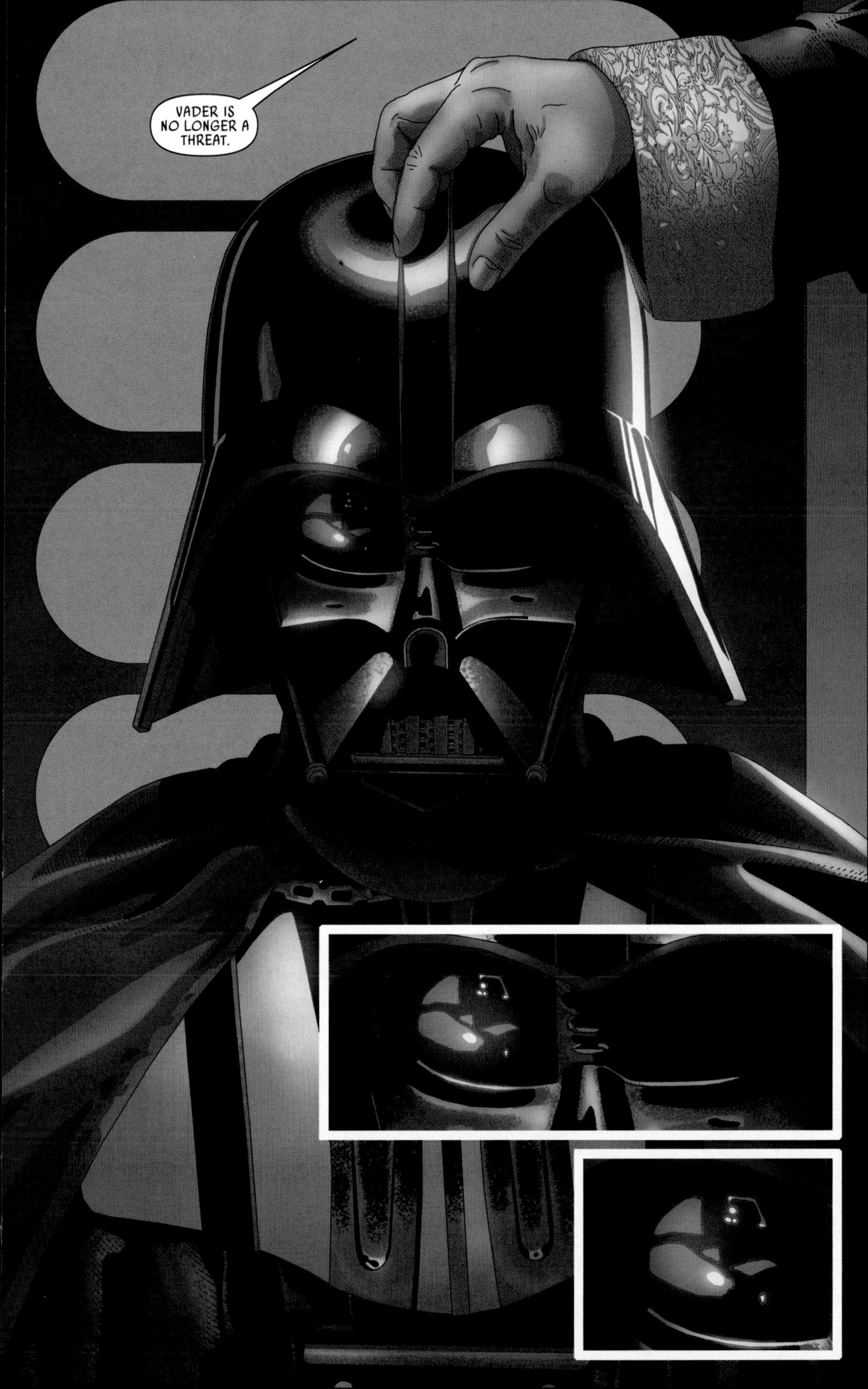
VADER IS NO LONGER A THREAT.

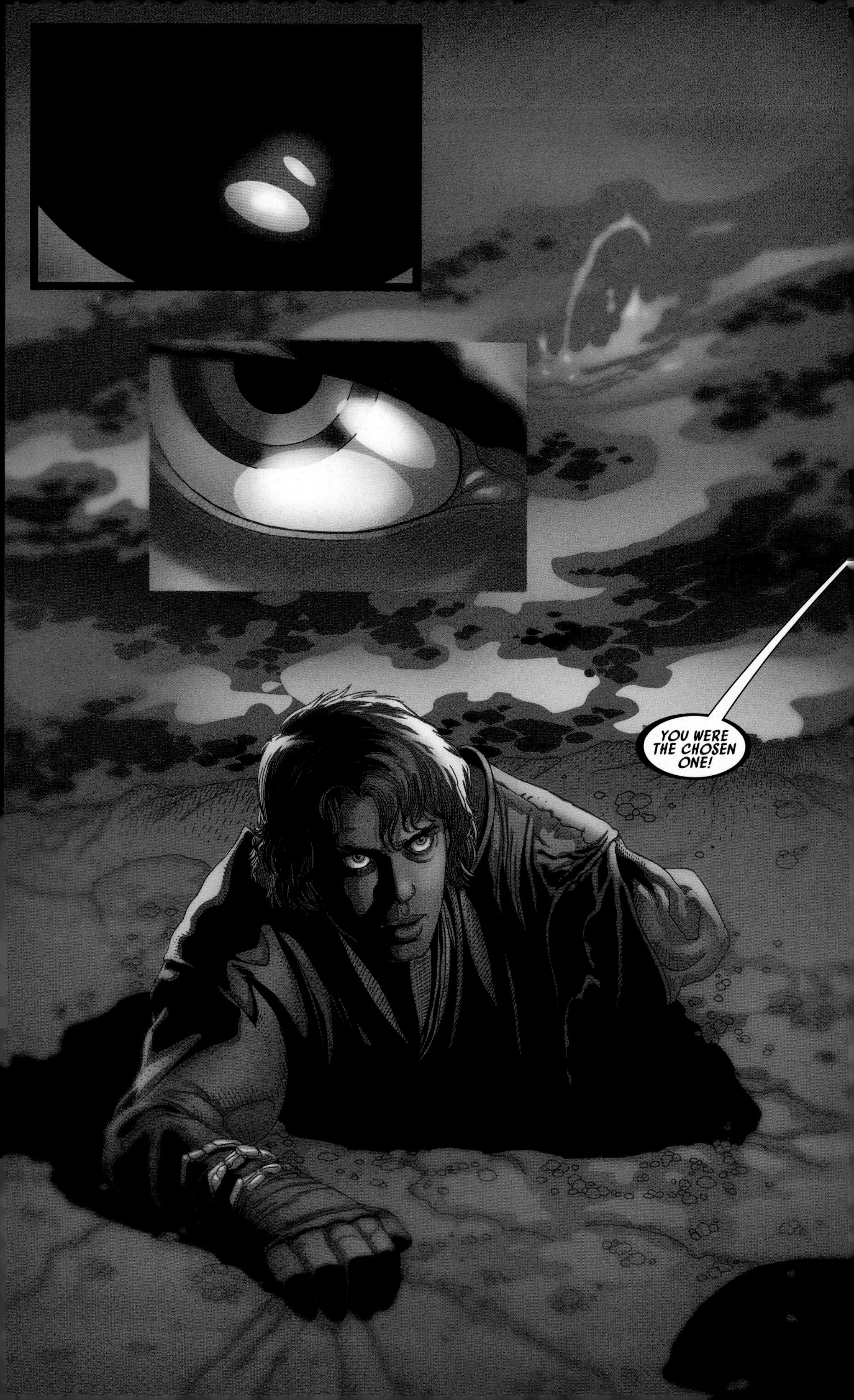
YOU WERE THE CHOSEN ONE!

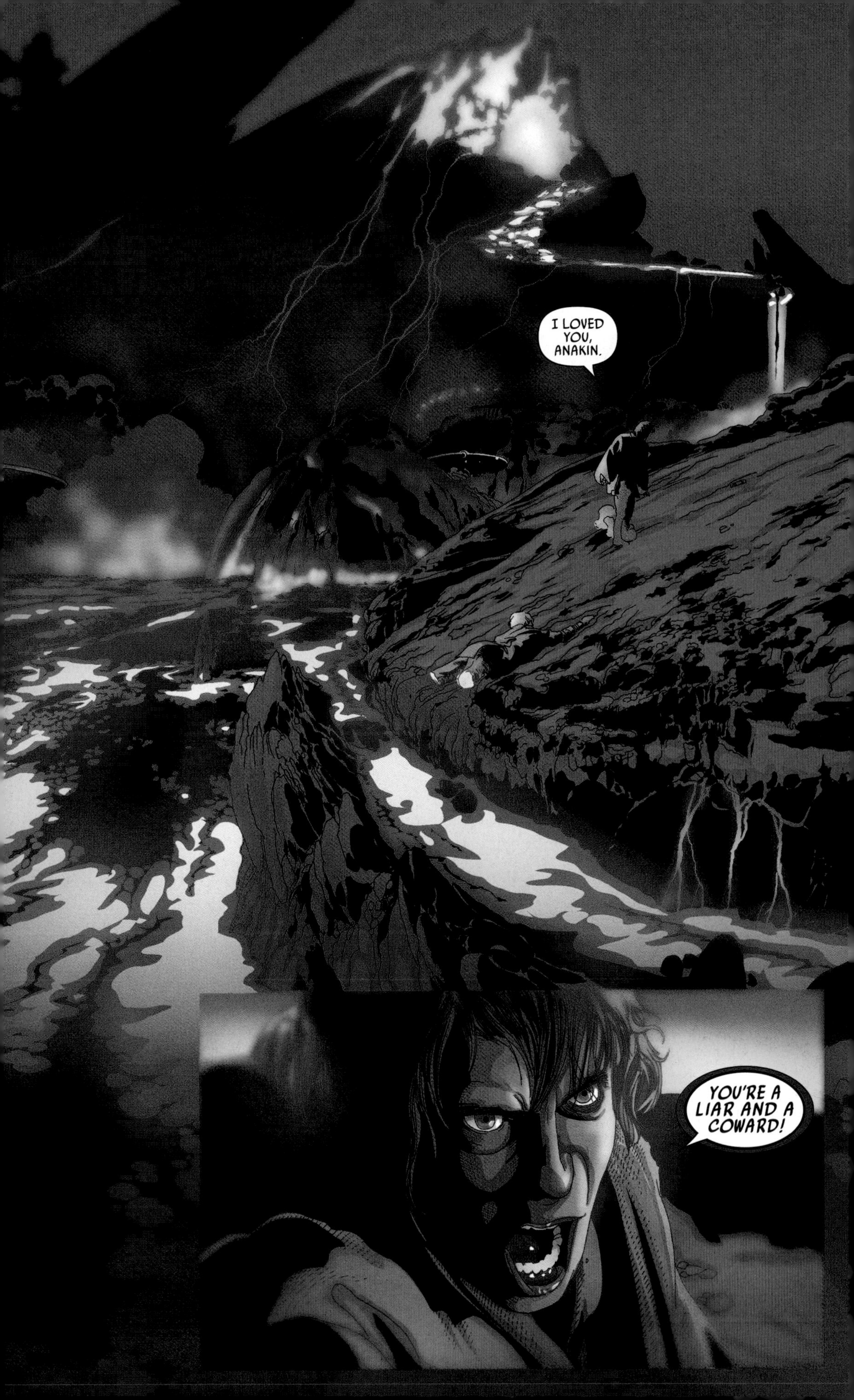
I LOVED YOU, ANAKIN.
YOU'RE A LIAR AND A COWARD!

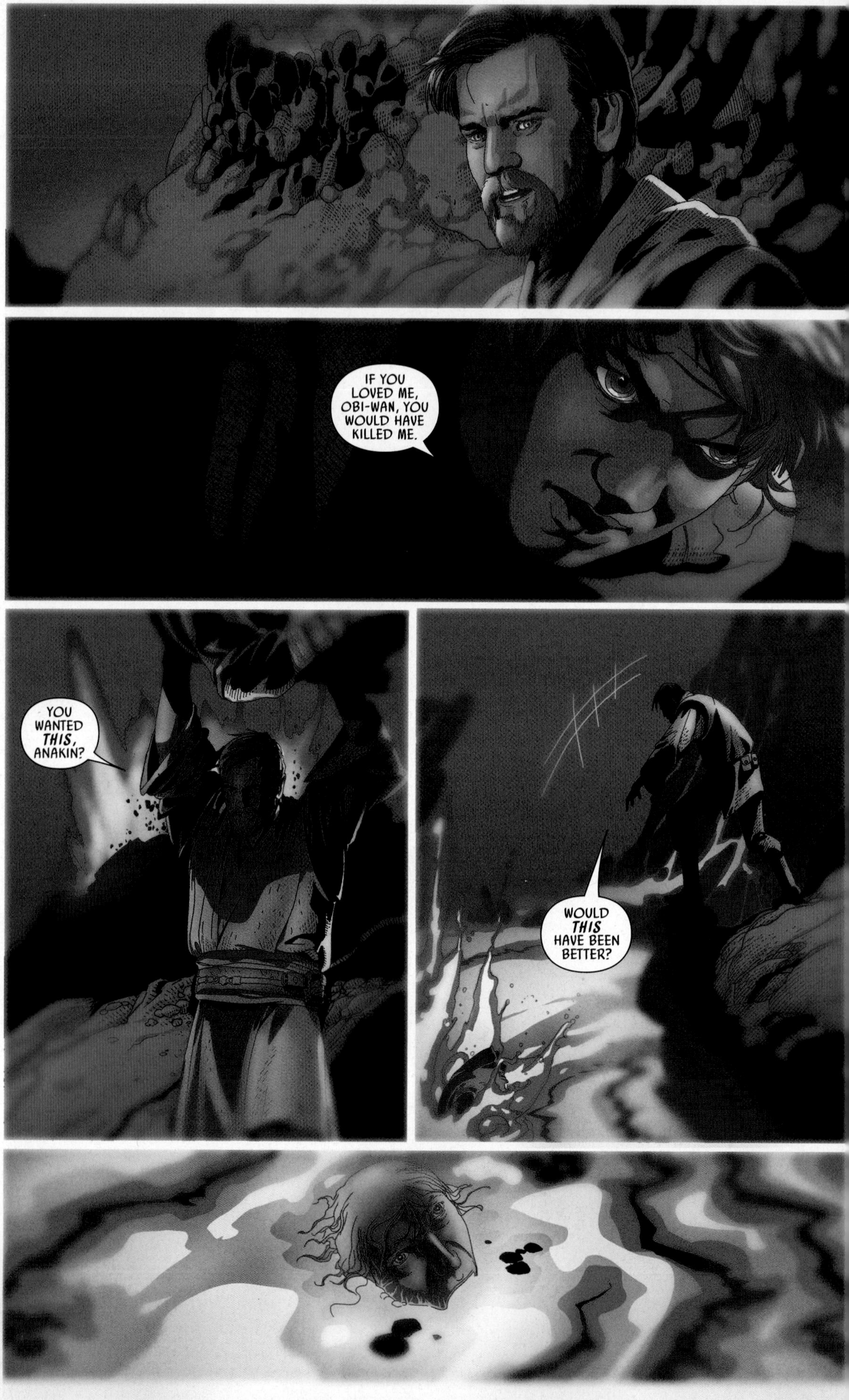
IF YOU LOVED ME, OBI-WAN, YOU WOULD HAVE KILLED ME.
YOU WANTED THIS, ANAKIN?
WOULD THIS HAVE BEEN BETTER?

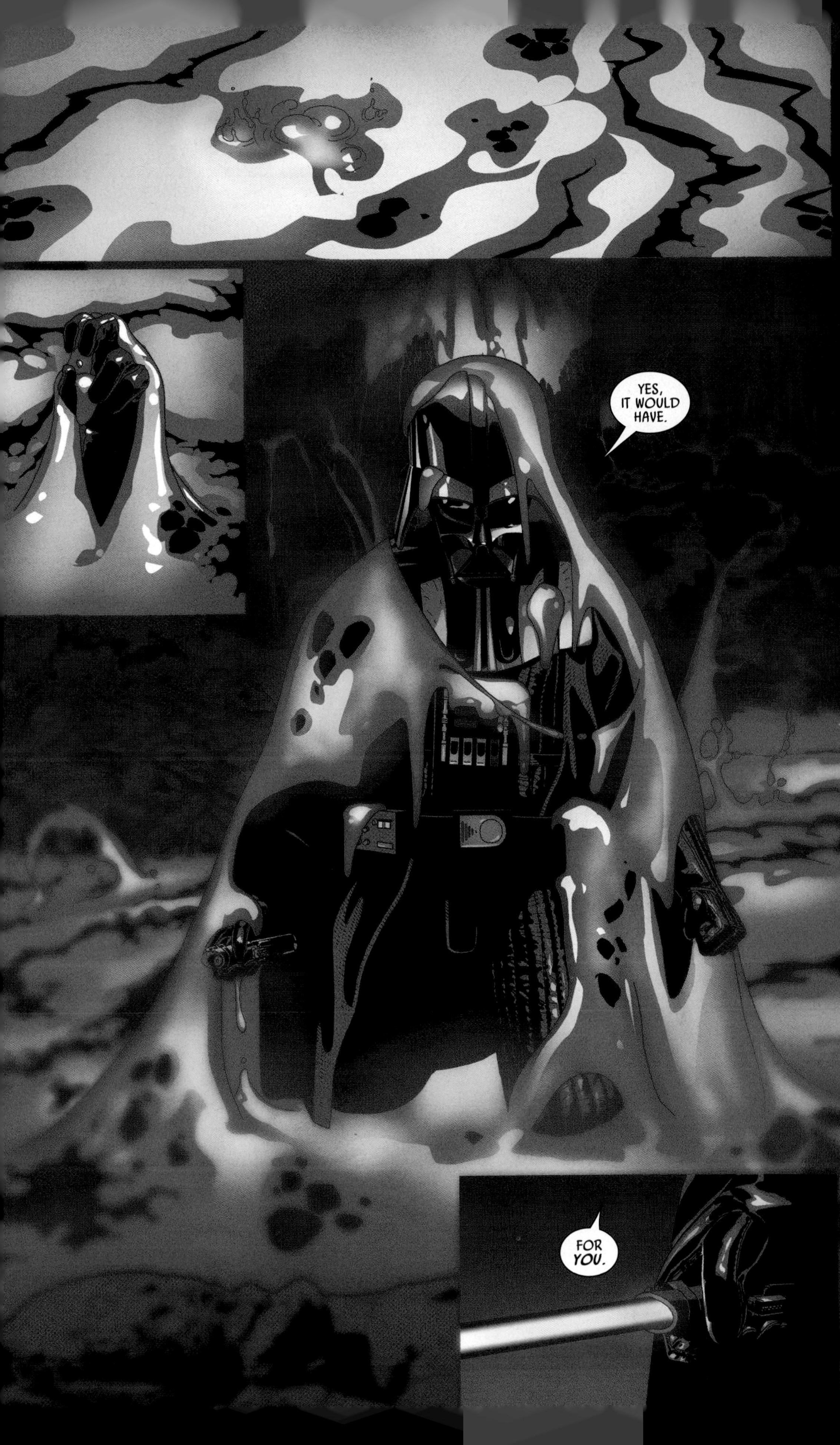
YES, IT WOULD HAVE.
FOR YOU.

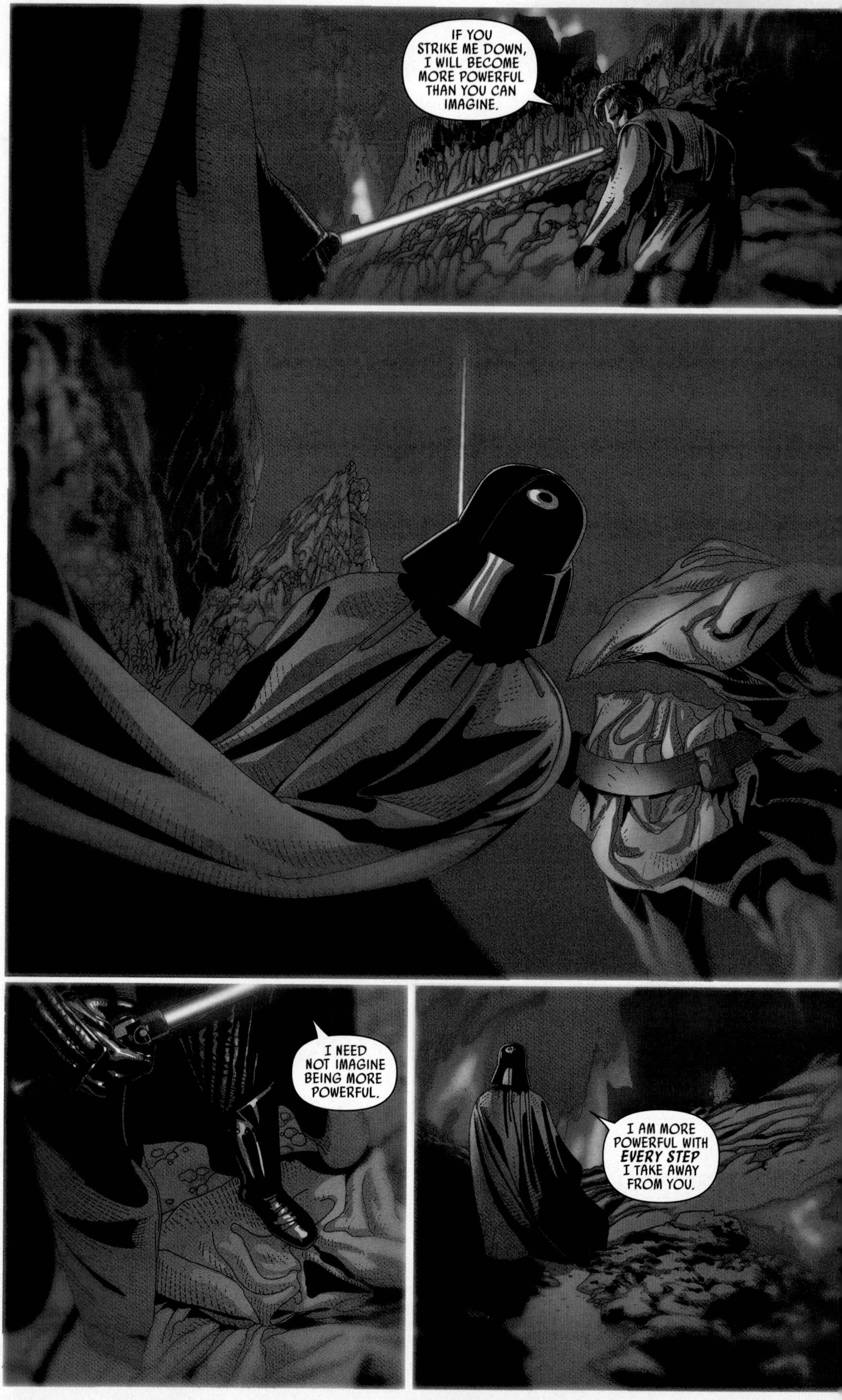
IF YOU STRIKE ME DOWN, I WILL BECOME MORE POWERFUL THAN YOU CAN IMAGINE.
I NEED NOT IMAGINE BEING MORE POWERFUL.
I AM MORE POWERFUL WITH EVERY STEP I TAKE AWAY FROM YOU.

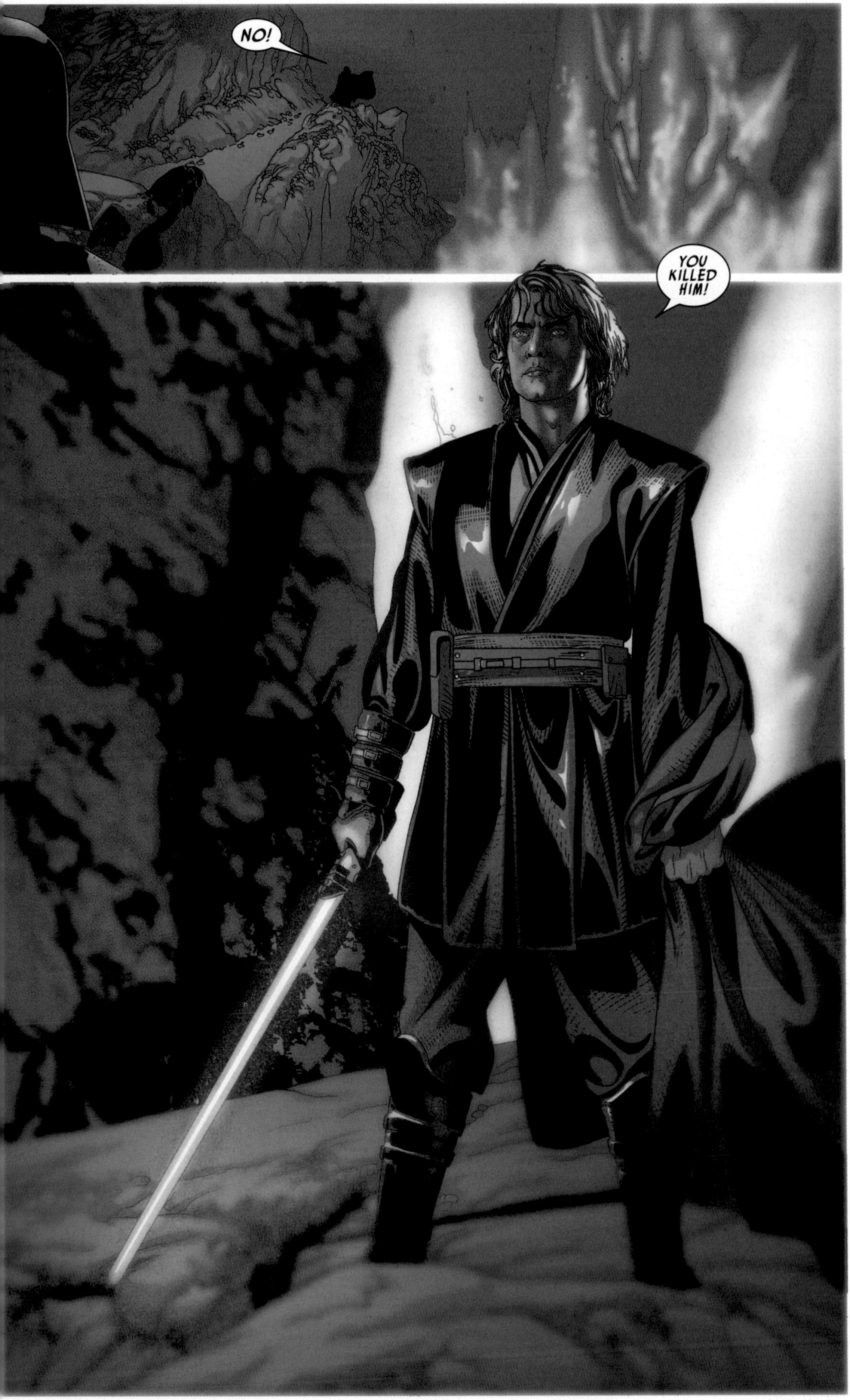
NO!
YOU KILLED HIM!

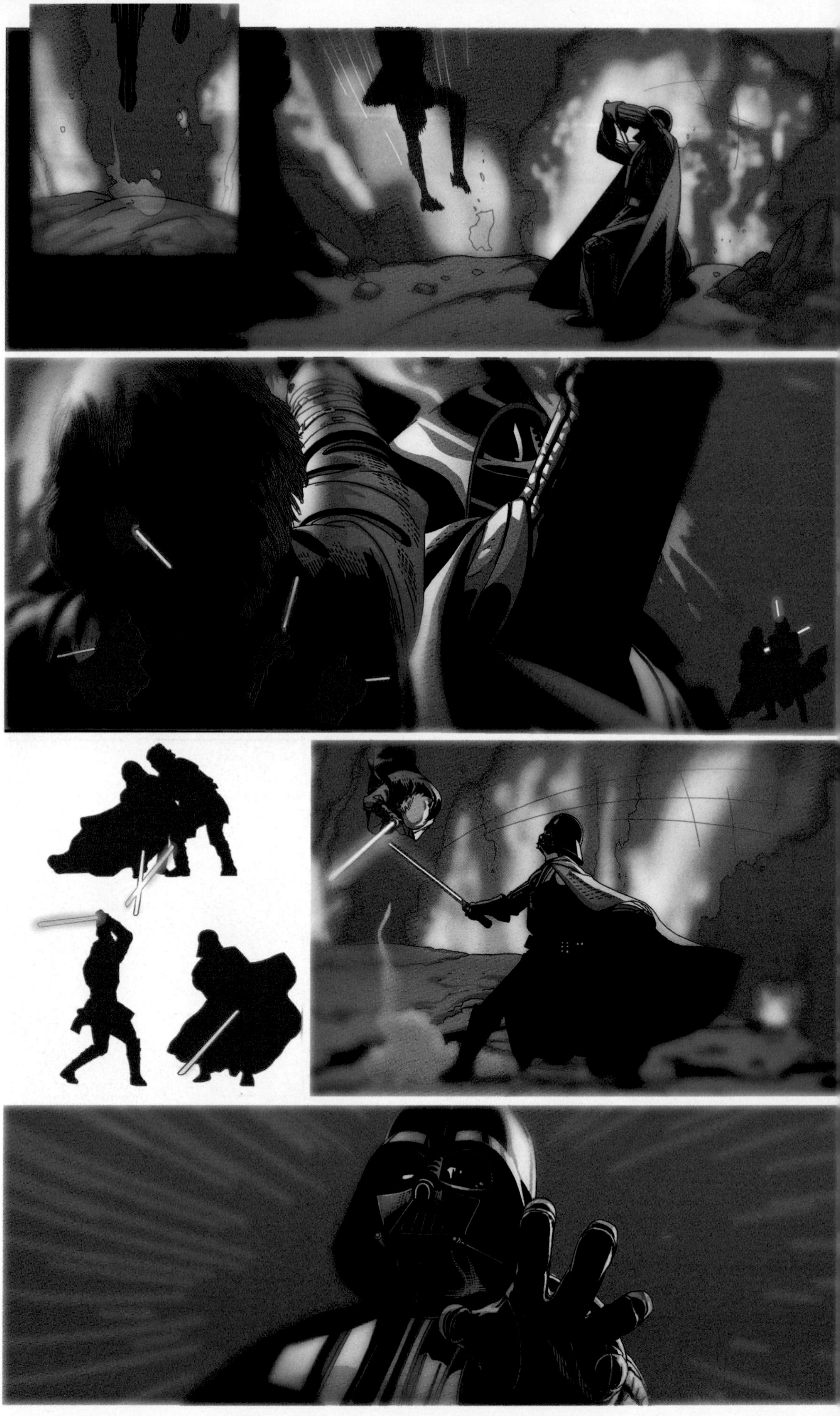

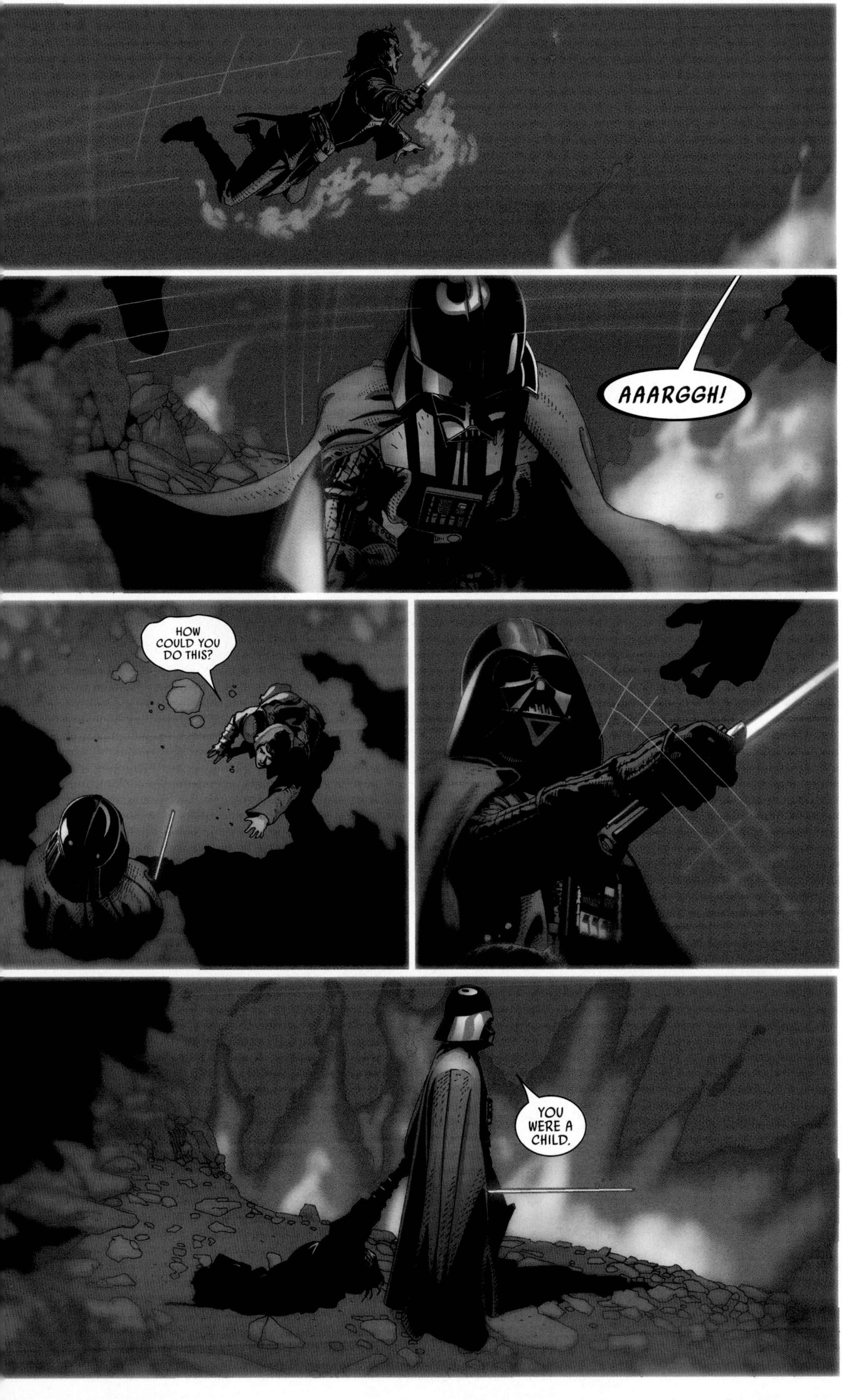
AAARGGH!
HOW COULD YOU DO THIS?
YOU WERE A CHILD.

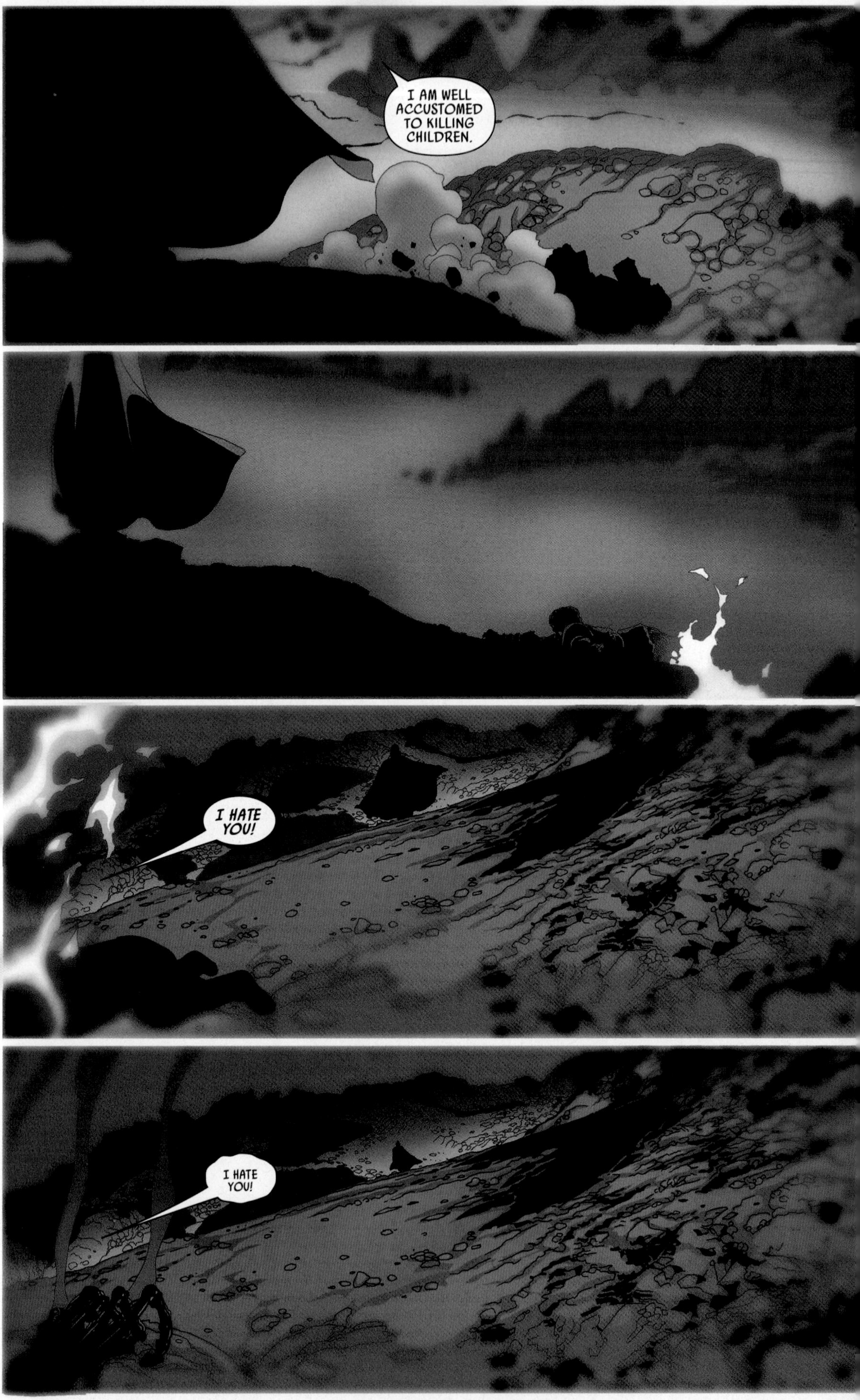
I AM WELL ACCUSTOMED TO KILLING CHILDREN.
I HATE YOU!
I HATE YOU!

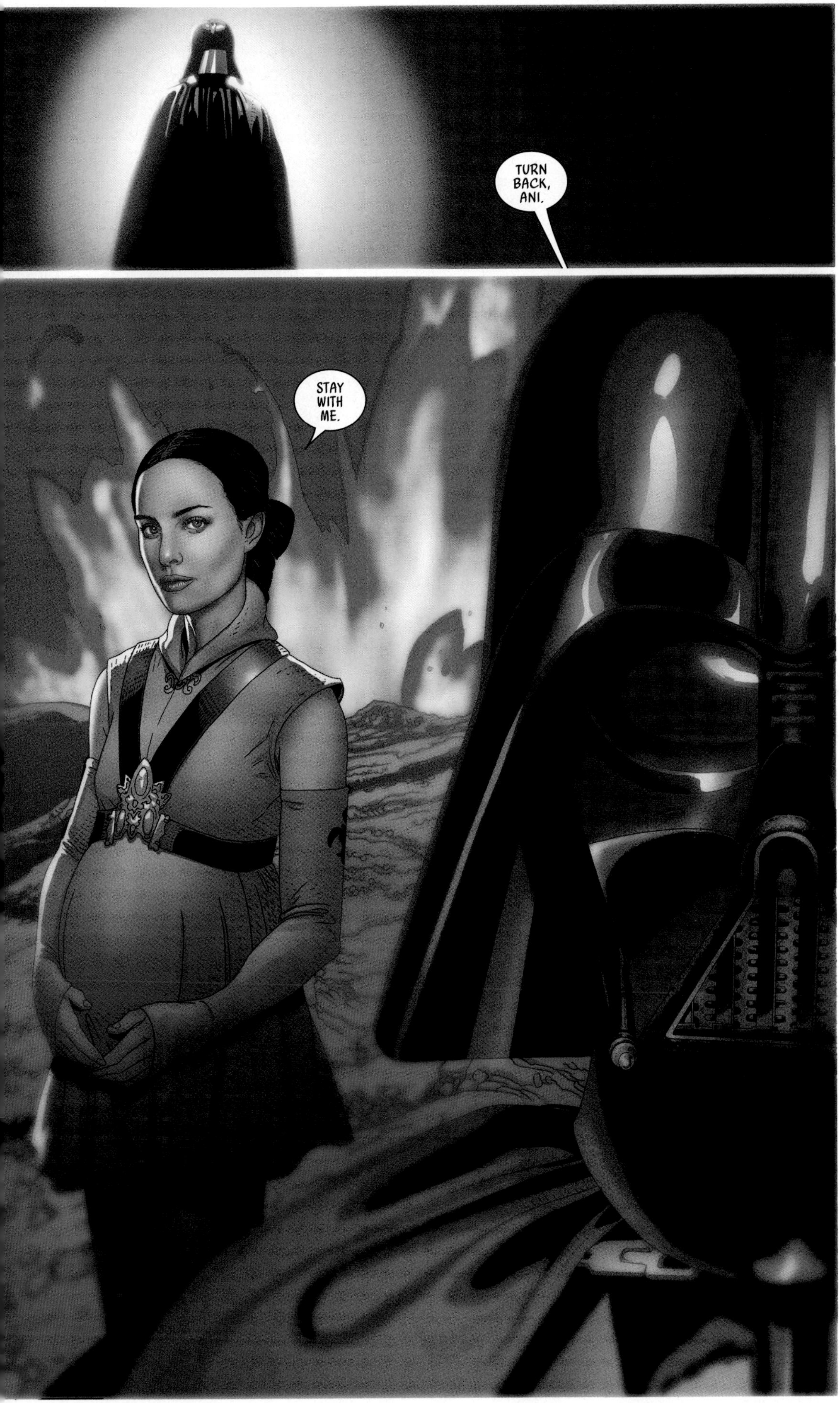
TURN BACK, ANI.
STAY WITH ME.

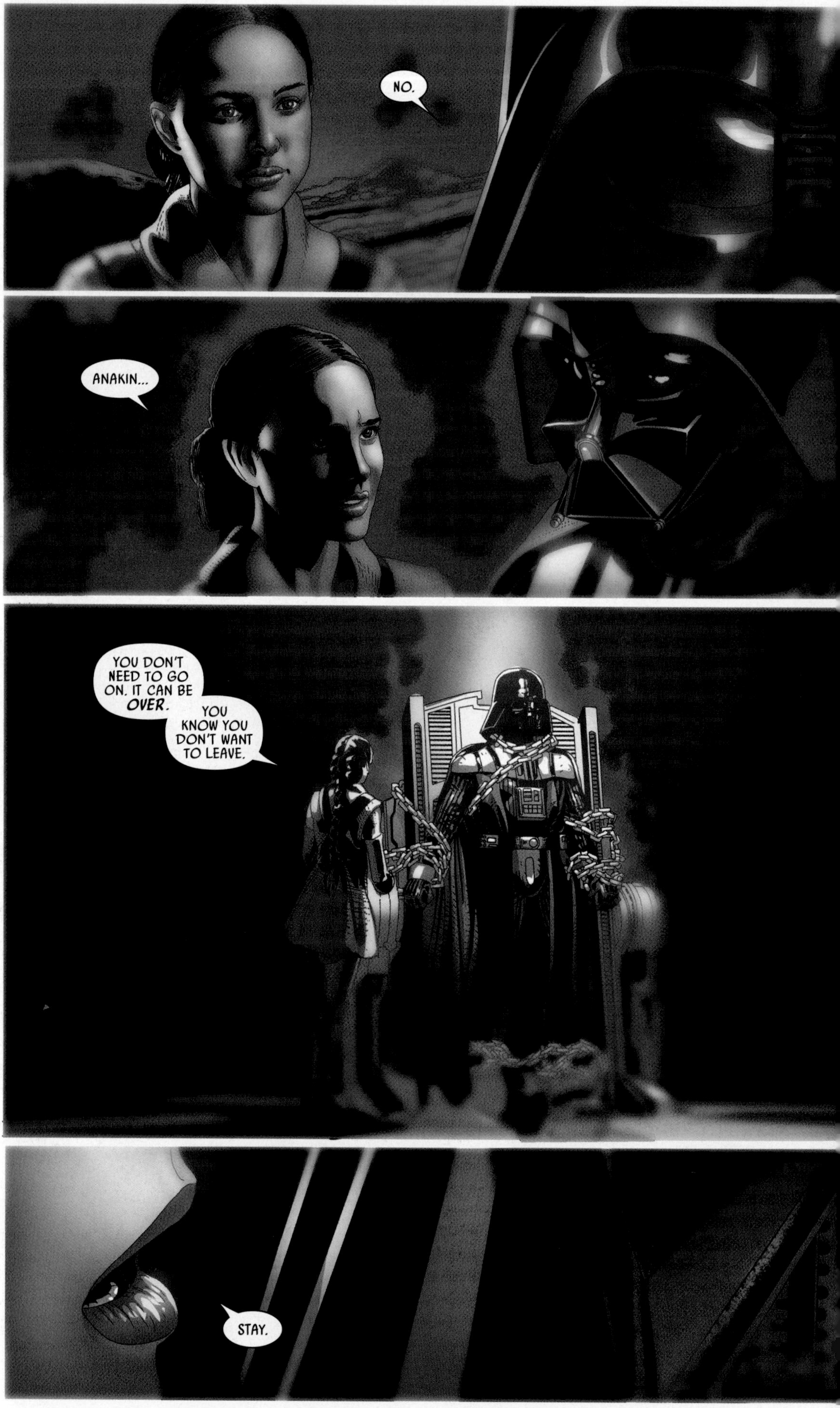
NO.
ANAKIN...
YOU DON'T NEED TO GO ON. IT CAN BE *OVER*.
YOU KNOW YOU DON'T WANT TO LEAVE.
STAY.

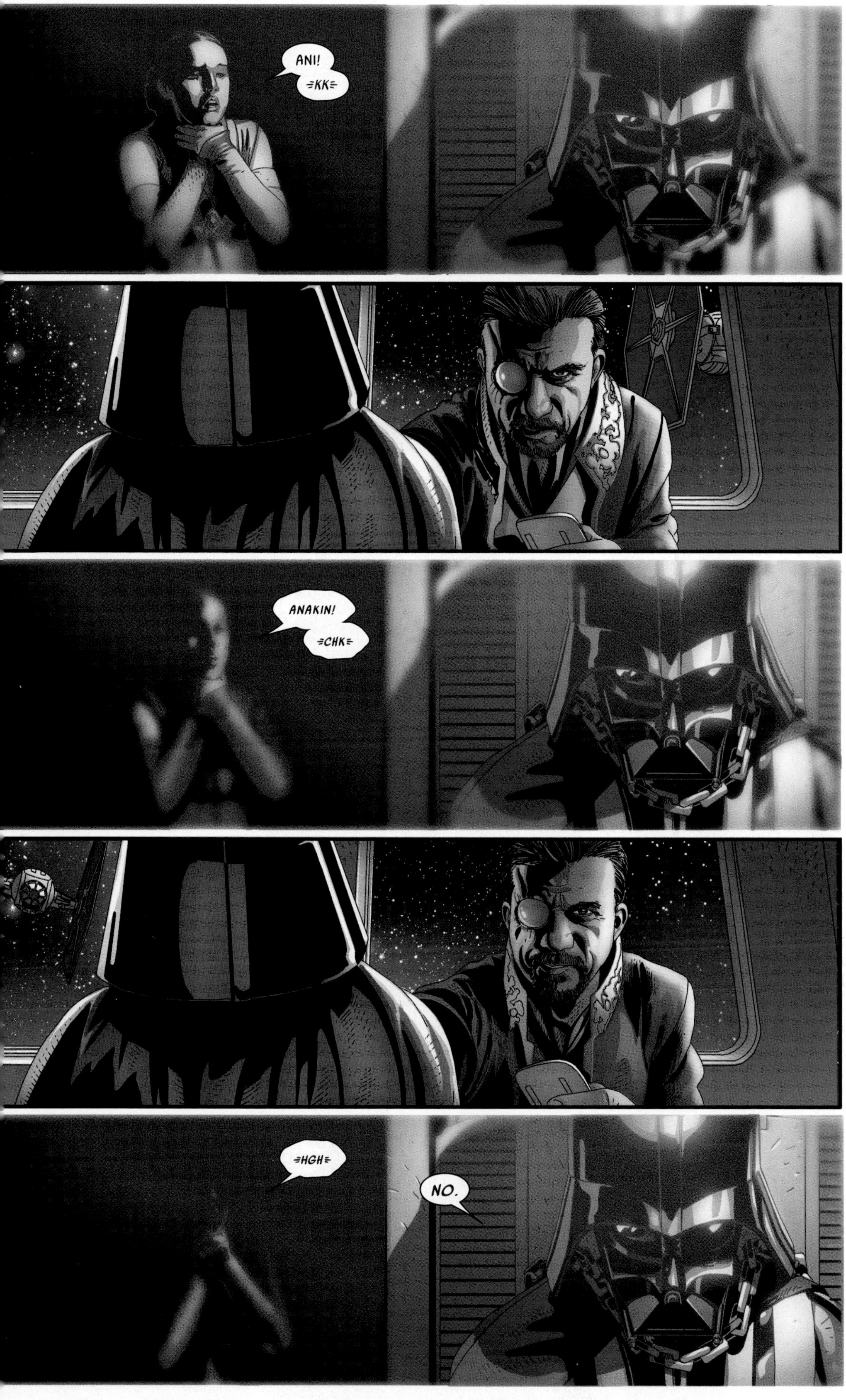
ANI!
=KK=
ANAKIN!
=CHK=
=HGH=
NO.

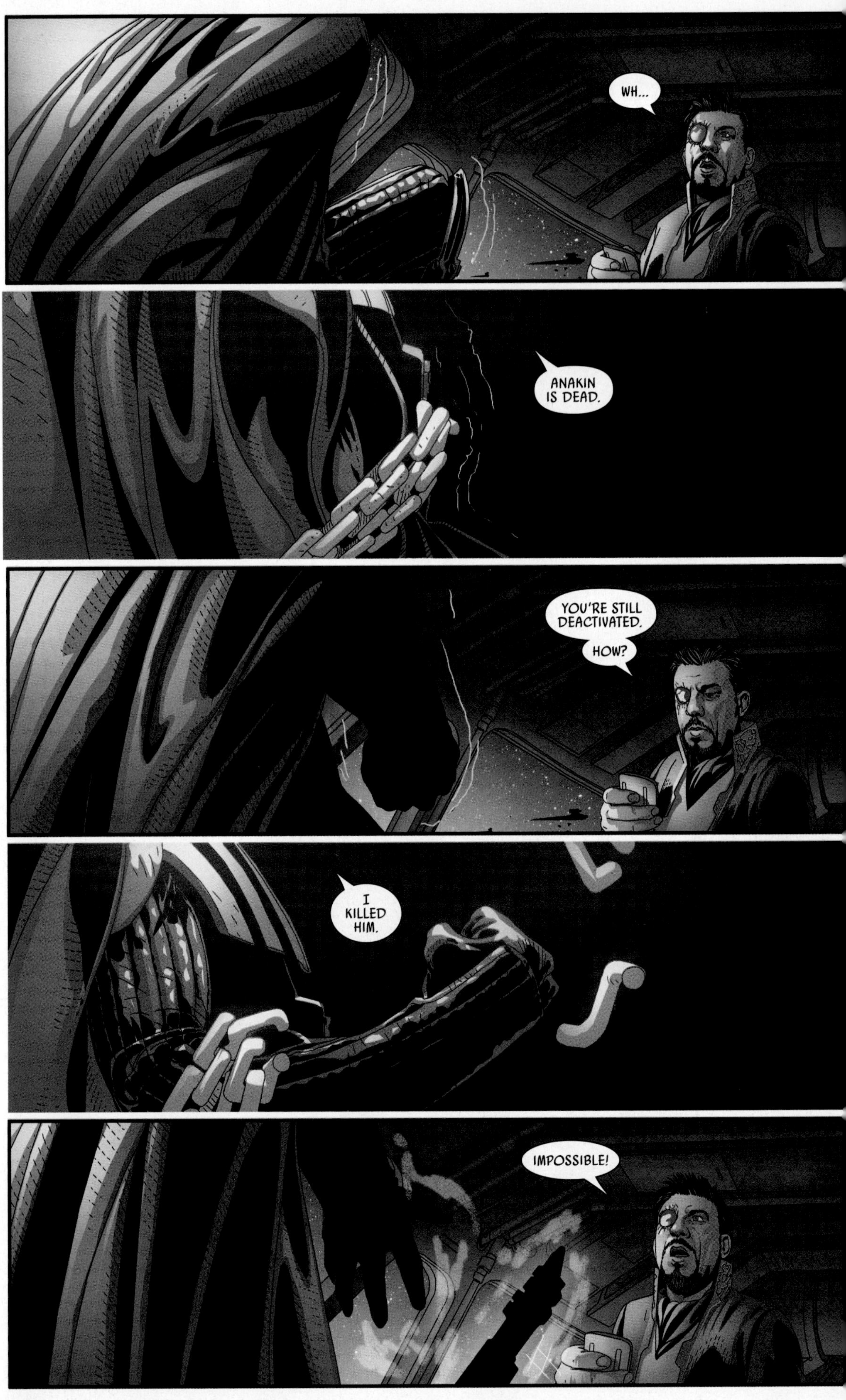
WH...
ANAKIN IS DEAD.
YOU'RE STILL DEACTIVATED.
HOW?
I KILLED HIM.
IMPOSSIBLE!

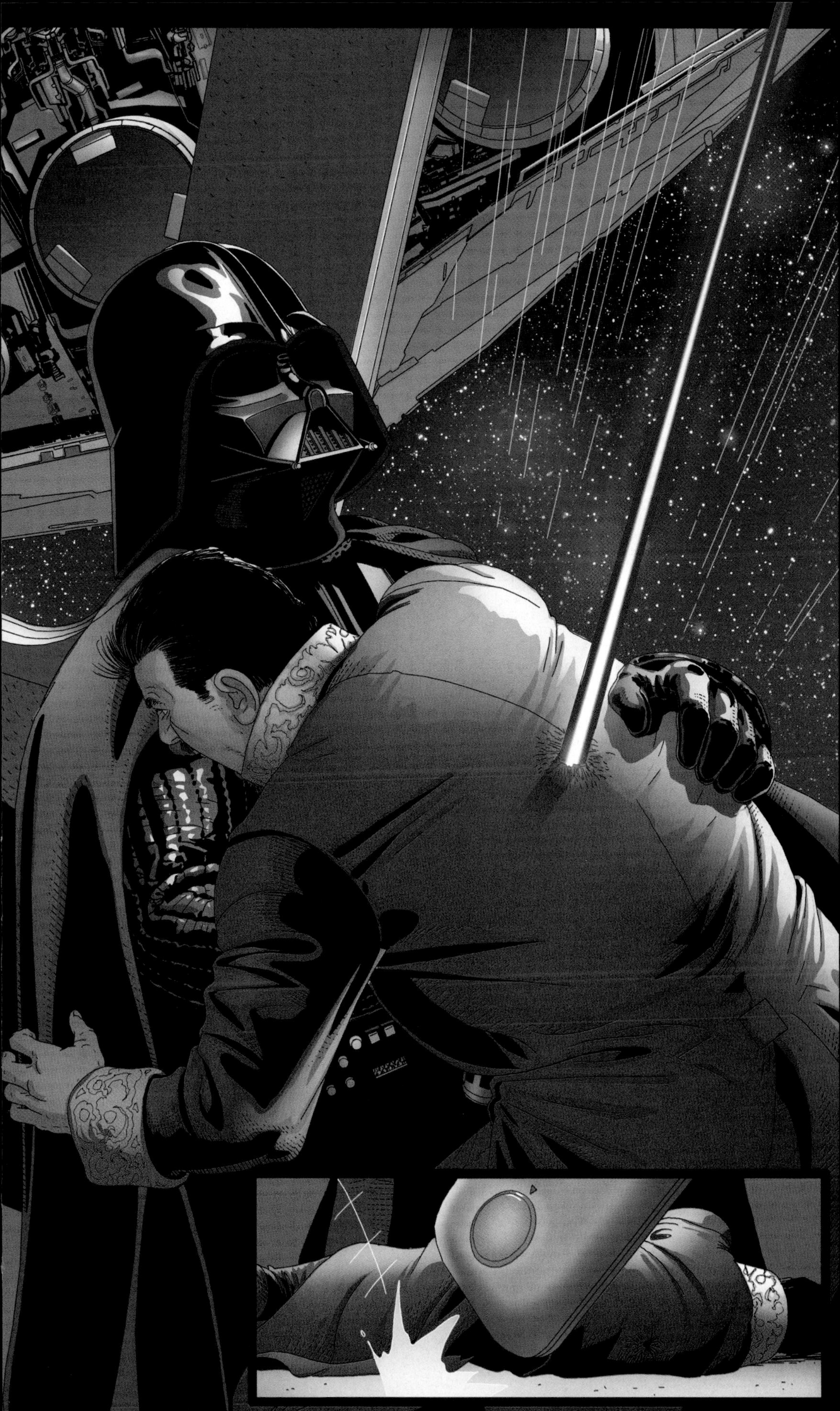

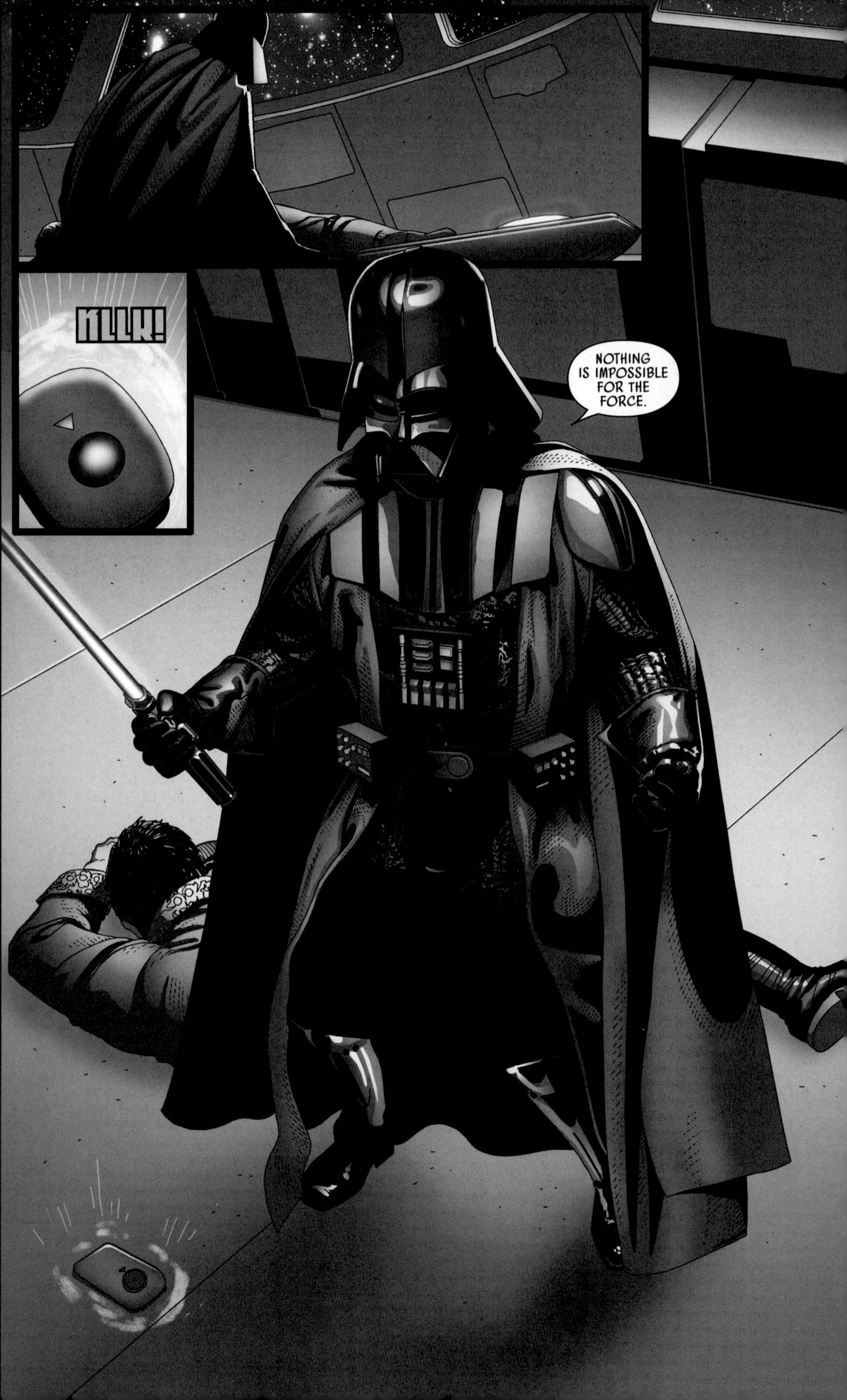
KLLK!
NOTHING IS IMPOSSIBLE FOR THE FORCE.

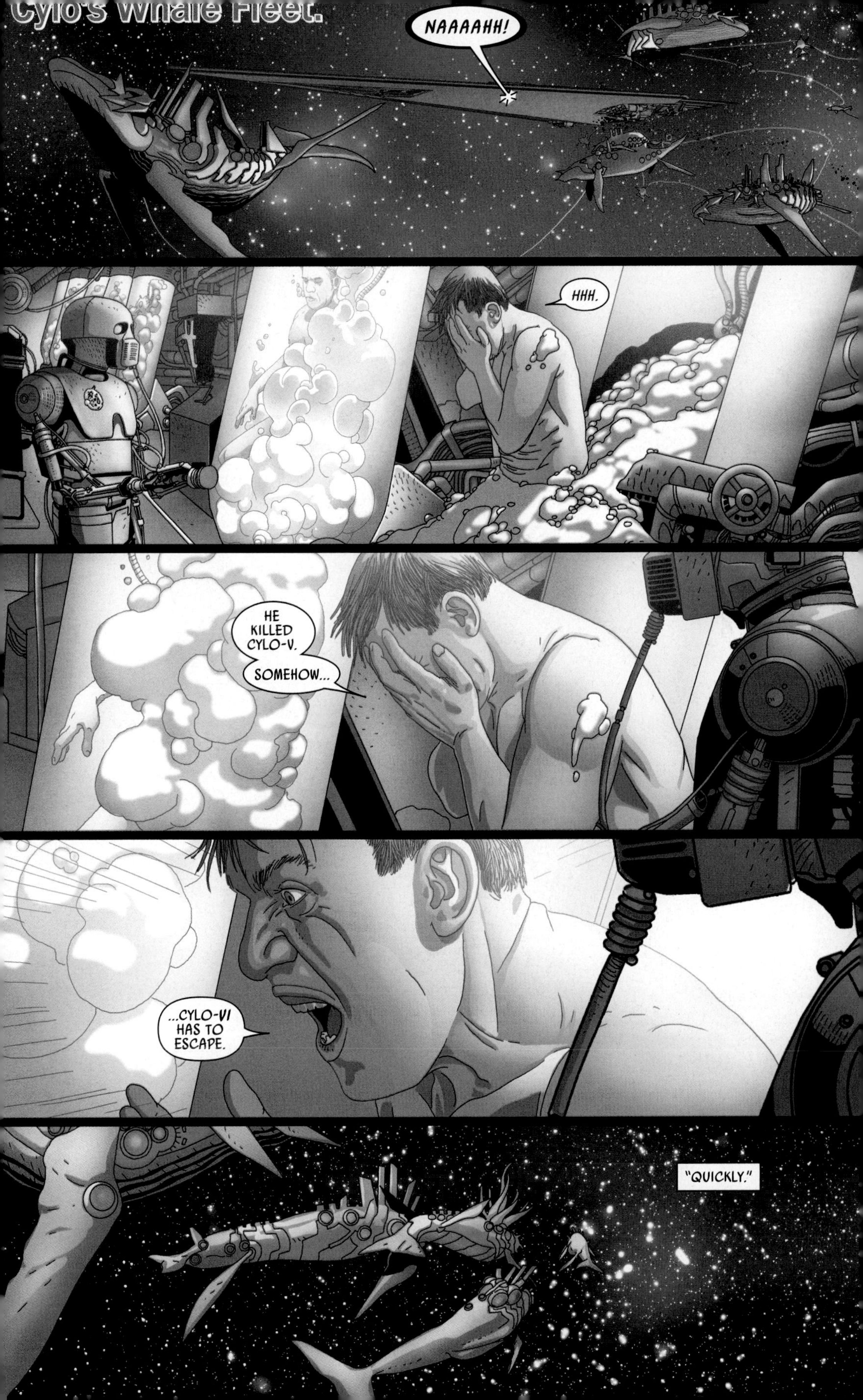
Cylo's Whale Fleet.
NAAAAHH!
HHH.
HE KILLED CYLO-V.
SOMEHOW...
...CYLO-VI HAS TO ESCAPE.
"QUICKLY."

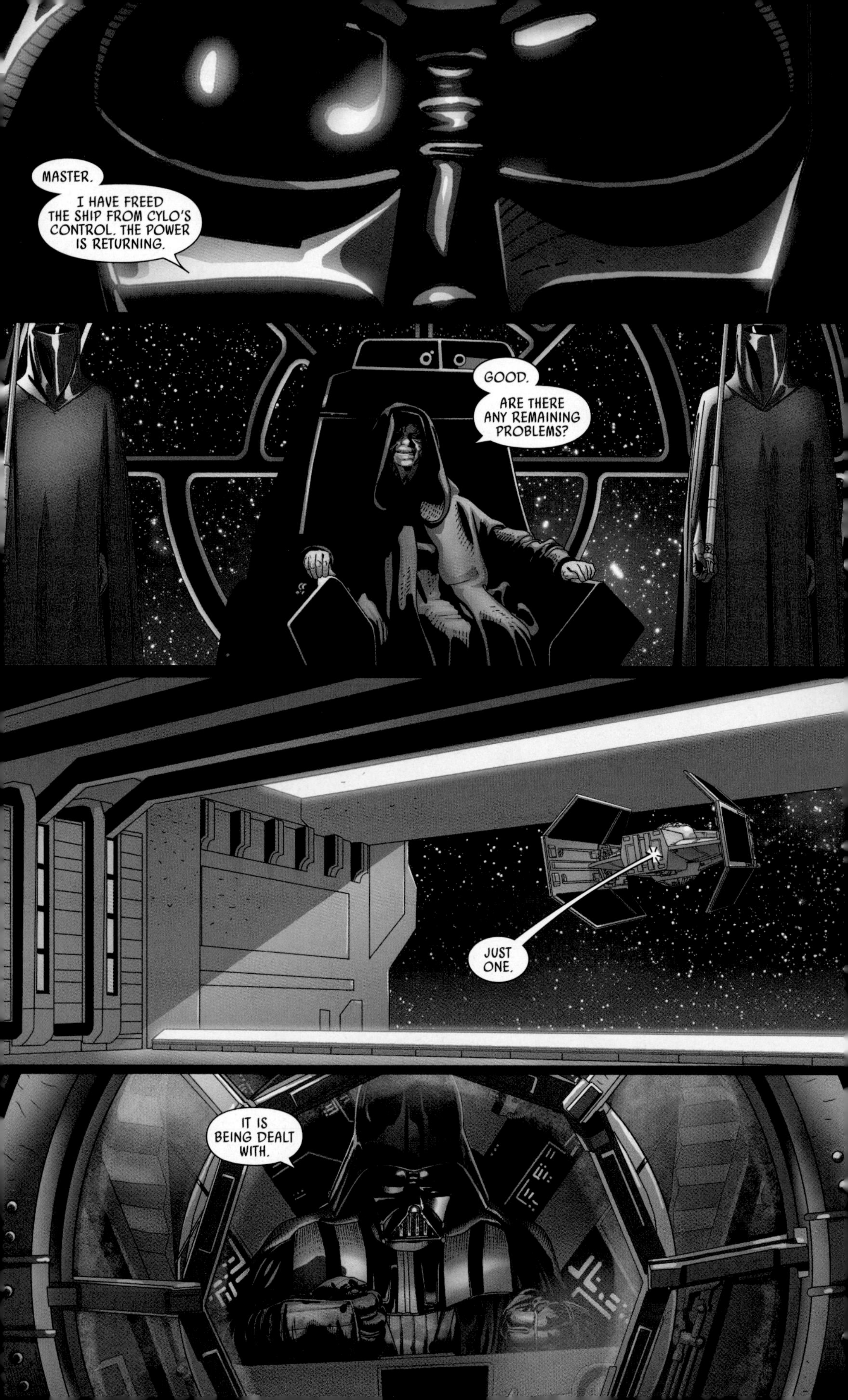
MASTER.
I HAVE FREED THE SHIP FROM CYLO'S CONTROL. THE POWER IS RETURNING.
GOOD.
ARE THERE ANY REMAINING PROBLEMS?
JUST ONE.
IT IS BEING DEALT WITH.

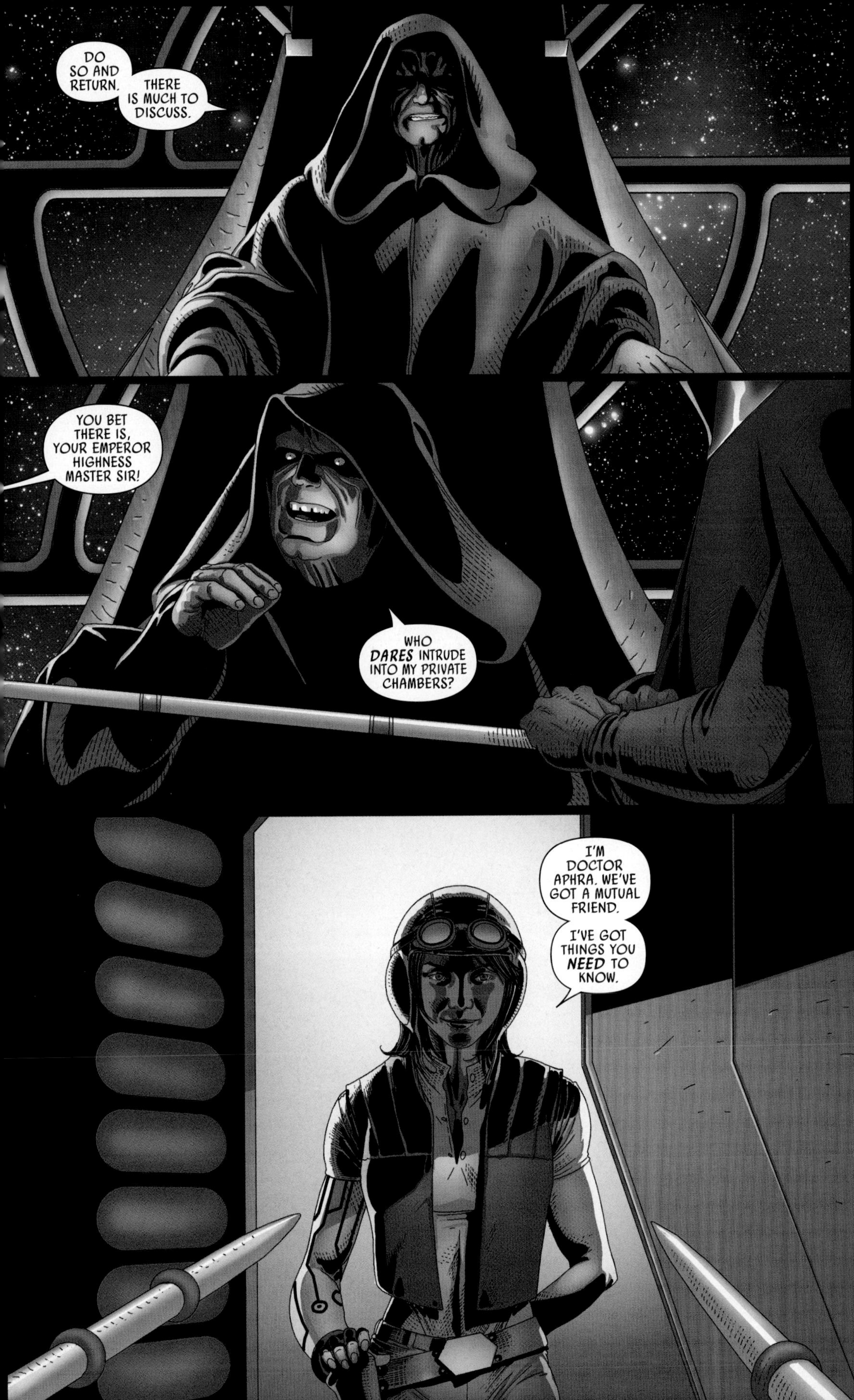
DO SO AND RETURN.
THERE IS MUCH TO DISCUSS.
YOU BET THERE IS, YOUR EMPEROR HIGHNESS MASTER SIR!
WHO DARES INTRUDE INTO MY PRIVATE CHAMBERS?
I'M DOCTOR APHRA. WE'VE GOT A MUTUAL FRIEND.
I'VE GOT THINGS YOU NEED TO KNOW.

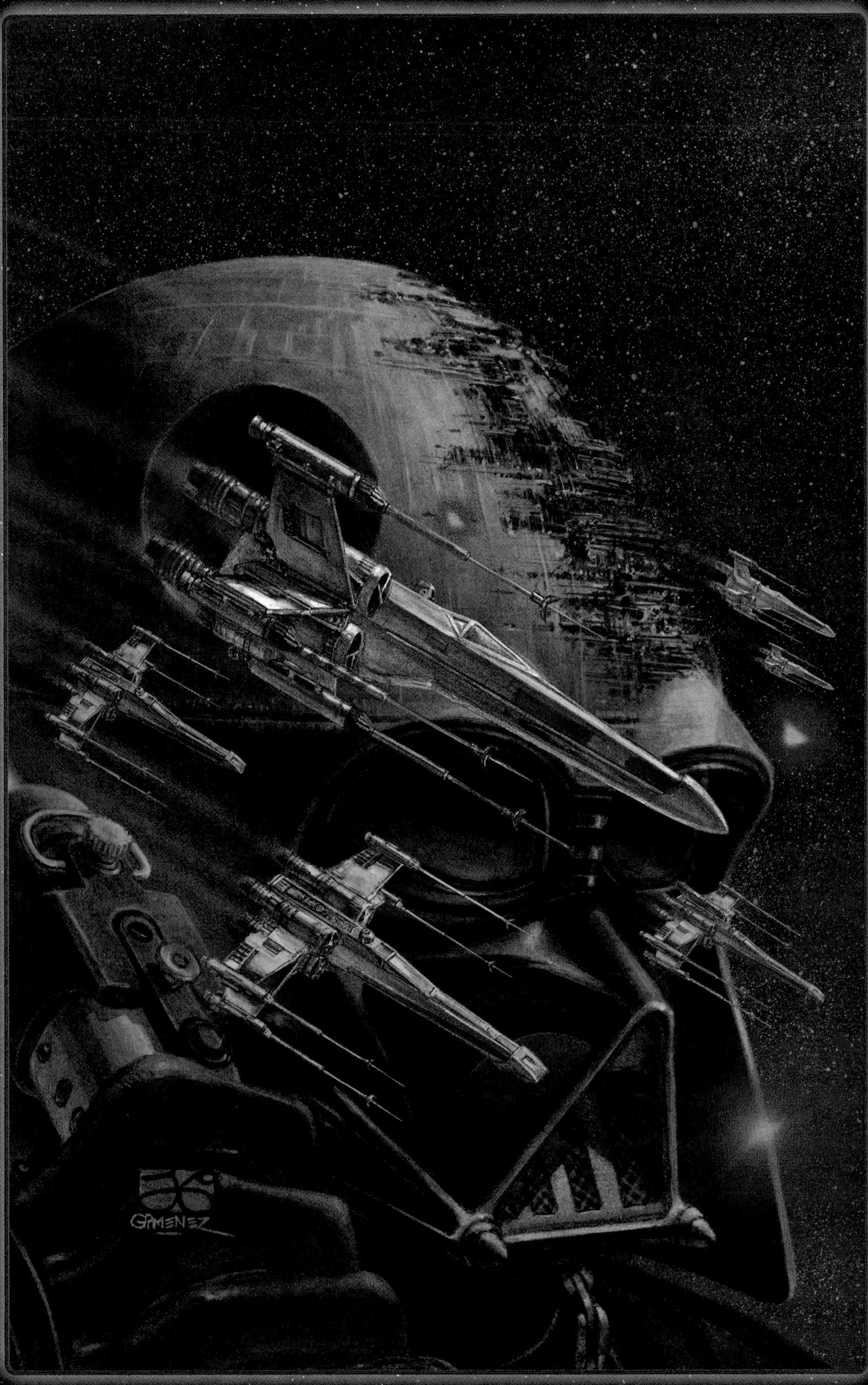
GIMENEZ

25

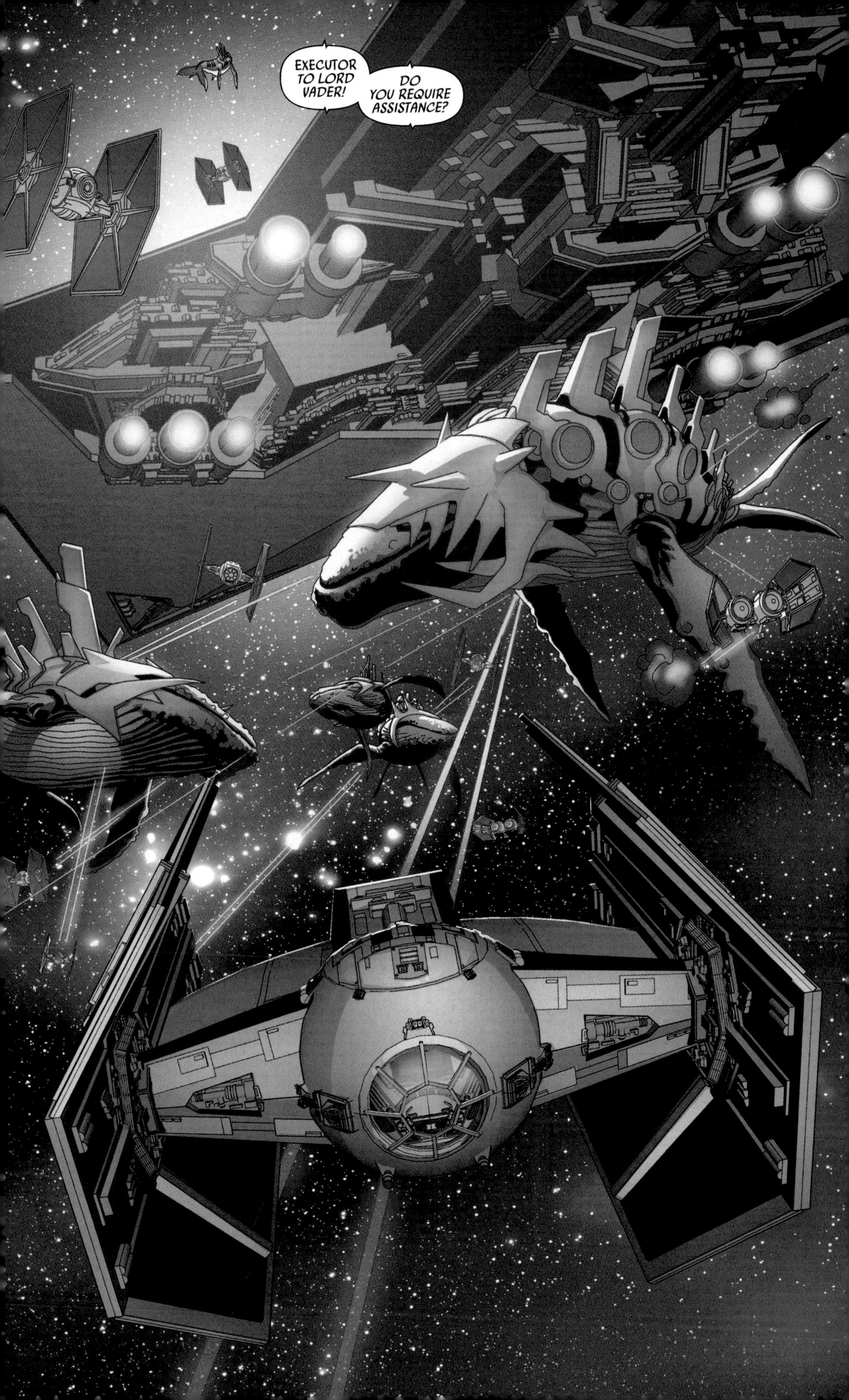
EXECUTOR TO LORD VADER!
DO YOU REQUIRE ASSISTANCE?

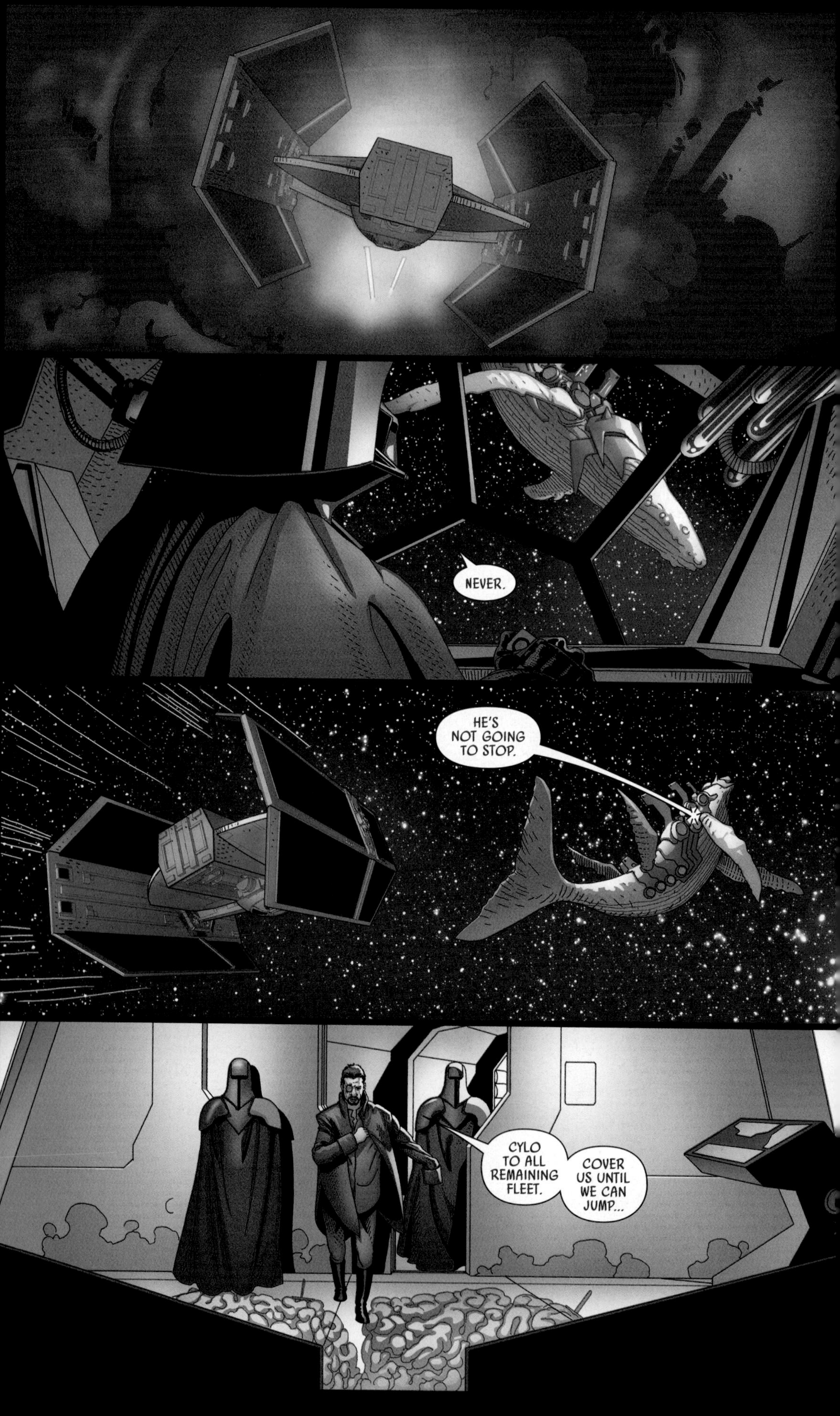
NEVER.
HE'S NOT GOING TO STOP.
CYLO TO ALL REMAINING FLEET.
COVER US UNTIL WE CAN JUMP...

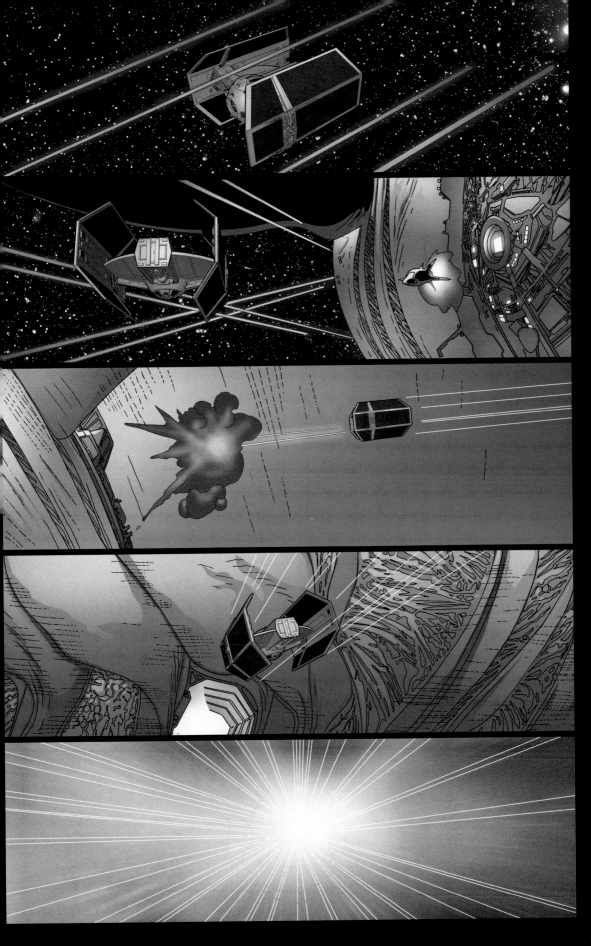

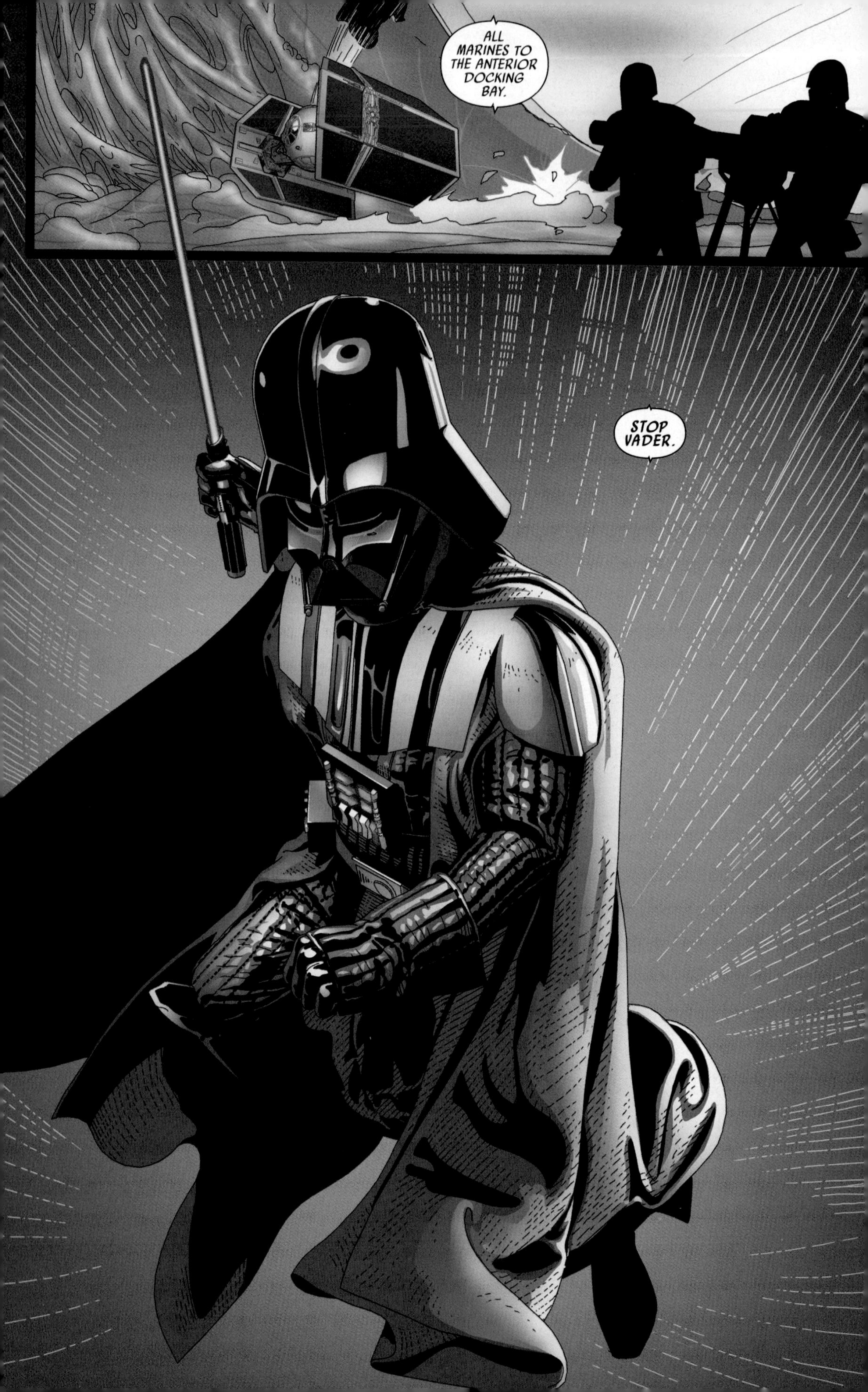
ALL MARINES TO THE ANTERIOR DOCKING BAY.
STOP VADER.

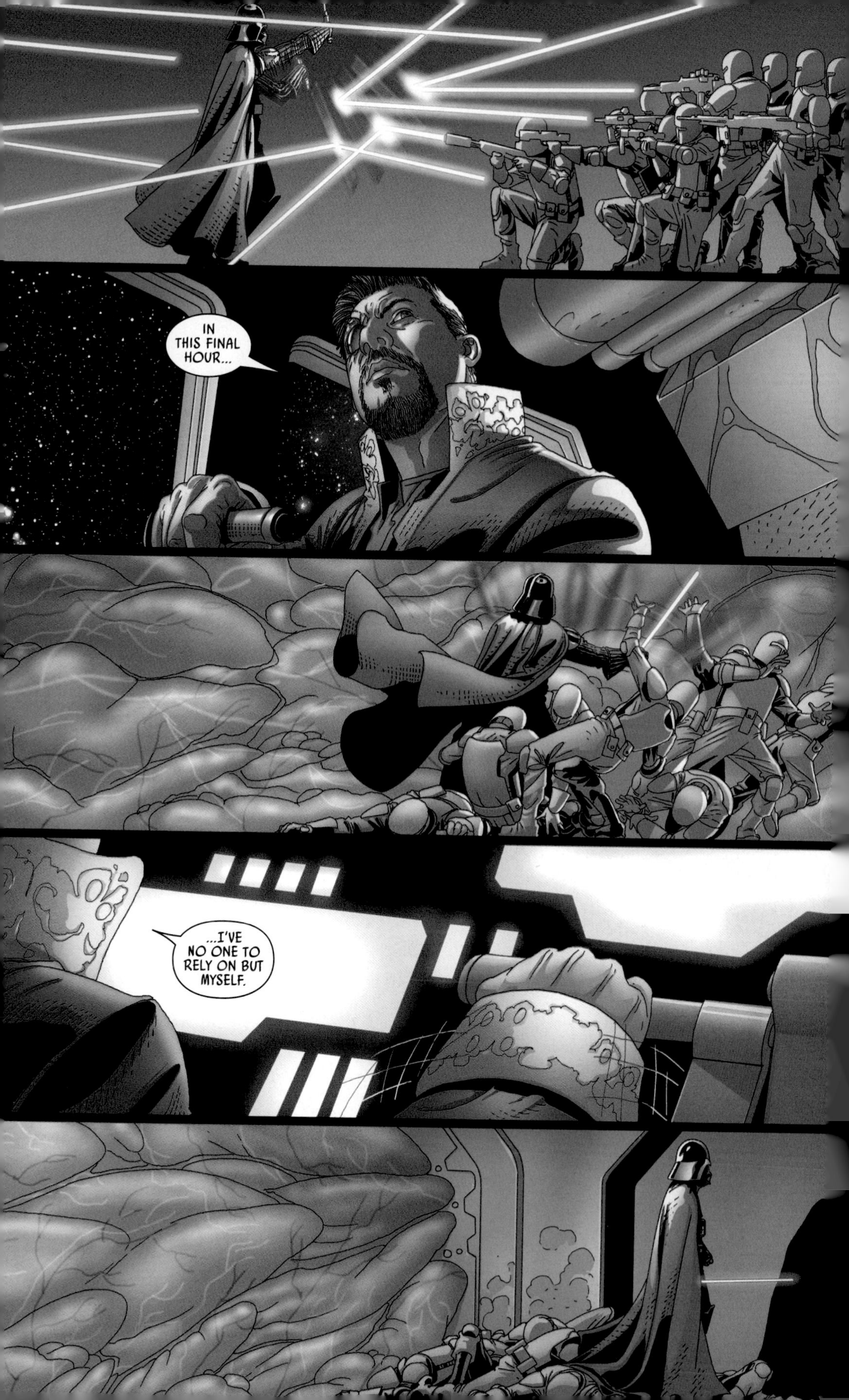
IN THIS FINAL HOUR...
...I'VE NO ONE TO RELY ON BUT MYSELF.

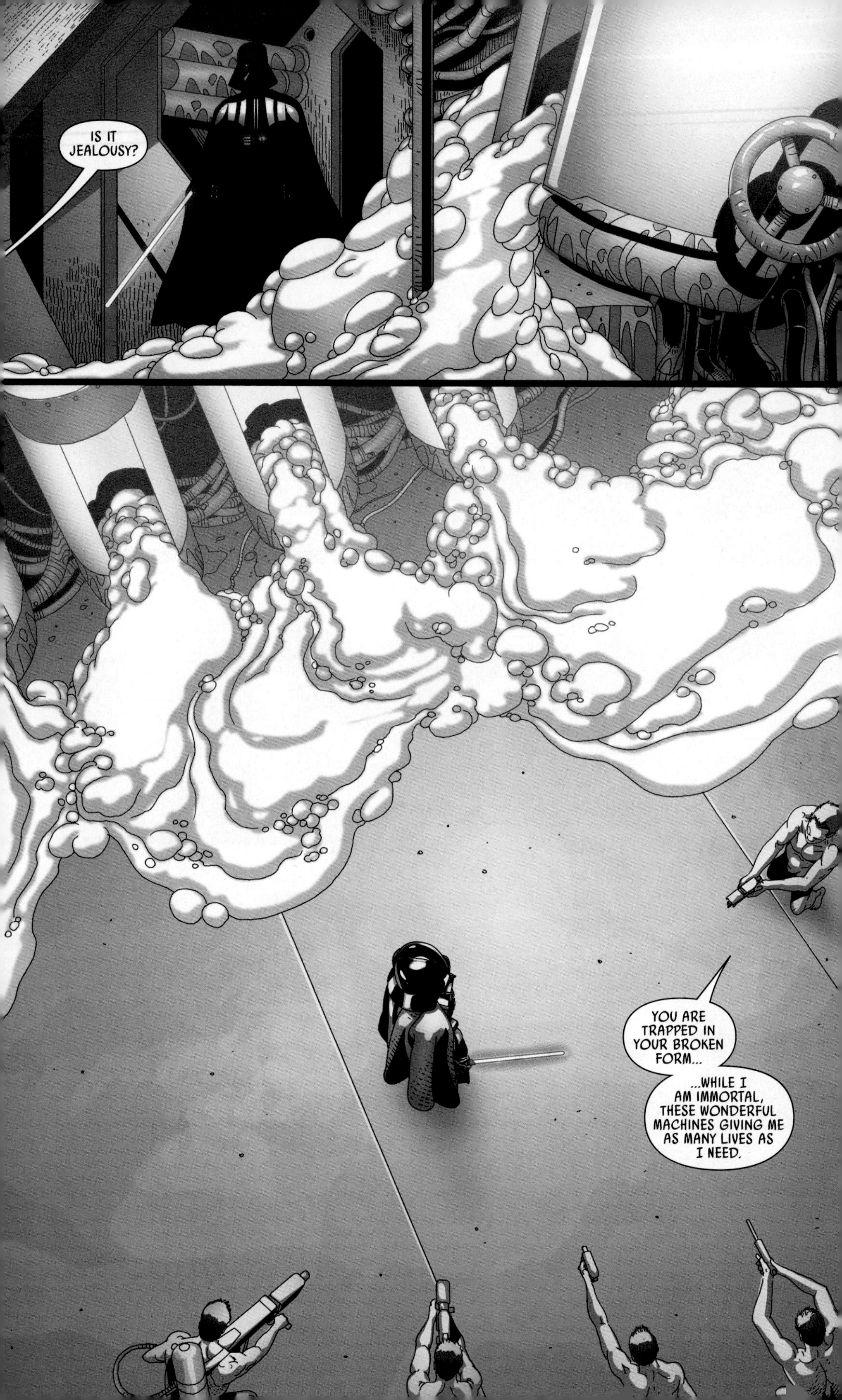
IS IT JEALOUSY?
YOU ARE TRAPPED IN YOUR BROKEN FORM...
...WHILE I AM IMMORTAL, THESE WONDERFUL MACHINES GIVING ME AS MANY LIVES AS I NEED.

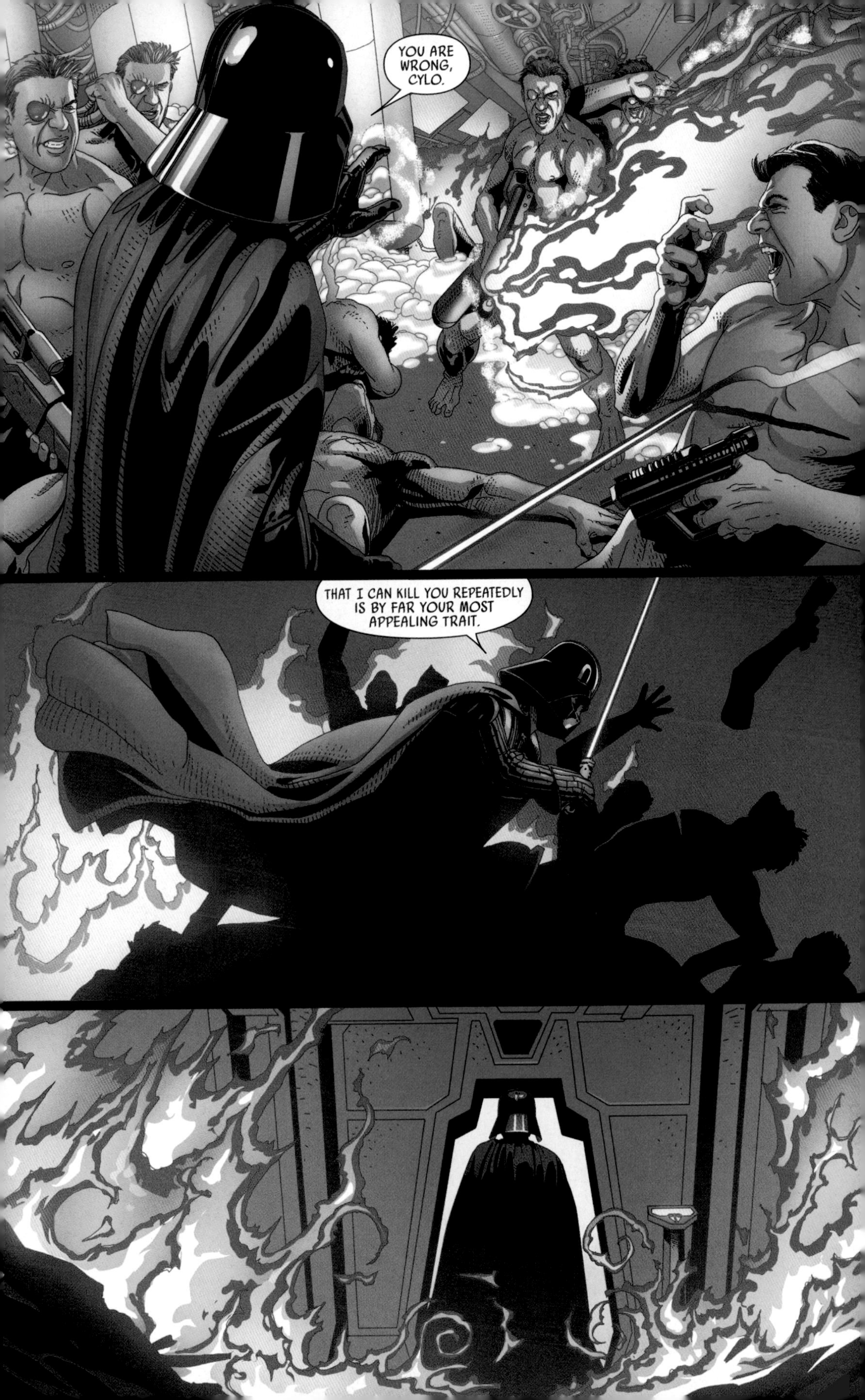
YOU ARE WRONG, CYLO.
THAT I CAN KILL YOU REPEATEDLY IS BY FAR YOUR MOST APPEALING TRAIT.

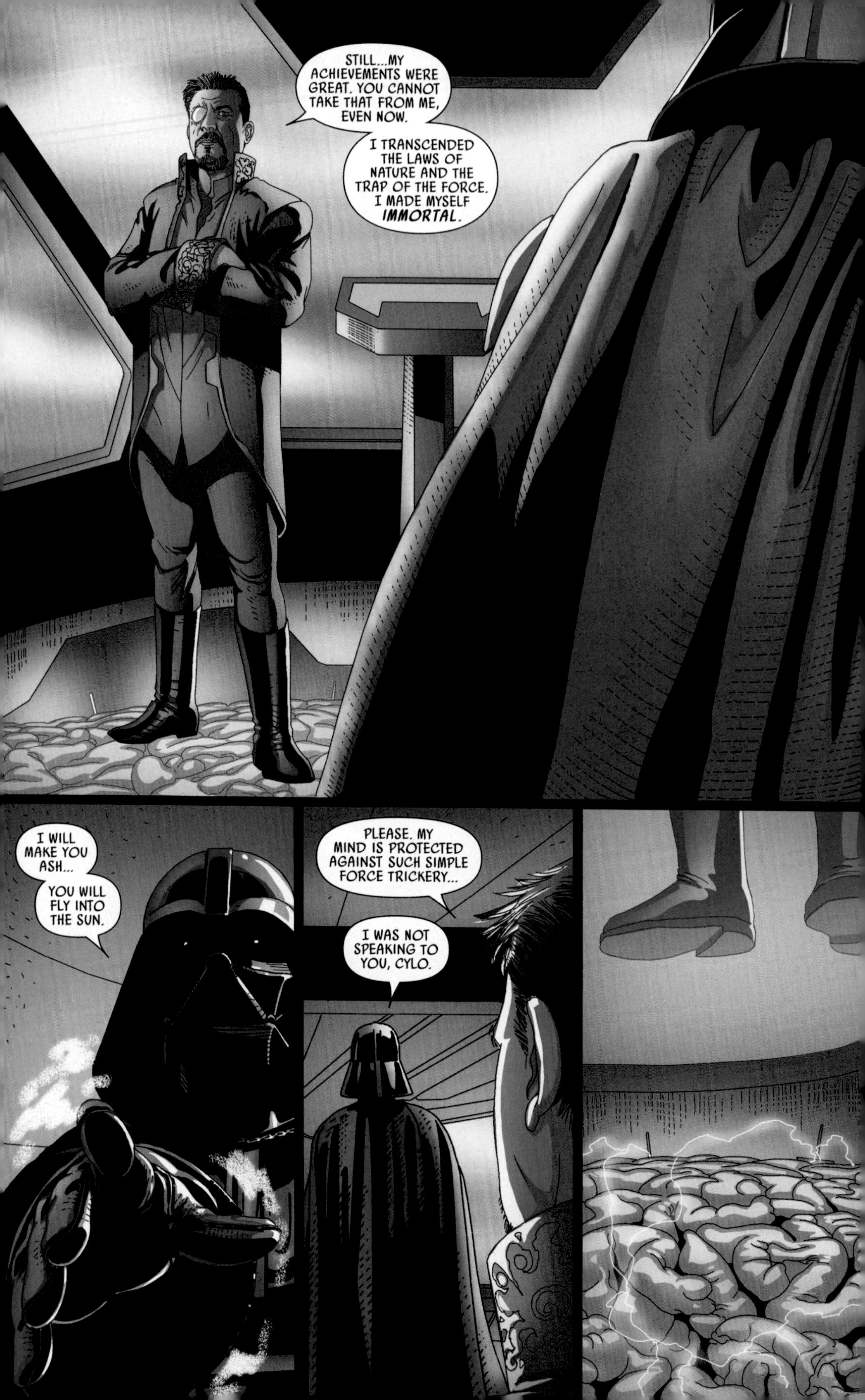
STILL...MY ACHIEVEMENTS WERE GREAT. YOU CANNOT TAKE THAT FROM ME, EVEN NOW.
I TRANSCENDED THE LAWS OF NATURE AND THE TRAP OF THE FORCE. I MADE MYSELF *IMMORTAL*.
I WILL MAKE YOU ASH...
YOU WILL FLY INTO THE SUN.
PLEASE. MY MIND IS PROTECTED AGAINST SUCH SIMPLE FORCE TRICKERY...
I WAS NOT SPEAKING TO YOU, CYLO.

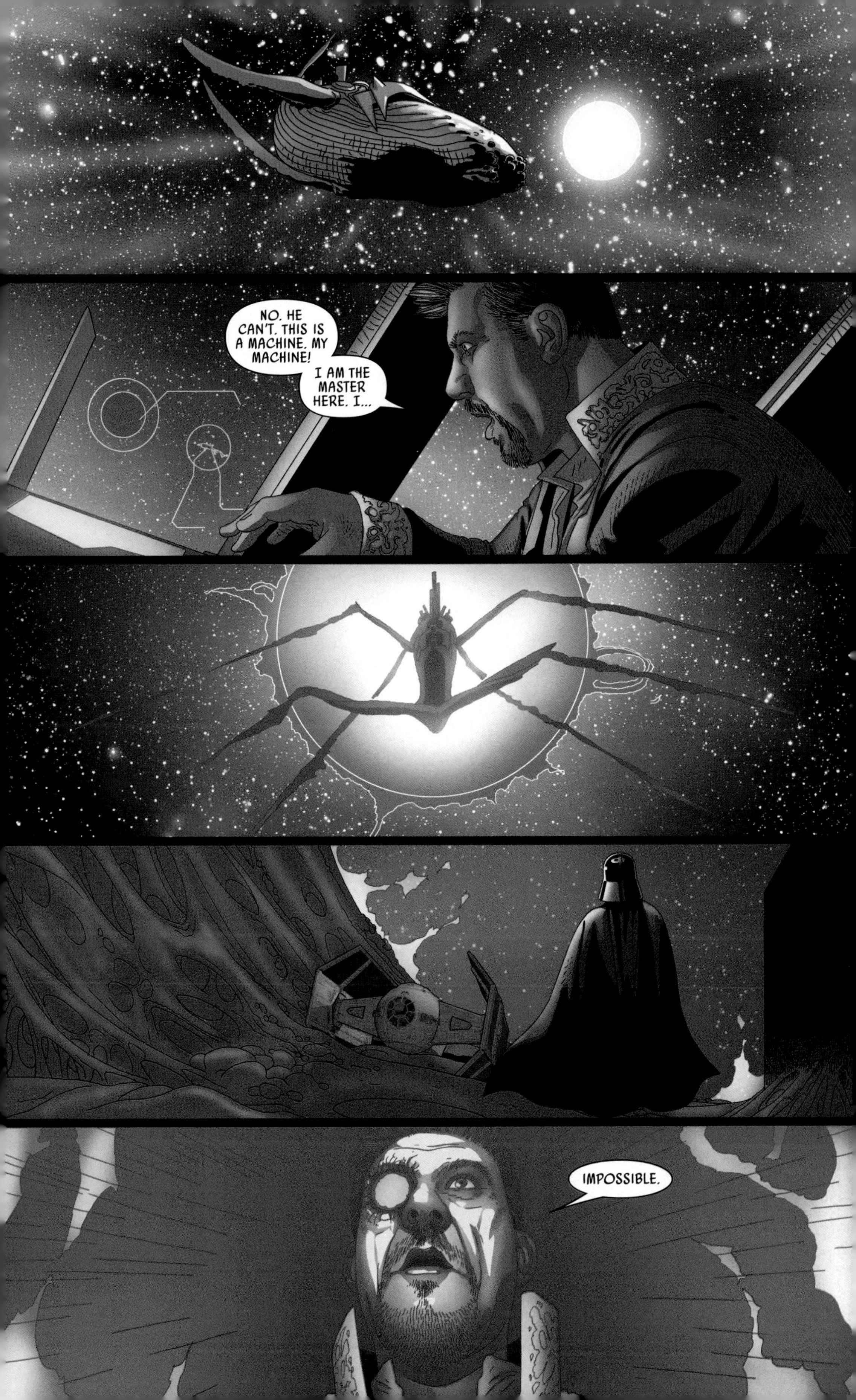
NO. HE CAN'T. THIS IS A MACHINE. MY MACHINE!
I AM THE MASTER HERE. I...
IMPOSSIBLE.

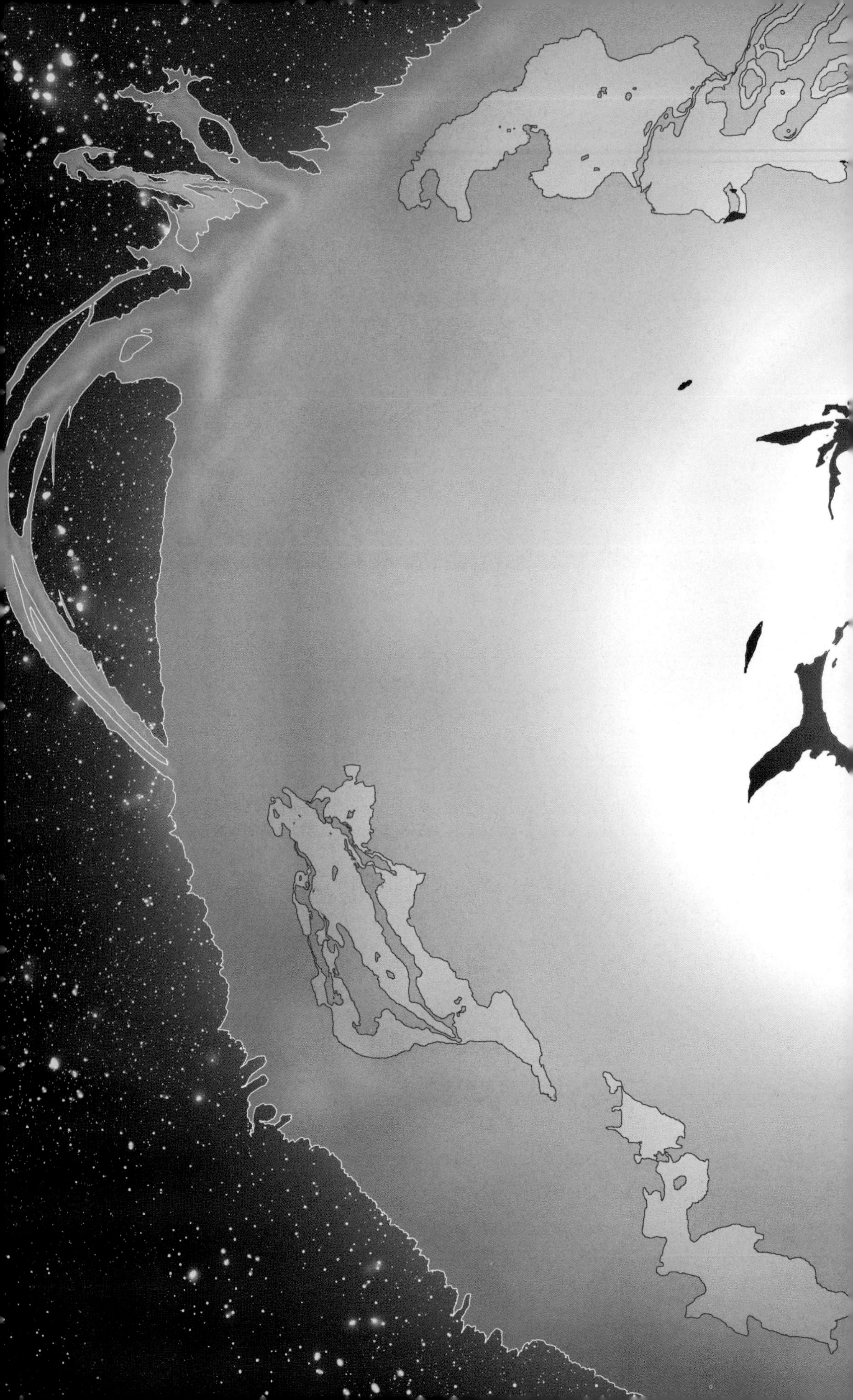

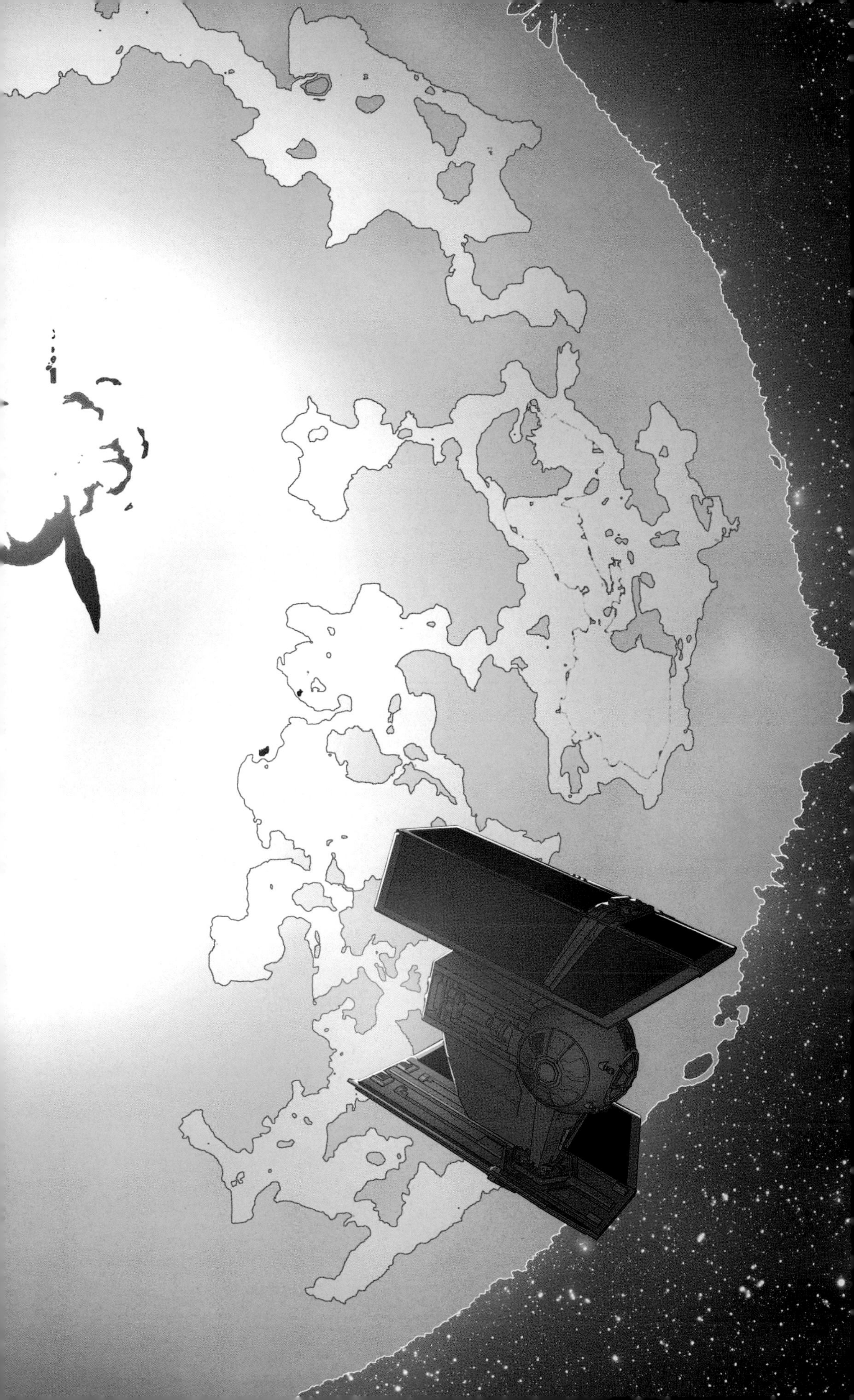

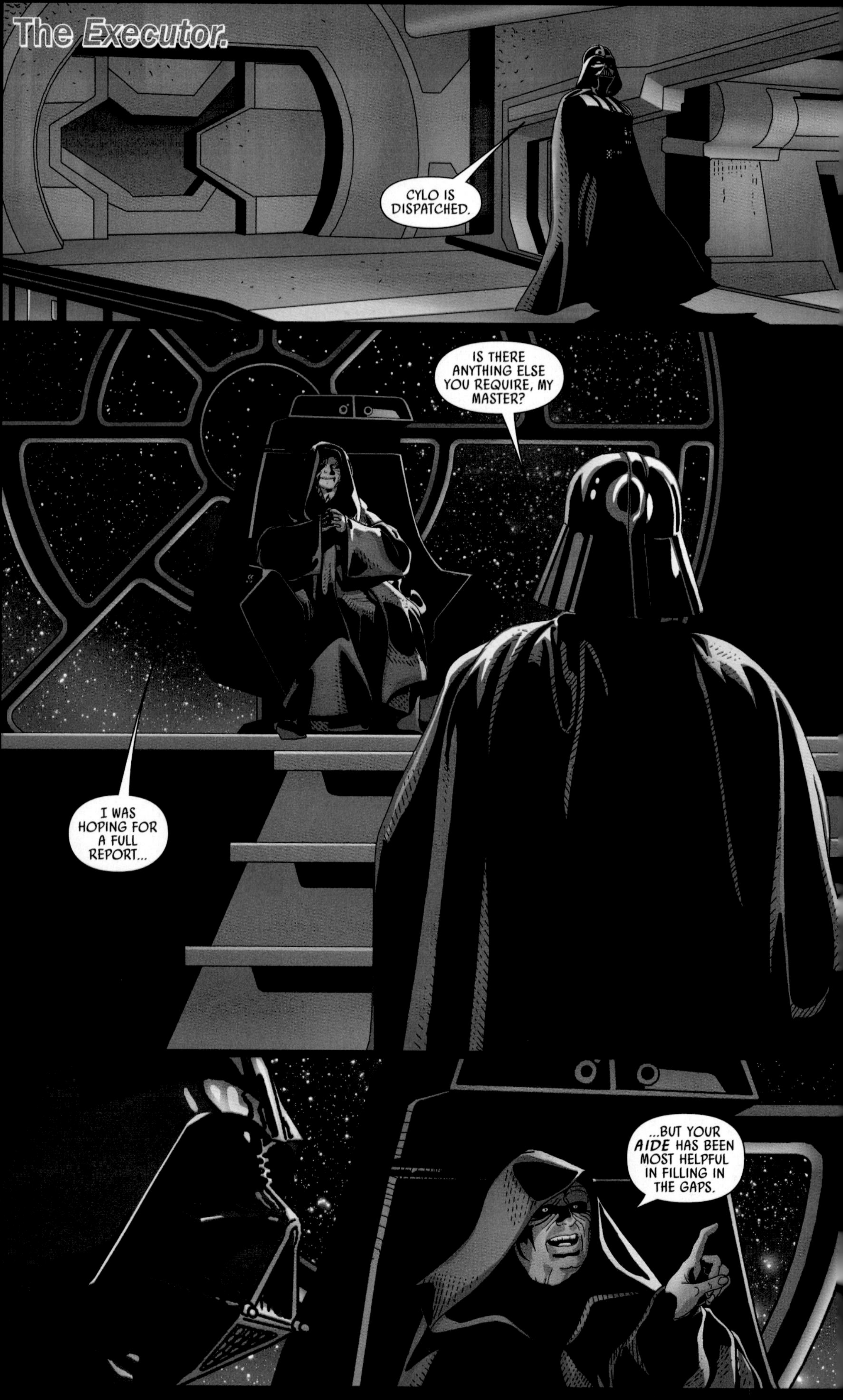

The Executor.
CYLO IS DISPATCHED.
IS THERE ANYTHING ELSE YOU REQUIRE, MY MASTER?
I WAS HOPING FOR A FULL REPORT...
...BUT YOUR AIDE HAS BEEN MOST HELPFUL IN FILLING IN THE GAPS.

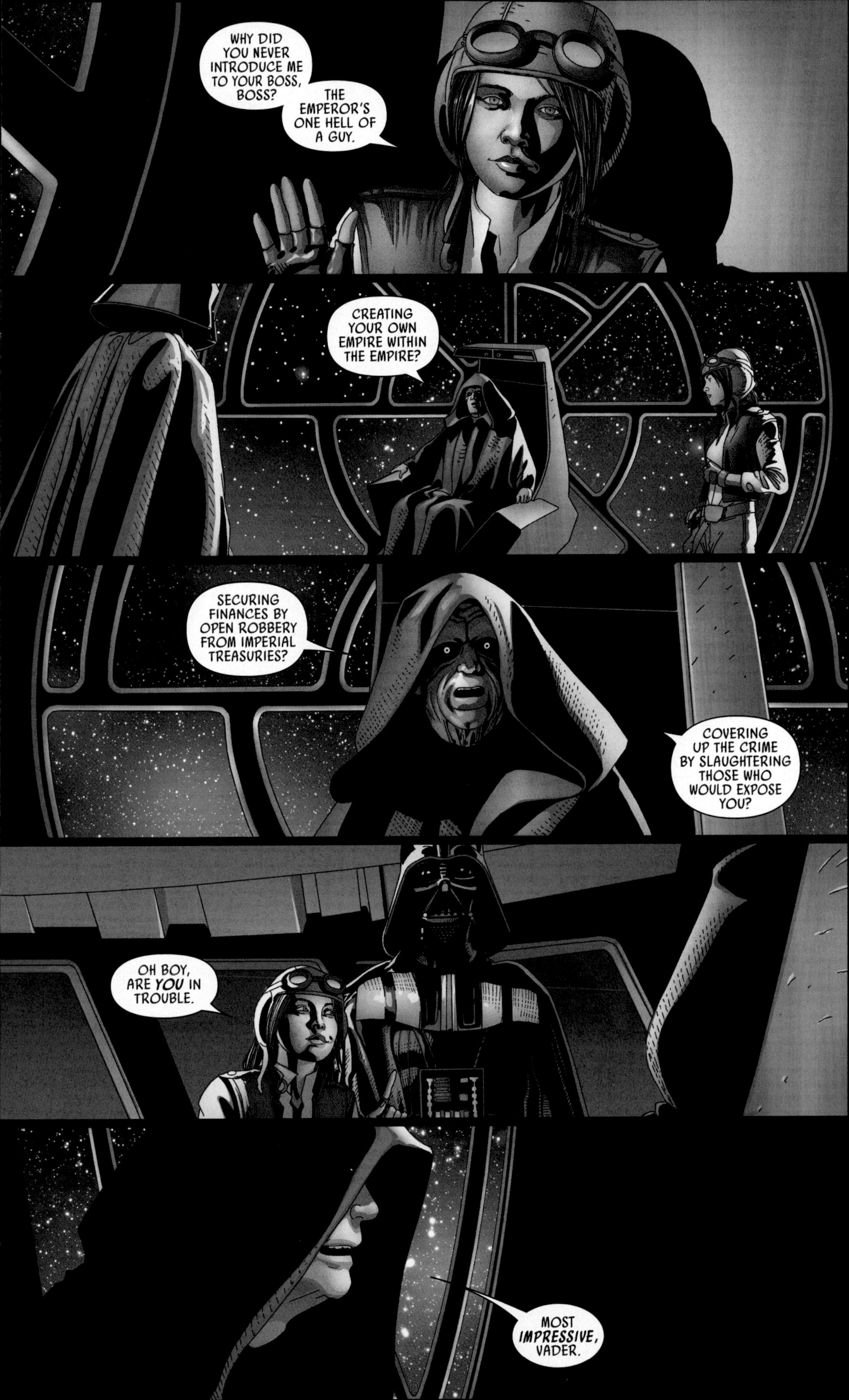

WHY DID YOU NEVER INTRODUCE ME TO YOUR BOSS, BOSS?
THE EMPEROR'S ONE HELL OF A GUY.
CREATING YOUR OWN EMPIRE WITHIN THE EMPIRE?
SECURING FINANCES BY OPEN ROBBERY FROM IMPERIAL TREASURIES?
COVERING UP THE CRIME BY SLAUGHTERING THOSE WHO WOULD EXPOSE YOU?
OH BOY, ARE *YOU* IN TROUBLE.
MOST *IMPRESSIVE*, VADER.

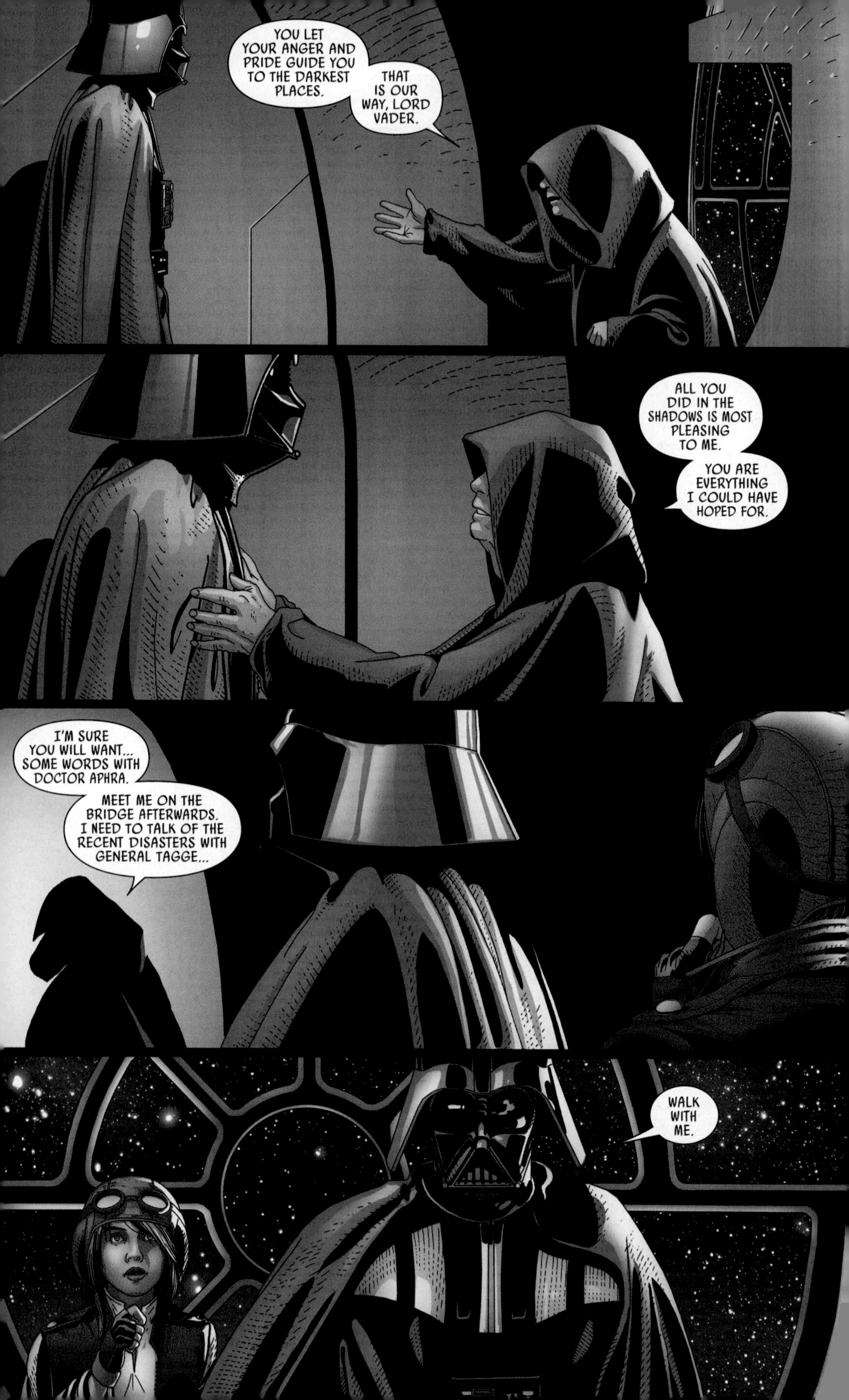
YOU LET YOUR ANGER AND PRIDE GUIDE YOU TO THE DARKEST PLACES.
THAT IS OUR WAY, LORD VADER.
ALL YOU DID IN THE SHADOWS IS MOST PLEASING TO ME.
YOU ARE EVERYTHING I COULD HAVE HOPED FOR.
I'M SURE YOU WILL WANT... SOME WORDS WITH DOCTOR APHRA.
MEET ME ON THE BRIDGE AFTERWARDS. I NEED TO TALK OF THE RECENT DISASTERS WITH GENERAL TAGGE...
WALK WITH ME.

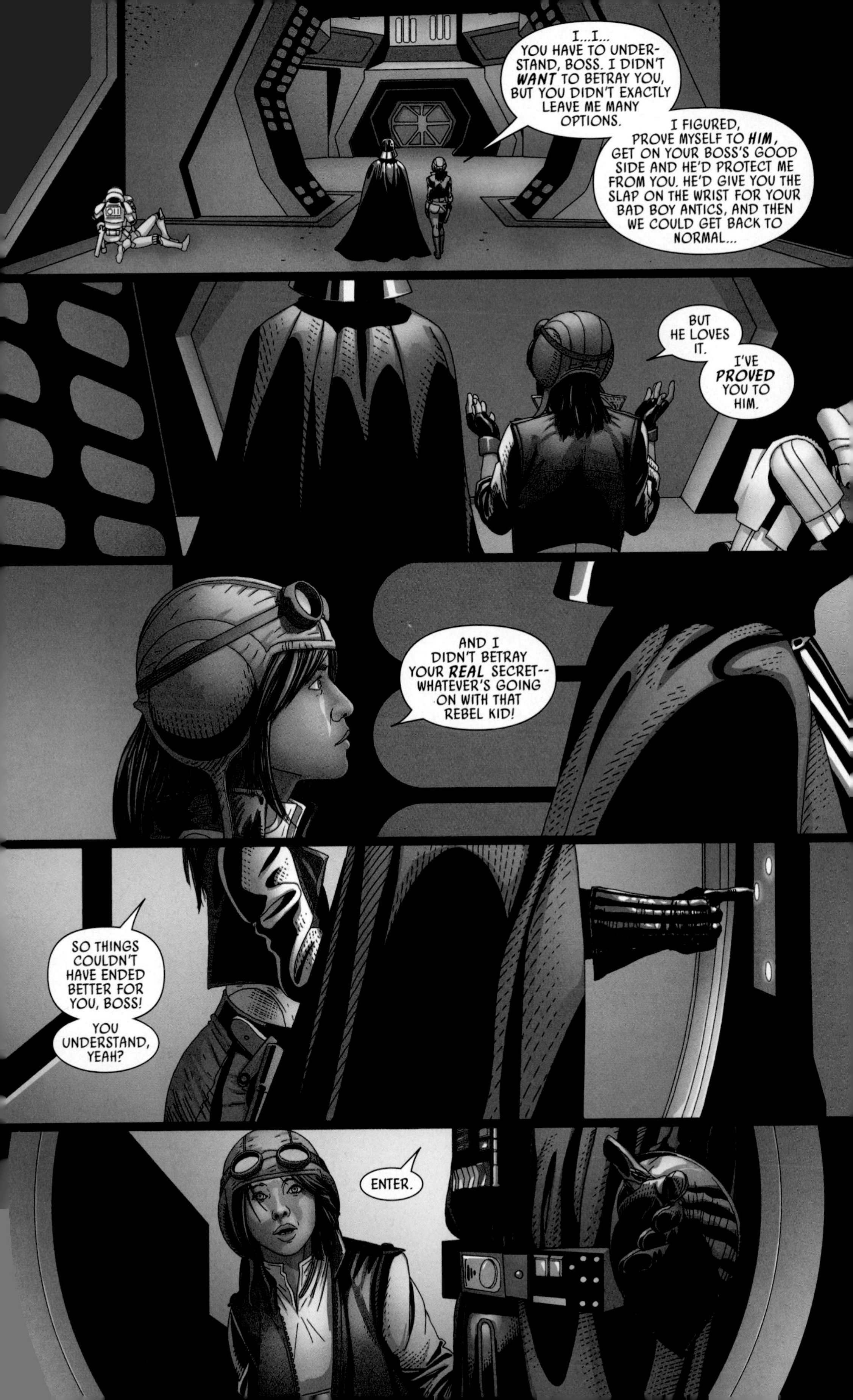
I...I... YOU HAVE TO UNDERSTAND, BOSS. I DIDN'T WANT TO BETRAY YOU, BUT YOU DIDN'T EXACTLY LEAVE ME MANY OPTIONS.
I FIGURED, PROVE MYSELF TO HIM, GET ON YOUR BOSS'S GOOD SIDE AND HE'D PROTECT ME FROM YOU. HE'D GIVE YOU THE SLAP ON THE WRIST FOR YOUR BAD BOY ANTICS, AND THEN WE COULD GET BACK TO NORMAL...
BUT HE LOVES IT.
I'VE PROVED YOU TO HIM.
AND I DIDN'T BETRAY YOUR REAL SECRET-- WHATEVER'S GOING ON WITH THAT REBEL KID!
SO THINGS COULDN'T HAVE ENDED BETTER FOR YOU, BOSS!
YOU UNDERSTAND, YEAH?
ENTER.

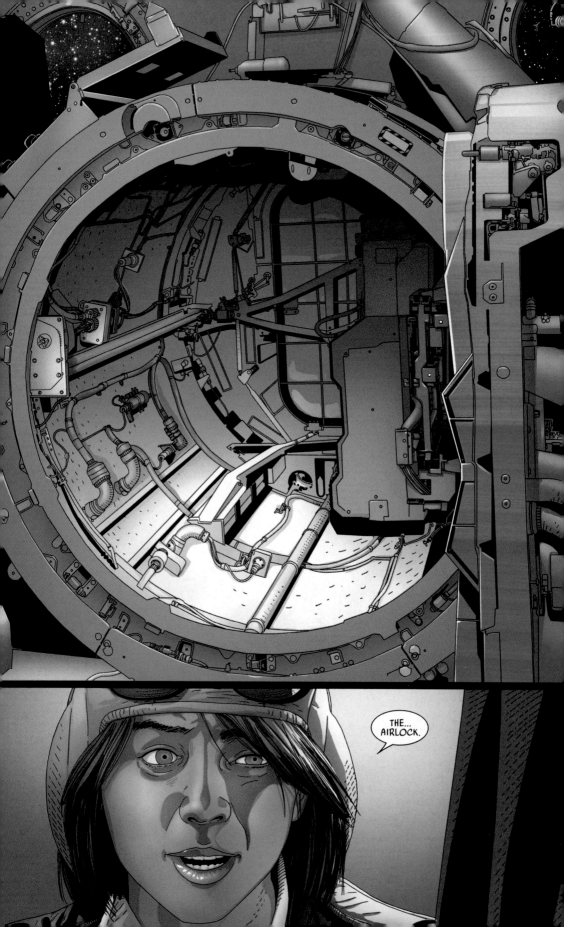

THE... AIRLOCK.

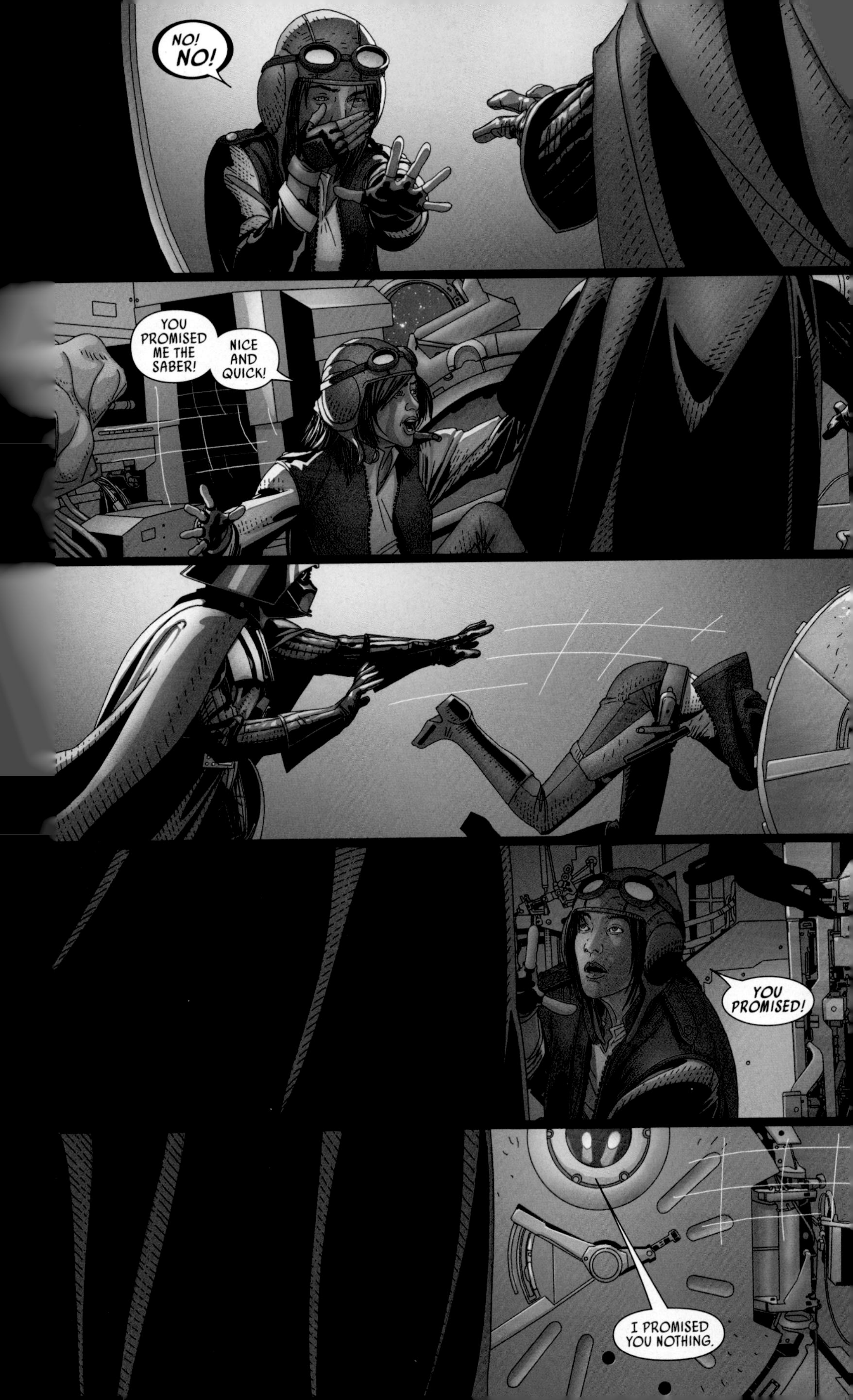
NO! NO!
YOU PROMISED ME THE SABER!
NICE AND QUICK!
YOU PROMISED!
I PROMISED YOU NOTHING.

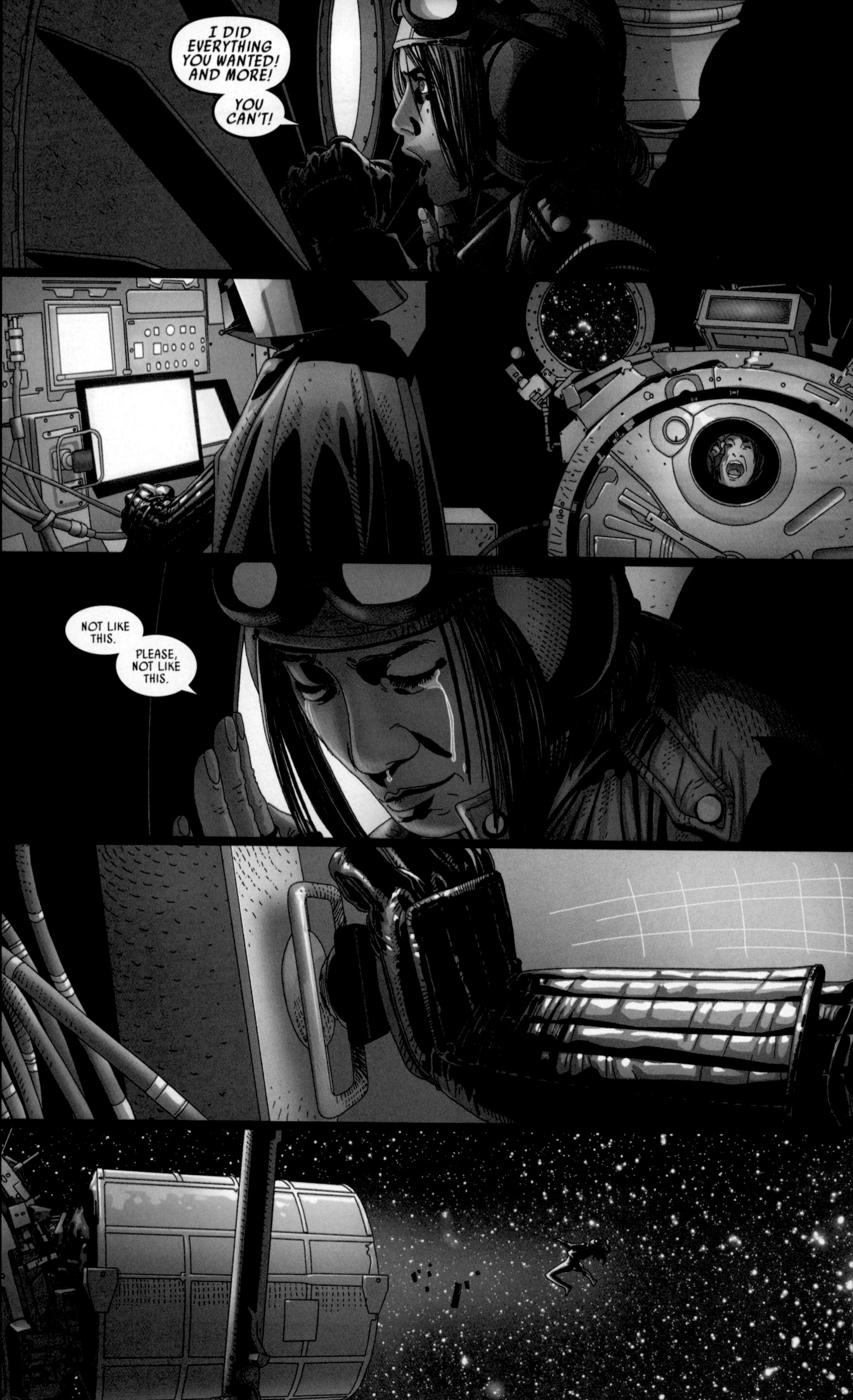
I DID EVERYTHING YOU WANTED! AND MORE!
YOU CAN'T!
NOT LIKE THIS.
PLEASE, NOT LIKE THIS.

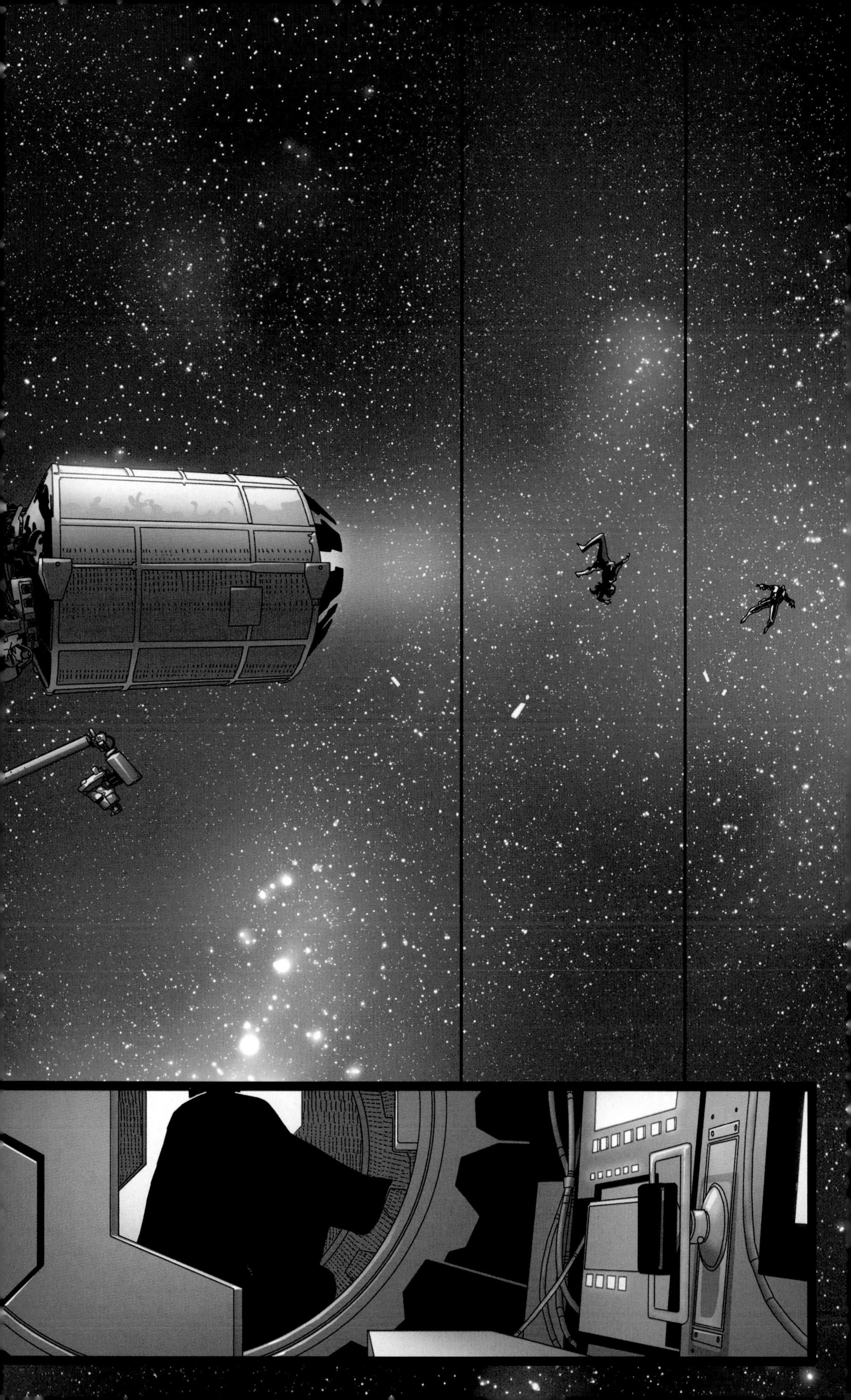

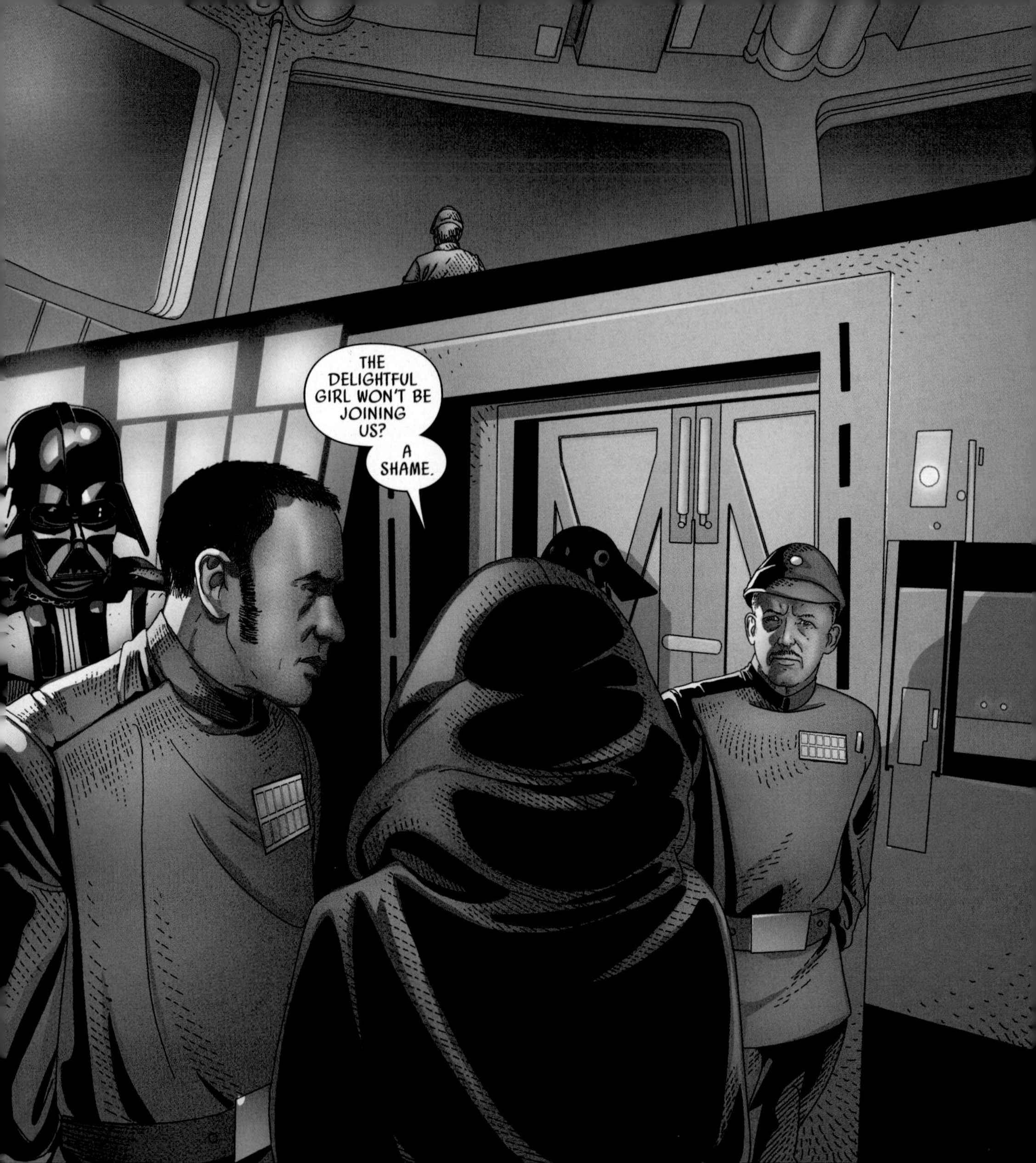
THE DELIGHTFUL GIRL WON'T BE JOINING US?
A SHAME.

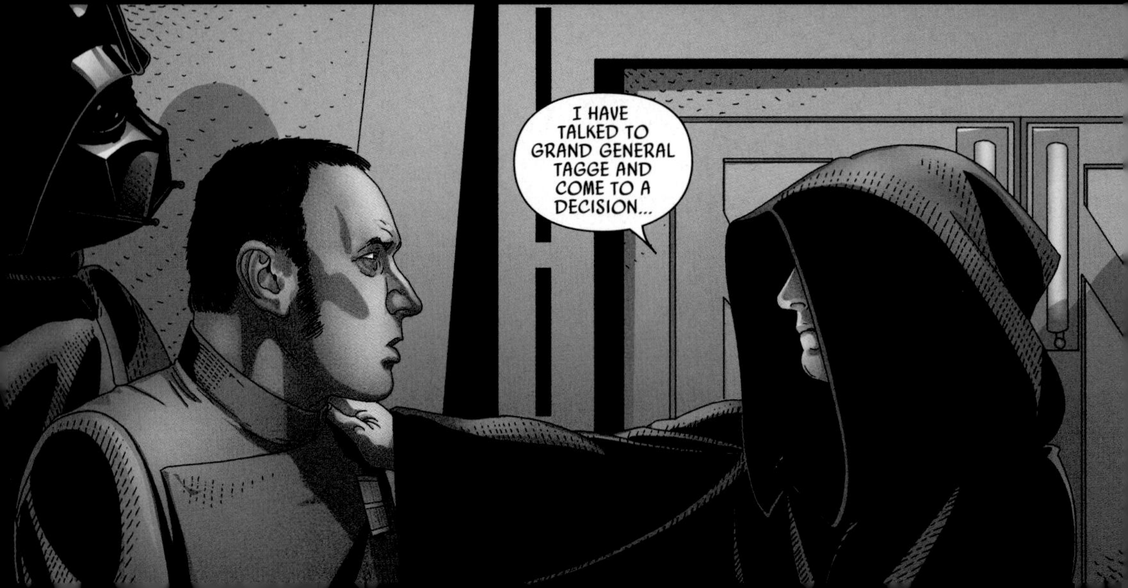
I HAVE TALKED TO GRAND GENERAL TAGGE AND COME TO A DECISION...

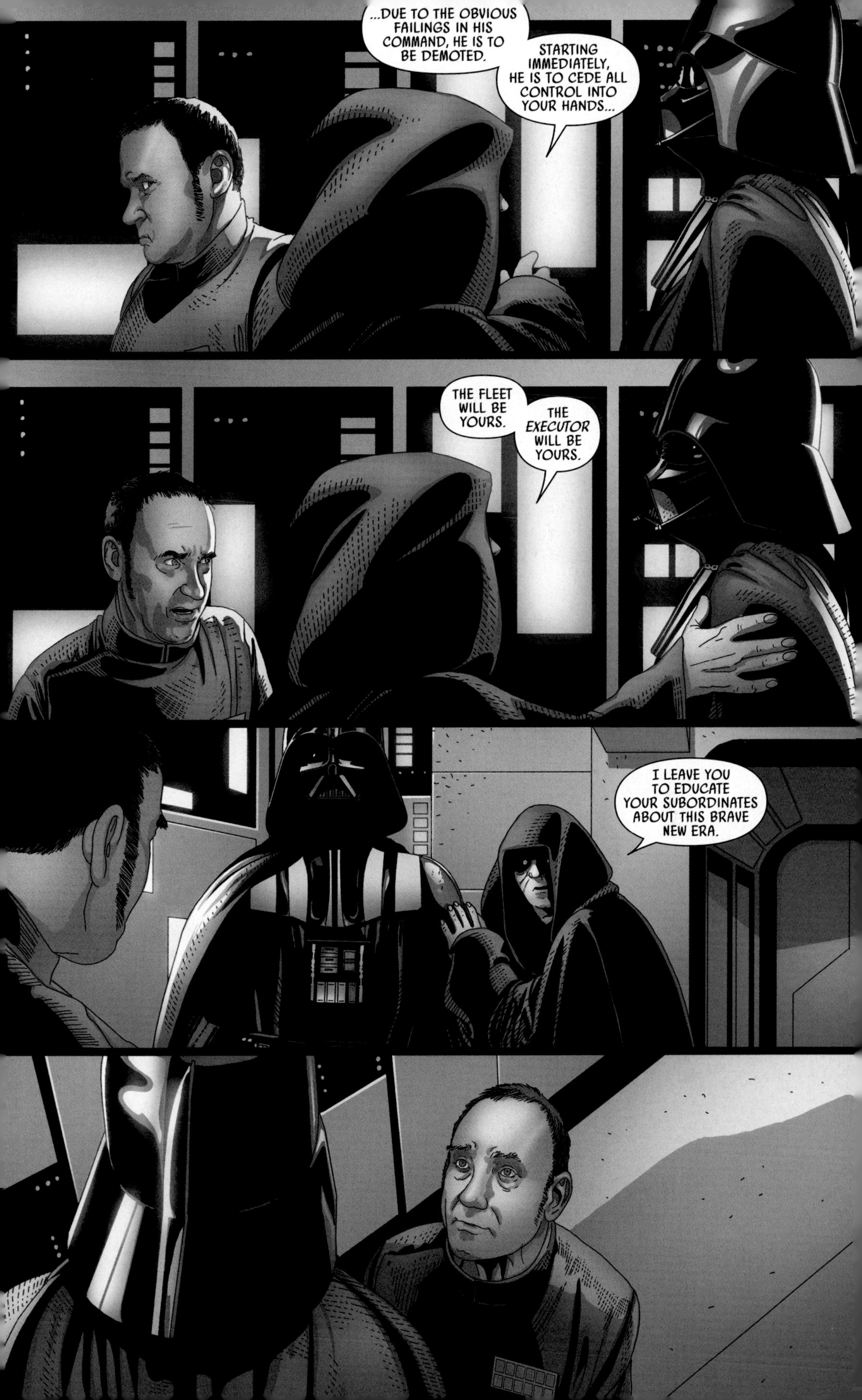
...DUE TO THE OBVIOUS FAILINGS IN HIS COMMAND, HE IS TO BE DEMOTED.
STARTING IMMEDIATELY, HE IS TO CEDE ALL CONTROL INTO YOUR HANDS...
THE FLEET WILL BE YOURS.
THE *EXECUTOR* WILL BE YOURS.
I LEAVE YOU TO EDUCATE YOUR SUBORDINATES ABOUT THIS BRAVE NEW ERA.

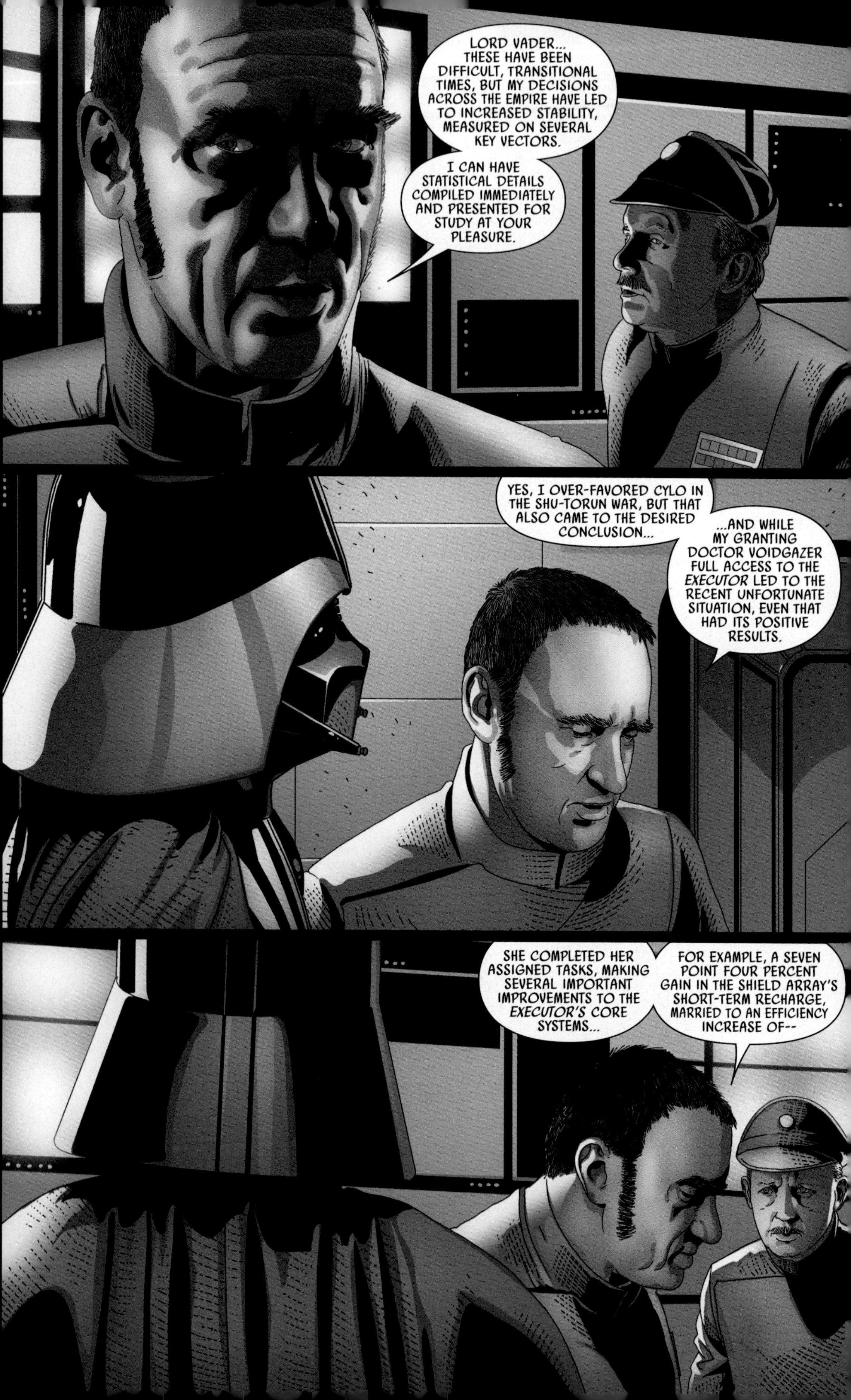
LORD VADER... THESE HAVE BEEN DIFFICULT, TRANSITIONAL TIMES, BUT MY DECISIONS ACROSS THE EMPIRE HAVE LED TO INCREASED STABILITY, MEASURED ON SEVERAL KEY VECTORS.
I CAN HAVE STATISTICAL DETAILS COMPILED IMMEDIATELY AND PRESENTED FOR STUDY AT YOUR PLEASURE.
YES, I OVER-FAVORED CYLO IN THE SHU-TORUN WAR, BUT THAT ALSO CAME TO THE DESIRED CONCLUSION...
...AND WHILE MY GRANTING DOCTOR VOIDGAZER FULL ACCESS TO THE *EXECUTOR* LED TO THE RECENT UNFORTUNATE SITUATION, EVEN THAT HAD ITS POSITIVE RESULTS.
SHE COMPLETED HER ASSIGNED TASKS, MAKING SEVERAL IMPORTANT IMPROVEMENTS TO THE *EXECUTOR'S* CORE SYSTEMS...
FOR EXAMPLE, A SEVEN POINT FOUR PERCENT GAIN IN THE SHIELD ARRAY'S SHORT-TERM RECHARGE, MARRIED TO AN EFFICIENCY INCREASE OF--

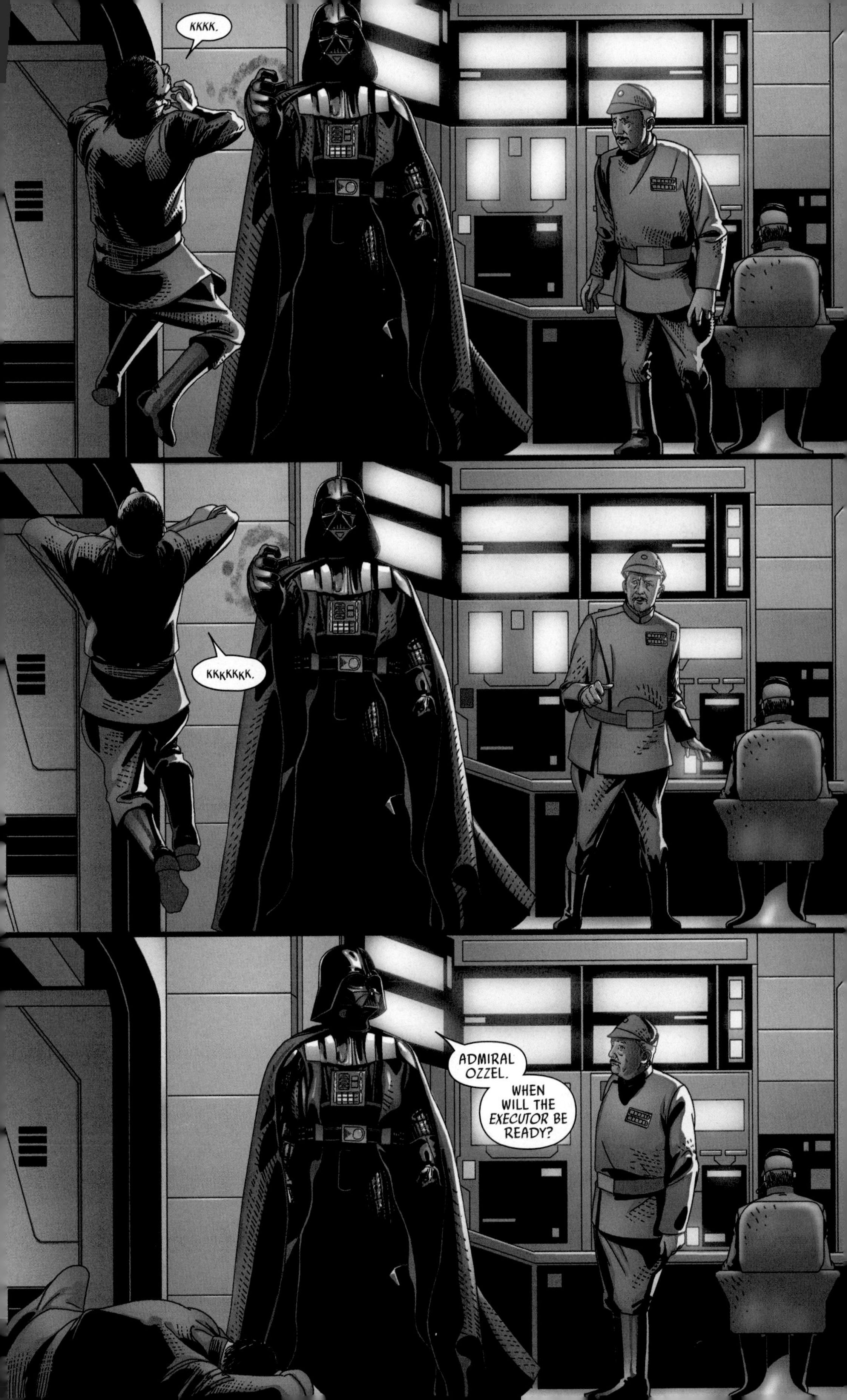
KKKK.
KKKKKKK.
ADMIRAL OZZEL.
WHEN WILL THE *EXECUTOR* BE READY?

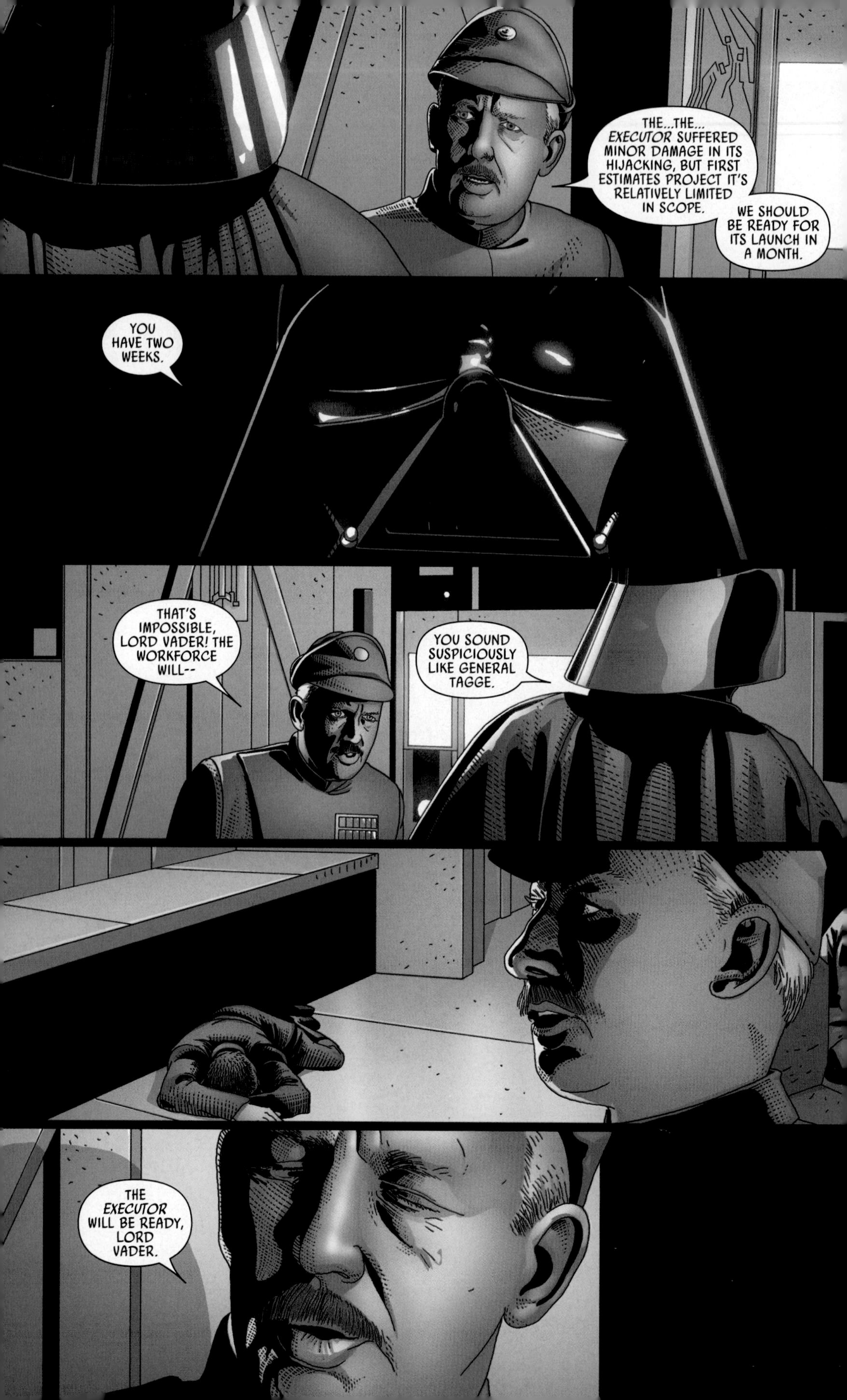
THE...THE... *EXECUTOR* SUFFERED MINOR DAMAGE IN ITS HIJACKING, BUT FIRST ESTIMATES PROJECT IT'S RELATIVELY LIMITED IN SCOPE.
WE SHOULD BE READY FOR ITS LAUNCH IN A MONTH.
YOU HAVE TWO WEEKS.
THAT'S IMPOSSIBLE, LORD VADER! THE WORKFORCE WILL--
YOU SOUND SUSPICIOUSLY LIKE GENERAL TAGGE.
THE *EXECUTOR* WILL BE READY, LORD VADER.

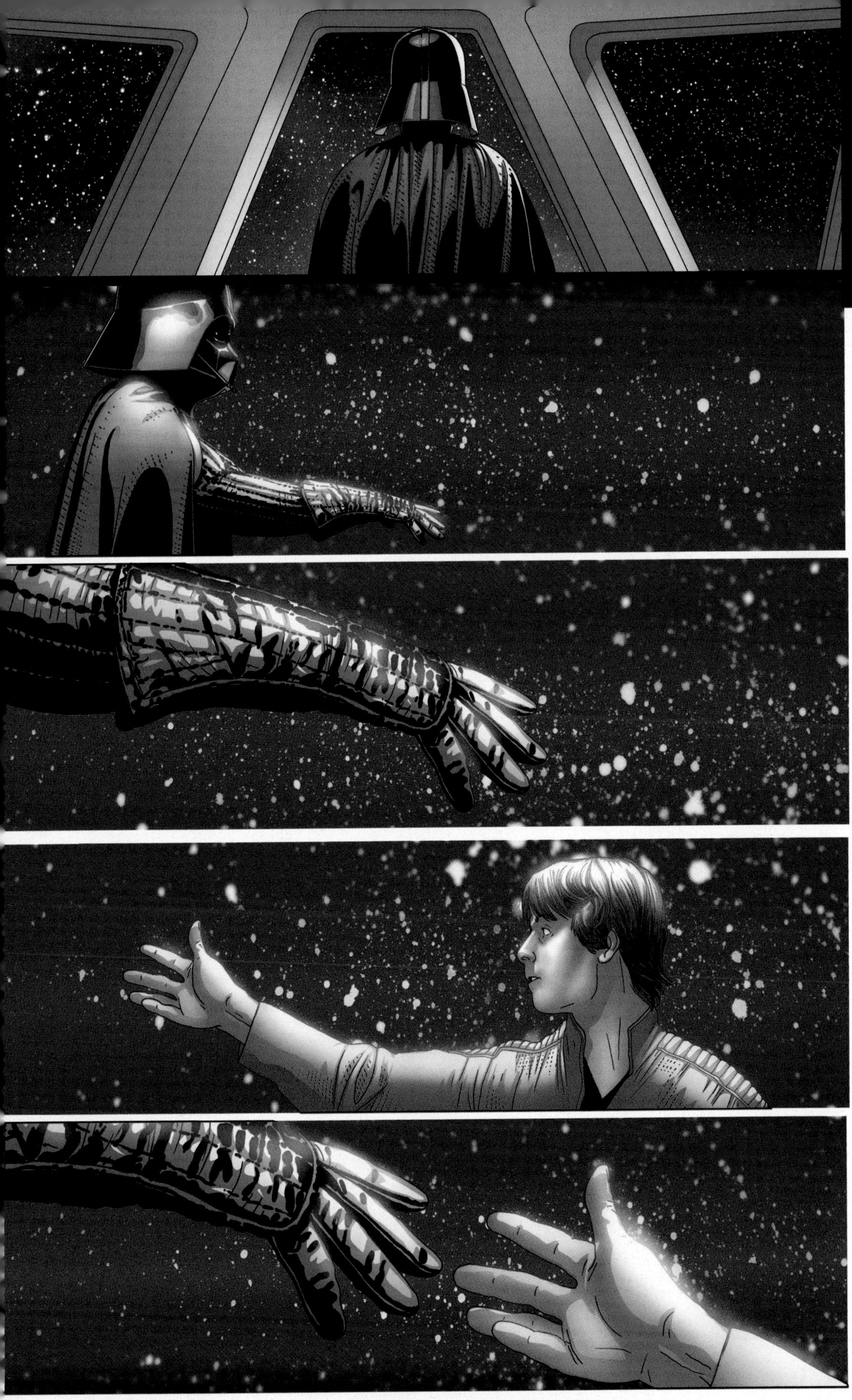

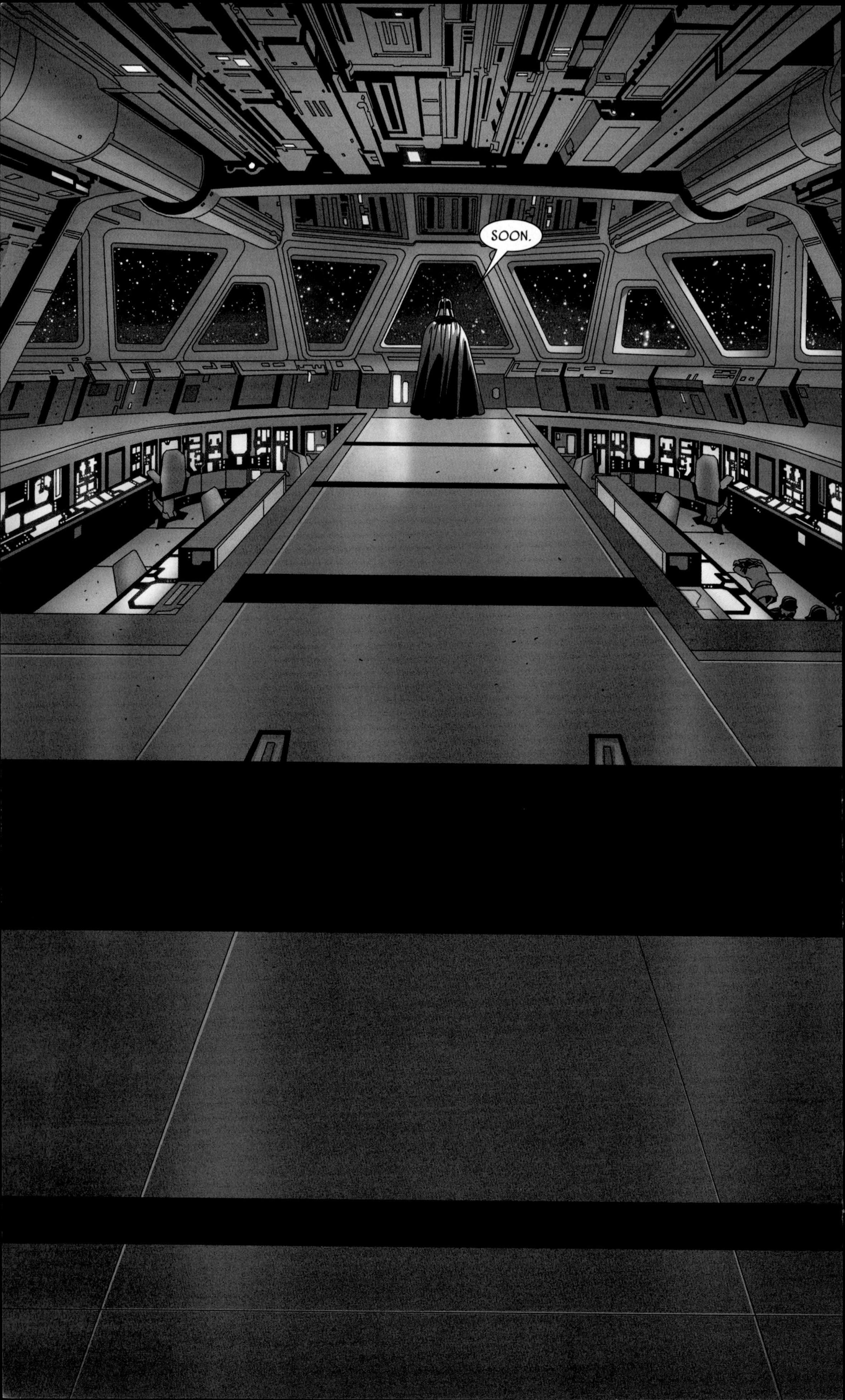
SOON.

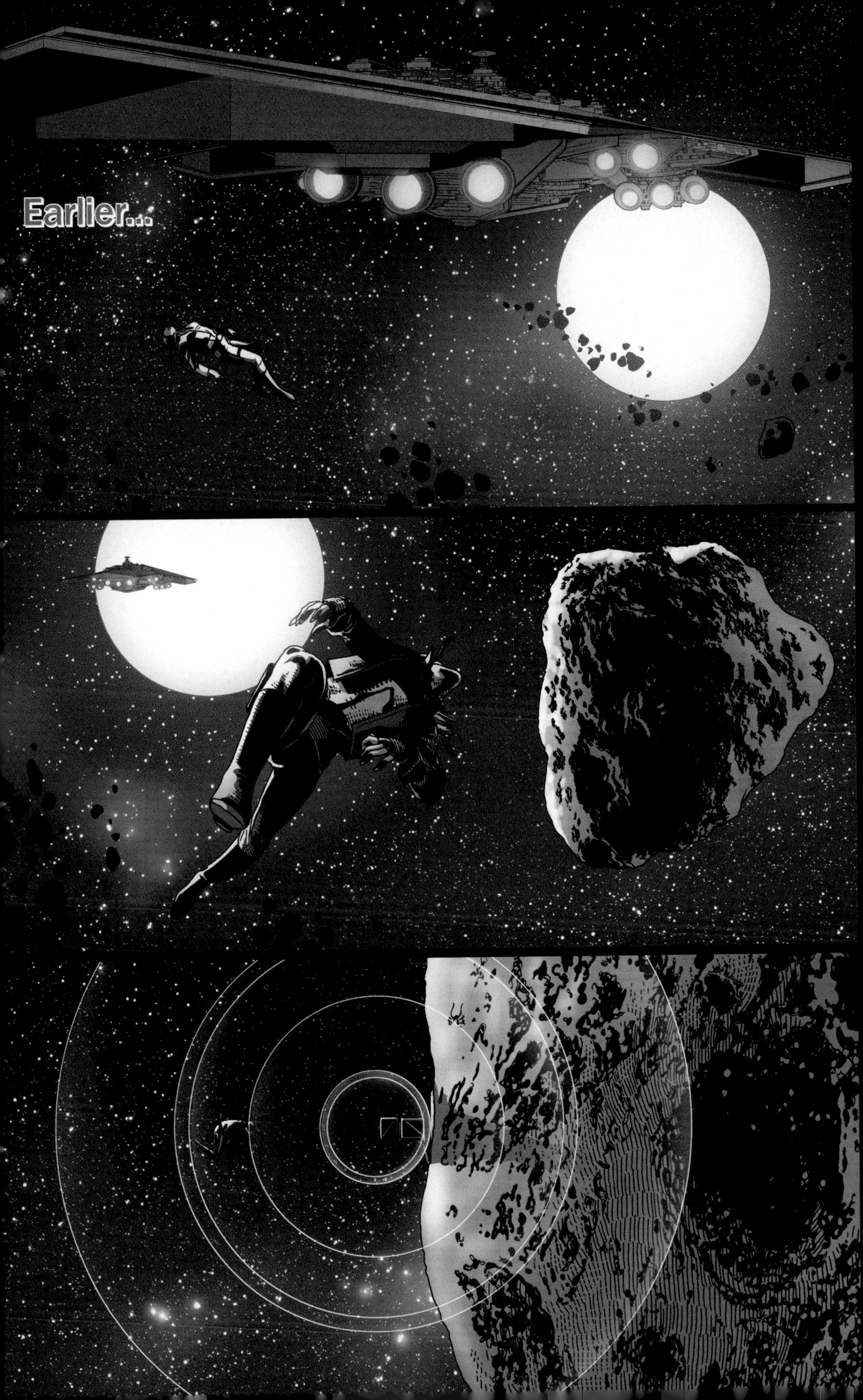
Earlier...

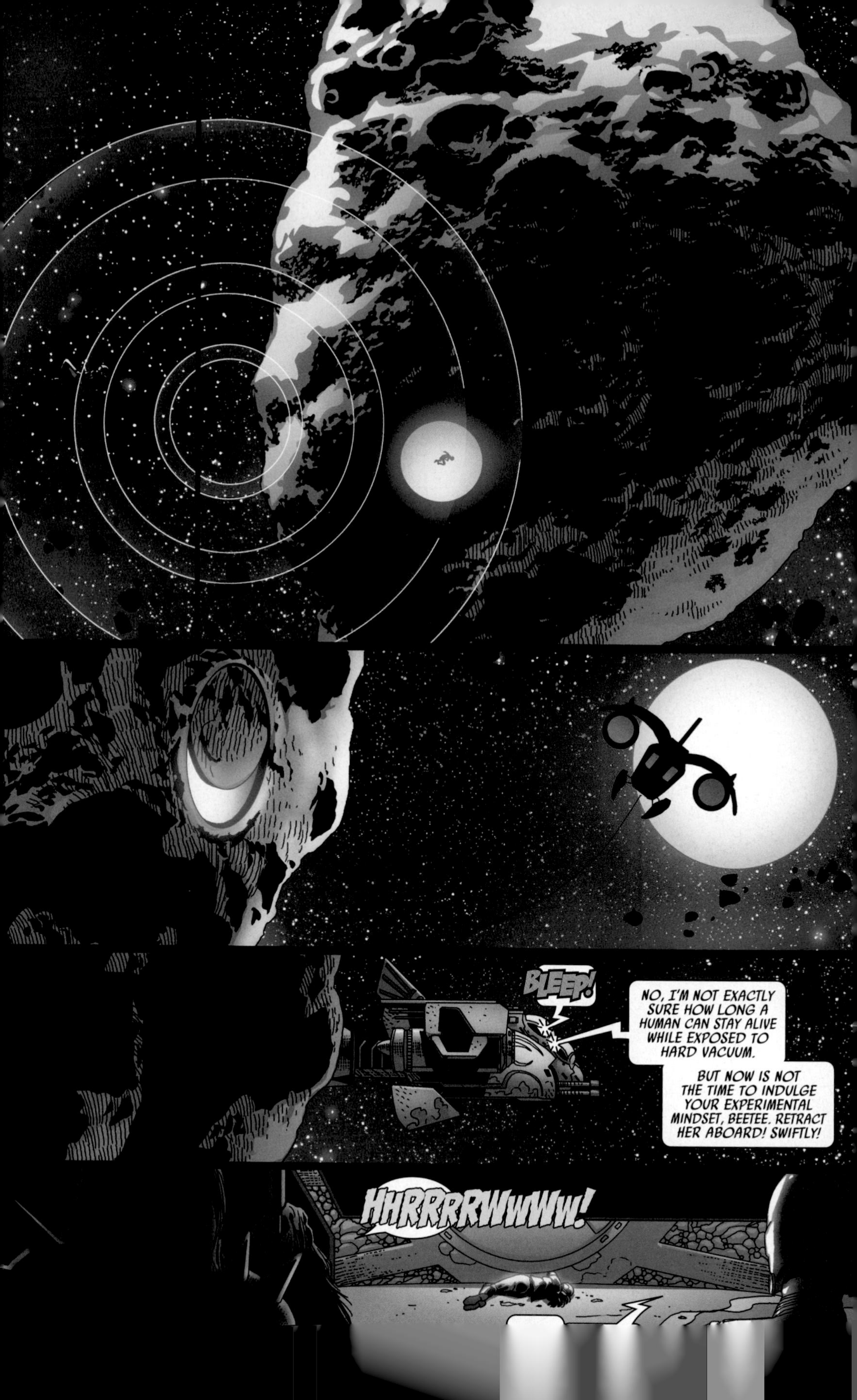
BLEEP!
NO, I'M NOT EXACTLY SURE HOW LONG A HUMAN CAN STAY ALIVE WHILE EXPOSED TO HARD VACUUM.
BUT NOW IS NOT THE TIME TO INDULGE YOUR EXPERIMENTAL MINDSET, BEETEE. RETRACT HER ABOARD! SWIFTLY!
HHRRRRRWWWW!

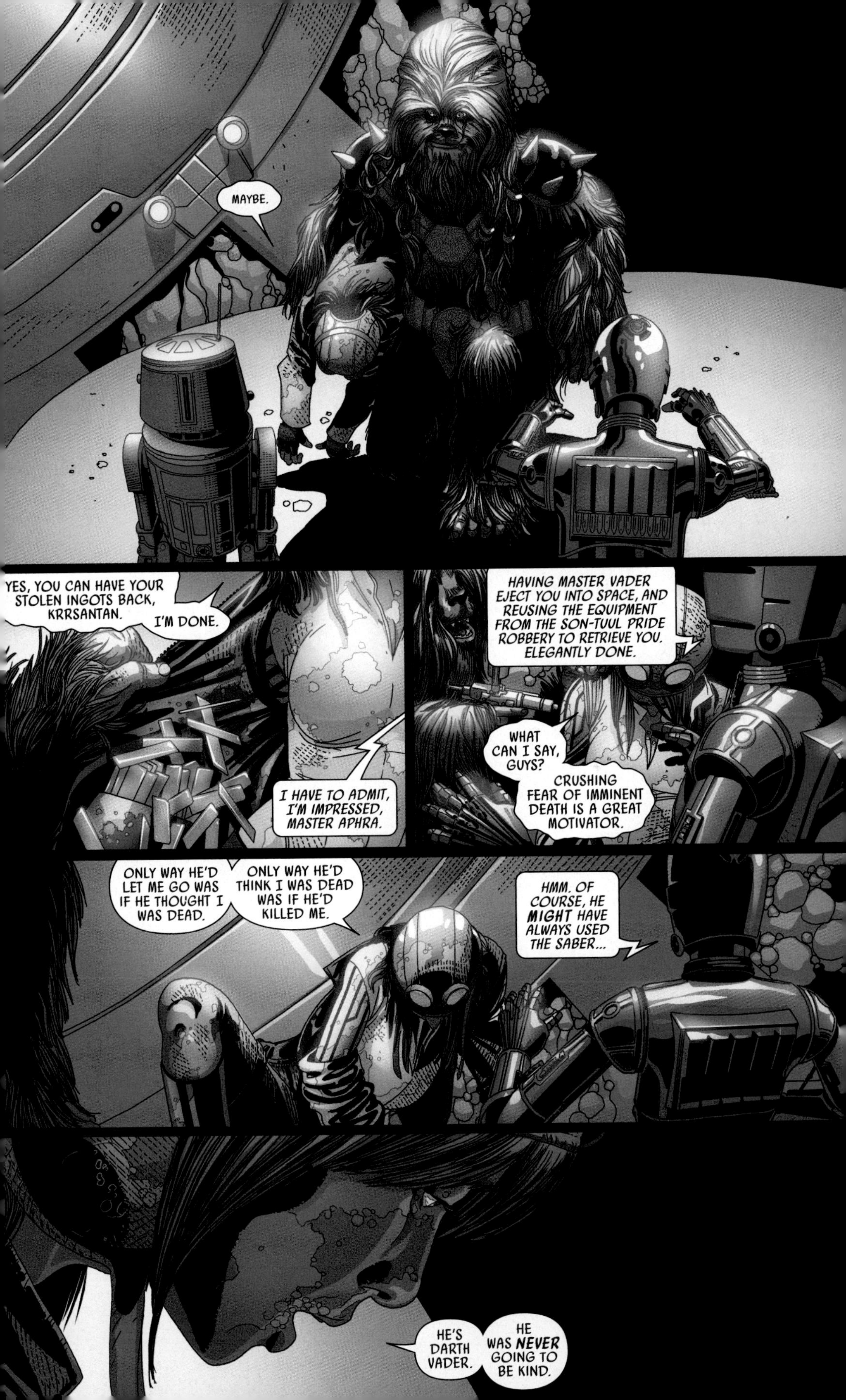
MAYBE.
YES, YOU CAN HAVE YOUR STOLEN INGOTS BACK, KRRSANTAN.
I'M DONE.
I HAVE TO ADMIT, I'M IMPRESSED, MASTER APHRA.
HAVING MASTER VADER EJECT YOU INTO SPACE, AND REUSING THE EQUIPMENT FROM THE SON-TUUL PRIDE ROBBERY TO RETRIEVE YOU. ELEGANTLY DONE.
WHAT CAN I SAY, GUYS?
CRUSHING FEAR OF IMMINENT DEATH IS A GREAT MOTIVATOR.
ONLY WAY HE'D LET ME GO WAS IF HE THOUGHT I WAS DEAD.
ONLY WAY HE'D THINK I WAS DEAD WAS IF HE'D KILLED ME.
HMM. OF COURSE, HE MIGHT HAVE ALWAYS USED THE SABER...
HE'S DARTH VADER.
HE WAS NEVER GOING TO BE KIND.

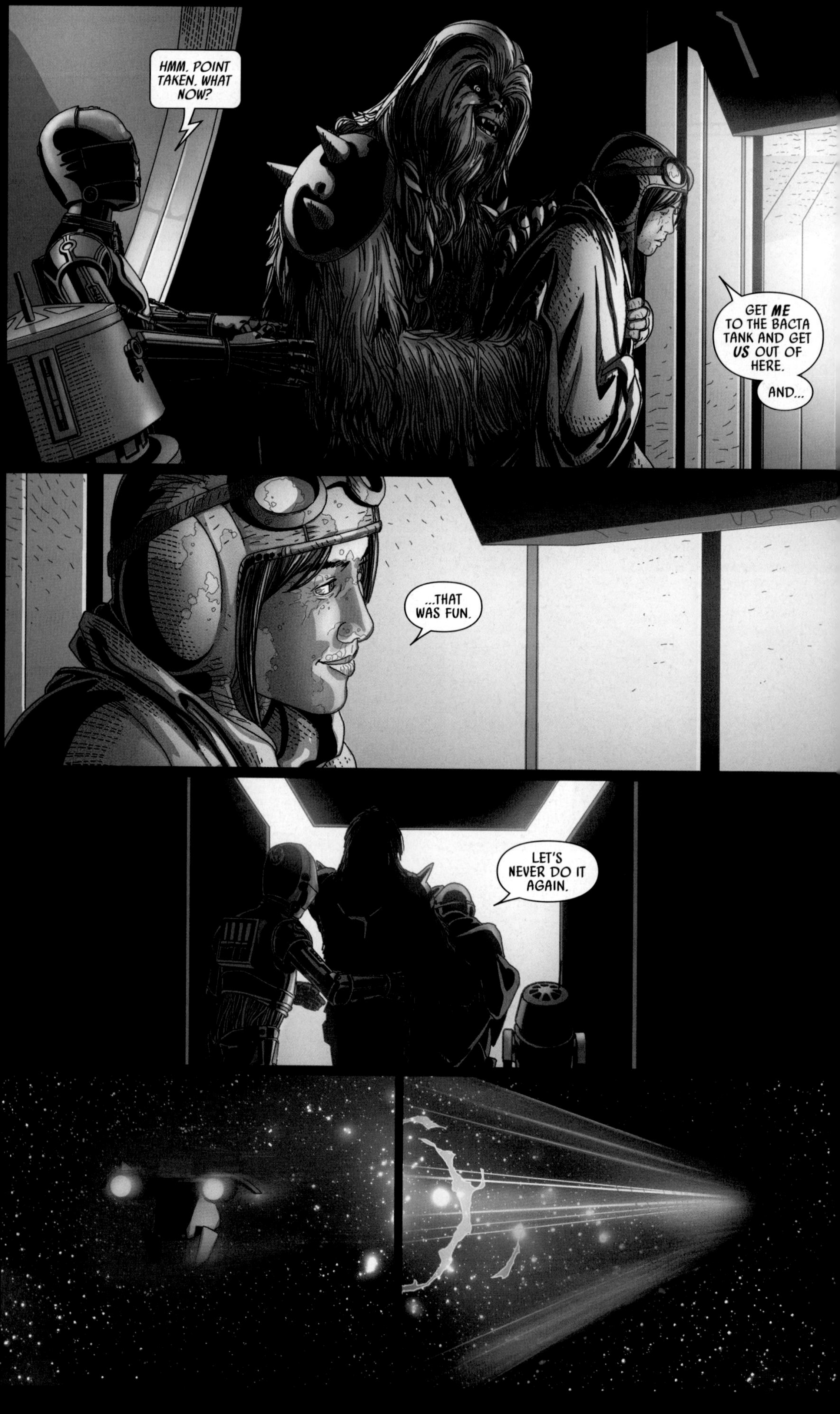
HMM. POINT TAKEN. WHAT NOW?
GET ME TO THE BACTA TANK AND GET US OUT OF HERE.
AND...
...THAT WAS FUN.
LET'S NEVER DO IT AGAIN.

CODA

Long ago, a boy named Anakin Skywalker, in a rage over the loss of his mother, butchered a whole village of Tusken Raiders. Soon after, he left Tatooine, never to return.

Months ago, Darth Vader arrived for the first time on Tatooine. While waiting for two bounty hunters, he passed the time by slaughtering a whole village of Tusken raiders.

Or so he thought.....

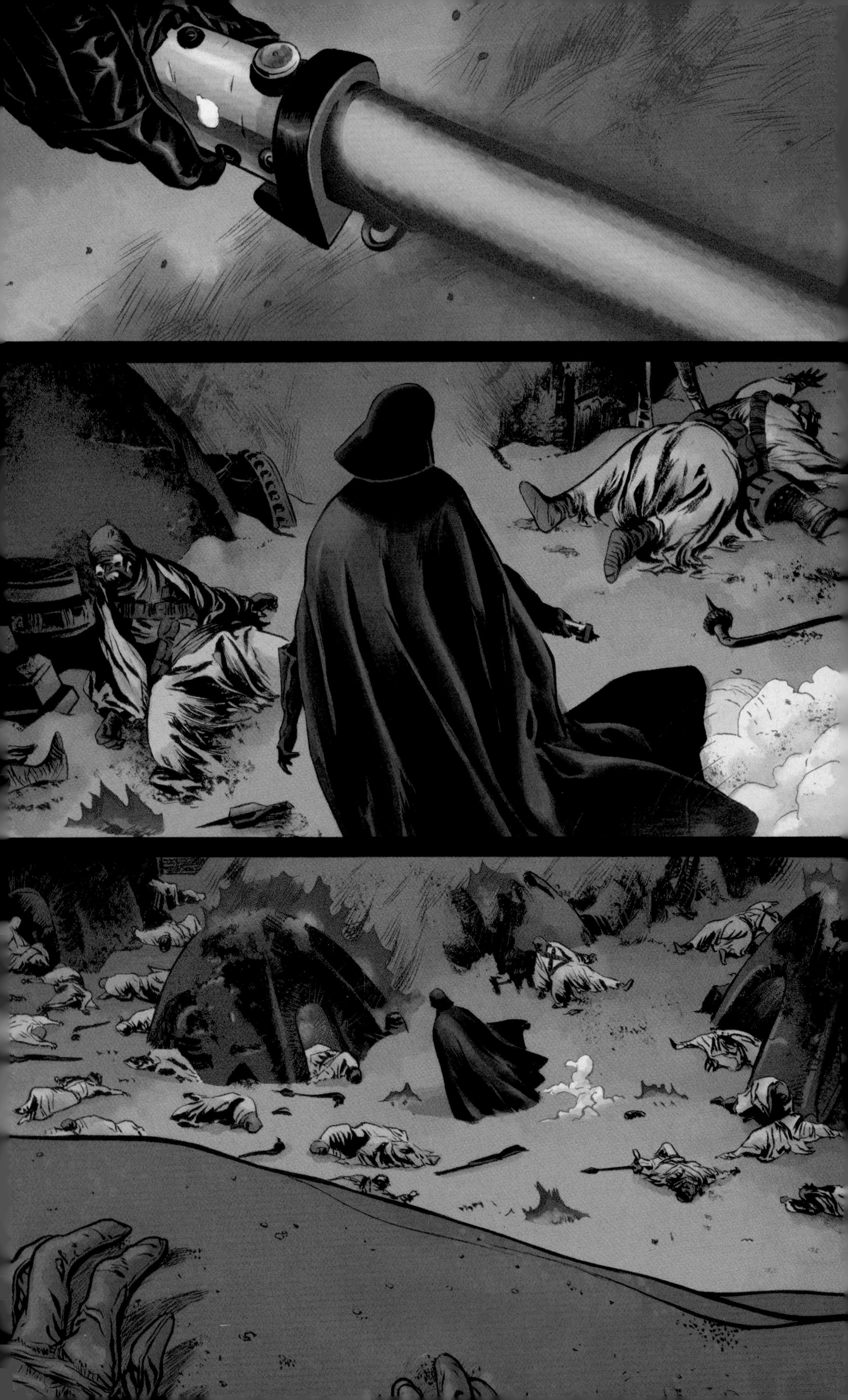

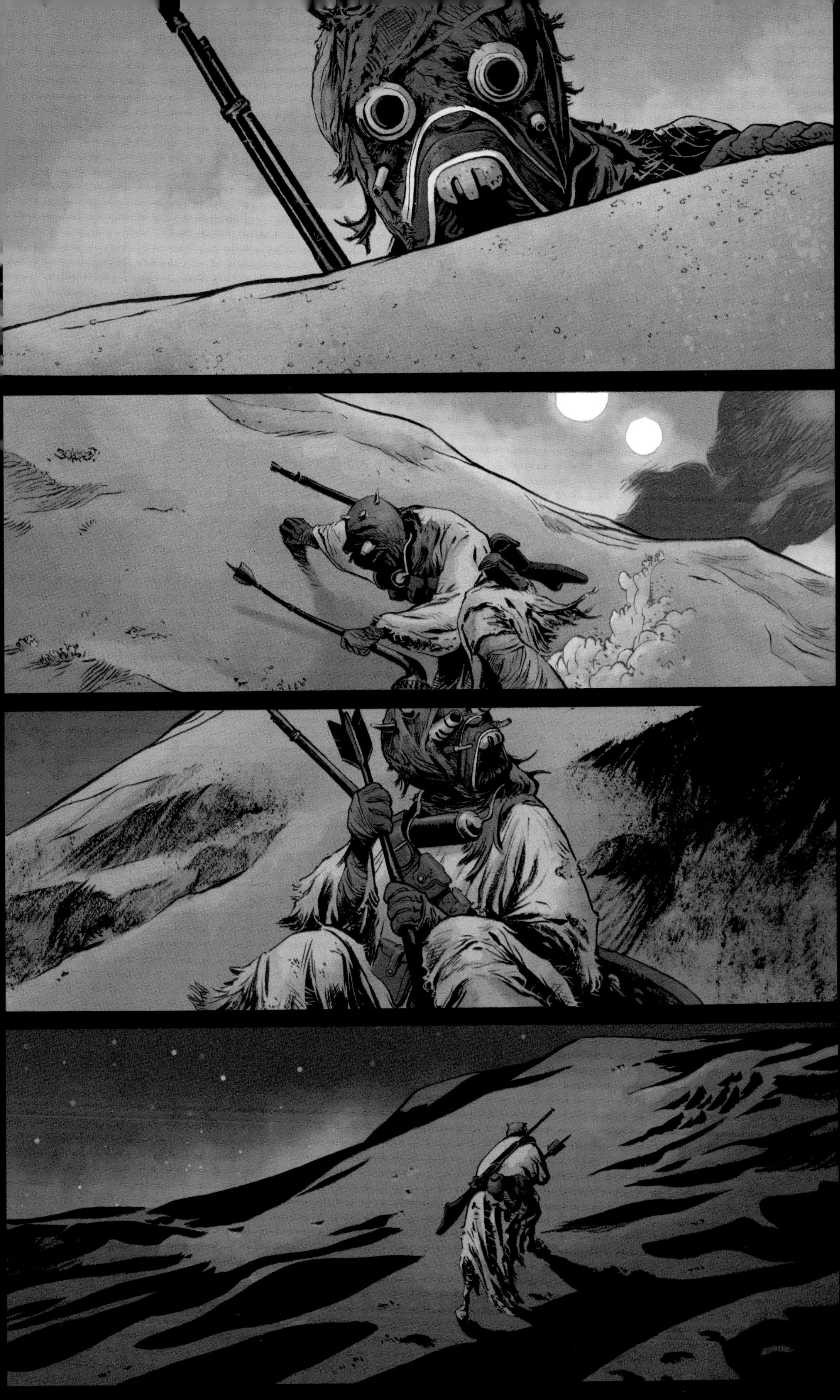

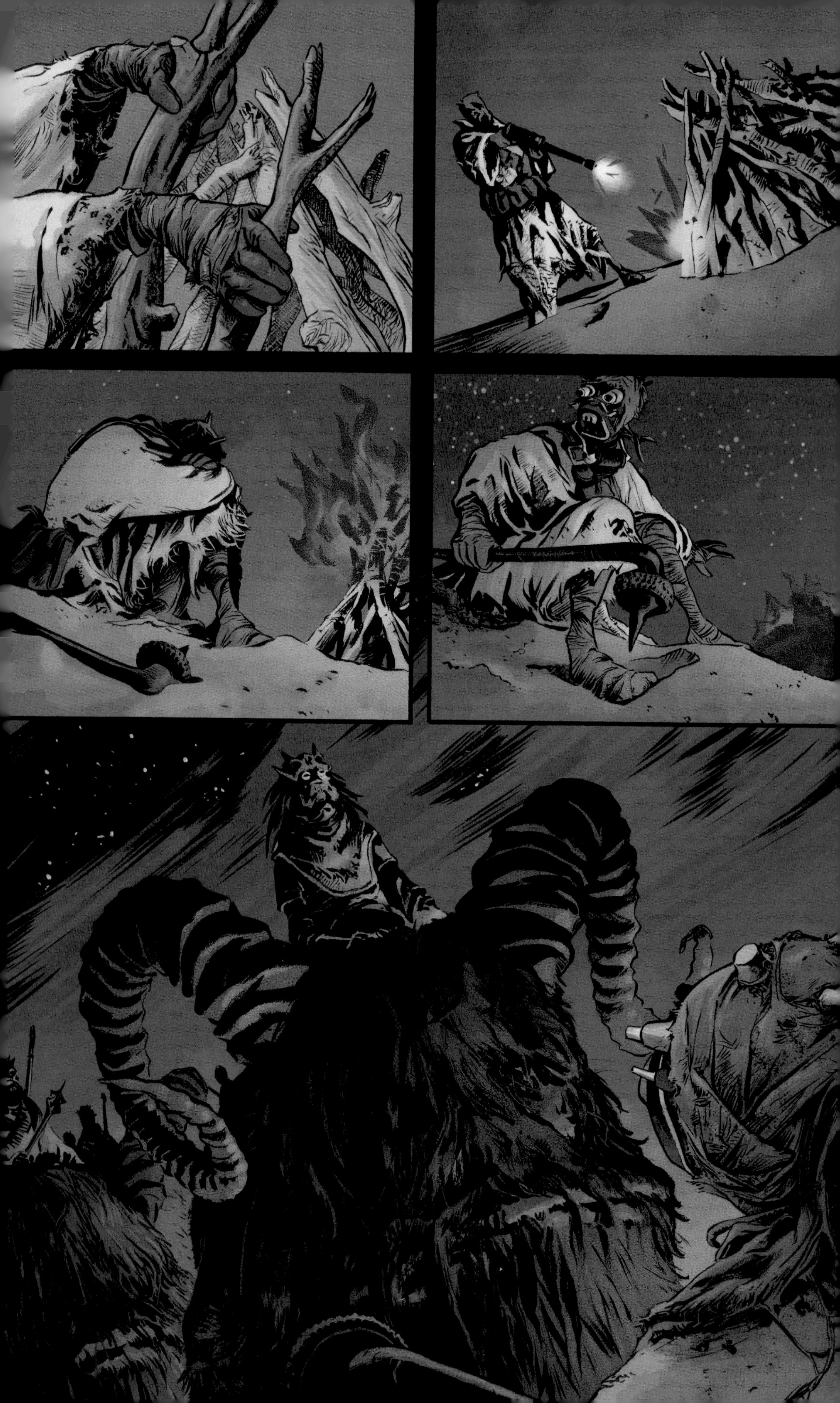

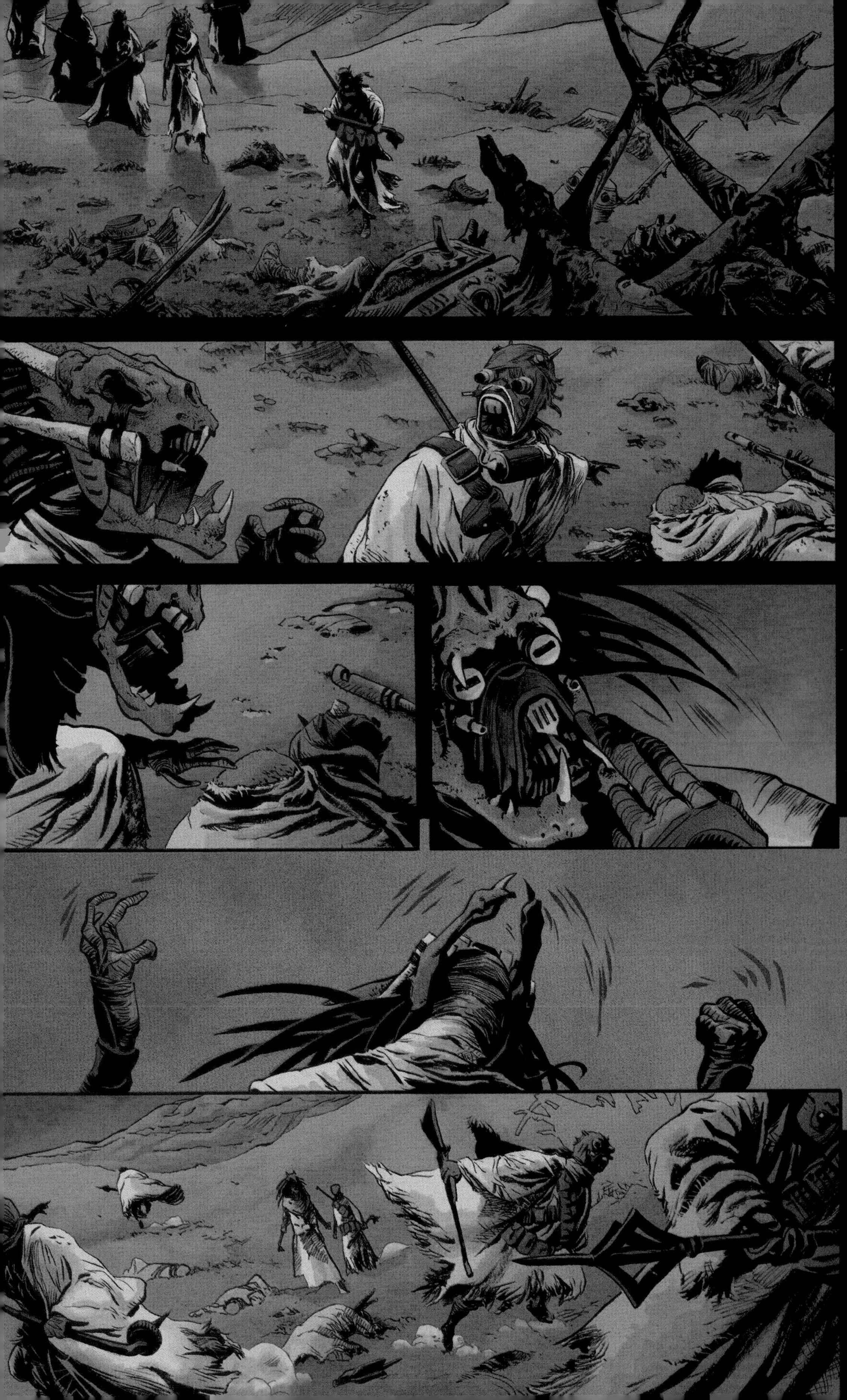

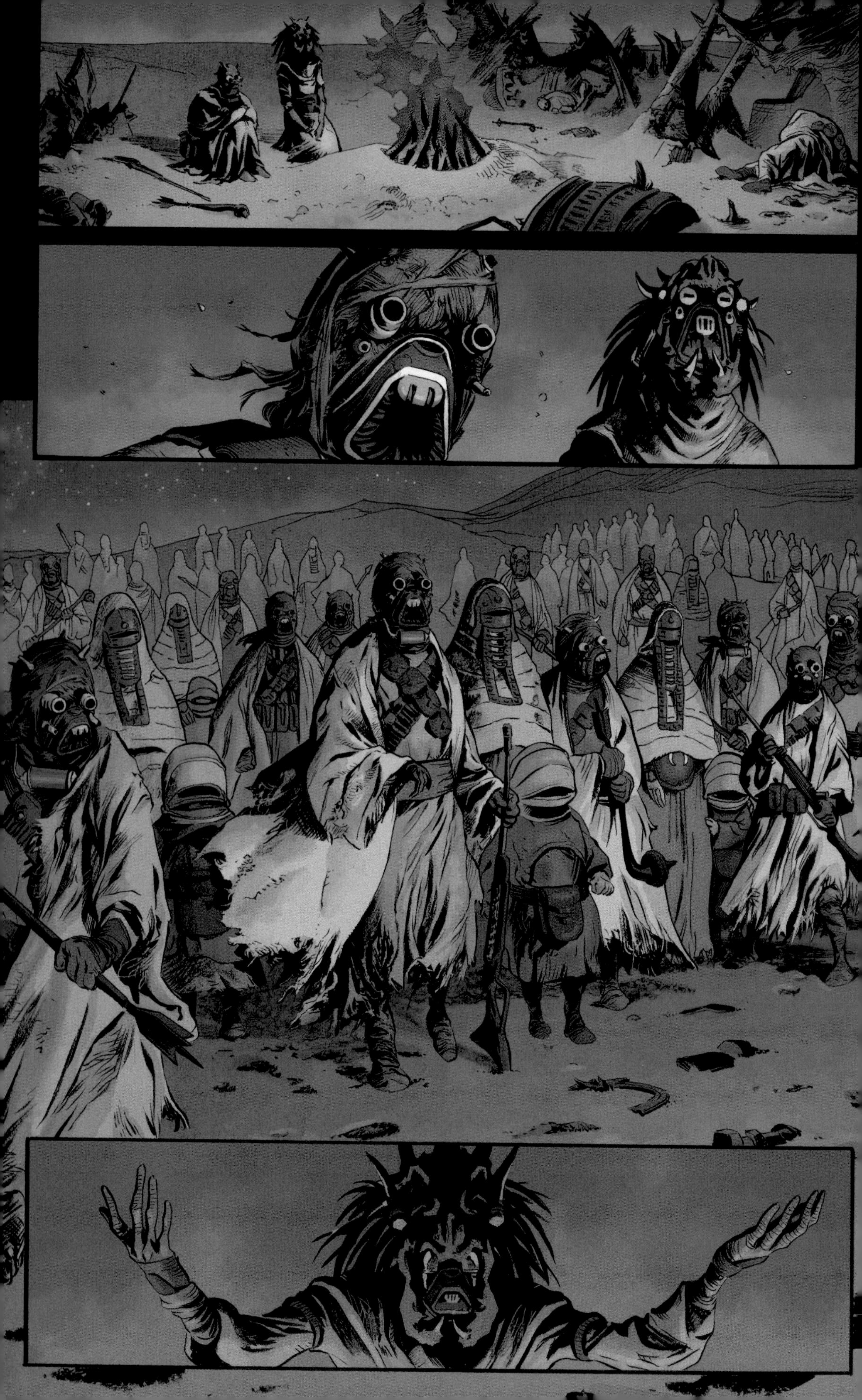

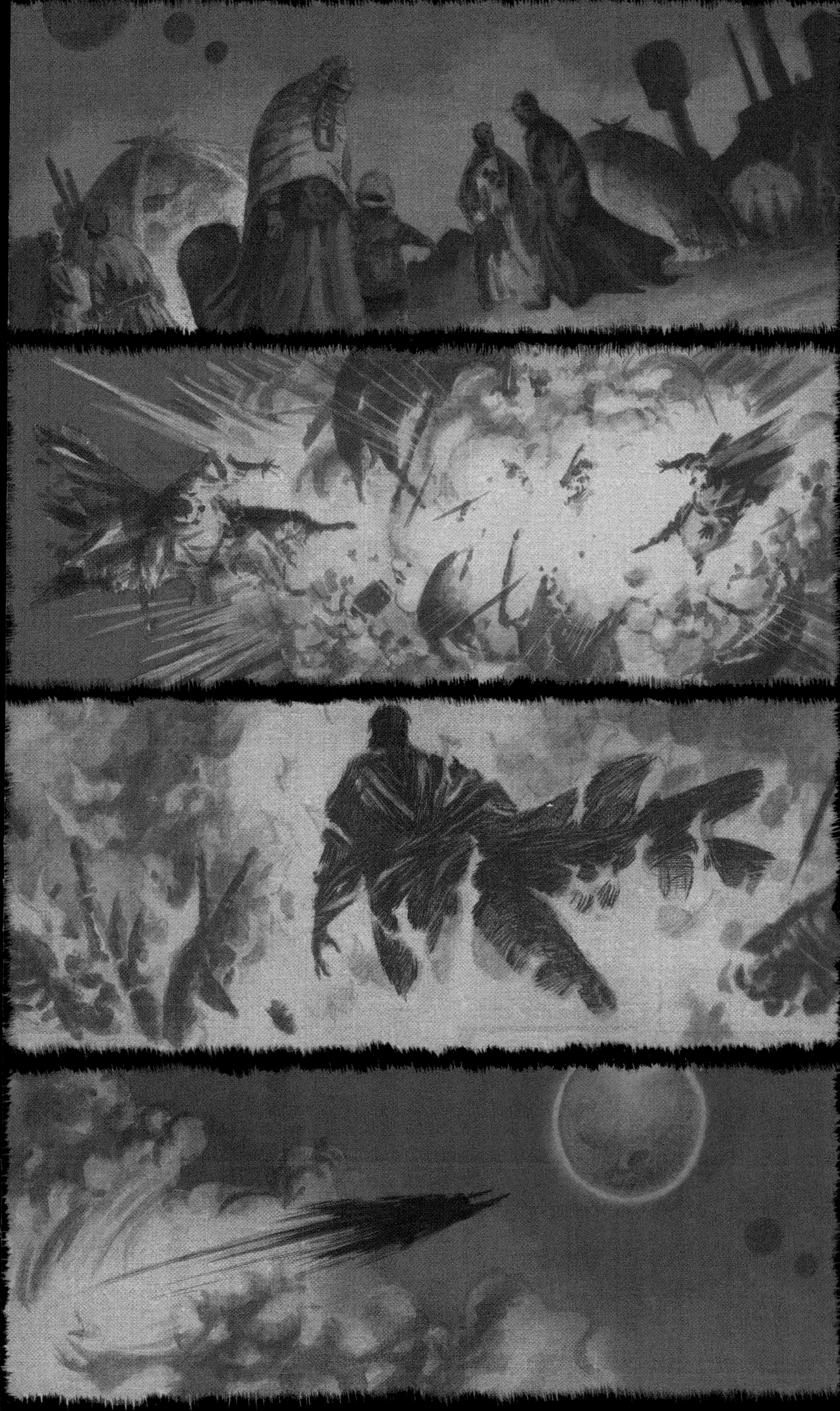

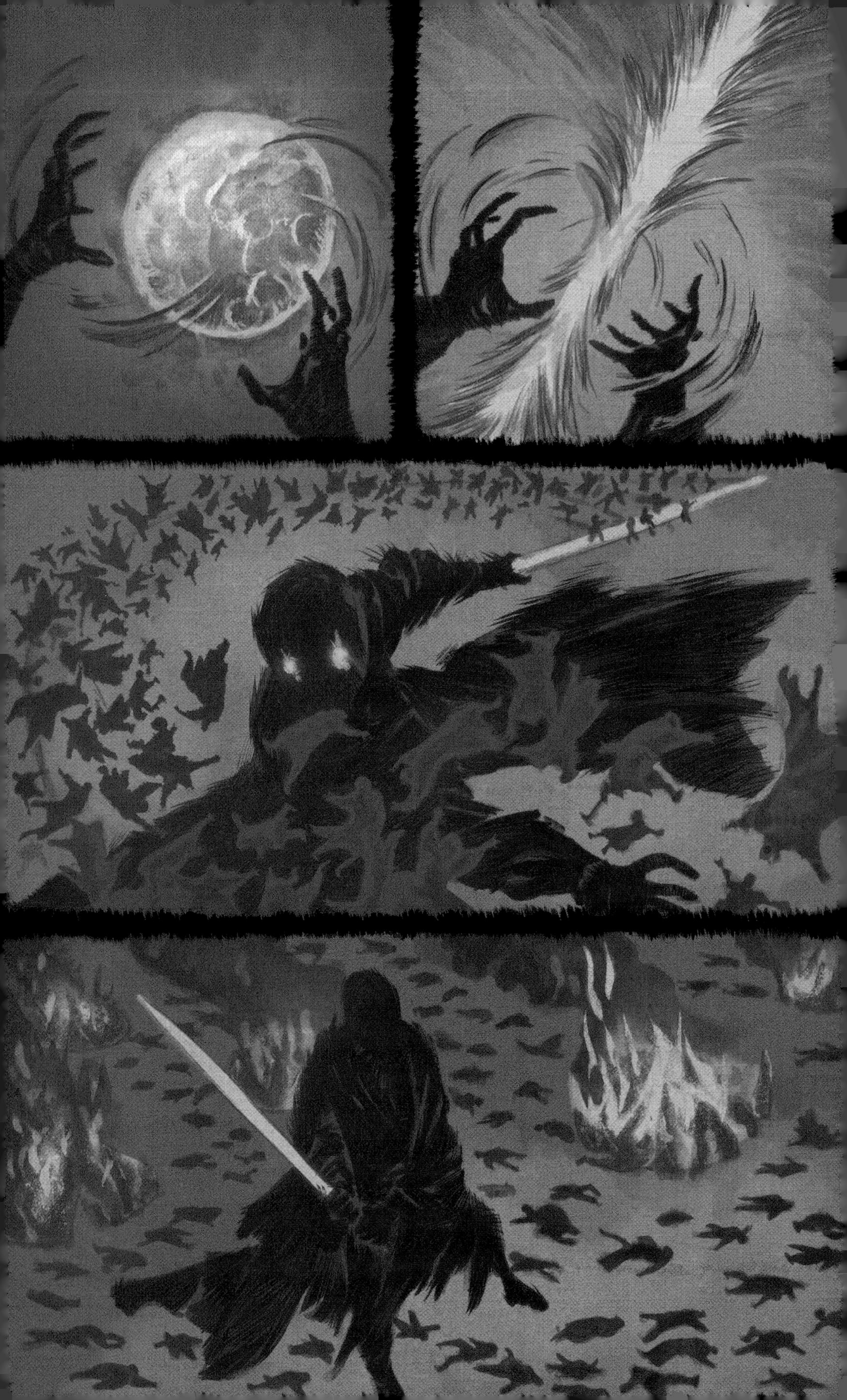

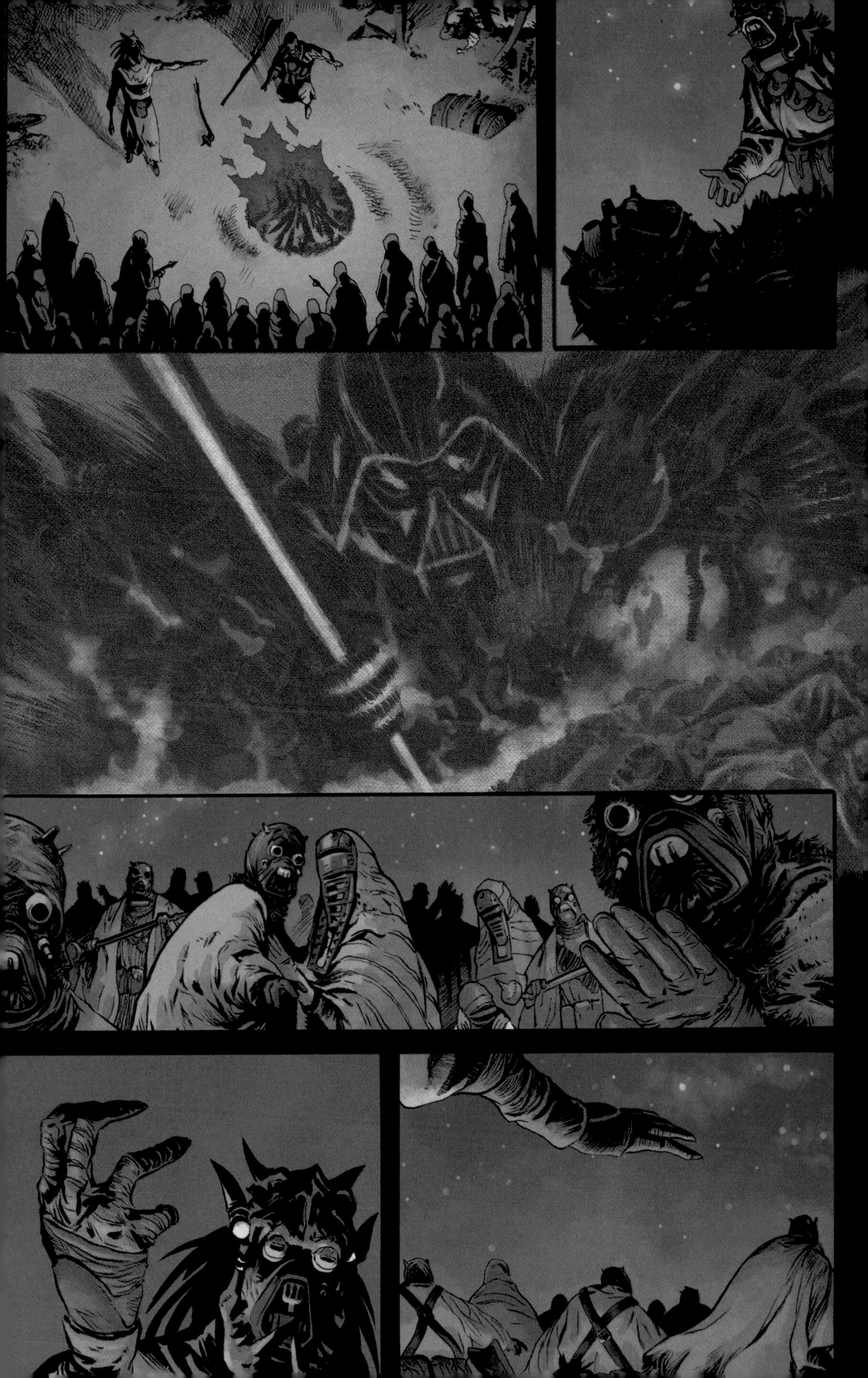

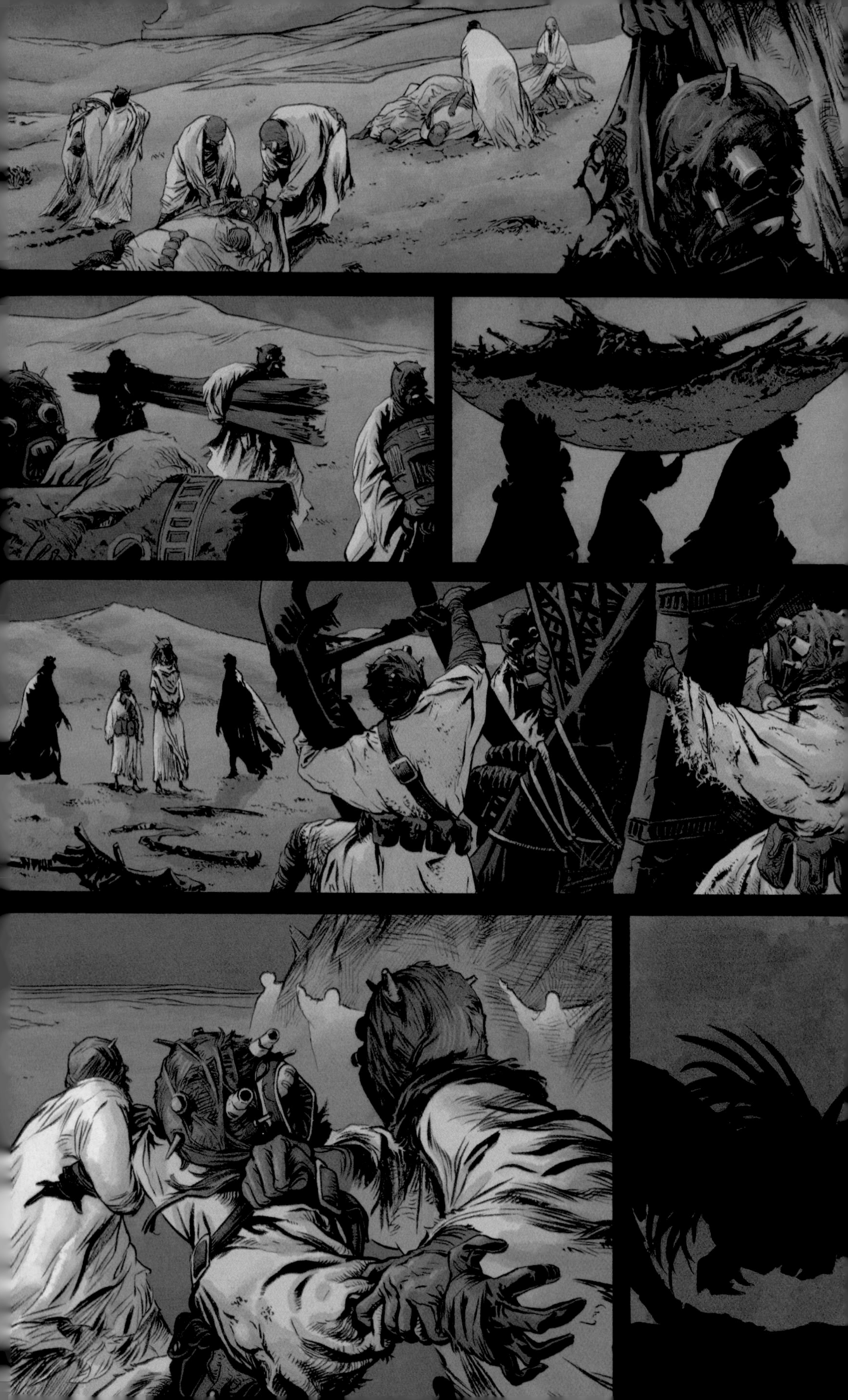

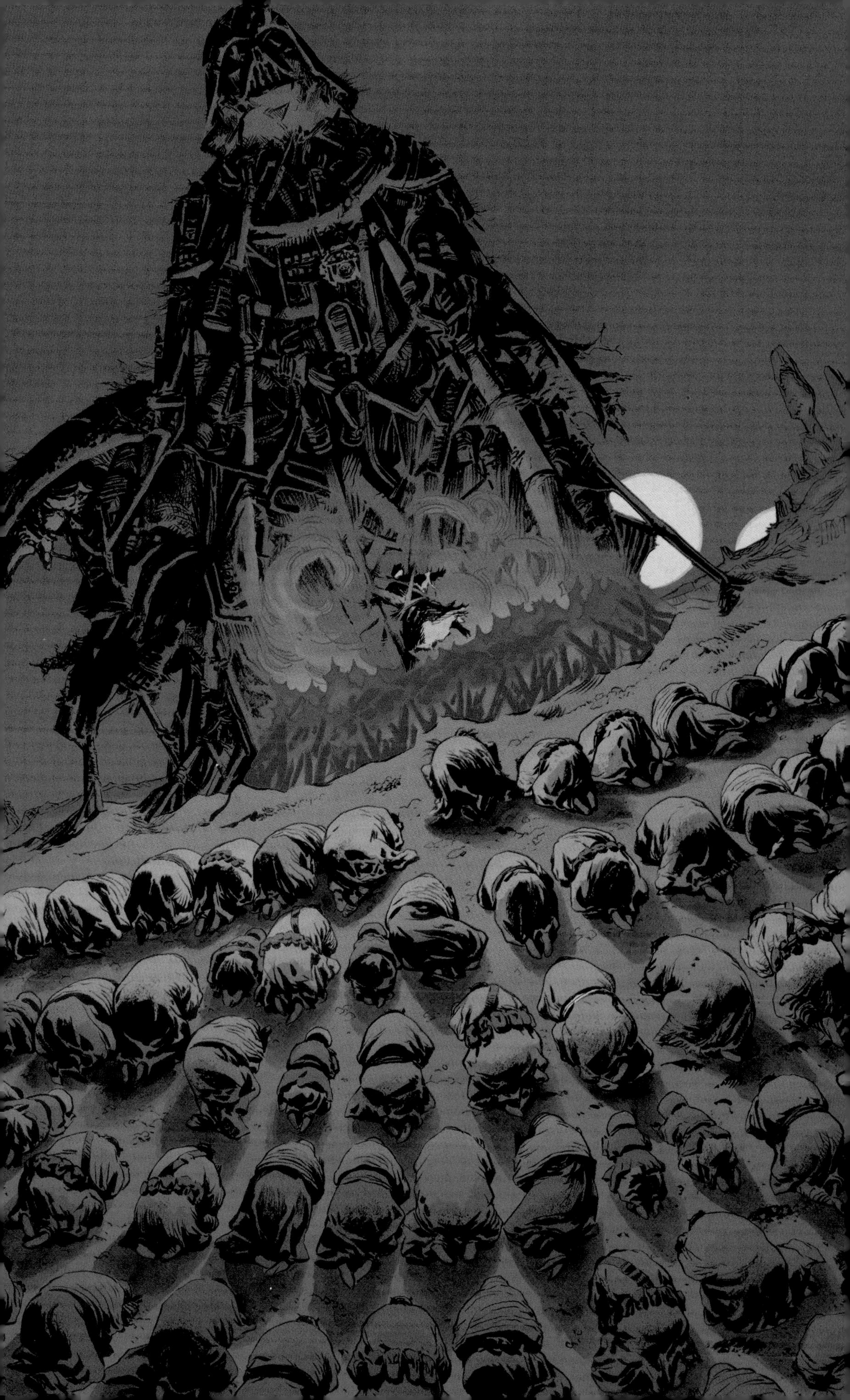

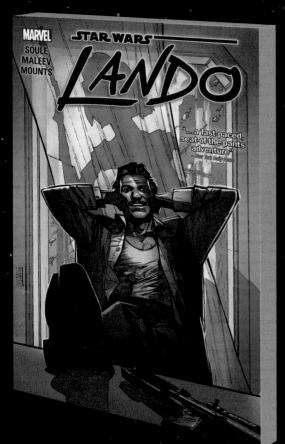

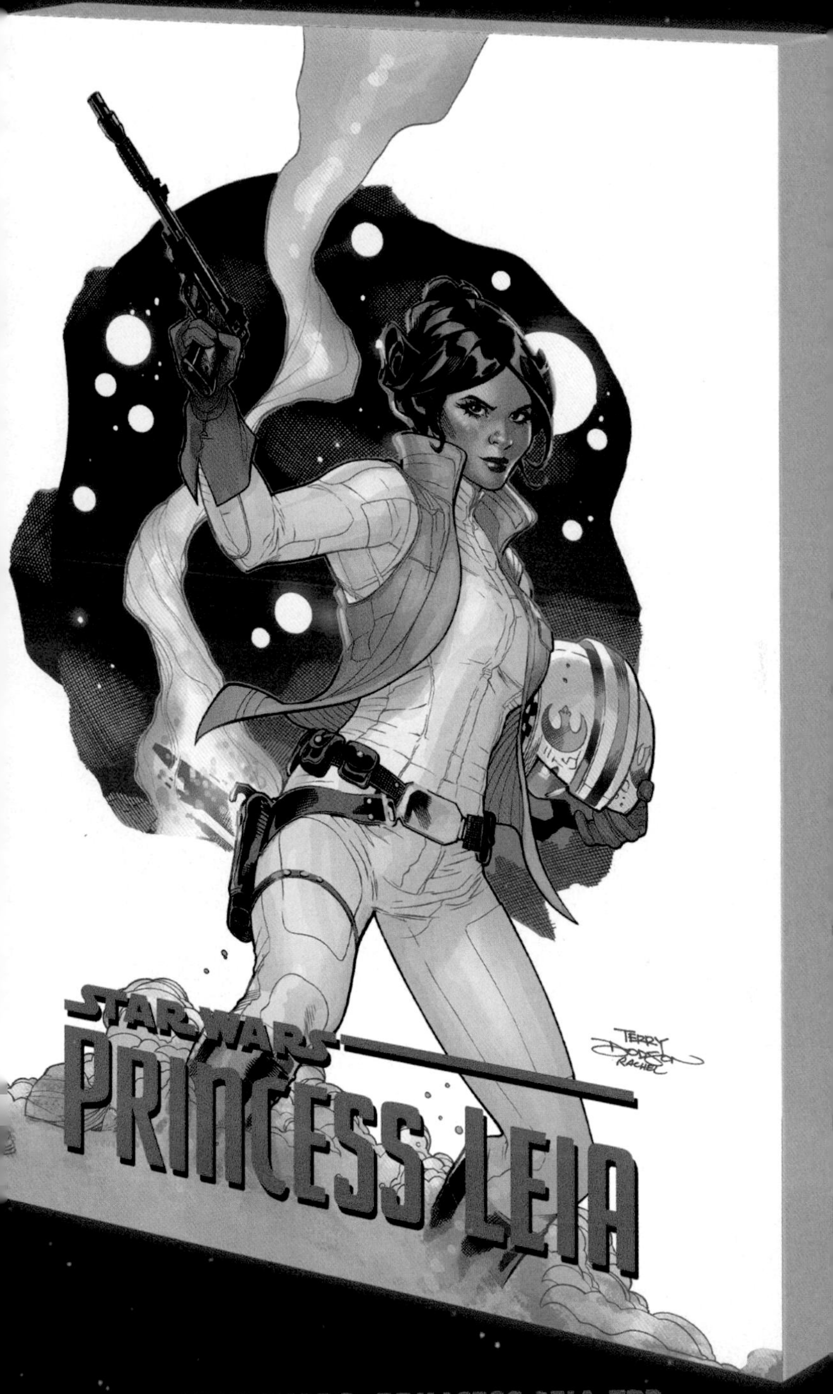
STAR WARS
PRINCESS LEIA

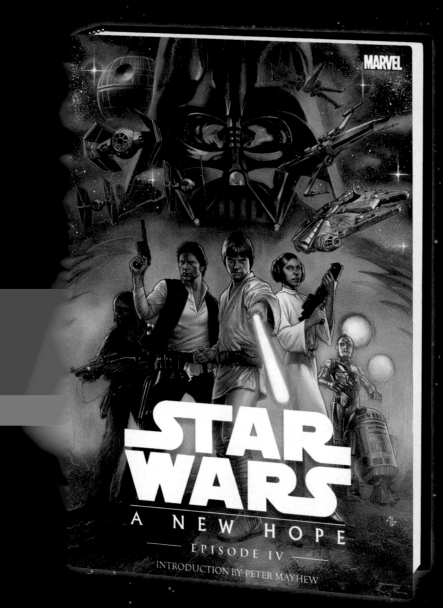

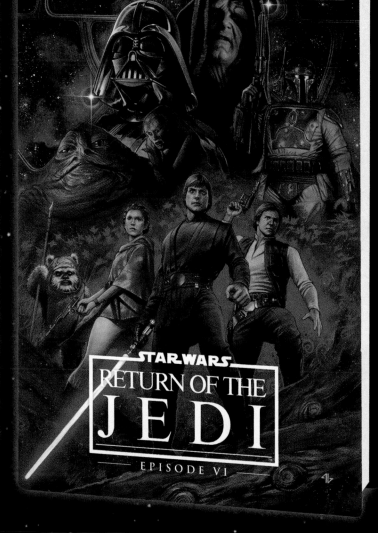

OFFICIAL GRAPHIC NOVEL ADAPTATION!

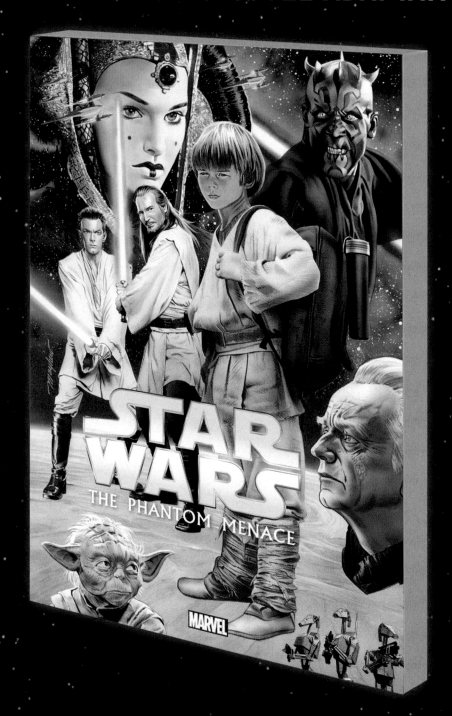

STAR WARS: EPISODE I – THE PHANTOM MENACE HC
978-1-3029-0074-8

AVAILABLE NOW WHEREVER BOOKS ARE SOLD

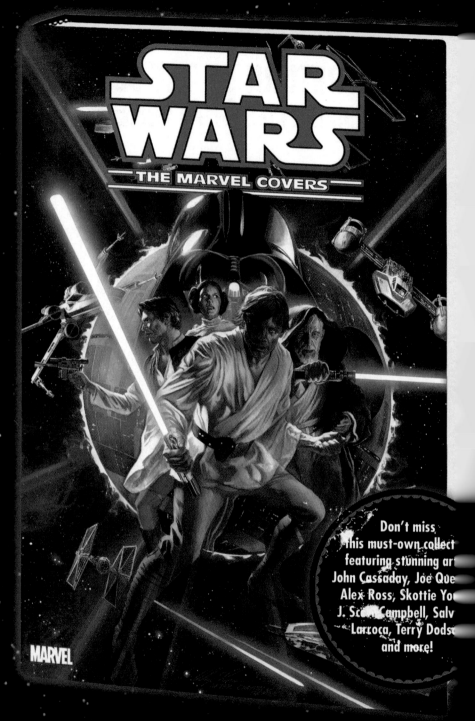